New technologies and the firm

In today's competitive world failure to invest sufficiently in innovation often means losing a vital competitive edge. An understanding of the motivating forces behind the development and use of new technologies in firms is now more important than ever. Why are some organizations more resistant to change than others? Are short-term considerations constantly blocking the way to generation and effective marketing of new technologies and to training in their use?

New Technologies and the Firm presents the findings of fourteen research teams involved in a major research initiative funded by the ESRC and DTI. In examining the initiation and response to innovation in firms, the authors draw together the many strands which were discovered to influence the successful generation and adoption of new technologies. The core issues in technology management are looked at, including skills and expertise, markets and marketing, finance and the issue of technology collaboration both on a domestic and international basis. Technology is shown to be at the very heart of corporate strategy and policy formation.

This volume offers a remarkable synthesis of new research and new conceptual frameworks drawn from a variety of perspectives and disciplines. The contributors are all widely known for their specialist areas and their findings will be important in advancing the understanding of the role of new technologies in firms. *New Technologies and the Firm* will be of interest to industry, government and unions as well as to the academic community.

Peter Swann is Senior Research Fellow at the Centre for Business Strategy, London Business School. His main research is in the economics of innovation. From 1990 to 1992 he was co-ordinator of the ESRC/DTI Research Initiative on New Technologies and the Firm at Brunel University, and he is also the Managing Editor (Europe) for the journal *Economics of Innovation and New Technology*. He is the author of *Measuring Price and Quality Competitiveness*, *Quality Innovation* and *Corporate Vision and Rapid Technological Change*.

New technologies and the firm

Innovation and competition

Edited by Peter Swann

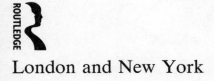

London and New York

First published 1993
by Routledge
11 New Fetter Lane, London EC4P 4EE

Simultaneously published in the USA and Canada
by Routledge
29 West 35th Street, New York, NY 10001

© 1993 Peter Swann

Phototypeset in Times by Intype, London
Printed and bound in Great Britain by
T.J. Press (Padstow) Ltd, Padstow, Cornwall

British Library Cataloguing in Publication Data
A catalogue record for this book is available from the British
Library
ISBN 0–415–08218–8

Library of Congress Cataloging in Publication Data
CIP data has been applied for
ISBN 0–415–08218–8

Contents

List of figures

List of tables

Contributors

Rob Ball, Department of Management Science, University of Stirling

Kate Barker, Programme of Policy Research in Engineering, Science and Technology, University of Manchester

Janet Biggar, Heriot-Watt Business School, Heriot-Watt University

John Board, Department of Accounting and Finance, London School of Economics

Mark Boden, Programme of Policy Research in Engineering, Science and Technology, University of Manchester

Derek Bosworth, Institute for Employment Research, University of Warwick, and Manchester School of Management, UMIST

Alan Cawson, School of Social Sciences, University of Sussex

David Cleary, University of Cambridge

David Collison, Department of Accountancy and Business Finance, University of Dundee

Sarah Y. Cooper, Heriot-Watt Business School, Heriot-Watt University

P. J. Robert Delargy, Department of Accounting and Finance, London School of Economics

Paul D. Foley, Department of Town Planning, University of Sheffield

Luke Georghiou, Programme of Policy Research in Engineering, Science and Technology, University of Manchester

Jas Gill, Department of Information Studies, University of Brighton

Alan Goodacre, Department of Accountancy and Finance, University of Stirling

Peter Grindley, Center for Research in Management, University of California, Berkeley

Leslie Haddon, Science Policy Research Unit, University of Sussex

Massoud Karshenas, School of Oriental and African Studies, University of London
John Kay, London Economics
Alasdair Lonie, Department of Accountancy and Business Finance, University of Dundee
Jim McGrath, The Queen's College, Glasgow
J. Stanley Metcalfe, Department of Economics, University of Manchester
Ian Miles, Programme of Policy Research in Engineering, Science and Technology, University of Manchester
Bill Nixon, Department of Accountancy and Business Finance, University of Dundee
Ray P. Oakey, Manchester Business School
Ken Pratt, Department of Accountancy and Finance, University of Stirling
Ian J. Smith, Teesside Business School
Paul Stoneman, Warwick Business School, University of Warwick
Peter Swann, Centre for Business Strategy, London Business School
Bruce Tether, Centre for Urban and Regional Development Studies, University of Newcastle upon Tyne
Richard Thomas, Department of Management Studies, University of Stirling
Alfred Thwaites, Centre for Urban and Regional Development Studies, University of Newcastle upon Tyne
Ian Tonks, Department of Accounting and Finance, London School of Economics
Joe Townsend, Science Policy Research Unit, University of Sussex
H. Doug Watts, Department of Geography, University of Sheffield
Janette Webb, Department of Business Studies, University of Edinburgh
Paul Willman, London Business School
Brenda Wilson, Department of Town Planning, University of Sheffield
Rob Wilson, Institute for Employment Research, University of Warwick
Pooran Wynarczyk, Centre for Urban and Regional Development Studies, University of Newcastle upon Tyne
Ivan Yates, formerly Deputy Chief Executive, British Aerospace, PLC

Foreword

Technology in its many forms profoundly affects almost every aspect of modern life, but it is not widely understood just how important is the effective management of technology to the sustained competitive performance and the profitability of the firms in all sectors of the UK economy. While there has recently been an increasing awareness amongst policy makers of the importance of manufacturing in a modern economy, which depends heavily upon both the performance of the firms themselves and the widespread and effective application of their products, there is as yet no agreement on the best way for the United Kingdom to achieve the steady economic growth attained by our European partners and international competitors.

Nearly all of us carry in our minds a model of the way we think the economy works and such concepts can be very influential in guiding the thoughts of policy makers and the actions of politicians. But it is increasingly evident that such models based only on macroeconomic thinking are too simplistic and that more attention must be paid to the functioning of the micro-economy. In particular we need a far better understanding of the 'industrial ecology' comprising not only the internal functioning of firms and the complex systems of interactions between them, but also between firms and the national 'education and training system' on the one hand and the various systems within the 'financial sector' on the other.

The processes involved in the development, acquisition and successful application of technology are extremely complex. Good management not only involves the organization of wide varieties of professional expertise and individual skills, it requires the establishment and continual updating of an extremely complex and extensive knowledge base which must be frequently accessed by many persons for different purposes. In addition, success critically depends upon the development of high levels of personal and interpersonal skills at all levels and a very high degree of motivation in individuals and teams.

Those who have had direct responsibility for managing in industry usually learn by experience as an essential part of a lifetime of personal development, and there are those of us who have also had the good fortune to learn directly from the operation of competitors. But in a busy professional life there is rarely time for reflection to analyse, explain and codify the large amount of mainly tacit knowledge acquired by the successful manager.

It is of vital importance that all the constituent processes should be properly understood and described so that not only may the appropriate policies be developed at a national level but the necessary skills can be developed and training given to those who will work in and manage industry in the future.

The scope and the focus of the work reported in the papers comprising this book is therefore very appropriate. The timing of its publication is also very opportune, coming as it does towards the end of the most severe recession for several decades and when it appears that the ability to achieve the long-term growth of our competitors still eludes us. Clearly we in the United Kingdom need some fresh insights and new thinking about the management of the economy and in particular what form the resulting industrial policy should take.

The wide-ranging talent and the experience of those who have participated in these studies speaks for itself. The large number of aspects covered reflects the complexities of the real technological and industrial world and it is greatly to the credit of the project directors that they have completed the work of managing the programmes and editing the results so effectively. The ESRC are to be congratulated in applying the concept of a co-ordinated research initiative in this way. There is much yet to be attempted, and hopefully with the support of the ESRC and the DTI such studies will follow using the same multi-disciplinary approach and drawing upon the great wealth of experience and knowledge within industry.

It is interesting that the wide range of approaches and methodologies employed allowed researchers from one background to obtain new insights into the results obtained by other disciplines. No less rich will be the perspectives and knowledge available to the reader who is prepared to learn from this very comprehensive study.

Ivan Yates
Formerly Deputy Chief Executive,
British Aerospace plc, and
currently Visiting Professor in the
Principles of Engineering, University
of Cambridge

Acknowledgements

The ESRC/DTI Research Initiative on *New Technologies and the Firm* was started in 1988, and a total of fourteen projects were funded, the last of which finishes work in December 1992. The Initiative has had two co-ordinators: Professor Paul Stoneman of the University of Warwick (from the start until December 1989) and Dr Peter Swann of Brunel University and London Business School (from January 1990 to April 1992).

The generous financial support of the ESRC and DTI is gratefully acknowledged by the editor and all authors represented in this book. We wish to thank the following publishers for permission to reproduce copyright material. Figure 6.1 is reprinted from P. Foley, H. D. Watts and B. Wilson 'Introducing new process technologies: implications for local employment policies', *Geoforum*, vol. 23, no. 1 with the kind permission of Pergamon Press Ltd. Chapter 2 appeared as a Centre for Business Strategy Technology Project discussion paper and we are grateful to the Centre for Business Strategy at London Business School for permission to reproduce it here.

A special word of thanks to Ivan Yates, formerly Deputy Chief Executive of British Aerospace plc and currently Visiting Professor in the Principles of Engineering Design at the University of Cambridge, for agreeing to write a foreword to the book. We also wish to express our gratitude and debt to John Barber of the DTI, for giving much time and advice on the progress of the Initiative. The editor would also like to thank Paul Stoneman, first co-ordinator, for all his work in setting it up, and subsequent advice to his successor. He would like to thank all members of the Initiative for their suggestions for clarifying and improving the Introduction and the Summary and Conclusions of the book. Particular thanks in this regard are due to John Board, Derek Bosworth, Alan Cawson,

David Collison, Alasdair Lonie, Paul Stoneman, H. Doug Watts, Rob Wilson and Romano Dyerson.

We would also like to thank the following: Ian Lawrence of the DTI for very helpful comments on several chapters; also Mike Phelps, Philip O'Neil, Colin Scott of the DTI, and Graham Walshe of the Cabinet Office; Richard Freeman, chief economist of ICI, who chaired our dissemination conferences in December 1990 and October 1991; and the following members of the ESRC: David Stout (chairman of the IEE RDG), Christine McCulloch, Iain Jones, Elizabeth Bell, Adrian Alsop, Tim Whitaker and Sarah Sleet. We are also grateful to Francesca Weaver, Laura Large, Alison Walters, Patrick Molson and their colleagues at Routledge for help in bringing this book to production. Finally our special thanks to Carole Jackson of Brunel University for all her hard work in typing parts of the manuscript and an enormous amount of correspondence in connection with it.

E·S·R·C
ECONOMIC
& SOCIAL
RESEARCH
COUNCIL

Introduction

Peter Swann

A recurrent theme emphasized by many observers of Britain's economic decline is that for one reason or another Britain has failed to invest sufficiently in new technologies to maintain her competitive position. In diagnosing the reasons for this, many observers place emphasis on one or more of the following five points: (1) organizations find change very hard to manage, (2) there are insufficient skills in the workforce to cope with new technologies, (3) the markets for (and marketing of) new technology-based products need to be better understood, (4) financial markets are too concerned with short-term considerations and (5) firms do not exploit fully the potential benefits of collaboration.

The ESRC/DTI Research Initiative on New Technologies and the Firm was designed around these same five central themes: technology management, skills, markets, finance and collaboration. Each of the projects in the Initiative addresses one of these five themes, and Chapters 1 to 15 give a summary of the main findings of each project. The Bibliography at the end of the book gives a list of the research output from these projects.

The introduction is in two parts. The first introduces the five main themes by briefly surveying the principal contributions of each project. In an area as complex as new technologies and the firm, however, there is a great deal of interaction between different research projects. Accordingly, the greater part of this introduction explores twelve key issues that keep reappearing in different contexts throughout the analysis of new technologies and the firm, and which cut across the themes of management, skills, marketing, finance and collaboration.

The prime objective of the initiative has been to advance understanding of the initiation and response to new technologies in firms, and to disseminate the findings of our research to industry, government and unions, as well as to the academic community. We hope that this book will play its part in that dissemination activity.

FIVE MAIN AREAS

The 'core': management of new technology

The centre of the 'core' has been a large project at London Business School analysing the management of new technology from an economic and organizational perspective. At the time of writing, this project is in the process of completing over twenty in-depth case studies of how firms manage the generation, implementation and marketing of new technology. Most of these firms come from the public sector, financial services, electronics and instrumentation, manufacturing and the motor industry. Each case study has been written up separately (see details in the Bibliography). Here we devote two chapters to this project. Chapter 1, by John Kay and Paul Willman, analyses firm architecture, trust and organizational relationships, which play a central role in the conceptual framework that has guided (and been shaped by) their case studies. Chapter 2, by Peter Grindley, gives more of an overview of the framework used to link organizational structure and economic performance, and summarizes some of the main case-study findings.

The 'core' also contains three smaller projects studying particular aspects of the management of new technology. Chapter 3 summarizes work by Ian Smith, Bruce Tether, Alfred Thwaites, Joe Townsend and Pooran Wynarczyk, on the factors affecting the survival and performance of innovative small firms. This chapter focuses on the characteristics of those small firms that introduce substantial innovations, their economic performance and survival, and their direct contribution to local and regional economic development. Chapter 4, by J. Stanley Metcalfe and Mark Boden, analyses the vital role of the technological paradigm in a firm's strategic planning and summarizes two case studies of how firms generate and revise their strategic paradigms. Chapter 5, by Janette Webb and David Cleary, describes the central importance of supplier-user relations for success in technology generation and implementation, and the role of experts in these relationships. Again, the analysis is informed by some in-depth case studies.

Skills and expertise in the workforce

This special area of the initiative had two projects. Chapter 6, by Paul D. Foley, H. Doug Watts and Brenda Wilson examines the extent to which skills shortages act as a constraint on the adoption of new technologies in a local labour market, and if so, what training strategies firms adopt to overcome these constraints. The chapter also explores the possibilities that new-technology adoption (in cases where the technology is 'user friendly') can offer a way *around* skills shortages. Chapter 7, by Derek Bosworth and Rob Wilson, summarizes the main results available at the time of writing the chapter (the work was still ongoing) of research on the employment of professional scientists and engineers in different companies, and the implications for the performance of these companies. The two main questions addressed are these: why do different firms make different use of scientists and engineers, and do those companies that employ greater numbers of scientists and engineers in positions of greater responsibility perform better?

Markets and consumers

This second special area contained four projects. Chapter 8 summarizes work by Paul Stoneman and Massoud Karshenas on the diffusion of new technology. This study makes several important new advances in the econometric analysis of diffusion, and uses these techniques to analyse the diffusion of a new industrial technology (computer numerically controlled, or CNC, machine tools) and a new consumer technology (colour televisions). Chapter 9, by Ray P. Oakey, Sarah Cooper and Janet Biggar summarizes the results of an innovative research project designed to assess the value of proactive marketing to small high-technology-based firms. The study argues that one of the main reasons for the inferior performance of some small firms is that they adopt a 'satisficing' attitude to marketing efforts, and the research shows that proactive marketing efforts (as supplied by the research team) can help to generate increased interest in the product, and ultimately increased sales. Chapter 10, by Peter Swann and Jas Gill, examines the twin propositions that rapid and *unexpected* technological change leads to reduced market concentration, while incremental and *anticipated* technological change – even if rapid – leads to greater market concentration. The chapter draws on five case studies to illustrate the argument. Chapter 11, by Alan Cawson, Leslie Haddon and

Ian Miles studies the dynamics of the innovation process for three consumer IT (information technology) products. The process is inherently cyclical, as market success (or failure) and user experience form a vital information feedback to guide current redesign and the development of future products. The chapter sees this and other information gathering about consumers and markets as helping to map out what they define as a 'product space' for a new technology.

Financing new technology

This third special area of the initiative contains three projects. Chapter 12, by Alasdair Lonie, Bill Nixon and David Collison, examines the internal and external pressures that may constrain firms from investing in new innovative technologies. As the case study companies were all innovators, the authors' approach is, in a sense, the other way round: how did the innovators get around the external financial pressures and internal control systems that might otherwise have prevented high-risk investment expenditures? That chapter explores the role of the technology champion in this, the concept of 'strategic override of financial criteria', and the role of selective disclosure of investments by innovators. Chapter 13 summarizes a study by Alan Goodacre, Rob Ball, Jim McGrath, Ken Pratt and Richard Thomas, of the accounting treatment of R & D expenditures. Using an experimental technique, they analyse whether investment analysts' valuation of firms is sensitive to whether R & D is treated as an expense, or capitalized, and accordingly whether analysts are 'short-termist' towards R & D expenditure. They also study whether small firms might be discouraged from investing in R & D because of the required accounting and disclosure treatment of R & D expenditure. Chapter 14, by John Board, P. J. Robert Delargy and Ian Tonks, examines the relationship between the financing or capital structure of the firm and its R & D intensity. They explore whether R & D intensive firms tend to have lower gearing ratios, and whether R & D-intensive firms in the United Kingdom have to pay a greater risk premium than those in the United States.

Collaboration in new technology

The fourth and final special area of the initiative had one project only, though as we shall see shortly the issue of collaboration crops up in many other studies. Chapter 15 summarizes the results of a study by Luke Georghiou and Kate Barker looking at the management of international collaboration. They examine those factors which underpin successful collaboration, and draw some lessons about best practice in the management of collaboration. They also study the circumstances in which firms choose to collaborate, whom they choose as partner, how the partnership is structured and operated, and what arrangements are made for the exploitation of the fruits of collaboration.

RECURRENT THEMES IN NEW TECHNOLOGIES AND THE FIRM

The remainder of this introduction identifies twelve of the most important issues that recur throughout the book and locates the interaction between these themes. While the choice of twelve is somewhat arbitrary, between them they cover some of the most important issues arising throughout the book. In what follows, the appearance of a chapter number in square brackets (e.g. [1]) indicates the chapters which are relevant to the present discussion.

Consumers and users

Consumers and users play an obvious role as buyers in the market studies [8–11]. It is recognized that while a variety of diffusion models can be applied to analyse industrial purchasing behaviour, some of these are unlikely to be relevant to the purchasing decisions of individual consumers [8]. Consumer (or buyer) preferences towards different technologies play a central role in determining market shares of different firms, and hence market structure [10]

Consumers also play a vital role as sources of information. This is particularly important for new products where producer information about 'the market' may be very limited. User feedback (whether formal as through focus groups, from pioneers testing subsidized prototypes, or more informally) is vital to a continuing and cyclical process of product innovation [11]. Consumers may indulge in postpurchasing innovation (making unexpected uses of the product), and that is important information to the producer [11]. The supplier-user relationship is important to both parties, as a source of feedback and perhaps prestige to the producer, and as a source of systems information to the user [5]. The user may be seconded to the supplier's technical groups, and may be asked to act as

mediator. At the same time, the supplier sometimes provides training to users [6]. Chapter 9 indicates that consumer evaluations of
products (and the marketing literature used to sell them) may be
very valuable to producers. It also suggests that the information
flow from potential consumers to the producer takes place over a
much longer period than just the time of purchase. Information on
consumer life styles is used as a basis for market segmentation [11].

The organization of the purchasing function within the firm may
impact on the user-supplier relationship [5]: the purchase committee
is seen by suppliers as 'soft' to deal with while the head of IT
services, for example, is seen as 'hard'. Feedback loops from users
to suppliers can be formal or informal, though the formal may
undermine the informal; they may be based on friendship, professional interaction, or they may be purely commercial [5]. Finally,
users can provide information for other users as in the epidemic
model of diffusion [8].

Collaboration

Collaboration was one of the four 'special areas' identified above
and is discussed most explicitly in Chapter 15. Firms have to decide
whether collaboration is worthwhile, if so with whom, how the
collaboration should be structured and managed, and how the
results from collaboration can be exploited. Collaboration across
national frontiers is seen (not surprisingly) to introduce further
complexities, and collaboration with Japanese companies calls for
long-term and top-level commitment, as well as patience. Collaboration is a source of competitive advantage and a strategic investment. It can be purely pre-competitive, it can be designed to share
production development, or it can go all the way to market-oriented
collaboration [15].

Collaboration arises as an issue in the management of user-
supplier relations [5], where contracts can range along a spectrum
from adversarial to collaborative, and various forms of collaboration
are recognized: long-term relationships with one supplier, inertial,
intervention, mediated and forced. Pre-competitive collaboration is
also required in the setting of standards, and that can be central to
the speed with which consumers will adopt a new product [2, 10, 11].

Collaboration also calls for a degree of trust, a theme discussed
under organizational structure and relationships below, and analysed particularly in chapters 1, 2 and 5.

Constraints on innovation: short-termism?

Chapters 12 and 13 recognize a whole array of constraints on innovation and ask which is the most important: finance, skills, management expertise, marketing, plant capacity, production knowledge, amongst others. Financial constraints on adoption, moreover, can be internal to the firm or external [12, 13], though internal constraints may be overridden by strategic considerations if a product champion is able to mount a sufficiently persuasive case to top management [12]. The major external constraint on innovation and R & D may be short-termism and the possibility of an unduly high risk-premium in the United Kingdom together with a relatively unsophisticated use of other financial instruments [12, 13, 14]. In many circumstances finance may be a more serious constraint on new-technology adoption than skills [6]. Indeed, when the new technology is 'user friendly', adoption of the technology can be a way around the problems caused by skills shortages. It is recognized, however, that technology acquired from another organization can be hard to assimilate; this can be a constraint on technology transfer [2, 10].

A traditional economic argument is that if the benefits of innovation cannot be appropriated by the innovating firm, then that will constrain innovative activity [1]. A mismatch between organizational structure, technological paradigms (or 'visions') and the emerging path of technological development can impose severe cost constraints on innovation [4, 10], and the theoretical rationale for this is further explored in Chapters 1 and 2. More generally, organizational change (see below) is often required to handle new technologies: such change will always meet some resistance at least, and this can easily be a constraint on innovation [1, 2, 5, 10, 11]. Finally, uncertainty about a new technology can often be a constraint on innovation, though in some cases such uncertainty can be managed by appropriate user-supplier relationships [5].

Diffusion and Market Penetration

Chapter 8 focuses on diffusion, and it is here that the topic receives the most detailed and rigorous analysis in this book. It is recognized that the speed of diffusion varies across firms, industries and technologies. While a variety of diffusion models may be applicable to industrial buyer behaviour, some of these are less relevant to the diffusion of individual consumer purchases. The economics literature on diffusion separates *exogenous* influences on diffusion from *endogenous* influences.

Chapter 11 is concerned with the diffusion of new consumer technologies and notes that this depends on the rival technologies available, the importance of standards for that technology and technological expectations. Chapter 10 summarizes a diffusion model over several competing firms' technologies in which what are commonly called 'bandwagon effects' operate (for example, around the *de facto* standard). The diffusion of an innovation is likely to depend at least in part on the skills available in different firms and regions [6], and part of the variability in purchase dates can be put down to the fact that some purchases are a response to a sudden and unexpected need [9]. Moreover, the various consumer responses to proactive marketing efforts ('interesting but no thank you', 'keep it on file', 'further enquiries', 'intend to purchase in near future' and 'purchase now') could be seen as distinct stages of the diffusion process [9]. The diffusion of a radical and risky innovation within an organization may require a high-level champion [12].

Expertise, competence, information, know-how, knowledge, learning and skills

By grouping these terms together it is not suggested that these words are interchangeable. Rather, it is done to emphasize just how pervasive these themes are in the analysis of new technology and the firm.

Chapter 6 is directly concerned with the skills of craft workers in traditional industries – their importance in determining new technology adoption and training strategies. Chapter 7 focuses on the role of experts (qualified scientists and engineers) in the firm, the reasons why different firms employ different numbers of scientists and engineers, and their effect on the performance of the firm. The chapter also discusses firms' strategies for investing in human-resource development and why short-termism may operate here. Chapter 5 is also directly concerned with the management of expertise inside and outside the firm, particularly with reference to the user-supplier relationship.

Most other chapters run up against these issues at some point. Successful management of technological change depends on exploitation of firm-specific capabilities, knowledge and skills, organizational routines and complementary assets [1, 2]. Successful organizational change requires mastering the dynamics of changing organizational knowledge bases and the routinization of change. The knowledge base is recognized to be tacit and diffuse, and the transfer of competencies between firms or even between divisions is problematic. Technological change can be competence enhancing or competence destroying; in some instances the rapid building of competencies may call for external as well as internal expertise.

The transfer of technological expertise between firms is important in determining their economic performance and some firms suffer because of technological ineptitude [3]. Technology strategy builds on a core of expertise, by exploiting the firm's knowledge base [4]. Expertise is frequently instilled by in-house training and the firm's strategic paradigm conditions the information signals that the firm can receive from outside.

Information and learning play a role in diffusion models [8] because information acquisition (or learning from other users) is a prerequisite for diffusion. Small firms are seen to have a marketing disadvantage compared to large firms in that marketing is often done by a senior manager as one of many duties, and this reactive response to marketing is inefficient [9]. Technology acquisition from another firm is recognized to be difficult because requisite knowledge bases are missing [2, 10]. Moreover, it is argued that competence-destroying technological change is deconcentrating, while competence-sustaining (or competence-enhancing) technological change (which can be dealt with by existing organizational routines) increases concentration [10].

Information is continually garnered from users, markets and others to feed back into the innovation process [11]. Again, it is recognized that much necessary knowledge is tacit rather than formal, and that informal networks play a vital role in the transfer of this tacit knowledge [5, 11]. Finally, successful management of collaboration requires distinct management skills and, if necessary, management training [15]; in seeking a partner in a joint venture, firms will look out for complementarities between their own knowledge and skills base and that of their partner.

Financial and accounting criteria for investment

Chapters 12, 13 and 14 consider financial and accounting issues directly. When do financial considerations constrain innovation and when do they not [12]? Do analysts undervalue firms that spend on R & D, and do analysts' valuations of firms depend on the firms' accounting treatment of R & D, [13]? Does the accounting treatment of R & D influence management attitudes to R & D spending [13]? Both these chapters [12, 13] recognize that financial constraints can be internal to the firm as much as external to the firm. How does the capital structure of R & D-intensive firms compare to that of other firms, and is there evidence that the risk premium for R & D projects is higher in the United Kingdom than elsewhere [14]? Chapters 12, 13 and 14 also discuss the firm's disclosure strategy: how much information should be released about R & D plans and to whom?

Again, finance and accounting issues inevitably arise in other contexts. Broadly speaking, finance may be a more serious constraint on the adoption of new technology than skills [6]. The technology strategies of finance- and accounting-led firms will be very different from those of engineering-led firms [7], and in comparison to our foreign competitors, the United Kingdom has a disproportionate number of the first type of firm. Chapter 9 recognizes that the time at which proactive marketing is most essential will also be the time of maximum financial stress for the firm, and this may in part explain the reactive and satisficing approach to marketing in many small high-technology firms. Chapter 9 also finds that retained profits are the main source of finance in high-technology firms of the types studied. Chapter 3 examines returns on assets as one key measure of the performance of small high-technology firms.

In a number of places it is suggested that conventional accounting practice may promote short-termism, though short-termism may also result from the misuse of accounting criteria [12]. This short-termism may lead to an underinvestment in training and human resource development more generally [6, 7]. Chapter 2 recognizes that the firm's stock market value will inevitably impact on technology strategy, because of the risk of hostile takeover.

Integration, communication and 'bridge-building'

In a sense, the themes of integration, communication and bridge-building arise along with the pervasive issues of expertise, competence, information, know-how, knowledge and skills – as discussed above. One aspect of this is the firm's *absorptive capacity* – its ability to absorb information and expertise from outside but also from inside the organization [1]: some competencies are transferable others are not. Communication between functions lies at the centre of technology strategy [1, 2]. Absorptive capacity can have a strong bearing on how rapid technological change impacts on market structure [10]. Moreover, bridge-building between different specialisms and knowledge bases is essential to the successful implementation of IT systems in the organization, and the communication of technology requirements and capacities are often mediated by experts [5]. It is recognized, however, that this cross-disciplinary or cross-functional transfer is difficult and demanding [5], and that informal networks are often the most important in effecting that sort of communication [11].

Another aspect of communication is developed in the book: the communication and acquisition of knowledge about technologies and markets [4, 11].

Organizational structure and relationships: organizational and user-supplier

Chapters 1 and 2 address the theme of organizational structure most directly. Chapter 1 in particular develops a model of the process of technology management around the triad of architecture, trust and organizational relationships. Successful management of innovation requires a firm architecture that ensures the firm can appropriate the benefits of its innovative efforts. Appropriability is an internal as well as an external issue: these benefits should accrue to the firm not to individual employees, and of course it is desirable to prevent too many benefits spilling over to rivals. To describe the architecture of the organization is to describe the network of contracts that define the firm. These contracts may be formal or informal, and that will depend on the degree of trust implicit in working relationships. 'Flat' organizational structures, with few levels of hierarchy, often exhibit high-trust relations and need only informal contracts, while hierarchic structures assume low-trust relations and need more formal contracts. In Chapters 1 and 2, firms are categorized according to whether technology is central to their operations. The case studies in Chapter 12 suggest that when technology is central, financial considerations are less likely to constrain innovation.

Structure is also a central issue for successful management of collaboration [15]. The appropriate structure depends on the character of the collaborative project, and important issues of trust, appropriability and the exploitation of collaborative results arise here. Moreover, it is recognized that the integration of two diverse structures (following an acquisition, for example) is difficult: this in turn makes it hard to exploit potential synergies from acquisition [2].

Chapter 5 also examines contracts and trust in organizational structure. Trust is required for informal trade in know-how. The contracts describing user-supplier relations are found to lie on a spectrum from collaborative to adversarial, while organizational structures lie on a *technical-entrepreneurial* spectrum (as well as the widely used *mechanistic-organic* spectrum). Organizational structures and user-supplier relations are designed to manage uncertainty and to cope with other aspects of the external environment. In particular, it is argued that the organic, entrepreneurial structure may better handle uncertainty while the mechanistic firm is better adapted to a stable environment [10]. In the same vein, the organization operating in an uncertain environment must have a structure to link diverse innovative processes [11].

The design of an organizational structure interacts with the articulation of a strategic technological paradigm (or corporate 'vision of the future' for a technology). These paradigms become embodied in organizational structure, and the structure filters the sorts and sources of information that can be acquired to inform and develop the paradigm [4]. The employment of scientists and engineers on the company board may influence the company's goals, structure and technology strategy [7].

Organizational change, paradigms and technological visions: radical versus incremental technology change

Organizations, even bureaucracies, can cope with certain types of change, so long as it is change for which they have a routine [1]. Organizations construct strategic paradigms or technological visions, which are paths along which they anticipate a technology will develop [4]. When these paradigms have been articulated, the firm can start to make organizational routines to manage the change. Change along a paradigm could perhaps be called *incremental*, in that the organization proceeds along this path in incremental attainable steps. Radical change could be classed as change inconsistent with this paradigm, which the organization will encounter much more difficulty in managing [10]. Alternatively, technological change can be classified as competence-destroying if it cannot be managed using existing routines and knowledge bases, and competence enhancing (or competence-preserving) if it can. The difference here is that even quite large technological leaps (between 'generations' of the same technology, for example) may be competence-preserving, even if too big to be incremental.

Technological change incompatible with an existing structure may precipitate organizational restructuring [5, 10, 11], though in some cases radical technology change is an *occasion* for rather than a driving force *behind* radical organizational restructuring [5]. Organizational change raises difficult problems of managing the disruption to organizational power relations [5] and managing the dynamics of a changing organizational knowledge base [1]. Moreover, acquisition presents many of the same difficulties [2], including the problems of standardizing information systems [5]. Some case studies suggest that a radical technological innovation will require a product champion if it is to overcome organizational resistance [12]. If managers shrink from such restructuring they are likely to experience a lower performance than the potential maximum, and indeed the more macro-economic effect of competence-destroying technological change is likely to be turbulence in market shares and market structure [10].

Technology paradigms act as a guide-post, but can also act as a constraint [4]. The paradigm becomes embodied in organizational structure, and conditions the organization's perception of external information [4]. Chapter 4 explores in detail how these paradigms are set, and similar questions arise elsewhere [10, 11] Chapter 7 touches on the question of the role played by scientists and engineers in setting technological agenda. Chapter 12 notes that in some cases, innovation is 'terror' not strategy – especially in markets with very short product life-cycles.

Comparable problems arise in the context of collaboration. If the circumstances of partners change – for example, if one develops a technological lead over the other, so that the joint venture is becoming one-sided – then transition to a new collaborative structure (or separation) presents a complex management problem [15].

Market structure and firm sizes

Many of the chapters in this book are concerned mainly with medium or large-sized firms [1, 2, 4, 5 (in part), 10 (in part), 11, 15]. Some, however, give explicit and particular attention to small firms [3, 6, 9, 12 (in part)]. Chapter 3 studies the performance and survival of small firms on a regional basis. The small firms studied tend not to develop radically new technologies but apply existing technologies in new ways; they usually operate in niche markets, and there is considerable sectoral and spatial diversity. Chapter 3 examines the characteristics of these innovating firms and finds that the very smallest and the medium-sized firms are least likely to survive, while the intermediate-sized firm is most likely to survive. The chapter studies to what extent these small firms are seedlings for new industries and a basis for industrial rejuvenation.

Chapter 9 studies the role of proactive marketing in small high-technology firms. It is suggested that small firms tend to satisfice rather than optimize in their marketing strategy, and this is one reason at least for the sometimes poor performance of small firms in this area. Part of the reason is that one manager in a small firm may be filling the marketing role as well as several others, and this lack of specialization makes optimization too difficult. It is suggested that such firms are introspective, and that in an attempt to reduce risks they are reluctant to seek external finance. The firms sampled in this study tend to have markets with a greater spatial (regional) dispersion if they are selling products than if they are selling sub-contracted services.

Innovative firms in the United Kingdom may face a risk premium especially on debt finance [14]. Chapter 10 suggests that small firms have a special role in the early stages of a product life-cycle, before a clear and widely accepted technology paradigm has appeared.

Chapter 10 is concerned directly with market structure – in particular, the market shares of different firms and their movements over time. Its main aim is to explore the interaction between rapid technological change (competence enhancing or competence destroying), technological paradigms or visions, organizational structure and the development of market structure. Chapter 10 also notes that technological change can be disruptive to market structure (in the sense of changing the league table of main players) but need not necessarily change the overall concentration ratio.

Performance and survival

Chapters 2, 3 and 7 pay most attention to the question of how technology strategy influences economic performance and firm survival, but several other chapters also touch on this. Chapter 2 draws on many of the London Business School case studies, and the conceptual framework developed in [1], to illustrate the linkage between technology management, organizational structure and economic performance. Chapter 3 examines the performance and survival of small high-technology firms: criteria of performance include return on assets and employment creation, especially regionally. It also examines the scope for regional policies and small-firms policies to improve performance. Chapter 7 examines questions of how the employment of scientists and engineers in companies, in particular the background of the managing director and the functional/disciplinary mix of the board of directors may affect the economic performance of the firm. The accounting and finance-led company is compared to the science and technology-led company.

Chapter 4 takes an evolutionary perspective on the development and survival of the firm. Chapter 8 argues that it is the *use* of new technology rather than its generation that is critical for improving economic performance. Chapter 9 examines the effect of a proactive marketing policy on the firm's performance. The history of the past market performance of products is a vital input into the innovation process [11], and it is easy for a potentially high-performing company to become a bankrupt company in the face of high interest charges [12]. Chapter 13 finds that analysts expect firms in R & D-intensive sectors to maintain a normal level of R & D expenditure to ensure satisfactory market performance. Finally, Chapter 10 explores the performance of different firms, with different organizational structures, in the face of rapid technology change.

Risk

R & D and innovation are very risky [1, 2, 12, 13, 14]. Because of this firms may have to pay a risk premium for investment in innovation [14] and this may underlie the frequently made references to short-termism in financial markets. Despite this, firms invest in innovation because the costs of not doing so may be worse [12]. Also, it appears that city analysts value the fact that firms do a 'normal' level of R & D in industries that are R & D-intensive, and in such industries disclosure of R & D plans (or at least selective disclosure) may be an appropriate strategy [13].

Chapters 1 and 2 argue that investment in new technology will not necessarily be successful even in firms where technology is central and in firms where it is not, such investment has very variable returns. Collaboration is seen as one way to reduce risk in technology investments [15] and the desire to avoid risk may explain the introspection of small high-technology firms [9].

DISCIPLINES REPRESENTED AND EMPIRICAL METHODOLOGIES

The research that is summarized here is informed by eleven different social-science disciplines. In alphabetical order, these are accounting, anthropology, business strategy, economics and econometrics, finance, geography and town planning, marketing, organizational behaviour, politics, science policy and finally sociology. While some projects are mono-disciplinary, one aim of the initiative has been to get different teams to learn from the different disciplinary perspectives of other projects. We hope that the discussion above highlights the many exciting points of connection between these different approaches. Related to this multi-disciplinary background, a wide variety of empirical methodologies have been used: case studies (longitudinal, interview-based, secondary sources), ethnographic studies, questionnaire surveys (postal and telephone), econometric analysis, other statistical analysis and simulation modelling. It is apparent that each of these methodologies brings its own rich insights, and the researcher from one different tradition has much to learn from the others.

Part I

The 'core' – management of new technology

1 Managing technological innovation

Architecture, trust and organizational relationships in the firm

John Kay and Paul Willman

1.1 INTRODUCTION

Discussions between sociologists and economists about matters of practical concern to business are often conspicuous by their absence. Where they do occur, they are often dialogues of the deaf. This is not only a matter for regret but also for concern, since the substantive concerns of both disciplines have tended to converge around issues which have clear commercial relevance. Economists have turned their attention to the analysis of organizations as well as that of markets; sociologists, in something of a return to their roots, have become concerned with rational choice models in the explanation of human activity.

These developments are important for the analysis of technological change. As Elster has noted, there have been two main approaches to the analysis of such change. The first, naturally favoured by economists, conceives technological change as involving rational goal-directed activity, seeking the best option within a given innovation set. The second emphasizes the incremental, cumulative and historically influenced nature of change in discussing evolutionary trajectories (Elster 1983: 9–11). Sociologists have been drawn to it, as have economists of the evolutionary school, such as Nelson and Winter (1982). The former approach has tended to sustain certain generalizations about change, perhaps at the expense of operating with rather rigid, counter-intuitive assumptions about the processes involved. Sociologists following the latter have tended to an idiographic approach, in some cases going so far as to argue that generalizations about either the process of technological change or its outcomes are impossible for theoretical reasons and that indeterminacy in outcomes is a consequence of the variable, socially created nature of the process itself (e.g. Barley 1986). Few predictive statements are possible. The middle ground between these two approaches is largely uninhabited.

Our knowledge of the process of change, particularly at the level of the firm, has been hampered by this lack of dialogue. As Tushman and Nelson note, the literature on both the selection of technology and the shaping of it by organizations is lamentably thin (Tushman and Nelson 1990:9). Questions about the factors underpinning successful technological innovation at the level of the firm, whether involving process, product or both, are difficult to answer. We lack a precise understanding not only of the organizational influences over the rate and direction of technical change, but also of the processes of deployment of any innovation – more specifically, of the ways in which organizations use innovation to attain competitive advantage.

The research discussed here has sought to fill part of this gap by developing a set of hypotheses about the process of innovation and its relationship to specific outcomes, notably competitive success defined as the generation of rents. These hypotheses, described more fully in Grindley (1989), initially concern the incentive to innovate and, subsequently, the organizational attributes of innovative success. At first, the spur to innovation is seen to lie in the perception of competitive pressure. Thereafter success is hypothesized to rely on organizational features such as cross-functional integration, flexibility, the accumulation of firm-specific skills and capabilities and on the ability to break down change into incremental attainable steps. These organizational features, which are described more fully below, together constitute the organizational capability of the firm to sustain long-term innovation. They concern not only the structure of the organization but also its knowledge base and its ability to deploy knowledge in pursuit of competitive success.

Our argument, based on the empirical data collected from over twenty case studies, is that firms are differentially capable of locating and appropriating their own knowledge bases, and that this differential capability relates to their innovative capacity. These case-study data, which will be referred to in an illustrative manner below, were collected between 1989 and 1992 in three sectors, namely, financial services (including public sector cases) instruments/electronics and manufacturing, particularly motor vehicles.

The purpose of this chapter is to articulate the theoretical basis for this argument. Put briefly, we argue that the organizational capacity to implement new technology is the key to success, that an examination of the organization's knowledge base is the basis for understanding this capacity and that an understanding of the dynamics of changing organizational knowledge bases can be generated by conceiving of the organization or firm as a network of implicit contracts.

The structure of the chapter is as follows. Section 1.2 indicates how a concern with organizational knowledge and capacity for change arose from our empirical work. Section 1.3 spells out a model of the firm as a network of contracts. Section 1.4 discusses the implications of this view. Section 1.5 concludes.

1.2 ORGANIZATION AND INNOVATION

We have been concerned with the relatively stable and long-term features of organization which sustain innovation streams. The debate here is primarily about the importance of bureaucracy or of its avoidance. In the seminal work, that of Burns and Stalker (1961), 'organic' structures, characterized by the absence of formality and hierarchy, ambiguity in reporting relationships and the absence of clear job definitions, are seen to support innovation more effectively than do 'mechanistic' structures with obverse characteristics. 'Bureaucracy', as commonly understood, is inimical to innovation. Subsequent popular literature tends to stress the need to avoid bureaucracy and to put considerable effort into the management of an innovative environment (e.g. Kanter 1983)

Our casework reveals the inadequacies of this approach. Our financial-services and public-sector cases relate, without exception, to bureaucratic organizations. They are, moreover, bureaucratic organizations for good reason. The processing of very large volumes of transactions to common criteria and standards and (in the case of the public-sector organizations) with a high degree of central accountability for all activities of the organization, demands hierarchic structure and an extensive body of organizational routine. In these cases, to advocate the breakdown of bureaucracy in the interests of an innovative culture is to misunderstand the primary purposes of the organization. The relevant issue is not how to dispense with, or circumvent, hierarchy or organizational routine but how to integrate technology in the context of hierarchy and organizational routine.

Our cases show that information technology projects tended to be more successful where relatively unambitious, focused applications were tried, as in the Inland Revenue, DVLC in the later stages and Halifax, than where the technology was seen as the basis for affecting major organizational change, as for example in Midland Bank.[1] This incrementalism is a feature of organization rather than a feature of technology (Pavitt 1990). Several firms were first-time users of this generic technology; their success in adopting it seemed to relate less to the precise technology chosen and more to the grafting of technological decision-making on to existing organizational routines. Organizational change through the use of technology did not work, but radical technological changes could be accommodated by use of existing procedures.

Other research on innovation patterns, such as that by Nelson and Winter (1980) and by Daft (1982), has tended to stress the importance of formality and routine in the process of innovation. Nelson and Winter speak of 'innovative routines', rooted in combinations of known, tried, sub-routines (Nelson and Winter 1980: 127–34). Daft emphasizes the importance of stable knowledge bases enhanced through stable communications channels (Daft 1982). In a slightly different vein, Van de Ven emphasizes the importance of *structural* integration and formal mechanisms for achieving it in the pursuit of success in innovation (Van de Ven 1986).

These routines are partly dictated by a perception that organizational success, even innovative success, depends on stable routine. Consider the following: 'Despite frequent, repeated structural change, endemic changes in products, processes and technology, people do need some sense of stability . . . *internal stability in these firms derives from strong, carefully nurtured organizational culture* (Jelinek and Schoonhaven 1990: 36). They speak of a 'dynamic tension' between stability and change, and stress the permanence of a strategy for change rather than a particular structural context. Their sample is of high-technology firms and their results may not be generalizable, but their work, populist but in the Burns and Stalker tradition, raises several interesting questions for the management of innovation, in particular the balance between of 'entrepreneurial' behaviour and bureaucratic structure in sustaining innovative activity.

These questions may be further considered by examining the often quoted cliché that 'change is normal'. This might be taken to imply that certain organizations exist which are capable of assimilating almost any kind of change, technological or otherwise. However, a more reasonable inference to be drawn is that organizations exist which have the capacity to operate with a relatively stable *rate* of change. Their forte is the routinization and bureaucratization of change itself. Procedures for incremental adaption to changed circumstances become part of the organization's rule structure. The appropriate empirical questions concern, first, the necessary conditions for the establishment of such innovative routines and, second, their durability over time.

1.3 INNOVATION AND THE KNOWLEDGE BASE OF THE FIRM

The development of an effectively innovative culture is not therefore a matter of finding alternatives to organizational routines for monitoring and control, but of establishing routines which stimulate appropriate innovation and achieve the integration of technology into the core activities of the business.[2]

In appraising these routines the test we apply is the contribution of technology to the competitive advantage, or rent-creating capacity, of the business. Thus the criteria used in measuring success in the management of technology are not technological ones. It follows that technological sophistication is distinct from our measurement of success. We believe, for example, that Halifax Building Society – who have made a relatively idiosyncratic and low-level technology meet the specific needs of their business very effectively – display better management of technology than Midland Bank where more advanced technology has been implemented with little evident benefit to the cost structure or competitive position of the firm. We therefore emphasize, first, the *relevance* of technology – in high-technology firms, in particular, there is a danger of emphasizing technological solutions at the expense of commercial application, second, the *integration* of technology, that is, the ability to match it effectively to user needs, and, third, the *appropriability* of technology, that is, the capacity of the firm to capture the benefits of technology *for itself*, and to defend them, both against employees and against competitors.

Each of these turns on the contribution of innovation and technology to the knowledge base of the organization. Incremental adaptation to change implies an existing knowledge base upon which to built. In the first instance, this knowledge base might not relate to the technology in question. At DSS, for example, knowledge of information technology remained in the hands of external consultants for some time during the early stages of the project; as internal expertise grew, the existing non-technical knowledge base of prospective users, relating to the administration of benefit provision, became a considerable influence on system design (Dyerson and Roper 1991). The knowledge base of an organization may not be explicitly acknowledged and articulated; it may be both tacit and diffuse, so that it is difficult to see in the first instance how new technological applications relate to it. It may be in the hands of a particular strategic group, whose relationship to new technology may be problematic; they may, for example, suffer status or pecuniary losses following technological change. If so, the firm will find the benefits of technological change difficult to appropriate, particularly if competitors can lure the strategic group away. Finally, the knowledge base itself might be reliant on a particular technology which new technology supplants. There is a clear distinction to be made between the knowledge base of an organization and the purely technological *expertise* it possesses.[3]

A correct appreciation of the relationship between a particular technology and business needs is thus important. We define the knowledge base of a firm as the sum total of information within the firm relevant to the conduct of its business. It will be greater in most cases than the sum of individual knowledge bases because such knowledge is a social and organizational construct not appropriable by individuals; however, it may not *in toto* be available to those managing the firm. The effective knowledge base will, however, be less than the sum total of information within the firm, some of which will be commercially irrelevant and some relating to redundant or divergent definitions of business need. We define 'know-how' as application of the knowledge base to particular problems.

Generation of know-how involves an understanding of the relationship between technical expertise and competitive advantage. It requires integration of functions, in particular it requires user involvement in and commitment to technological change. In many businesses considering the adoption of new technology, the preliminary requirement of an understanding of the core-knowledge base of the business is absent. In such circumstances, the firm exercises little influence over the extent to which new technological applications may be competence enhancing or competence destroying.

In Tushman and Anderson's original formulation, competence enhancement or competence destruction were conceptualized as consequences of adoption of in-coming technology (Tushman and Anderson 1986: 439–65). However, where generic technologies such as information technology are concerned, the organization may, through its management or mismanagement of the innovative process, enhance or destroy the pre-existing knowledge base.[4] The firm's knowledge of the in-coming technology and definition of the strategic importance of expertise related to it may be an intervening variable. The pre-existing level of understanding of the technical expertise involved – as well as the firm's understanding of its own knowledge base – will be important.

Enhancement of the knowledge base may involve research of various forms but is likely, following the Nelson and Winter argument, to follow from practice – learning by doing. Enhancement may involve the drawing in of expertise from outside. Examples from our own cases would include both DSS and DVLC, in both of which expertise initially held by outside consultants became know-how in the possession of employees involved in the use of information technology. However, it may also involve the selective inclusion of groups within the firm in the process of innovation. Over time, the locus of both expertise and know-how may shift, and in order to capture a greater proportion of the available knowledge base, senior managers may have to share information with certain strategic groups. In doing so, they run the risk that employees will leave, taking know-how to competitors. In failing to do so, the firm may forego competitive advantage.

1.4 FROM EXPERTISE TO KNOW-HOW

The knowledge base

We are now close to establishing the necessary organizational conditions for successful long-term innovation – the durability of innovative routines. The firm must establish organizational arrangements which generate and appropriate commercial know-how through the application of technological expertise. It is the conversion of individual and external expertise into business specific know-how which is at the heart of the effective appropriation of technology by the firm.

By our definition, any firm operating with some success will deploy know-how in pursuit of competitive advantage. This statement does not imply either that the body of know-how within the firm is codified and programmatic or that there is consensus about the best way to pursue competitive advantage within the business. On the one hand, much know-how may be tacit and localized within particular functions of the firm. On the other, there may be competing definitions, or at least substantial differences of emphasis, between functions in discussions about what constitutes know-how. Both may affect the reception and performance of any new technology adopted by the firm. Consider the example of generic technologies such as information technology. Such technologies support a variety of applications with varying relationships to overall business objectives. Broadly, these may be in the process of production, in the product itself or in reforming the administrative systems within the firm. Engineering or production personnel may be expected to consider applications such as process control or computer-aided design in the interests of enhanced process or product performance. Marketing may consider inclusion of information technology into products or its use in enhancing the firm's market responsiveness. Other functions, such as accounting, may consider the use of information technology for cost control and cost projection purposes.

Within the firm there will also be various forms of technical *expertise* relating to the different product and process technologies, current and perhaps prospective, within the firm. The relationship between expertise and know-how which deploys the knowledge base is, however, problematic. In some firms expertise is the core of know-how. A good example is Cosworth, the manufacturer of racing and high-performance road engines, where expertise in engine technology to all intents *is* the business (Aston 1991). What might be termed 'technology push' firms driven by R & D may generally fall into this category. However, in many firms technical expertise is a necessary but not sufficient condition for competitive success. It may be impossible to function as a major banking institution without good systems, but it does not follow that developing more advanced systems will generate competitive advantage. Even in a relatively high-technology industry such as telecommunications, the most advanced digital switching systems are not necessarily the most successful in the market-place. An understanding of the *centrality* of technical expertise to business know-how is essential.[5]

In short, each function will define the information technology opportunities of the business initially in functional rather than strategic terms. More importantly for the argument here, they are likely to do so by assessing the relationship between new technology and the pre-existing functional knowledge base. If the distribution of information technology opportunities is uneven across functions and if the functions in any event hold to competing, functionally based definitions of the essential knowledge base of the business, then there may be conflict over the strategic opportunities presented by information technology. This creates scope for misinterpretation of the centrality of technology.

The Chief Executive Officer or strategic group charged with the direction of the business must operate with an understanding of the relationship between technical expertise and know-how.[6] This does not simply relate to adoption decisions but also to the implementation process and the ways in which technology is subsequently used. To pursue our earlier example from financial services, it would be impossible to operate a large-scale financial institution without an automated money-transmission system. However, to suggest that further investment in more advanced systems will yield competitive advantage because of its effect on costs and margins is to make further assumptions about the behaviour of the market which raise the status of information technology from a necessary to a sufficient condition for business success. Our argument is that technological leadership is a sufficient condition for business success in very few industries.

Appropriability and contract structure

There are thus intra-organizational issues involved in the management of the knowledge base and in its appropriation by the firm. In Cosworth, for example, selective decentralization of knowledge and expertise prevented any group of employees from understanding the whole process of engine design and emerging as potential competitors; the owners retained key expertise relating to engine design and component manufacture which was difficult to replicate through reverse engineering. In Halifax Building Society employees who are involved in IT tend to have developed competencies which, because of location and because of the computer languages used, are not readily transferable. Within any organization, there may be groups of employees possessing know-how which is neither available to the firm, because of employee retention of information, nor exportable elsewhere, because of its tacit and idiosyncratic nature.

In any firm there may be tensions between the generation and enhancement of the knowledge base on the one hand, which may imply extension of involvement in process or product redesign, and appropriability on the other. If there are different definitions, say between functions, about what constitutes the appropriate knowledge base, these tensions may break out into covert or overt conflict, involving information retention, competing objectives and a failure to co-ordinate actions. In order to manage the knowledge base successfully through sequences of technological change in the long term, the firm must identify, locate and capture the pre-existing knowledge base, understand how successive changes can be related to it in a competence-enhancing way, and appropriate the returns to innovation. Similar conceptual issues arise here in the intra-firm context to those discussed by Georghiou and Barker in Chapter 15.

These considerations serve to introduce some of the difficulties involved in capturing the know-how in a firm. It should not be assumed that such capture occurs naturally. The associated problems have been tackled in different ways by both economists and sociologists; their approaches are convergent (see Willman 1986).

The economic approach is one which emphasizes the game-theoretic nature of the problem and points to the contract structure of the firm as a means of dealing with it (Kay 1993). From a game-theoretic perspective there are two familiar problems associated with the development of firm-specific know-how. The transfer of capabilities – either from the individual to the firm or in the other direction – is an activity which invites strategic behaviour. There is not only some direct cost to effecting the transfer, but the loss of a valuable asset which (from the individual's perspective) can no longer be bargained over and (from the firm's perspective) can be transferred to a competitor. Thus, although there are potentially clear advantages to both parties in successful transfer, the game has a clear prisoner's dilemma structure. Moreover, although the formal contract structure can impose obligations and restrictions, these are largely incapable of being monitored or enforced in practice. This activity is a particularly clear example of Williamson's distinction between perfunctory and consummate co-operation (Williamson 1975, 1985).

It was quickly evident from our case studies that this is not a purely theoretical issue. We observed the frustration of DSS managers at their inability to secure an effective transfer of skills from their consultants who, as they saw it, realized that to effect such a transfer was to diminish their future role. We saw the routine drain of expertise from VG, with the loss of both firm- and industry-specific know-how in the process. We observed Cosworth's success in largely preventing a similar problem from eroding their expertise, and noted the importance which their senior management had attached to the issue (Aston 1991, Dyerson 1992a).

The second group of game-theoretic issues are those which arise from the need of both parties to engage in idiosyncratic expenditure, through the transfer (from the firm) or the acquisition (by the individual) of the firm-specific know-how. To do this exposes each to the risk of opportunistic behaviour. Again, it was apparent that this was a real issue. Halifax information technology staff were effectively locked into that organization, as were many Cosworth engineers (and, importantly, did not appear to be unhappy with that position in either case). Other financial services organizations noted the difficulty they encountered in retaining information technology personnel and resented the bargaining position which they enjoyed in relation to the rest of the organization. In order to sustain idiosyncratic investment, it is necessary to obtain credible commitments from both sides that ensure *ex post* consistency of *ex ante* behaviour.

We have therefore come to emphasize the role of the firm's structure of formal and informal contracts – what Kay describes as the firm's architecture (Kay 1993) – as key to the development of competitive advantage through the creation and enhancement of firm-specific know-how. A key characteristic of architecture is that because of the high degree of informality in contracting – contract design and terms are predominantly relational rather than classical – the structure defies easy replication. This leads directly to the key issue of appropriability. The establishment of competitive advantage through architecture, together with the development of firm-specific know-how, enables the gains from technology to be appropriated by the firm itself rather than by those who provide the technological expertise. 'Ownership' of technology by the firm in this sense has a commercial as well as a social significance.

The sociological perspective

The sociological literature says strikingly similar things, although in very different language. The approach is best characterized by Fox (1974). His argument is that organizations operate with different combinations of institutionalized trust, an expression which embraces both the strictly contractual and non-contractual elements of the employment relationship. Low-trust employment relations are characterized by close supervision, impersonal rules, the encouragement of performance through disciplinary arrangements and by low levels of task discretion. In high-trust relations, by contrast, close supervision is seen as inappropriate, task discretion is high, and the typical career path involves promoting an individual through a series of posts with increasing discretion. Simple reciprocity is assumed on the part of employees; low-trust relations foster low-trust responses such as indifferent performance, absenteeism and information hoarding, while the individual advancing through a series of high-trust posts will display increasing commitment to and identification with the organization in question. Moreover, 'spirals' of respectively increasing and decreasing trust may be established, making a shift from one form of relationship to another extremely difficult to effect; each regime has its own equilibrium.[7]

The picture of the firm emerging from Fox's work is, despite differences of detail, one of a network of idiosyncratic exchanges conducted against a background of shared expectations about the continuity of the relationship and the rules for managing change. Under low-trust relations, characterized by classical contracting, change will be bargained over with opportunistic employees hoarding information. Under this regime, one has a complex contingent claims contract. On the other hand, under Fox's high-discretion syndrome, which intuitively seems to describe the conditions governing most managerial work, one has an authority relationship based on shared assumptions about rewards, contribution and the ways in which authority will be exercised.

The ability both to generate innovations and to adapt to change will be influenced by the nature of the employment relationship. Most large organizations operate with a mixture of high-trust and low-trust employment relations. The logic of both Williamson's argument and that of Fox suggests that low-trust, opportunistic relationships will generate conflict in the face of change. On the one hand, the firm will seek to document and control the development of task and team idiosyncrasies in low-trust roles in order to appropriate the emerging knowledge base, while job incumbents will seek to retain such knowledge in order to bargain over its sale. On the other hand, technological change may be used to eliminate or to further curtail discretion in low-trust roles to minimize the prospects of subsequent resistance. This dynamic has generated considerable debate within the sociological tradition (Willman 1986, Offe 1976). It is highly unlikely that innovative behaviour intended by or appropriable to management within the firm will emerge from such relations.

There are, however, complex issues involved in the generation of innovative behaviour in high-trust roles. One approach to the encouragement of innovation might suggest the provision of direct financial rewards to innovate individuals according to their contribution to a given innovation and its subsequent success. However, the potential for opportunism and the disincentives to team working here are considerable. A second opinion implied by the adoption of the high-trust syndrome is not to reward innovative behaviour directly but, in effect, to guarantee to a specific group long-term shares in the rents accruing to the innovative firm. Under this option, the firm establishes a reputation for rent sharing with present and prospective employees in particular categories which encourages efficient transactions around the knowledge base.

The location of the boundary between high-trust and low-trust roles is thus a critical question. Inclusion of employees within the high-trust network who either have low-trust responses or who do not possess significant amounts of know-how raises overall costs and risks loss of know-how to competitors or to sub-groups within the firm. Exclusion of employees from the high-trust network who *do* possess significant know-how is to forego sources of competitive advantage and to encourage resistance to technological change. If the firm is unaware of the underlying distribution of know-how, or if the competitive environment shifts so that previously excluded groups become significant to the generation of new know-how, successful innovation will be difficult, not least because high-trust initiatives towards inclusion are likely to meet with low-trust responses. However, in attempting to enhance its own knowledge base during periods of technological change, the firm may be faced with the need to extract information about task idiosyncrasies from recalcitrant groups in order to implement changes originated by high-trust employees. In our case studies, the most common case concerned user-held information in public-sector information technology applications.

Innovative effectiveness is thus closely tied up, not simply with the existence of expertise within the business, but with questions of organizational design. A strategic group within the firm may reach an accurate and durable understanding of the centrality of a particular set of technologies for business success, but there are separate questions related to the ability of the firm's organization to be able to generate competitive advantage from that knowledge. The empirical relationship between technical competence and this organizational capacity needs to be explored in more detail.

Any firm will consist of a network of high-and low-trust roles. Put another way, it will have an idiosyncratic network of contracts. Our contention is that this architecture may substantially enhance or impede the firm's ability to generate rents from innovation. The contractual structure must, on the one hand, encourage the generation of innovation and, on the other, secure its retention and appropriability by the firm rather than by employees or competitors.

1.5 CONCLUSIONS

Here we summarize some of the implications of the preceding analysis, based on the project casework. The main issues concern centrality, firm-specific knowledge and the contractual structure of the firm.

Centrality of technology

We have come to attach considerable importance to the idea of centrality of technology; the extent to which it is a prime source of, or a support to, competitive advantage in specific industry sectors. The key issue is that where technology is central the credibility of the long-term commitment to a technology-based value system allows informal contracting between the firm and those who contribute technological expertise, while where technology is non-central this is necessarily the subject of an explicit bargain. The difference in styles of relationship is in turn reflected in the shape of the reward structure, and the status of those implementing technology within the organization. Notice that this is not to say that technology 'ought' to be central for all firms. In the sense in which we use the word, the centrality of technology is very largely something which is defined for the firm rather than by it, and where technology is not central the firm achieves more effective monitoring and control of its technological activities at the price of much greater difficulty in achieving integration.

Firm-specific knowledge

Our conclusion here is that firms which implement technology successfully take the development of firm-specific knowledge beyond the point at which this is actually required by the nature of the technology itself, because of the requirements of integration and appropriability. It appears that in some cases firms encourage the development of further technological expertise, confident that this will enhance commercial know-how in the longer term. However, even in the absence of such encouragement, learning-by-doing by job incumbents develops further expertise which may or may not generate know-how, depending upon the architecture. User knowledge tends to be highly idiosyncratic and tacit, but it may be either a source of competitive advantage if appropriated or of resistance to change if not.

The nature of the contract structure

We believe that in most circumstances organizations which are successful in implementing technology are characterized by some degree of relational contracting (although not necessarily in all areas of the organization). This will be reflected in pay and remuneration structures and in the form of organizational controls over job incumbents (flat hierarchies, pay related to organizational rather than individual performance, loose supervision), length of employee service, balance of direct pay and benefits, and other less tangible aspects of employee attitudes. It is not clear yet, beyond what has been said already, what generalizations may emerge here. Our argument is that the architecture might generate appropriable innovations around technological expertise relevant to the firm's knowledge base. We also regard much of the knowledge base as tacit and idiosyncratic. But it does not follow that there are no general principles about the construction of organizational architecture. The key factors appear to be the nature of technological changes, the nature and location of the pre-existing knowledge base and the experience of competitive pressure.

In summary, we have developed an approach to the study of technological change which locates it squarely in the context of firm organization, employing ideas from industrial economics and organizational sociology. Our emphasis, supported by the data from our cases, is a contract structure and information exchange. Our concern is not with the technical success of innovation, but with its impact on the performance of the firm. In this chapter we have outlined the thinking behind the approach and attempted, by reference to our case studies, to show its empirical relevance.

ACKNOWLEDGEMENT

This chapter is a paper which forms part of the output of the 'New Technology and the Firm' project at London Business School. The paper has benefited from comments from other project members, in particular Romano Dyerson. It relies on fieldwork conducted by Beverley Aston, Romano Dyerson and Michael Roper.

NOTES

1 See Dyerson (1989), Dyerson and Roper (1990) and Dyerson (1992a).
2 The argument presented in the following paragraphs has many parallels with the discussion of 'technological paradigms' by Metcalfe and Boden in Chapter 4.
3 For a fuller discussion, see Willman (1992).
4 The idea here is similar to that of Clark *et al.* (1988), who argue that the 'engineering system' surrounding any technological application gives degrees of freedom to decision makers within the firm which leave open many key design parameters.
5 The concept of centrality parallels Daft's idea of the 'dominant innovation issue' confronting the firm (Daft 1982: 152–3). In both cases, the firm may choose, mistakenly, a technological solution when some other form of organizational change would have been more appropriate.
6 There are issues here relating to the nature of the firm's strategic group which are discussed more fully by Bosworth and Wilson in Chapter 7.
7 Fox is implicitly describing a repeated prisoner's dilemma game. The argument that both high- and low-trust regimes are self-sustaining parallels the 'folk theorem' in economics. For a similar analysis of these issues, see Casson (1991).

REFERENCES

Aston, B. (1991) 'Unlimited horsepower: innovation at Cosworth engineering' *Technology Project Paper* 10 London Business School.
Barley, S. (1986) 'Technology as an occasion for structuring', *Administrative Science Quarterly* 31: 78–108
Burns, T. and Stalker, G. M. (1961) *The Management of Innovation*, London, Tavistock.
Casson, M. C. (1991), *Economics of Business Culture; Game Theory, Transaction Costs and Economic Performance*, Oxford University Press.
Clark, J., McLoughlin, I., Rose, H. and King, R. (1988) *The Process of Technological Change; New Technology and Social Choice at the Workplace*, Cambridge University Press.
Daft, R. (1982) 'Bureaucratic versus non-bureaucratic structure and the process of innovation and change', in S. Bacharach (ed.) *Research in the Sociology of Organizations*, Greenwich, Conn.: JAI, pp. 129–66.
Dyerson, R. (1989) 'The DVLC and technological change: one-time failure, long-term success' *Technology Project Paper*, London Business School.
—— (1992a) 'VG instruments', *Technology Project Paper* 21, London Business School.
—— (1992b) 'Halifax Building Society', *Technology Project Paper*, 23, London Business School.
Dyerson, R. and Roper, M. (1990) 'Building competencies: the computerization of PAYE' *Technology Project Paper*, 6, London Business School.
—— and —— (1991) 'When expertise becomes know-how: the management of IT projects in financial services' *Business Strategy Review* 2(2): 55–73.
Elster, J. (1983) *Explaining Technical Change*, Cambridge University Press.

Fox, A. (1974) *Beyond Contract: Work, Power and Trust Relations*, London: Faber.

Grindley, P. (1989) 'Technological change within the firm: a framework for research and management', *Technology Project Paper 1*, London Business School.

Jelinek, M. and Schoonhaven, C. B. (1990) *Innovation Marathon*, Oxford: Blackwell.

Kanter, R. M. (1983) *The Change Masters*, London, Allen & Unwin.

Kay, J. A. (1993) *The Structure of Strategy*, Oxford University Press.

Nelson, R. and Winter, S. (1982), *An Evolutionary Theory of Economic Change*, Harvard University Press.

Offe, C. (1976) *Industry and Inequality*, London: Edward Arnold.

Pavitt, K. (1989) 'What we know about the strategic management of technology', *California Management Review* 32: 17–26.

Tushman, M. and Anderson, M. (1986) 'Technological discontinuities and organizational environments', *Administrative Science Quarterly* 31: 439–65.

Tushman, M. and Nelson, R. (1990) 'Technology, organizations and innovation', *Administrative Science Quarterly* 35:1–8.

Van de Ven, M. (1986) 'Central problems in the management of innovation', *Management Science* 32:590–607.

Williamson, O. E. (1975) *Markets and Hierarchies: Analysis and Anti-trust Implications*, New York Free Press.

—— (1985) *The Economic Institutions of Capitalism*, New York: Free Press.

Willman, P. (1986) *Technological Change, Collective Bargaining and Industrial Efficiency*, Oxford University Press.

—— (1992) 'Bureaucracy, innovation and appropriability', *Technology Project Paper 15*, London Business School.

2 Managing technology
Organizing for competitive advantage

Peter Grindley

2.1 INTRODUCTION

The aim of this research programme has been to investigate the links between economic and organizational management of technology and to identify keys to successful and unsuccessful performance. The premise has been that we cannot understand the firm's economic performance in technology without also understanding the organizational relationships within it. The integration of technology into the firm's business operations is crucial to its successful management and hence its competitive advantage. Research has focused in parallel on the development of an analytical framework and on a series of case studies. The framework has identified key features for technology management. This has both guided case research and in turn been modified by it. Generalizations about organizational structures and procedures have been made using a contracts-based approach, derived from synthesis analyses of the case histories. The overall aim has been to add perspective to the study of technology management. This echoes some of the issues from other sections of the New Technology and the Firm initiative.

The research framework has stressed three management features: functional integration, learning and strategic direction. Particular issues involved in this are the appropriability of the core-knowledge base by the firm or by individuals, the influence of the centrality of technology to firm performance on the interfaces between technical and other functions, and how strategic control may combine flexibility with overall guidance. Many hypotheses have evolved as the investigation has progressed. Two principles for organizational structure have emerged. The first is that within functions engaged in innovation (or adoption) of technology the managerial requirements are best achieved using a system of 'relational' (loosely defined, flexible) rather than 'specific' (fully defined, explicit rewards) contracts. The second is that the interfaces between different functional groups may be best governed by 'specific' contracts. Interface specificity depends on how dissimilar the functional organizations are. Firms continually involved in innovation may be totally organized around creativity and flexibility, while firms only peripherally involved may segregate the innovation functions from the main operations, which remain bureaucratically organized.

This chapter provides an overview of the research programme. It describes the framework, reviews the case findings and discusses management implications. The theoretical basis for the cross-disciplinary approach, the reasons for focusing on the knowledge base of the firm and an explanation of the contractual analysis are given in Kay and Willman (1993). The current paper describes the application of the approach to technology management and the analysis of the case studies. The cases are in three groups, involving the adoption of information technology in financial services, product innovation in electronics and instrumentation and combined product and process innovation in manufacturing.

In the following, Section 2.2 describes the key features of innovation management in the framework and the implications for organization and strategy. Section 2.3 discusses organizational types appropriate for technology management using the contracts approach. Section 2.4 gives an overview of the case studies, including remarks on methodology, and collects some of the findings. Section 2.5 makes concluding remarks.

2.2 RESEARCH FRAMEWORK

Performance objectives

Technology and the capacity for innovation are vital elements in the long-term success of most enterprises. What is more important for the firm is not technology itself but its impact on commercial or operational performance. This means that the criteria for judging success or failure are not just technical but relate to the firm's ability to exploit technology in the market-place. A basic proposition is that technology needs to take its place with other business capabilities. It is evaluated alongside other sources of competitive advantage and can only be understood and managed as an integrated part of the business. Rather than reducing the importance of technology, this may be the only way that it can be made effective.

This also means that we are concerned with long-term capabilities for continual innovation rather than individual product success.

There are two related parts to technology management. The first is the appropriate organizational structure and processes for managing innovation itself. The second is how technology is integrated with the other functions of the firm. This includes questions of strategic management and its contribution to performance. Clearly strategy and organization must be closely related.

Key elements of innovation management

Having made this link the next step is to identify key features of the innovative and adaptive organization, able to develop and retain competitive advantage. The aim is an organization which can develop streams of new products or repeatedly introduce new process technology to give the firm lasting advantage in the marketplace. Three basic elements have been identified, stressing the management of the knowledge base of the firm (Grindley 1989, 1991a).

Functional integration

Cross-functional integration between areas such as research and development, design, manufacturing and marketing ensures that products fill user needs, can be manufactured at low cost and that these and other complementary assets are available on time (Teece 1986). It involves communication, knowledge sharing and substantial understanding within the firm, and to some extent outside it. It requires openness and trust within the firm, as well as some form of controlled information sharing outside. This may arise from job rotation and cross training as well as from routines for involving different areas in the innovation process. It requires attention to the interfaces between innovation functions and the rest of the firm (Reich 1989).

Learning and capability building

Core capabilities and learning include business skills and organizational integration as well as technical knowledge. Capabilities are built up over relatively long periods and need constant replenishment. This implies an orientation towards encouraging learning. As much of this is firm-specific 'know-how' it depends on long-term commitment as well as identification with firm objectives. This requires continuity of employment for trained and knowledgeable personnel, to keep the 'know-how' and 'know-why' inside the organization. Skills are difficult to acquire 'off the shelf' or change quickly (Imai *et al.* 1985).

Strategic direction

Integration and learning may occur but we still need strategic direction to guide the capabilities into commercially rewarding areas. Strategy provides the overall guidance towards long-term goals. It may be seen as a shaping function, which selects and forms capabilities into basic competencies which are applied over series of products. However, strategy also evolves as technological and market opportunities arise. It is a combination of forward planning and responsiveness to ideas inside and outside the firm. It should combine broad direction with flexibility, top-down leadership with bottom-up ideas. Ultimately the motivation for innovation is from competition, though the link may be long term and indirect (Prahalad and Hamel 1990, Teece, *et al* 1991).

Management dynamics

Each of the key features, integration, learning and strategy, follows a similar dynamic. Development works in cycles. Short-term projects depend on the capabilities and cultural attitudes built up over the long term and in turn strengthen them and add new ones. The dynamic is shown in Figure 2.1. The same mechanism may be applied to learning, which builds know-how over time, to integration, which is built up via individual experiences, and to strategy, which couples overall long-term direction with short-term expediency and redirection as technology unfolds. Flexibility is part of all these features, to allow the evolution of the organizational structure, knowledge base and strategy (Nelson and Winter 1982, Dosi 1982, Pavitt 1990).

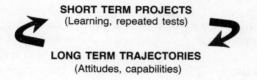

SHORT TERM PROJECTS
(Learning, repeated tests)

LONG TERM TRAJECTORIES
(Attitudes, capabilities)

Figure 2.1 Short- and long-term development cycles

Specific concerns

Appropriability

Appropriability of technology, the protection from imitation, is a crucial strategic variable. It is the basis for competitive advantage, affecting profit margins and options for exploiting technology. Appropriability rarely depends solely on the technology itself; more often it is a function of the network of skills. Technology embedded in an integrated organization cannot easily be appropriated by individuals within the firm or by competitors outside. In such cases personal knowledge is most valuable as part of a team, so individuals are unlikely to leave and competitors will find it hard to imitate a complete organization, built up over a long period. Integration and tacit skills provide their own protection, especially if the firm is producing streams of innovations which competitors cannot imitate without a time lag.

As one component of commercial success, this is part of a virtuous cycle which enhances the coherence and continuity of the organization and thus promotes open communication and competence building. However, appropriability is only part of the picture and must be balanced against other considerations. As an overriding aim protection of knowledge may make the organization too restrictive and defensive, stifling creativity and isolating the firm from outside sources of technology. Also, unless employees share in the benefits via the reward system they may feel exploited and withhold effort.

Centrality

The value of integration and learning across functions involved in technology need not mean that the entire firm should be organized in the same way. The extent of the innovative organization within the firm depends on the contribution of technology to the firm's competitive advantage, referred to as centrality. For some areas, such as electronics, technology is central to commercial success. For others, such as financial services, technology may be important but is unlikely to be the prime source of advantage. Where technology is peripheral the different functional types may call for different management styles – the non-technological functions having a bureaucratic structure with hierarchy and rules, the innovation functions using a flat structure, fostering open communications and flexibility. Problems arise in the interfaces between these types of organization and present a major challenge for management. Imbalances between the *modus operandi* for technological functions and the rest of the organization are at the heart of difficulties integrating technology into the firm. The interfaces may need to be relatively formal and limited to those performance measures which both sides can commit to. This may be a reason why development is often managed within project groups separated from the main organization, with special attention to the overlaps between the two. This may also help explain difficulties of introducing technology in mature businesses and traditional problems of R & D management.

Centrality is partly linked with the concepts of high-tech and low-tech firms. In high-tech sectors, working at the leading edge of technology, innovation is necessarily a key to competition. In low-tech sectors, operating with known technology, competitive advantage lies elsewhere. It depends on the nature of the technology involved, on the competitive structure of the industry and on the firm itself.

Strategic control

A fundamental paradox of technology management is the balance of creativity and control. How can firms be flexible and creative at the same time as maintaining control over operations and directing innovation towards commercial aims. The need for cross-functional integration and unstructured learning implies that rule-based, hierarchic control will be ineffective, other than for very complex, large-scale projects where it may be unavoidable. The problem is how to control and motivate loose 'integrated' teams, so as to give them clear, if non-specific, goals but leave them free to decide how to get there. Precise financial goals may be rejected in favour of 'strategic intents' which at the same time as being readily comprehended are expressed in qualitative terms, such as to be number one in a market or develop the industry's leading products (Hamel and Prahalad 1990).

2.3 ORGANIZATIONAL STRUCTURES

Architecture: the contractual network

Incorporating these elements of innovation management in the firm requires a combination of organizational structures and reward systems. This combination is referred to as architecture. To understand this it has been necessary to develop a common cross-disciplinary approach to characterize the many different types of relationships within the firm. A view is that the firm may be seen as a network of implicit and explicit contracts, the precise nature of which differs from firm to firm (Coase 1937, Williamson 1975). Managerial relationships are identified in the nature of these contracts. The main distinction is between *relational* (broad, loosely defined) and *specific* (narrow, fully specified) contracts. These are similar to the 'organic' and 'mechanistic' distinctions of Burns and Stalker (1961). An important advantage of the approach is that it gives us a common unit of analysis for relationships at different levels within the firm: between individuals, functional groups, divisions and owners. It also extends outside the firm to alliances with suppliers, customers and competitors. This allows a unified analysis of contracting problems. It may also help explain some pathological conditions in which firms are locked-in to inefficient game equilibria. Changes in management are effected by changing the contractual rewards (pay-offs) or by modifying the rules, such as by moving to a repeated long-term game (Kay 1992).

Structures define formal relationships in the organization. Basically they may be flat or hierarchical. Reward systems concern the nature of the contracts. For technology these should ensure that employees have individual incentives towards integration, learning and strategic goals as above. Individuals should be satisfied that the system is fair and this is their best alternative, otherwise they may withhold effort or leave. Similar relationships apply between functions of the firm, between the firm and its suppliers, partners, even its competitors. These relationships are founded on trust, itself built-up through repeated tests over time (Grindley, Kay and Willman 1991, Kay and Willman 1992, Grindley 1991b).

Appropriate organizational forms

This leads to our main questions of what are appropriate architectures for innovation and how technology fits within the firm. The emphases on open communications, on avoiding the withholding of private information for personal advantage and on mutual long-term investment in firm-specific skills, imply an architecture with flat organizational structures characterized by shared goals and trust relationships. This innovative organization is characterized by relational contracts within the firm, and outside it, for those functions involved in the technology base. In contrast, an organization which depends less on private information and more on individual incentives, as may occur in more mature sectors, may use a more hierarchical structure with differentiated rewards. This more bureaucratic organization would rely on specific contracts (Simon 1976, 1991; Lazear 1991). In most organizations there is a mix of forms: relational for innovation management, specific for bureaucratic functions, the combination of which is related to the centrality of technology. The mix of different architectures gives rise to the interface problem.

Strategy in this analysis is different from some of the usual ideas of generic strategy (Porter 1980, 1983). Its role is primarily one of setting up the contract networks incorporating the organizational structure and reward systems. It steers activity towards areas of greatest competitive advantage via general objectives reflected in the architecture and project selection. This combines a directive strategy with the use of varied sources of ideas, inside and outside the firm. Within guidelines individuals have discretion over how best to achieve the aims. Clearly, to be able to evaluate performance requires deep knowledge by top management of both the technology and the business (Rosenbloom and Abernathy 1982).

Management implications

This has several implications for management. One is in integrating the technology functions into the business of the firm, as in the case of managing the R & D function. A typical problem for corporate R & D is that it is isolated from the mainstream business, following its own agenda but by the same token having little influence. An organization which treats R & D as a continuous contributor to product and process development (rather than as an overhead expense), integrated in fact as well as in theory, will start with the terms under which development is performed. Exhortations to central R & D to have closer contacts with manufacturing and marketing, even with formal communications channels, may have little effect without real incentives to encourage the spirit as well as the letter of integration. More effective may be the direct incentives to communication, cross-training and effort provided by the inclusion of design personnel within multi-disciplinary project teams, focused on a particular product or process and organized relationally.

A second is the management of the interfaces between those functions involved in technology and the rest of the firm, which may use different architectures with incompatible contract types. Even for high-technology firms exploitation requires access to complementary assets in manufacturing and marketing, so it is rare for there to be no interface problem (Riggs 1983). To avoid a clash the interfaces between the two different architectures may be best managed using specific contracts with clear performance goals and conditions for exchanging information. Both areas may then make internal operations decisions as they wish. Information exchanges needing more relational arrangements may need to take place within the development functions, using methods such as multi-disciplinary teams and cross-training. Steering committees at the boundaries may help handle remaining areas where interests overlap. Part of the role of the product champion is to relate development to overall strategy and provide the barrier with corporate management.

Another consequence is that we may expect different types of architecture to be effective at different stages of the firm's development and for different parts of its business. Managing organizational change is a well-known problem for firms as they grow or are challenged by new technology (Tushman, et al. 1986). The most effective architecture is not always the most obvious. Paradoxically, although the small entrepreneurial core is relational, a start-up venture may mainly use a specific organization, especially where contracting out, to give the entrepreneur direct control over resources. Incremental changes to established product lines usually point to looser relationships to allow networks of individuals each to make their contribution. Firms which become overly 'mature' forget this.

Acquisitions in technological areas may be particularly hard to integrate into the parent firm because both the architecture and the deep knowledge needed to manage them effectively are likely to be different from that of the new parent. These problems are avoided by growing the business organically, if possible. Joint ventures and partnerships, on the other hand, have much more confined aims and their performance depends on the quality of the contracts involved.

2.4 CASE STUDIES

Research outline

Case research has focused on a number of studies of the development and adoption of new technology in different organizational and institutional contexts. The aim has been to develop a case library of between twenty and thirty cases covering a range of issues and industries and to synthesize the results in a series of analytical reviews. Research has included a combination of literature and secondary-source reviews and interviews with company personnel. Some cases are in-depth longitudinal studies, involving historical analysis and repeated site visits, while others concentrate on a specific episode. The cases fall into three broad areas.

Financial services IT

These study the adoption of information technology (IT) in a series of large private and public-sector organizations. Issues include the growth of expertise within the organization, the centrality of technology, the interfaces between innovative and bureaucratic organization, project management techniques and the influence of competition in private and public sector. Cases include three major public sector organizations and three commercial lending institutions.

Electronics and instrumentation

These study the management of product innovation in high-technology firms, where technology is the prime means of competition. Issues include the build-up of core competencies in technology and its commercialization, the generation of streams of innovations over long periods, functional integration and use-oriented development, the appropriability of technology and strategic leadership. Cases also raise governance issues of the importance of informed ownership, operational problems of 'holding company' diversification and the influence of financial markets on operating decisions. Cases include ten small to medium-sized electronics companies (six of which are involved in scientific instruments), two semiconductor companies and an automobile racing engine company. Five of the companies are diversified.

Manufacturing

These study the development and adoption of new technology in mainstream manufacturing. Issues include the combination of product and process innovations, managing the interfaces between functional groups and between lead manufacturer and suppliers, technology transfer and the motivating effect of competition. Cases include two engineering companies, two automobile companies, a pharmaceutical company and a newspaper.

Companies included in the case studies are listed in Figure 2.2.

Area	Cases
Financial Services IT	1. DVLC
	2. DSS
	3. Inland Revenue
	4. TSB
	5. Midland Bank
	6. Halifax
Electronics/Instrument	7. Oxford Instruments
	8. Link Scientific
	9. Cosworth Engineering
	10. Quantel
	11. Solid State Logic
	12. UEI Group
	13. Queensgate Instruments
	14. Cambridge Instruments
	15. VG Instruments
	16. Peek
	17. Bowthorpe Holdings
	18. Ferranti (ASICs)
	19. Inmos
Manufacturing	20. Richardson Sheffield
	21. Volvo Transport
	22. Edwards High Vacuum
	23. Today Newspapers
	24. Rover-Honda
	25. Glaxo

Figure 2.2 Case-study groups

Methodology

The research approach has been more intent on theory development than deductive testing of preconceived beliefs. Hypotheses have evolved as the project has gone forward. They are often quite different from the ones at the start of the research. This implicitly follows the idea of grounded theory development, for situations which are too complex and unexplored for conventional theories to cover (Glaser and Strauss 1967, Mintzberg 1978, Pettigrew 1979). Having begun with the management framework it was found that the value of cases was as great in suggesting new hypotheses within this as in verifying the original ideas. The basic propositions concerning the combination of organization and economics and the impact of technology on business have generally been confirmed. However, many of the links between performance and management have only arisen as the casework has progressed. This includes the distinction between 'relational' and 'specific' organizational networks. The financial services cases were embarked on to test ideas about the importance of market competition but instead suggested more clearly the link between centrality and the organization of innovation. The electronics cases have been useful sources of ideas about relational networks, the protection of technological know-how, the importance of technically competent top management and informed ownership. The manufacturing cases have also changed preconceptions about how strategy evolves.

Developing the managerial framework

At each stage the case research has been informed by and in turn contributed to the development of the managerial framework. Some main illustrations are given below.

Technical and commercial capability

The emphasis on the business aspects of managing technology is underscored in all the cases. For example, Halifax Building Society, using technically modest systems but with development staff experienced in that organization and sensitive to user needs, has successfully introduced information technology which other financial services firms have found hard to match. Oxford Instruments has been technically brilliant in its core area of super-conducting magnets, a world-leader, but it came near to failure due to poor commercial judgements. Quantel's success in computer graphics has relied more on its attention to user requirements and ingenuity with new features than on the technology itself. We need only contrast the success of Glaxo with its Zantac ulcer drug with the failure of Thorn-EMI with its CAT scanner and other breakthrough innovations, to illustrate that the larger technical achievement is often commercially less effective. Similarly, Ferranti's invention of the ASIC semiconductor never led to major commercial success as the firm lacked the drive and ability to take it out of military niche markets, leaving other firms, including start-ups, to take away what is now a multi-billion-dollar industry.

Integration and learning

These key issues occur throughout the cases. The importance of close contact between design, manufacturing and marketing are most evident in the electronics group. By the nature of their products, in technical equipment, development is very close to manufacturing and to the customer. However, this has not always gone smoothly. At Inmos, one of the United Kingdom's last semiconductor producers, technical enthusiasts ignored messages from marketing and presented the Transputer microprocessor as a revolutionary method of computer design rather than as a marketable product. There was a complete lack of integration between the US division, interested in immediate sales of memory devices, and the visionary UK division pursuing the Transputer. It was years before strategic changes at the top reshaped the organization. The firms have also treated the build-up of technical and market competencies as crucial. Oxford Instruments has a policy of not taking on development contracts unless they contribute to the knowledge base of the firm. Cosworth, a manufacturer of racing engines, for years had an untapped reservoir of knowledge in its engineering teams, only fully exploited later in commercial engines such as the Ford Sierra-Cosworth series (Aston 1991, 1992).

These issues are also very apparent in the manufacturing cases in the relation between process and product innovation. Richardson revived its fortunes as a cutlery producer by concentrating on the single area of kitchen knives and building firm-specific expertise in grinding technology and salesmanship. These allowed it later to take advantage of an opportunity to produce a break-through product innovation with an 'everlasting' knife. It now makes a range of related products (Grindley, McBryde and Roper 1990). Rover was able to develop its technically successful K-series engine partly as a result of skills learned during collaboration with Honda (Mueller and Roper 1991). In financial services integration has mainly been a question of interfacing IT with the rest of the organization, discussed below. The problem of learning has been to ensure that competencies reside within the organization rather than with external contractors (Dyerson and Roper 1991a).

Appropriability

The link between appropriability and organizational networks is illustrated by Cosworth. With the basic technology well known, the firm's superior design and production capability rested on close teamwork together with the key design skills of the founder. Individual engineers, who had 'grown up' with the firm, found it difficult to take their skills outside and competitors were unable to duplicate such a team. The firm's engines dominated racing for over a decade, which in turn also helped retain personnel. Halifax Building Society's dominance of the local labour market and the non-transferability of skills associated with its idiosyncratic in-house IT systems, allowed a build-up of experience which other institutions could not match. On the other hand VG Instruments's policy of setting up a new subsidiary for each new product line made it very easy for managers to leave and set up their own enterprises when dissatisfied with their position. VG was the unwilling parent of over twenty entrepreneurial ventures in two decades. Quantel, which applies well-known and easily reproducible technology to computer graphics, has had to rely on constant innovation to keep ahead of competitors and frequent patent suits to defend its products, specifically the non-technical-user interfaces. These methods depend on a close-knit team of designers and a cultural emphasis on non-disclosure.

Centrality and the 'interfaces'

Centrality is an issue of varying importance. Integration takes a very different form at a company such as Cosworth, where technology is central, than at Inland Revenue and Midland Bank, where technology, though important, takes its place alongside other capabilities. At Cosworth the whole firm is oriented around developing racing engines, and any integration problems have only come as Cosworth has moved into commercial production. The introduction of information technology in financial services show the more familiar problems of interfacing development with the rest of the organization. In its computerization exercise the Inland Revenue developed systems using a project approach with more flexible internal organization and reward system and greater individual management authority than usual civil service practice. This was a quite different internal architecture from the main organization. The interface with other operations was carefully nurtured and managed via steering committee. This has been a very successful experience. With the main development now over the IT operations structure is returning to standard and being reabsorbed into the main organization. In contrast, Midland Bank has attempted to manage its systems development efforts within the hierarchical structure of its banking operations. Development has been plagued with delays and cost problems (Dyerson and Roper 1991b).

Appropriate architecture

The use of a relational architecture for innovation is typical of the collection of high-tech firms which until recently made up the UEI group. These include Quantel, Solid State Logic, Link Scientific and Cosworth. Each of these is a young firm which has grown to medium size based on consistently successful innovation. Though in a variety of sectors, they have similar organizational characteristics, including an egalitarian, open organization, flat pay structure, and a concern for the long-term coherence of the workforce. For most of their existence each has been led by the original entrepreneurs, who are technically expert, have close involvement in product innovation and are more concerned with the growth and autonomy of the firm than personal financial reward. At the UEI group level, although share-holding was concentrated in one individual, the board members were equals in argument, and had the freedom to manage their own firm as they saw fit. A contrast is Peek, a mini-holding company producing electronic components. This is managed hierarchically by a non-technical chief executive and has had difficulty developing and exploiting innovation. Problems introducing information technology at DSS have been almost exclusively organizational, stemming from the attempt to develop systems using a formal structure inappropriate for a creative process.

Ownership and finance

Problems of governance, the ownership structure, are evident to some degree in each of the electronics cases. Inmos provides the clearest example of the problems of 'disengaged' ownership. The original owner, the UK government, had little understanding of the industry and allowed strategy disagreements between the UK and

US divisions to stall development. The second owner, Thorn-EMI, put the firm on a firmer commercial footing but lacked the vision and motivation to make forward investment. The current owner, SGS-Thompson, is the first to be based in the semiconductor industry and belatedly has given the Transputer the backing it needed to make it a commercially viable product. Informed management has been a major part of the success of each of the UEI firms, each of which was headed and owned by technical experts, and at Oxford Instruments, where most of the board members have technology PhDs. Pressures from the city for more stable earnings have forced Oxford Instruments to diversify into areas outside its core competencies, so far with only mixed success.

2.5 CONCLUSION

The project has had broad goals, to develop a framework for relating the management of technology to the performance of the firm. The research project began motivated by a belief that technology may only be understood by combining economics and organization. This focused not on the technology as such but on the role of technology in the competitive behaviour of the firm. Consideration of the strategic requirements for innovation led to the key features for technology management, which were confirmed and extended by the case work. This in turn led to the contractual approach, merging strategic and organizational concerns, which has brought us back to the links between economics and organization with which we started.

REFERENCES

Aston, B. (1991) 'Unlimited horsepower: innovation at Cosworth Engineering', *Technology Project Paper* 10, London Business School.
—— (1992), 'Oxford Instruments', *Technology Project Papers* 13, London Business School.
Burns, T. and Stalker, G. (1961) *The Management of Innovation*, London: Tavistock.
Coase, R., (1937) 'The nature of the firm', *Economica* 4: 386–405.
Dosi, G., (1982), 'Technological paradigms and technological trajectories', *Research Policy* 11: 147–62.
Dyerson, R. and Roper, M. (1991a) 'Building competencies: the computerization of PAYE', in B. Williams (ed.) *IT in Accounting: The Impact of Information Technology*, London, Chapman and Hall.
—— and —— (1991b) 'When expertise becomes know-how: managing IT in financial services', *Business Strategy Review* 2 (2): 55–74.

Glaser, B. and Strauss, A., (1967) *The Discovery of Grounded Theory: Strategies for Qualitative Research*, New York: Aldine.

Grindley, P., (1989), 'Technological change within the firm: a framework for research and management', *Technology Project Paper* 1, London Business School.

—— (1991a) 'Turning technology into competitive advantage', *Business Strategy Review* 2 (1): 35–48.

—— (1991b) 'Managing technological innovation: culture and organizational relationships within the firm', *Technology Project Paper* 14, London Business School.

Grindley, P., Kay, J. and Willman, P. (1991) 'Technological change processes and outcomes within the firm: project outline and completion plan (1991–92)', mimeo, London Business School.

Grindley,· P., McBride, R. and Roper, M. (1989) *'Technology and the Competitive Edge: The Case of Richardson Sheffield'*, *Technology Project Paper* 2, London Business School.

Hamel, G. and Prahalad, C. (1990) 'Strategic intent', *The McKinsey Quarterly*, Spring, pp. 36–59.

Imai, K. Nonaka, I. and Takeuchi, H., (1985) 'Managing the new product development process: how Japanese companies learn and unlearn', in K. Clark, R. Hayes and C. Lorenz (eds) *The Uneasy Alliance*, Harvard Business School Press.

Kay, J., (1992) 'The Structure of Strategy', Centre for Business Strategy, London Business School (manuscript).

Kay, J. and Willman, P., (1993), 'Managing technological innovation: architecture, trust and organizational relationships in the firm', Chapter 1, this volume.

Lazear, E. (1991) 'Labour economics and the psychology of organizations', *Journal of Economic Perspectives* 5 (2): 89–110.

Mueller, F. and Roper, M., (1991) 'Technological innovation and commercial success: the development of the K-series engine at Rover', *Technology Project Paper* 15, London Business School.

Nelson, R. and Winter, S. (1982) *An Evolutionary Theory of Economic Change*, Cambridge, Mass.: Harvard University Press.

Pavitt, K., (1990) 'What we know about the strategic management of technology', *California Management Review*, Spring, pp. 17–26.

Pettigrew, A., (1979) 'On studying organizational cultures', *Administrative Science Quarterly* 24 (4): 570–81.

Peters, T. (1987) *Thriving on Chaos*, London: Macmillan.

Porter, M. (1980) *Competitive Strategy*, New York: Free Press.

Porter, M., (1983) 'The technological dimension of competitive strategy', in R. Rosenbloom, (ed.) *Research on Technological Innovation, Management and Policy*, vol. 1, Greenwich, Conn.: JAI Press, pp. 1–33.

Prahalad, C. and Hamel, G., (1990), 'The core competence of the organization', *Harvard Business Review*, May-June, pp. 79–91.

Reich, R., (1989) 'The quiet path to technological preeminence', *Scientific American*, October, pp. 19–25.

Riggs, H., (1983) *Managing High-Technology Companies*, New York: Van Nostrand.

Rosenbloom, R. and Abernathy, W. (1982) 'The climate for innovation in industry', *Research Policy* 11: 209–25.

Simon, H. (1976) *Administrative Behaviour*, 3rd edn, New York: Macmillan; (1st edn, 1947).

—— (1991) 'Organizations and markets', *Journal of Economic Perspectives*, 5 (2): 25–44.

Teece, D. (1986) 'Profiting from technological innovation', *Research Policy* 15: 285–305.

Teece, D., Pisano, G. and Shuen, A. (1991) 'Firm capabilities, resources and the concept of strategy', CCC Working Paper No. 90–8 (rev.), Centre for Research in Management, UC Berkeley.

Tushman, M., Newman, W. and Romanelli, E., (1986) 'Convergence and upheaval: managing the unsteady pace of organizational evolution', *California Management Review* 29: 29–44.

Williamson, O. (1975) *Markets and Hierarchies*, New York: Free Press.

3 The performance of innovative small firms
A regional issue

Ian J. Smith, Bruce Tether, Alfred Thwaites,
Joe Townsend and Pooran Wynarczyk

3.1 INTRODUCTION

The small technologically leading firm has become the subject of
increasing academic and policy-making interest in recent years. Its
study and promotion is based upon a perceived link between this
type of firm and rapid or sustainable economic growth, especially
at the local level, where it provides the focus for locally determined
policy designed to stimulate indigenous development. At present,
relatively little is known of the economic inter-regional performance
of this type of firm. Research undertaken at the University of
Newcastle upon Tyne under the ESRC New Technology and the
Firm Initiative, is attempting to contribute to knowledge in this
field. Space dictates that only part of the research can be reported
here, concentrating on the characteristics of small manufacturing
firms which introduced substantial innovations in The United Kingdom between 1975 and 1983, and their direct contribution to local
economic development.

3.2 BACKGROUND TO THIS RESEARCH

A persistent factor characterizing the development of the UK and
other industrial economies over the last century has been spatial
variations in economic advance. These disparities have attracted
the attention of academics who have tried to conceptualize the
process by which economic advance takes place at the sub-national
level, and how such disparities might be reduced, so as to converge
on a common growth trajectory which would benefit all regions and
the national economy as a whole (e.g. Richardson 1973, Armstrong
and Taylor 1985, NEDO 1991). In practical terms, however, and
over a large part of the post-war period, the removal or reduction

of economic disparities between UK regions has been seen in terms of redistributing industry, particularly manufacturing, from the southern core to less-favoured areas in the north and west. These actions have been supported by modernization of the economic and social infrastructure in depressed areas as well as through substantial transfer payments to the economically inactive population resident there. In addition, 'foreign' direct investment has been encouraged in designated 'development areas'. It was hoped that through such actions synergetic developments would take place over time in depressed regional economies to improve their prosperity and prospects for self-sustained growth. This approach to local economic development was not without its successes (Moore *et al.* 1981) but has not overcome the basic problems of continued disparities in employment, income and wealth in these regions in comparison with core regions located mainly in the south of England.

The limitations of past policies have been highlighted in the recessions of the late 1970s and early 1980s. It is argued that the constraints on the effectiveness of past regional redistribution policies have thrust to the fore the concept of indigenous economic development which requires local actors to take greater responsibility for their future development (Goddard *et al.* 1979). These responsibilities include the generation of new economic activities which can be efficiently produced and exploited in both home and overseas markets (Ciciotti *et al.* 1990). However, such responsibilities cannot be developed simply in local terms but must be set within wider national and global contexts. This has prompted the search for a more adequate conceptualization of the local economic development process and re-evaluation of the nature and value of factors contributing to what is currently seen as a new and changing environment for economic progress. Two factors which have emerged as important, perhaps critical, are technological change and the small firm.

The arguments supporting technology as an important factor in local economic development are essentially a translation to the sub-national of arguments expressed at national and global scales. Pioneering research by Solow (1957; see also Denison and Poullier 1968) suggested that national economic growth could not be satisfactorily explained in terms of the traditional inputs of labour and capital alone; he attributed the balance of unexplained growth to technical changes or advances in knowledge. In support of this analysis research-intensive industries and enterprises have also been found to lead economic advance (e.g. OECD 1986) when measured in terms of sales growth (Odagiri 1985), export success (Katrak 1985), productivity growth (Mansfield 1968) or profitability (Schott 1981). Technological advances have been shown to form the basis for new industries (e.g. the transistor and electronic industries; Dosi 1984) and the rejuvenation of more established product areas (e.g. the substitution of microprocessor for electro-mechanical controls). These advances have provided the capability to create new markets or increase the penetration of existing markets (Sweeney 1985). New technology in productive and other functions of business is also associated with improved cost, quality and reliability. The technologically advancing firm, and – in aggregate – region or nation, has the capability to develop advantages which help it compete successfully with other firms, regions or nations, in both home and overseas markets. On the other hand, the markets of technologically lagging firms are in danger from more dynamic firms which may result in the former's loss of market share, decline and closure. Increased generation and more rapid adoption of technology by firms in depressed areas is therefore seen as a mechanism for stimulating local economic growth.

A second force for economic change and the focus of considerable attention in recent years has been the small firm. Research suggests that large firms have been shedding labour in recent years and that smaller firms have become increasingly important in employment creation and therefore income generation. (Birch 1979, Storey and Johnson 1987). In the 1980s small firms have been seen as a vehicle for individual expression and as a valuable and flexible response mechanism to rapidly changing economic conditions (Storey and Johnson 1987). A further factor in support of the small-firm argument is the perceived link to technological advance. Research suggests small firms are making an increasing contribution to significant innovations and diffusion (Townsend et al. 1981, Rothwell 1984, Pavitt et al. 1987).

In combination, the small and technologically advanced firm would seem, therefore, to provide a potentially powerful force for bringing about positive economic change at a variety of spatial scales. In addition, they are claimed to be more susceptible to policy influence, including local authority or local agency influence, than larger firms. As a result, the small firm which makes a significant contribution to technological advance has become the focus of attention in a number of policy-making circles. The European Commission has, for over a decade, supported innovation and technology transfer in small firms within selected less-favoured regions and sub-regions of the Community, including those in the United Kingdom (e.g. non-quota section of the ERDF, SPRINT and more recently STRIDE).

Similarly, the UK central government has focused greater attention on support for the small technologically advancing firm in recent years. For example, the Department of Enterprise has recently introduced the two schemes SMART and SPUR (DTI 1991a, 1991b). The objectives of SMART are to stimulate small firms to develop and market new science and technology-based products; to encourage and facilitate the formation of viable and durable science and technology-based small firms; and to contribute to a climate which encourages investment in highly innovative technology by individuals and financial institutions. This is a competition which helps selected firms to carry out feasibility studies (total 180 in one year), and if successful, support is extended to the development stage.

SPUR supports the costs of developing new products and processes which involve significant technological advance in firms with a total workforce of less than 500 employees.

In the 1980s regional policies have also laid greater stress on technological developments through the creation or transfer of research and development jobs to the depressed areas. Selected financial assistance has also been used to support technological developments favourable to designated less-favoured areas. In addition, regional-policy aid has been modified to focus on the two apparently disparate strands of large-scale inward investment and indigenous small-enterprise development. At the local level, local authorities have also become involved in the stimulation of innovative small firms by a variety of means, including support for technology audits and establishing innovation centres.

Despite the interest, few theories of regional or local economic development have tried to incorporate a technological dimension, greater interest has been shown in the contributions of small firms and small firm networks to economic development (e.g. Brush 1982, Storey 1982). Crevoisier claims that traditional models of regional economic development have been limited in their ability to explain 'changes in the economic map of Europe and the United States' (Crevoisier 1990: 17). He argues that these models emerged in periods of particular forms of production which are no longer relevant. Under the new conditions technological change becomes an important focus in local development which should not be viewed independently but is seen to be dependent upon 'the capability of regions to create a dynamic local innovative milieu' (*ibid.*) in which small firms have a significant role to play (Ciciotti *et al*. 1990; see also Pompili 1990, Aydalot 1986). Numerous authors have commented on the value of new and small firms to local development (e.g. Wynarczyk *et al*. 1993, Storey *et al*. 1987, Gallagher and Steward 1986).

Evidence from the regional level would seem to provide some support for the identification of technological change as a factor in local economic development even if the evidence is primarily one of association rather than causation. Ten years ago Thwaites *et al*. (1981, 1982) found systematic regional variations in product development by small firms and the absorption of advance subcomponents into products notably to the disadvantage, of the less-favoured regions of the United Kingdom. The most comprehensive studies of the spatial incidence of technological change in small firms have been undertaken by Oakey (1984, 1988), which confirm that innovation in the small-firm sector is in general weak in the already disadvantaged regions of the UK economy. Studies undertaken in other countries tend to arrive at similar conclusions (Ciciotti 1983, Brugger and Stuckey 1987, Todtling 1990). These studies have provided valuable insights into the regional patterns of innovation, or innovative potential, but only limited attempts have been made to differentiate between incremental and leading edge technological development. (See Harris 1988 for an exception). The latter might be expected to exhibit a stronger influence on the level and pace of local economic development, than will lower levels of incremental change or customization (see Thwaites 1981). Moreover, few spatial studies have attempted to measure the contribution of small innovative firms to either national or local economic development.

The research reported below attempts to contribute to this field by providing some evidence of the characteristics, survival and performance of innovative small firms in the United Kingdom, and briefly exploring inter-regional variations in their activities.

3.3 METHODS OF RESEARCH

The research used three basic methods (although this chapter draws mainly on the first method for its evidence):

- The assembly and analysis of data and information obtained from secondary sources.

- An interview survey of a structured sample of small innovative firms and of organizations acquiring such firms.
- A postal questionnaire of a broader population of innovative small firms.

The focus of the research was on the small technologically-leading manufacturing firms. The overall concern was with product, process or material innovation. These types of firm and innovation were identifiable on the Science Policy Research Unit's (SPRU) Innovation Data Base which provided a population from which a sub-population could be selected for study.

The definition of innovation used by SPRU followed the Schumpeterian tradition of 'the successful commercial introduction of a new or improved product or process' (new materials were also included) (Townsend *et al.* 1981: 21).

The SPRU data-base was assembled by requesting experts knowledgeable in particular industries to identify technological advances in the industry(ies) with which they were familiar and where possible to identify the innovating firm. In total, over 400 experts were consulted in the data assembly exercise. Once a set of innovations was identified, and with common agreement as to their technological importance, innovative firms were sent a questionnaire requesting them to confirm the facts of the innovation and to supply information about their firms: the date of innovation, its type (product, process, material), the employment size, ownership status and principal product of the firm at the time of innovation. After careful scrutiny a list of 4,576 innovations allocated to specific innovating firms was constructed. The data set was estimated to cover the important technological changes taking place in the United Kingdom between 1945 and 1983 inclusive, in twenty-five industries which produced approximately 58 per cent of the UK net output in 1975. The advantage for the research in using this data base is that innovations were identified as significant by independent experts and did not rely upon executives' own assessment of their technological achievements.

A sub-set of firms (detailed below) were drawn from the SPRU data-base and to which were attached information and data from a variety of secondary sources. *Who Owns Whom, Kompass, MacCarthy Cards*, Jordans and ICC were among the directories used to provide background information on each firm. In addition, selected information from Companies House was attached to each case. This included, whenever declared, information such as turnover, assets and profits, as well as more qualitative data on directors, shareholdings and changes in holdings. In addition a number of spatial variables were attached to the data.

Firms were selected from the data base on the criteria that, at the time of innovation were independent (directors owned at least 50 per cent of the issued share capital); small (were enterprises or part of an enterprise in which total employment was less than 500 employees world wide); and introducing products, processes or materials new to the United Kingdom in the years 1975 to 1983 inclusive. The selection of this period was designed to allow exploration of the effects of innovation in the period after innovation up to 1989 but would at the same time avoid some of the problems, associated with assessing events in the very distant past. Although it is recognized that most firms are not single-innovation firms, the interview survey revealed that the identified innovation usually had, in the opinion of executives, a significant, if not crucial, influence on the firm's survival and subsequent performance. In addition, most firms claimed that the innovation was also the source of subsequent flows of innovation in the company and therefore was important to its continued economic health.

The SPRU Innovation Data Bank identifies 261 organizations with less than 500 employees world wide and introducing innovations in the United Kingdom between 1975 and 1983 inclusive. Sixteen organizations were found to be in the public sector and were rejected as not being small independent firms by definition. In addition, it was estimated that fifty-two cases are misclassified on the SPRU data base, as at the time of innovation these were already part of larger organizations with over 500 employees world wide. They were therefore eliminated from the analysis. After exhaustive searches sixteen firms listed on the data-base remained untraced. Two further firms were eliminated because they operated in the service sector, whereas the focus of the research was on manufacturing industry. The sub-population of firms meeting the criteria and providing the focus for investigation and analysis is therefore 175.

A selection of thirty-one surviving firms have been interviewed representing various experiences of firms at and after innovation until 1989; those remaining independent throughout, those acquired, and in different sectors. The structured interviews concentrated on the development of the technology, its impact on the firm and the ways in which a market for the new technology was developed and extended both in the United Kingdom and abroad.

Finally, a postal questionnaire was dispatched to all remaining traceable enterprises identified from the SPRU data base outside the interview survey (N = 98). The questionnaires concentrated on the same areas of enquiry as those covered in the interview survey but were restricted by technique to a more limited set of structured questions.

3.4 CHARACTERISTICS OF INNOVATING FIRMS AND THE INNOVATIVE ENVIRONMENT

The size distribution of the 191 (including those which could not be traced) firms at the time of innovation is given in Table 3.2. This shows that the vast majority of innovating firms (71 per cent) in the 1–500 employee category listed on the SPRU data-base claimed to employ less than 150 workers at the time of innovation, and 37 per cent had less than fifty workers.

A further examination of the SPRU data-base allowed the allocation of firms (by primary product) to the 1980 Standard Industrial Classification. This confirmed earlier findings (e.g. Townsend *et al.* 1981) that the firms were heavily concentrated in a few industries, in particular within:

- Electronic data-processing equipment
- Electrical and electronic components and equipment
- Measuring, checking and precision instruments
- Medical and surgical equipment
- Plastic products

There were also substantial numbers in a broad range of what might be termed the machine-building industry, notably textile machinery. However, due to time and resource constraints it was necessary to concentrate analysis within the five sectors noted above. These five sectors together accounted for 51 per cent of innovations in the small-firm category 1975–83 listed on the SPRU Innovation data-base.

Table 3.1 shows that these firms were set up mainly in the post-war period, although a few date from an earlier era. While 45 per cent were set up before 1970, further scrutiny indicated that the

Table 3.1 Incorporation years for innovative small firms

1920s	1930s	1940s	1950s	1960s	1970s	1980s
2.8%	0%	7.1%	9.8%	25.4%	42.2%	12.7%

Source: Companies House data.

Table 3.1 Number of firms by employment size at the time of innovation

No. of employees at innovation	1–24	25–49	50–99	100–149	150–199	200–299	300–399	400–499	Total
Corporate Status (1989)									
Independent N	33	16	27	19	8	18	6	2	129
%	26	12	21	15	6	14	5	2	100
Acquired N	12	4	7	7	5	5	2	4	46
%	26	9	15	15	11	11	4	9	100
Untraced N	5	1	3	2	2	2	1	0	16
Total N	50	21	37	28	15	25	9	6	191
%	26	11	19	15	8	13	5	3	100

Sources: SPRU Innovation data base; Companies House data.

vast majority were incorporated before the significant innovation was developed. Thus, older firms seem as likely as new firms to produce significant innovations (see also North *et al*, 1991).

Over 90 per cent of innovations in this small-firm sample were product innovations with relatively few in process or materials. The largest proportion of material advances was found in plastics. Far from introducing fundamental new technologies, the majority of small firms saw themselves applying existing technology in new ways or developing technologies to resolve known problems.

The economic contribution of the innovation to small firms' performance is reflected in the fact that over three-quarters estimated the significance to enterprise performance as 'essential to important' and two-thirds had used the first innovation as a platform for subsequent innovations. The technology was claimed to have given one-quarter of the firms a relatively long-term advantage in their field, whilst the remainder generally found their technological lead eroded over time by competitors' technological and/or commercial actions. This led to the claim that these innovations had spurred technological progress in their industries.

The research did not discover any small firms supplying what are generally termed mass-consumer markets. The vast majority of firms are producing goods for other firms or organizations and not for final demand. Even those firms which serviced consumer markets were found to serve market niches (e.g. very high-quality ends of a market; elements of the disabled population). Markets were extended beyond the United Kingdom with approximately 80 per cent of respondent firms exporting part of their production. Most firms saw their markets as small or niche, from the outset, only about a third won markets larger than they had originally expected.

While the extent and scale of markets addressed by small firms place some limits on growth and development, all the interviewed firms claimed to operate in a competitive environment where substitutes or potential substitutes existed. This suggests that there were real possibilities for expansion but also threats to the technologically inept or inefficient. It was in this context that the performance of the sample of innovating firms was examined.

3.5 THE PERFORMANCE OF INNOVATIVE SMALL FIRMS

One of the major contributions that firms can make to local and national economic development is through continuous trading into the longer term.

Overall (and on the assumption that the sixteen untraced firms have closed), it is estimated that sixty-two of the sample firms, or 32.5 per cent, closed after innovation (Table 3.3). Notably it is the firms below twenty-five employees and with 300 or more employees which seem most prone to closure. Those firms employing between twenty-five and 299 employees appear to be more stable. While there do not appear to be any official statistics on closure rates of innovative small firms, other research undertaken on closure rates (e.g. Storey et al. 1987, North et al. 1991, Ganguly 1983) suggests that this type of firm, particularly the independent firm, may be more robust than its counterparts in the general small-firm population.

In the five sectors which provide the focus of our analysis, long-term survival was highly inconsistent. Enterprise survival was highest in the medical and surgical equipment industry with no post-innovation closures, as opposed to the electronic data-processing equipment industry in which nearly two-thirds of firms closed after innovation. On the other hand, acquisition, which occurred in approximately one-third of our sample, is evenly distributed between sectors. The period from 1975 to 1980 was one of relatively low takeover and merger activity nationally; it was not until the 1980s that the surge of activity began. In line with those trends the majority of acquisitions in the sample are of relatively recent date and dominated by acquisitions from abroad and outside the European Community.

The size and characteristics of the original sample have changed considerably over time. At the time of innovation all of the firms were classified as independent, by 1989 after closure and acquisition, two-thirds of firms were still operating independently in the medical equipment and measuring instrument industries, but less than 40 per cent were operating and independent in the electrical and electronic components and equipment, plastic products and electronic data-processing equipment industries.

Another important characteristic of firm performance is employment change over time. The SPRU Innovation data-base provides information on the employment size of innovating firms in the year of innovation. In the five sectors providing the focus of this analysis a total of 8,080 workers were estimated to be employed at the time of innovation, an average of ninety-eight workers per firm (Table 3.4). Numerous sources were consulted to calculate the employment in 1989 and it is estimated that the surviving independent and acquired firms employed 7,527 workers. While overall employment

Table 3.3 Ownership and closure after innovation to end year 1989 by employment size of firm

	1–24	25–49	50–99	100–149	150–199	200–299	300–399	400–499	Total
Independent and closed* %	36	25	26	16	0	22	33	0	25
Acquired and closed† %	50	25	0	29	20	0	50	75	30
Untraced assumed closed N=	5	1	3	2	2	2	1	0	16
Total closed‡ %	46	29	27	25	20	24	44	80	32

Sources: Various directories; Companies House data.
Notes:
* Total number of independent firms at time of closure or surviving to 1989 = 129
† Total number of acquired firms at time of closure or surviving to 1989 = 46
‡ Total closed N = 62

Table 3.4 Employment by industry in firms at the time of innovation and in the late 1980s

	Time of innovation employment total†	Total employment in 1989*	x̄ employment at time of innovation†	x̄ in employment in 1989*	Change in employment by survivors	
					Acquired %	Independent %
Measuring, checking and precision instruments	2,798	3,549	108	187	+ 27	+ 49
Plastic products	1,703	825	114	92	+ 13	− 40
Electric and electronic components and equipment	1,591	1,083	88	98	+ 42	− 49
Electronic data-processing equipment	1,043	212	95	53	‡	+165
Medical and surgical equipment	945	1,858	79	155	+189	+ 38
Total	8,080	7,527	98	137		

Sources: SPRU data base; Companies House data; KBE and other directory sources; interview survey.
Notes:
* Date for 1989 but a few 1988 and 1991.
† Variable by data of innovation.
‡ No survivors.

is estimated to have declined, the average survivor appears to have grown substantially over the period, resulting in an average size of 137 workers per firm. In particular, there appears over time to have been increases in average employment size in the measuring instrument and medical equipment sectors, with a decline in the size of firms in the plastics and electronic data-processing equipment industries. As already noted, these last two industries have been hit by closure, in particular the electronic data-processing equipment industry. Those few remaining independent firms in this sector have shown employment growth but from a very small base and their combined employment was estimated to be just over 200 employees in 1989. In terms of employment performance those surviving firms in plastic products, electrical and electronic, and medical equipment industries appear to do better after acquisition than those which remain independent. This may reflect reasons why they have been acquired, but also the benefit of the greater support available within a large company group than is possible while remaining independent. Post-acquisition growth in employment in surviving firms is found in all industries with the exception of the electronic data-processing equipment sector. Acquired company growth was outstripped by independent companies in the measuring instruments and medical equipment sectors.

A further measure of performance in surviving firms is total asset (i.e. fixed plus current assets) growth where assets are taken to reflect not only investment but also the 'wealth of the firm'. Table 3.5 suggests that in those thirty-four firms able to provide information in 1975 and 1987, assets have grown quite considerably with

Table 3.5 Total assets of small innovative firms, 1975 and 1987

(£)	1975 (%)	1987 (%)
Up to 9999	8.8	–
10,000–499,999	17.6	–
50,000–99,999	11.8	2.9
100,000–499,999	35.3	11.8
500,000–999,999	11.8	17.6
1,000,000–plus	14.7	67.6
Mean	£441,872	£4,146,046
Median	£145,528	£2,574,187

Only firms which have provided data for both 1975 and 1987 are included (a total of 34 firms).
Source: Companies House data.

two-thirds of firms now having assets of over one million pounds. In the thirteen-year period, assets for the average firm have increased tenfold. This is obviously an over-estimate due to inflation, the effects of which are not easily calculated in an area in which debate continues as to the most appropriate deflators to use, particularly in the small-firm sector (Watson 1990). Crude estimates using a number of deflators ranging from the retail price index to the more appropriate plant and machinery investment indices by industry, suggest that real growth in assets for the average firm has taken place.

Further analysis of the data permitted the investigation of the return on total assets achieved by the same thirty-four firms in the period 1975 to 1987. This is calculated as the percentage of operating profit to total assets. Operating profit is defined here as pre-tax profit before deduction of directors' remuneration and interest payments. This is meant to provide a measure of the gross earning capability of small firms before allowance is made for differences in the methods and costs of financing. The results of this analysis (Table 3.6) suggest that with exceptions in 1977 and 1981, the average firm in the sample achieved between 20 per cent and 27 per cent return on assets. The results show that the average small firm possesses the funds to reinvest in the business if they are not subject to excessive tax or loan charges or removal of funds from the firm in the form of directors' fees or remuneration.

In order to assess the effects of these factors on company results the rate of retained profit in the business was assessed. Here retained profit is defined as profit retained in the business after tax and after deduction of other payments including directors' fees and interest charges. As such it reflects the funds available in the business for future investment. The results (Table 3.7) indicate that returns on assets on this measure are quite variable and do not move in parallel with the returns of operating profits to assets, suggesting that retained profit is more sensitive to other financial movements and decisions both within and outside the firm which perhaps affects their future growth potential.

However, comparisons of the results displayed in Tables 3.6 and 3.7 with that of high-growth firms in Storey et al.'s analysis suggest that these innovative small firms have relatively higher rates of return on their assets than those observed in Storey et al.'s high-growth firm (Storey et al. 1987, 1989). In turn, Storey et al. found high-growth small firms did not appear to have a significantly greater rate of return on their assets than their 'matched', more

Table 3.6 Percentage return on assets (operating profit/total assets × 100)

	1975	1976	1977	1978	1979	1980	1981	1982	1983	1984	1985	1986	1987
Mean	22.6	23.3	21.7	16.0	23.2	20.4	26.4	11.4	21.1	22.3	20.5	24.7	25.2
Median	22.6	27.3	22.0	25.9	23.9	20.9	19.5	18.4	20.9	23.1	18.8	23.3	22.8

Source: Companies House data.

Table 3.7 Return on assets (net profit/total assets × 100)

	1975	1976	1977	1978	1979	1980	1981	1982	1983	1984	1985	1986	1987
Mean	3.0	−2.0	6.1	7.0	8.3	6.1	7.2	−3.5	−1.4	9.7	4.4	5.0	6.7
Median	5.0	5.6	6.7	8.6	8.1	8.0	6.1	5.7	4.5	7.3	4.6	4.6	6.3

Source: Companies House data.

run-of-the-mill firms, both in terms of operating profits and retained profits during the 1980s. They concluded that their results were mainly due to the greater size of the assets of the high-growth firms. The results of the study reported here, however, suggest that innovative small firms increased their total assets substantially over the period 1975 to 1987 and appear to be more profitable than the high-growth firms (particularly those firms located in the South East) which could be due to their capacity for innovation.

The foregoing analysis is concerned with the 1975 to 1987 period and the general performance of small innovative firms. There is, however, some difficulty with the above analysis due to the fact that the innovations took place in different years in that period and so the post innovation experience is unstandardized. In order to overcome this anomaly, data on seventy-one traceable firms in the five selected sectors were standardized using percentage changes in financial performance at the time of innovation and four years later.

The first row of Table 3.8b illustrates for all firms changes in total assets, turnover, retained profits, operating profits and exports in the four-year period following innovation. (The formulae and definitions are presented in Tables 3.8a and 3.8c). The information in Table 3.8b suggests there are considerable inter-firm variations in

Table 3.8a Financial performance measures

$$(1) \ \% \ TA = \frac{\text{Total Assets in year 4} - \text{Total Assets in year 1}}{\text{Total Assets in year 1}} \times 100$$

$$(2) \ \% \ T \ = \frac{\text{Turnover in year 4} - \text{Turnover in year 1}}{\text{Turnover in year 1}} \times 100$$

$$(3) \ \% \ RP = \frac{\text{Retained Profits in year 4} - \text{Retained Profits in year 1}}{\text{Total Assets in year 1}} \times 100$$

$$(4) \ \% \ OP = \frac{\text{Operating Profits in year 4} - \text{Operating Profits in year 1}}{\text{Total Assets in year 1}} \times 100$$

$$(5) \ \% \ EX = \frac{\text{Exports in year 4} - \text{Exports in year 1}}{\text{Exports in year 1}} \times 100$$

Note:
Year 1 = year of initial innovation
Year 4 = four years after the year of initial innovation
Operating profits = pre-tax profits before interest payments and directors
  remunerations

Table 3.8b Univariate results for the financial performance measures of innovative small firms located in the South East and Other Regions

	% change in total assets		% change in turnover		% change in retained profits		% change in operating profits		% change in exports	
	Mean	Median	Mean	Median	Mean	Median	Mean	Median	Mean	Median
All firms	162.6	89.7	140.7	67.3	− 9.7	−0.4	834.6	10.5	288.8	120.7
South East firms	210.3	89.4	105.4	74.8	27.0	6.2	98.5	69.3	528.9	255.4
Other regions firms	123.8	90.2	168.5	53.2	−40.4	−3.6	1457.4*	23.2	75.3	69.2
	z = 0.88		z = 0.816		z = 2.02†		z = 0.145		z = 2.12†	

Source: Companies House data.

Notes:

z = Mann Whitney U-test of the difference between South East and Other Region located firms.

* = An examination of the data indicates that there are a few extreme values incorporated into the analysis. Due to the small size of the sample the authors did not wish to exclude any cases.

† = Significant at 0.05 level of confidence.

Table 3.8c Definitions

Total assets	= Total fixed assets + current assets.
Total fixed assets	= Net book value of land, buildings, plant and machinery, motor vehicles but retains government grants.
Total current assets	= Stocks and WIP deletions, investments, cash and loans to directors.
Turnover	= Total value of sales excluding VAT or other sales tax.
Exports	= Total value of sales the company makes directly to foreign customers, and is part of the turnover figure.
Operating profit	= Pre-tax profit before the deduction of directors' remuneration and interest payments after depreciation but before charging taxation, dividends and extraordinary items.
Pre-tax profit	= Total profits from trading and other activities after interest, depreciation and directors' remuneration but before charging taxation, dividends and extraordinary items.
Retained profit	= Profit after deduction of tax (both current and deferred), dividends and after adjustment for extraordinary items. It reflects the profit retention in the business.

performance where the mean firm increased total assets by 162 per cent with a median of approximately 90 per cent. The mean change in turnover was not quite so high but still substantial at 140 per cent, although the median of 67.3 per cent suggests that a few firms are biasing the mean. In the post-innovation period the average firm seems to have increased exports nearly twice as fast as turnover increasing its penetration of the international market. A similar exercise was conducted at the sectoral level; the results of which are illustrated in Table 3.9. The results suggest that there were no significant differences in the growth of turnover between sectors, although the growth in turnover between firms in the electrical and electronic components equipment and electronic data-processing equipment industries would appear to be quite varied. The former sector appears to show a steep fall in operating profits post-innovation which differentiates it from the other sectors, apart from those firms operating in the plastic products industry. Changes in the rate of profit retention would appear to vary considerably

Table 3.9 Performance by sector

	Change in retained profits CRP		Change in total assets		% change in turnover		% change in operating profits	
	Mean	Median	Mean	Median	Mean	Median	Mean	Median
Plastics products	−17.4	−10.6 (4)	49.0	28.8	41.3	63.1	− 55.1	− 30.1
Medical equipment	1.33	− 1.14 (10)	138.7	101.1	80.3	81.2	− 28.2	4.4
Electronic data-processing equipment	55.4	33.1 (5)	350.4	155.8	97.2	13.6	− 40.4	10.0
Measuring instruments	−53.8	− 1.5 (15)	152.5	76.7	99.8	59.2	− 31.3	10.0
Electrical and electronic components	11.7	4.7 (12)	125.6	79.9	132.9	49.8	−131.9	−105.6
	F-Ratio		F-Ratio		F-Ratio		F-Ratio	
	2.0*		4.7*		0.73		3.38*	

Source: Companies House data.
Notes:
* = significant at 0.05 level of confidence.
F-Ratio = Kruskal Wallis one-way anova.
Inter Industry Differences

between sectors with electronic data-processing equipment showing the highest growth while general decline is experienced in the plastics products sector. Significant differences between sectors are found in growth (which can be negative) of operating and retained profit and of total assets. Even though operating profit growth would seem to be difficult to attain in the electronic data-processing equipment industry, there seems to be a desire, or pressure, to plough any profit back into the business which results in rapid asset growth.

The structure of the industry in each of the five sectoral groups appears to be quite different and perhaps helps to explain their varying performance and survival (Patel and Pavitt 1990). The electronic data-processing equipment industry is dominated by a few large firms (1980 C5=70 per cent) in the United Kingdom and to a large degree in the international field too. The five largest companies operating in the electrical and electronic components and equipment industries or in the plastics products industries also produce approximately half of total industry output per year. On the other hand, the measuring instrument and medical equipment industries have few large players. The competitive environment in which firms operate and conditions of entry to the market may therefore affect their performance.

In the medical equipment industry, sales, profits and export performance have been impressive during the 1980s and a positive trade balance has been maintained (ICC 1989), despite the fact that the high-technology areas are becoming increasingly dominated by foreign competition and weakening prices in the domestic market have been accompanied by unfavourable exchange rates in major export market areas. These export surpluses and domestic market share have, it has been argued, been maintained in low-technology products made by small producers with an accompanying deficit on high-technology electronic-based medical equipment – a sub-sector in which smaller firms are less visible. The low-tech sectors have also not suffered such intensive domestic competition as the high-tech sectors (ICC 1989).

A second and contrasting experience is available from the electronic data-processing equipment industry. This industry is part of one of the fastest-growing sectors in the economy over the 1980s according to various business ratio reports (ICC 1989). However, these same reports suggest contrasting performance within the industry between large and small firms. The reports suggest that it was the smaller firms which tended to be the loss makers, the majority of which were independent manufacturers. One explanation offered for this finding is that the high rates of new firm entry into the industry in the 1970s and the activities of multi-national corporations led to over-crowding in the 1980s. This the smaller firms could not withstand as severe price-cutting took place. Moves towards standardization have also tended to erode the advantage of the market specializations (niches) which many small firms try to capture. Internationalization of production on the part of the transnational corporations has also caused problems for the small producer in this market.

3.6 THE REGIONAL DIMENSION

The location of the innovating firms in the five selected sectors shows a tendency for concentration in the south of England (Figure 3.1). This is not a new finding; Harris's analysis of both large and small firms listed on the SPRU Innovation data-base came to the same conclusions (Harris 1988). Harris also came to the conclusion that this is not simply a structural problem. Due to the spatial concentration of small innovative firms, the following spatial analysis has been restricted to comparisons between those firms located in the South East economic planning region and those located elsewhere in the United Kingdom ('Other Regions').

In terms of continuing production and employment an equal proportion of small firms closed after innovation in the period to 1989 in both the South East region and elsewhere in the United Kingdom. No particular regional environment could therefore be claimed to be more conducive than another to innovative firm longevity. However, a larger proportion (37 per cent) of innovative small firms located in the South East were acquired by other firms than was the case for their counterparts in Other Regions (22 per cent). South East located innovative small firms appear to be either particularly attractive or vulnerable to takeover bids. As a result the surviving and independent-firm sector in the South East shrank considerably over the period to 1989.

In terms of job generation, Table 3.10 provides information on the original employment in sample firms at the time of innovation and in survivors to 1989 for the South East and Other Regions of the United Kingdom. The evidence suggests that at the time of innovation the average South East located firm was already slightly larger than its counterpart in the rest of the country and that over time, in those surviving, this discrepancy has increased. As a result it is estimated that while the overall employment in the innovative

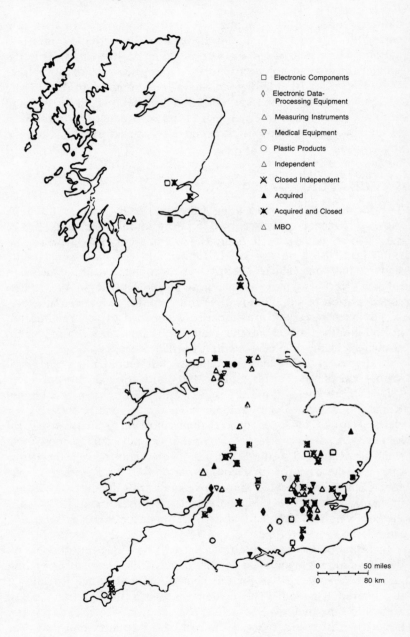

Figure 3.1 Location and status of new-technology companies

Table 3.10 A comparison of employment change in surviving firms located in the south of England and in the rest of the UK

	Total employment at time of innovation	Total employment in 1989	$\bar{x}$ in employment at time of innovation	$\bar{x}$ in employment in 1989
South East and East Anglia	3983	4166	102	160
Other Regions	4097	3361	95	115
Total	8080	7527	98	137

firms, including closures, has declined by approximately 700 in the Other Regions it has increased by 200 in the South East region.

Using the same criteria and methods of analysis used at the national scale Table 3.8 illustrates the 'regional' dimension to changes in total assets, turnover, retained profits, operating profits and exports in the four-year period following innovation in firms located in the South East region and Other Regions of the United Kingdom. At the spatial level it would appear that in terms of total asset growth, operating profits and turnover growth these are not significantly changed by location. However, there appear to be marked differences between the growth in retained profits and exports for the two groups. For example, the median South East located firm experienced a positive growth of 6.2 per cent in retained profits over the four years compared with negative growth of −3.6 per cent for the median innovative firm located in the Other Regions over the same period. Negative growth in retained profit can obviously threaten the viability of the firm in the longer term.

Furthermore, the median South East firm exhibited a positive growth of 255 per cent in exports compared with the positive growth of 75 per cent for the median Other Region firm. Thus while growth of turnover is not significantly different between firms located in the South East or Other Regions, South East located firms seem to focus on exports with greater success than their counterparts in the rest of the United Kingdom. Storey *et al.* suggest that fast growth firms are more likely to be competing in overseas markets (Storey *et al.* 1989). They showed that 45 per cent of fast-growth firms exported at least part of their production compared with only 15 per cent of matched firms. Furthermore, 20 per cent of fast-growth firms were significant exporters, compared with only 5 per cent of matched firms. The evidence of considerable involvement with, and growth of, exports in the innovative small-firm sector would seem to allow them to be classified (on one characteristic at least) as part of the fast-growth-firm sector. In particular, the South East region appears to be benefiting from this activity.

3.7 SUMMARY AND CONCLUSION

The research reported here can only be regarded as a small contribution to our understanding of the links between technological change in the small firm and national or local economic development. While it will be possible to explore the existing data further to confirm or extend these results, there remain many areas in this field for future fruitful research. While the limitations of this research and analysis are obvious, it proved impossible to examine the subsequent performance of the innovations and innovative firms which were acquired and became undifferentiated parts of larger organizations. The results therefore reflect, to a greater extent than originally intended, the performance of surviving and separately identifiable innovators in the small-firm sector.

The results confirm that significant innovations introduced into the United Kingdom by the small-firm sector were clustered in a few industries: electronic data-processing equipment; electrical and electronic components and equipment; measuring checking and precision instruments; medical and surgical equipment; and plastics products. They also suggested that the majority of these firms were already producing in those industries some time before innovation and therefore substantial innovation and new firm formation did not necessarily coincide. These innovations were important to the economic and future technological performance of participating firms, but there was no evidence from this study that this type of firm addressed other than niche or specialized markets.

The direct effects on regional and national economic development seem to be somewhat limited. However, the capacity for innovation appears to be associated with the performance of the firm which, for survivors, is more akin to Storey *et al.*'s 'high-growth firms' than their more run-of-the-mill 'matched' counterparts. On average this type of firm appears able to resist closure and for survivors to create employment. In the four-year period following innovation it is also associated with growth in assets, turnover, operating profits and exports. Returns on assets appear to approximate the performance of high-growth firms rather than those of the average small firm.

These general results are neither sectorally nor spatially evenly distributed. The post-innovative survival is highest in medical and surgical equipment firms and lowest in electronic data-processing equipment. Similarly, in the period to 1989 employment doubled in the firms in the medical and surgical equipment industry but was reduced very substantially in the electronic data-processing equipment industry. The results also showed that changes to operating profit, and retained profit over total assets, were significantly different between industries, illustrating the complexity of the innovation/economic process.

In comparisons between firms located in the South East region and the rest of the United Kingdom it was found that differences in performance in terms of employment, retained profits and exports worked to the advantage of the South East region with no offsetting advantages to Other Regions on the other tested variables.

Overall, this type of firm appears to have a number of attributes other authors have associated with success. These attributes could be claimed to be beneficial to economic development. However, these factors appear to be neither sectorally nor spatially constant in their benevolence which results in the core region of the country gaining further advantage over its less-favoured counterparts.

Policy makers, on the fragmentary evidence provided here, seem justified in supporting this type of firm. However, the evidence also suggests that the support of firms in some industrial sectors and locations seems to provide a greater chance of success than others. Examination of the aggregated data does not suggest that this type of firm will have more than a marginal impact on current economic problems at either the national or local levels.

ACKNOWLEDGEMENT

We would like to acknowledge the financial support for this research received from the ESRC under its New Technologies and the Firm Initiative. We gratefully acknowledge the generosity of the SPRU researchers who allowed us access to and use of their unique innovations data-base. We also thank all those industrialists who provided information for our research, and also Mike Coombes, Neil Alderman and other members of CURDS for their invaluable assistance. Any errors remain the responsibility of the authors.

REFERENCES

Armstrong, H. and Taylor, J. (1985) *Regional Economics and Policy*, Oxford: Philip Allan.

Aydalot, P. (ed.) (1986) *Milieux Innovateurs en Europe*, Paris: GREMI.

Brush, S. (1982) 'The Emilian model: productive decentralisation and social integration', *Cambridge Journal of Economics* 6(2): 167–84.

Birch, D. (1979) 'The Job Generation Process', MIT Program, Cambridge, Mass.: Cambridge U.P.

Brugger, E. and Stuckey, B. (1987) 'Regional economic structure and innovative behaviour in Switzerland', *Regional Studies* 21: 241–54.

Crevoisier, O. (1990) 'Functional logic and territorial logic and how they inter-relate in the region', in E. Ciciotti *et al.* (eds) *Technological Change in a Spatial Context*, Heidelberg: Springer-Verlag.

Ciciotti, E. (1983) 'La diffusione regionale delle innovazioni in Italia', paper presented at the IV AISRE Conference, Firenze, November.

Ciciotti, E., Alderman, N. and Thwaites, A. T. (1990) *Technical Change in a Spatial Context*, Heidelberg: Springer-Verlag.

Denison, E. and Poullier, J. (1968) *Why Growth Rates Differ* London: Allen & Unwin.

Dosi, G. (1984) *Technical Change and Industrial Transformation*, London: Macmillan.

DTI (1991a) *The Research and Technology Initiative: SMART Competition*, London: DTI, Pub. 305.

—— (1991b) *Support for Products Under Research* DTI. London:

Gallagher, C. and Steward, H. (1986) 'Jobs and the business cycle in the UK', *Applied Economics* 18: 875–900.

Ganguly, P. (1983) Life-span analysis of business in the UK 1973–1982, *British Business* 12 (12 Aug.): 838–45.

Goddard, J. B. and Thwaites, A. T. (1979) 'The mobilization of indigenous potential in the UK'. Report to the Regional Policy Directorate of the European Community, CURDS, University of Newcastle upon Tyne.

NEDO (1991) *Reducing Regional Inequalities*, London: Kogan Page.

Harris, R. D. (1988) 'Technological change and regional development in the UK: evidence from the SPRU database on innovations, *Regional Studies* 22(5): 361–74.

ICC (various dates) *Business Ratio Reports*, London: ICC Information Group.

Ingersoll Engineers (1991) *Change the Good, the Bad and the Visionary*, Rugby: Ingersoll Engineers Ltd.

Katrak, H. (1985) 'R & D in United Kingdom Industries', *Discussion Paper* 103, NIESR, London.

Mansfield, E. (1968) *The Economics of Technical Change*, London: Longman.

Moore, B., Rhodes, J. and Tyler, P. (1981) 'The impact of regional policy on regional labour markets', mimeo, Department of Applied Economics, University of Cambridge.

North, D., Leigh, R. and Smallbone, O. (1991) 'A comparison of surviving and non-surviving small and medium-sized manufacturing firms in London during the 1980s', W.P. No. 1, ESRC Small Business Research Programme, Middlesex Polytechnic.

Oakey, R. P. (1984) *High Technology Small Firms*, London: Pinter.

Oakey, R. P., Rothwell, R. and Cooper, S. (1988) *Management of Innovation in High Technology Small Firms*, London: Pinter.

OECD (1986) 'R & D, invention and competitiveness', *Science and Technology Indicators* 2, Paris: OECD.

Odagiri, H. (1985) 'Research activity, output growth and productivity increase in Japanese manufacturing industries', *Research Policy* 14: 117–30.

Patel, P. and Pavitt, K. (1991) 'Large firms in the production of the world's technology', *Journal of International Business Studies* 22(1): 1–22.

Pavitt, K., Robson, M. and Townsend, J. (1987) 'The size distribution of innovating firms in the UK: 1945–1983', *Journal of Industrial Economics* 35(3): 297–316.

Pompili, T. (1990) 'Differentiation, entry, innovation in the system of cities', in E. Ciciotti *et al.* (eds) *Technological Change in a Spatial Context*, Heidelberg: Springer-Verlag.

Richardson, H. (1973) *Regional Growth Theory*, London: Macmillan.

Rothwell, R. (1984) 'The role of small firms in the emergence of new technologies', *Omega* 12: 19–29.

Schott, K. (1981) *Industrial Innovation in the UK, Canada and the United States*, London: British-North American Committee.

Solow, R. M. (1957) 'Technical change and the aggregate production function', *Review of Economics and Statistics* 39:312–20.

Storey, D. J. (1982) *Entrepreneurship and the Small Firm*, London: Croom Helm.

Storey, D. J. and Johnson, S. (1987) *Job Generation and Labour Market Change*, London: Macmillan.

Storey, D. J., Keasey, K., Watson, R. and Wynarczyk, P. (1987) *The Performance of Small Firms*, London: Croom Helm.

Storey, D. J., Watson, R. and Wynarczyk, P. (1989) 'Fast growth small businesses, Research Paper No. 67, Department of Employment, Sheffield.

Sweeney, G. (1985) *Innovation Policies: An International Perspective*, London: Allen & Unwin.

Thwaites, A. T., Oakey, R. P. and Nash, P. A. (1981) 'Industrial innovation and regional development', Final Report to Department of the Environment, CURDS, University of Newcastle upon Tyne.

Thwaites, A. T., Edwards, A. and Gibbs, D. (1982) 'Interregional diffusion of production innovations in Great Britain', Final Report to Department of Industry/European Community, CURDS, University of Newcastle upon Tyne.

Todtling, F. (1990) 'Regional differences and determinants of entrepreneurial innovation: empirical results of an Austrian case study' in E. Ciciotti *et al.* (eds) *Technological Change in a Spatial Context*, Heidelberg: Springer-Verlag.

Townsend, J. (1981) 'Innovations in Britain since 1945', *Occasional Paper* 16, SPRU, University of Sussex, Brighton.

Watson, R. (1990) 'Employment change, profits and directors remuneration in small and closely held UK companies', *Scottish Journal of Political Economy* 37: 259–74.

Wynarczyk, P., Watson, R., Storey, D. J., Short, H. and Keasey, K. (1993) *Managerial Labour Markets in Small and Medium-sized Enterprises*, London: Routledge, (forthcoming).

4 Paradigms, strategies and the evolutionary basis of technological competition

J. Stanley Metcalfe and Mark Boden

4.1 INTRODUCTION

Few if any students of management would quarrel with the claim that the formulation and implementation of technology strategies are critical factors in determining patterns of technological innovation and, by direct implication, the competitive advantages enjoyed by firms. The research reported in this chapter is concerned with a key, if not *the* key, determinant of a firm's performance in technical innovation: the nature and development of a technology strategy.

For the firms we have investigated, technology strategy is central to the conduct of competition. They all have a significant R & D spend, they operate in global markets and each places technological excellence at the core of its competitive strategy.[1] The companies also differ considerably in size, technologies and market scope, and so strategy is realized in very different ways. But for each one the issues of how to build competitive advantage from technology, and of how to maintain a sequence of profitable innovations which keep the business ahead of competitors, are pervasive. The following are typical examples of the management problems which colour any discussion of strategy. How should R & D be organized and funded? How much should be spent on 'blue skies' research unrelated to current business needs? How can marketing and production be linked more effectively to research and development activities? In a multi-dimensional business, how can various technology activities be co-ordinated and best-practice technology be diffused through the group? How can joint ventures, acquisitions and technology licences be exploited to enhance the performance of the internal R & D effort? We shall argue that these issues are addressed and resolved in terms of business specific strategic paradigms, frameworks of thought adopted by the top management team which focus and constrain their innovative creativity.

Perhaps to our surprise we have been led to a view of the firm's strategy as an intellectual construct built and sustained in ways similar to those which shape the growth of knowledge more generally (Loasby 1991, Kelly 1964). This is not to deny the importance of resources in shaping patterns of innovation, but rather it is to put the disposition of resources to innovate in their proper context. Firms are more or less creative as they adopt strategic paradigms which encourage or limit, conjecturing, hypothesis formation and experimentation. Firms act according to how they think.

The literature on technology strategy scarcely touches these issues. The critical concerns are often expressed in terms of rules and algorithms to identify market niches, the sources of differential advantage, and the scale and timing of investments to secure the desired outcome (Porter 1985, Newman et al 1989, Ramanathan 1990, Stacey and Ashton 1990). We do not object to this except in so far as it is a view of strategy which is akin to a clock without a spring. It is mechanism not energy. Our perspective is much closer to one recently expressed by Teece and colleagues which presents a dynamic approach focusing on learning mechanisms and the accumulation of firm-specific skills and distinctive capabilities (Teece et al. 1990, Pavitt 1987). Expressed succinctly, our approach has come to view strategic paradigms as the frameworks within which the top management team learns and conjectures different futures for the firm. Strategy in this sense reaches to the very core of a firm's operations and, we suggest, emerges at the intersection between three elements – namely, technology, organization and competitive market environment. Thus we have defined strategy for our purposes as the framework chosen by the firm to reconcile the development of technology and the pursuit of competitive advantage in specific organizational and market environments. From this perspective technology strategy is an integral, not an independent, component of business strategy more generally, and not one of the firms we have investigated would see it otherwise (Grindley 1992). In short, we have explored the idea that the way strategy develops is not unlike the way other bodies of knowledge develop. Consequently, the philosophy of science and technology provides important insights into the fundamental competitive differences between rival firms, and an integrating framework in which to understand strategic questions. In our investigations we have been forced to take a snapshot view of each business. Future research would be greatly strengthened by following the development of strategy through a period of at least five years to understand more fully how strategies evolve. The various differences and similarities between our case studies clearly reflect and condition the technology strategies adopted. However, they are not matters of the first importance. Our concern is with the formal and informal frameworks within which such issues are addressed and which are reflected in two central elements of the firm's creative activities – namely, the processes which construct the agenda of future technological opportunities perceived by the top management team, and the process by which items on this agenda are accepted or rejected. To understand why these are critical elements in strategy we need to dwell a little on the nature of competition and of technology.

Competition

Each of the firms we have investigated continually seeks to find competitive advantage and recognizes that the markets in which it sells are highly competitive. However, the degree of competition they face relates not to the number of rivals against which they compete but rather to the ever present possibility that their rivals may innovate and gain a decisive cost or product-quality advantage. The competition they face is evolutionary competition driven by distinctive variety in behaviour, and no difference between rivals in the longer term is more significant than their ability to maintain a momentum of profitable innovation. Superior products or process attract customers and enhance profit margins so providing the basis for expanding market share relative to rivals. In a world of identical behaviours there is no scope for dynamic competition, for competition is driven by variety of behaviour and ultimately by the creativity of firms. Exactly as Schumpeter claimed, the gale of creative destruction is far removed from the idea of competition as a static market equilibrium between equal and lifeless competitors (Schumpeter 1944); an idea which, as many have noted, has lost touch with the reality of the commercial world (Clark 1961, Hayek 1948). Competing is about performing better than rivals, and this is where strategy becomes relevant, for technology strategy sets the rules for the creativity of the firm and the basis for competition differentiation. This leads directly to the view of competition as the outcome of interactions between two evolutionary processes: an external process taking place in market environments, and an internal process taking place within firms to determine the products and processes with which each firm competes externally. It is not difficult to see that long-term competitive advantage depends on having a suitable correspondence between the external and internal evolutionary processes. It is the internal selection environment that is at the heart of the strategy formation process. It provides the processes and criteria by which technological options reach the agenda, are evaluated and selected or rejected. It both determines the generation of technological variety and forecloses potential directions of development. It interacts with the firm's technological vision, where the firm sees its own technological activities in relation to current and prospective developments in the technological environment.

If changes in the external selection environment require adaptive behaviour on the part of the firm, it is the internal selection environment which articulates this need and conditions the creative responses which enable the external conditions to be met. From this it is a short step to see that the internal evolutionary process is conditioned by the firm's perception of its technology and the way it organizes the process of hypothesis formation and hypothesis testing.

Technology

There are few more complex aspects of the modern firm than its technology. Technology can be identified at all levels of its operation, in many cases it is difficult to separate technology from other questions of organization, and, most significantly for our purposes, technology covers a whole spectrum of activities and concepts ranging from artefacts to skills to knowledge of various kinds (Layton 1974). The strategic issues facing the firm vary across the spectrum, as does the way in which technology is developed and acquired and the degree to which technology lies outside the business. In our investigations the distinction between technology as artefact and technology as knowledge has played an important role. Technology as artefact plays a major role in evolutionary theories of competition and industrial change, for it is the products and methods of production articulated by firms which are the primary objects of selection in markets. Every firm has to pay attention to how the performance dimensions of its artefacts relate to those of its competitors. Positioning is a major strategic task, where the firm is located relative to its rivals, and in which directions to move and how quickly relative to rivals. It is with respect to performance characteristics that trajectories of technological advance can be identified, in the *ex post* sense of a record of performance at different dates and, more problematically, in the *ex ante* sense of expected improvements in performance generated by new technological hypotheses (Swann and Gill 1992). It is clear that an important role for mapping exercises of this kind is to identify limits on functional performance beyond which an artefact cannot be pushed. We suggest that mapping of trajectories is a valuable strategic tool for firms.

Our second dimension of technology is technology as knowledge, those concepts, theories and actions which enable a transformation process to operate. This knowledge is necessarily contained in the minds of individuals who either know directly or know how to find, for example, by library search, concerning some piece of information. Here we find the obvious link between technology and the science knowledge base, and the cross-cutting distinctions between different kinds of technological knowledge, such as the codified, tacit distinction versus the procedural, descriptive distinction (Vincenti 1990). We can also draw a connection here with the idea of technologies as communities of practitioners (Constant 1980, 1984) carrying out their activities within traditions of practice which focus problem solving, suggest solutions and provide methods for the comparative appraisal of solutions (Laudan 1984). These traditions reflect the division of labour in the growth of technological capability. Any one of our firms is typically an embodiment of a number of such traditions which it seeks to integrate, paying due attention to the boundaries between the conduct of different traditions. Pilkingtons identifies five key traditions in its knowledge base, while Lucas identifies twelve traditions.

One implication of this is that members of the firm belong to wider technological and scientific communities than are contained in the firm. They share educational backgrounds in common and can thus communicate readily with other discipline members. However, their knowledge is also focused more precisely by the particular transformation processes in which they claim expertise.

With this as background we must now be more precise about the relation between artefacts and the knowledge base. As we have already suggested, a business unit is organized around some specific transformation process which embodies quite specific design principles as to the nature of the product and the method of its production. This interconnected set of principles defines the artefact rather precisely so we can distinguish a jet engine from a steam turbine or a petrol internal combustion engine. This set of principles we call a *design configuration*, defining precisely the purpose, mode of operation, construction materials and method of manufacture of the relevant artefacts. It defines the evaluation framework for the technology and it is within the configuration that specific design puzzles emerge. It is at root a shared intellectual construct. There is considerable evidence that the temporal sequence of innovations which trace the development of a configuration are linked to the patterns of puzzle formation. Sahal's (1981) concept of technological guideposts, Rosenberg's (1983) concept of technological bottlenecks and Hughes's (1983) concept of reverse salients all fit within this idea of the configuration as the puzzle-generating framework. Notice that any design configuration may enable the production of a wide range of products and designs for different market segments, and that it may experience substantial improvements in revealed technological performance over time.

Organization

The final element in our triad is the formal and informal organizational structure of the firm which we see as an operator, translating the skills and knowledge of the individual members into a collective competence.

The organizational operator is defined in terms of rules of communication, both internally and with respect to the outside world, which filter, transform and store knowledge in the organization. They constitute what Arrow has called a code of communication, which determines who communicates with whom, about what, with what authority, and with what frequency (Arrow 1984). As Arrow indicates, there is no one operator which is best in all circumstances and firms must be expected to vary considerably in their internal codes, and as Burns and Stalker, among others, have pointed out, the operators which optimize with respect to static efficiency are unlikely to be the operators which stimulate creative experimentation (Burns and Stalker 1961). Necessarily the knowledge which is filtered is always a subset of what is available (Jacob 1982).

Since the operator is firm-specific it is not surprising to find that the same individual may perform quite differently in different firms, or that attempts at technology transfer or joint ventures between firms often run into severe difficulties relating to the lack of connectivity of different codes. Conversely, changes in the membership of a firm may entail large variations in competence.

Once we see the organization as an information-gathering and manipulating system, some immediate issues are raised, including (1) the openness of the organization to external information and the way in which this is allowed to mould its competence, (2) the capacity of the organization to systematically explore its technological and market environment by entertaining different conjectures about its future and (3) the ability of the organization to learn from its errors. All of these are well recognized in the literature (e.g. Morgan 1987) and often recur in debates about the relative creativity of large and small organizations (Quinn 1985) or about the tension between the organizational requirements of efficiency and creativity. We suggest that the concept of the strategic paradigm allows these different findings to be related in a coherent way.

The notion of the organization as a competence-defining operator has a further dimension, namely as a competence-changing operator, a competence to change competence (Pelikan 1989). In this respect we shall emphasize its crucial role as an internal-selection environment which determines the evolution over time of the firm's knowledge base and its revealed technological performance. Having clarified the idea of strategies as built around design configurations supported by a particular organizational structure, we can turn to a brief synopsis of two of our case studies.

4.2 TRADITION AND CHANGE IN GLASS TECHNOLOGY: PILKINGTONS PLC

Pilkingtons is a long-established UK company specializing in the production of flat and safety glass for the building and automotive industries world wide. It is the least diversified of our companies, with flat and safety glass sales accounting for three-quarters of the world-wide turnover in 1990. Characterized in the past as a conservative, family-dominated company, it has in the last five years undergone a major restructuring of its activities, with three major overseas acquisitions, Libby Owens Ford in the United States, Flachglas in Germany and a series of Visioncare Ophthalmic businesses in Australia and the United States.

Of all the companies in this study, Pilkingtons arguably has the most mature technology. Improvements in technology are primarily related to cost reduction, although glass products with new properties have also been developed in recent years. A small division has been established to introduce glass into radically new product areas. However, the critical point is the stability and long-accepted nature of the design configurations in glass making, which is not to say that the scope for incremental improvement is necessarily limited. Pilkingtons' substantial commitment to R & D indicates otherwise. The development of coating technology, in particular, has been extremely significant in the past two decades, with many of the ideas being transferred from microelectronic and semi-conductor manufacture.

To match the new circumstances of the company, the former UK research facility, Lathom Laboratories, has become the long-term research facility for the Group as a whole, with the bulk of development work devolved to the operating divisions. The role of Group Research (GR) is to develop positions of excellence in the key enabling technologies which support and extend the business strategies of the divisions. To accomplish this role GR carries out high-quality research and engineering on projects with a five- to ten-year horizon to exploitation. The objectives of GR are related to the Group's own business strategy, the intention being to facilitate reductions in production cost and improvements in product quality to sustain high-profit margins for what is virtually a commodity product.

To achieve these objectives a number of approaches are employed to enhance the effectiveness of the R & D spend. Up to 10 per cent of the research budget is spent on collaborative support for work in universities and other research establishments, to extend technical capabilities and identify new areas of science and technology. Group participation in pre-competitive collaboration programmes supported by the EEC and the UK government is actively promoted. Within the group, mechanisms have also been established to facilitate the secondment of employees into and out of the operating companies and GR. In these principal ways the Group is integrated into a wider technological community just as its own internal effort is more effectively integrated within a Group community.

Setting the agenda

In the new and complex company structure the strategy formation process inevitably has a number of levels at which hypotheses are generated and selected between. Each of the operating divisions has a technical director who is in continuous dialogue with GR, with the latter accountable to a main board committee which contains the chief executives of all the operating divisions. The primary purpose of this structure is to ensure that the technology strategy is integrated with the business strategy. Below this level is a technology steering committee for the main glass business, charged with deciding the main elements in the R & D programme and where this work should be carried out. It is supported by a series of technology management groups whose purpose is to generate the agenda for the steering committee. Programmes of potential projects are put together to match the business strategies of the divisions with the technical capabilities within the Group. The steering committee comprises the technical directors from the main operating divisions together with the Group Research and Engineering directors. Each member of this committee leads and supervises the activities of one of the technology management groups each of which contains appropriate specialists from GR and the operating divisions. In broad terms, three of the technology management groups are focused on product technology and three on process technology. Although the agenda creating process is essentially 'bottom-up', the steering committee can also shape the thinking process of the management groups by setting targets for improved technological performance, for example with respect to reduced environmental emissions or greater energy efficiency. Considerable emphasis is placed on informal contacts across divisions and between technical and marketing specialists in the company.

Selection

Of our case studies, the selection process in Pilkingtons GR gives the impression of being the most informal, no attempt being made to evaluate options with rigorous investment appraisal techniques. However, appearances belie the fact that this is a company with very strong technological traditions in a technology where experience and tacit knowledge count for a great deal. It is also a company where market pressures, including perceived competitive threats, exert a major influence on the agenda. The technical directors of divisions are fully briefed by their own marketing functions. Thus projects are in practice rigorously assessed for their chances of success with judgement and a feel for what is practical counting a great deal. Those projects which are selected, roughly one-tenth of all possibilities, are intended to keep the company at the forefront of glass technology, to be exploited internally or licensed out when this is compatible with the company maintaining its competitive position.

4.3 SYSTEMS TECHNOLOGY AND THE FUTURE OF THE AUTOMOBILE: LUCAS INDUSTRIES PLC

Lucas Industries plc is also a long-established company with its core business in the automotive and aerospace industries, primarily associated in the past with electrical technology, batteries, lighting systems, generators and so on. In the past ten years it has experienced a fundamental strategic and organizational transformation driven in the first instance by the collapse of the automotive market in the late 1970s, but more fundamentally by a radical restructuring of automobile technology. Characterized in the past as having an inward-looking and highly centralized management, the company was slow to respond to its rapidly changing market and technological environment and made losses for the first time in its history in 1981. The resulting restructuring of its business into three divisions (automotive, aerospace and industrial, the latter subsequently reorganized as Lucas Applied Technology), combined with a reduction in the role of group activities, has contributed to a return to the current levels of profitability. At the same time a good number of its business interests were sold, whenever they did not fit into the corporate strategy (e.g. the 50 per cent stake in the Lucas-Cookson Sialon business), while other more appropriate ones have been acquired.

The strategic intent of the company is clear, to maintain a leading international position in the supply of automotive components based on an underpinning of advanced technology. This strategy is reflected in the following three objectives: reduction in exposure in UK markets; reduction in dependence on low-technology, commodity products; and creation of a better balance between the activities of the three company divisions.

With respect to each of these considerations, matters of technology strategy are highly relevant, and this is reflected in the technological intent of the company, namely:

- to command a strong position in all chosen markets world wide, based on leading-edge technology, total quality and high manufacturing efficiency; and
- to utilize investments in innovation, training and better management of change, to generate a professional flexible and enterprise-based organization.

The nature of recent changes in automotive technology enter at this point. A fundamental trajectory on which the automobile industry is now placed, involves the development of a comprehensive and integrated set of in-vehicle control systems which define a new design configuration. Instead of independent systems for braking, engine management and other functions, each operating on different hydraulic electrical or mechanical principles, the goal is to manage each of these functions with the aid of electronic devices interconnected via power and data management systems. Ultimately, these systems will be active not reactive, anticipating road and traffic conditions independently of the driver. It is this technological concept which currently drives Lucas's strategy in its automotive division. As such, it represents a radical change in the definition of core businesses, competencies and technologies. The organization of the restructured company reflects this technological strategy and this is particularly clear in the position of the newly formed Advanced Engineering Centre (AEC).

AEC and the technological vision

To the external observer, one of the striking features of Lucas plc is the presence of a clear cut and powerful technological vision, and it is the responsibility of the AEC to drive this forward by building the requisite knowledge base to support the new design configuration within Lucas. This vision has clear paradigmatic qualities, shaping the kinds of innovation hypotheses that can be generated and focusing the attention of its researchers and engineers on objectives and future possibilities to be achieved within clearly established boundaries. In this sense, it acts as a clear focusing device for the development of technology, just as the float glass configuration does in Pilkingtons.

A crucial issue here is the relationship between the AEC and the operating divisions, and the way in which the desired synergy is to be generated. The thrust of the AEC programme is to build enabling, or competence-enhancing technologies, the underpinning science and engineering required by the technological vision. In this, the AEC takes a proactive role with respect to the divisions: performing advanced work which the divisions cannot afford or which is too remote; integrating programmes involving cross-divisional activity; and, performing work which is outside the competence of the scientific and engineering teams within the divisions. To achieve this clearly requires, communication, co-operation and collaboration between group research and the divisions, not a previous strength of the company. In part, this is achieved by locating

AEC within the automotive division to achieve a focused attack on the automotive side of the business. Currently, however, the evident synergy in technology between the auto and aero sides of the business have led AEC to adopt an evenhanded approach to both parts of Lucas. More generally, it is to be achieved by a particular style of operation for research projects.

There is a continuing awareness of the need to integrate central R & D with the divisions. While the AEC has the remit to develop generic capabilities, the divisions are more narrowly focused on specific market segments, have their own technological capabilities and consequently communication problems are considerable. To overcome this problem a Group Technology Council was formed in 1990 to bring together the technological needs of the different divisions and the AEC in a single forum. In this way it is intended that duplication can be avoided, group-wide projects identified and best practice diffused more effectively throughout the company. Moreover the Council provides a sounding board for proposals from anyone in the company to ensure that creativity is not stifled by established management structures.

Setting the agenda

How then is the agenda for research determined? Obviously it is strongly shaped by the broad technological vision and appears to be generated primarily by suggestions which 'bubble up' from the engineers and scientists working with AEC. Staff are expected to liaise closely with divisions and with the automobile producers to provide 'market information' independently of Lucas's marketing activities. About a fifth of the suggested projects emanate directly from the divisions. The entire portfolio of projects, current and prospective, is then the subject of a monthly review meeting chaired by the head of the AEC. This committee grants and withholds approval, allocates resources and locates projects firmly within an appropriate demonstrator programme. Thus the central ethos is to let the AEC staff draw up the agenda in technology-push fashion, but keep control of this with market-directed demonstrator programmes. In general, a demonstrator programme will not be sanctioned unless there is a customer with specific interest, and a market appraisal carried out. Thus the monthly review committee is the primary instrument for generating and evaluating the technological agenda.

There is a deep awareness at the top levels of management that external technological threats can emerge at any time and that the AEC must not be dominated by an inward-looking approach. The methods for achieving this are threefold: first, close contact with customers and suppliers; second, formal liaison with external knowledge base bodies such as universities; and third, participation in collaboration programmes with competitors and other firms with common technological interests. About 20 per cent of the budget is spent on these external links, which include European programmes, such as BRITE and PROMETHEUS.

Selection

Determining the agenda is one thing, selecting from it within the constraints of the overall budget is quite another. To deal with the question of choice, AEC operates a pragmatic procedure to highlight and favour activities which fit with the broad objectives of Lucas, the particular capabilities of the AEC, and the technology paradigm. Broadly speaking, projects are favoured when they are consistent with the technological vision, typically involving integrated system elements, when the potential market is of sufficient size and when the potential market promises rapid growth. The favoured time scale to exploitation is five to ten years with a distinct bias against time scales in excess of twenty years. In practice, each project is scored with respect to more than twenty criteria which divide along the lines of market prospects, and consistency with the existing technological capability of the AEC. Each criterion is weighted and the scores are summed. No attempt is made to use sophisticated investment appraisal techniques or to establish the sensitivity of the estimates which emerge, although the weights applied to the different time scales have an effect akin to discounting the distant future.

The informality of the process for generating and selecting from the research agenda of the AEC seems to reflect a clear awareness of technological strategy as an open-ended learning process. Advice is sought and discussions regularly held with a wide range of people, and the outcome is a process of incremental trial-and-error learning. This system searches for improvements (not necessarily optimal solutions) relative to the current state of the art.

To summarize, Lucas is a company which has been transformed in the 1980s. Central to this transformation has been the gradual discovery of a technological paradigm which reached its current level of articulation in 1988. This paradigm not only shapes the development of the company's technology, it also determines patterns of acquisition and divestiture, stopping the company diversifying in random ways. It provides focus and discipline, it is an exclusion principle for the development of the company.

4.4 IMPLICATIONS

Of course, each of our case studies relates to a quite distinctive business operating in different technological and market environments. But since each one has a strong commitment to gaining competitive advantage via technological innovation it is not surprising to find that common themes emerge. Not one of the companies can be said to lack a comprehensive system for generating and evaluating information on technology and markets. Their external antennae appear to be particularly well developed. Similarly, the time horizons for developing new technology give no sign of short-term attitudes, substantial commitments are made in every case to an unknowable future. Each of the companies has a clear view of the various technologies which constitute its knowledge base and recognizes that it cannot rely on internal development alone and must create and manage linkages with a wider technological community. Not one of the companies fails to devote considerable effort to ensuring that technology strategy develops in harmony with the established business policy and *vice versa*: they are certainly not technology-push companies. Where R & D is to be located and how it is to be funded are matters of continuous concern.

We have been led to the view therefore that none of these matters is likely to be of decisive importance in explaining differences between companies in their creativity. Rather we consider that explanations lie more deeply in terms of the frameworks of thought which integrate technology and business need. As suggested above these frameworks determine the process of hypothesis generation, and set the boundaries to what will be tolerated in terms of a proposed innovation. Each of our companies can be identified with a clear strategic framework which guides the development of its technology through a process of interaction with perceived market pressures. To understand the nature of their strategy frameworks we must turn for guidance to the history and philosophy of the development of science and technology – the epistemic connections.

Strategy and paradigm in the competitive process

We have suggested that a firm is competitive by virtue of its ability to differentiate its technological performance from its rivals. Now, it is elementary that every business unit must specialize to survive, it cannot do everything: it cannot develop in an *ad hoc* way, and if it is to be even moderately efficient and creative it must eliminate debate about fundamentals at an early stage in its development. The question then arises of how its business policy is given the necessary focus while permitting the requisite creativity to ensure its longer-term survival and growth. We now suggest that this dual requirement of focus and development is met by the company's technology strategy paradigm, always taken in conjunction with the other elements of business policy, and that strategy is built around the chosen design configuration. The paradigm becomes the framework for generating and managing non trivial changes in the firm's activities.

In these terms, strategy is a framework of thought – in Kelly's terms an instrument for probing the future, for inviting the company to conduct particular innovation experiments (Kelly 1964). In each of our case studies there are well-defined formal and informal frameworks which determine how technology is to be developed and linked with business policy. They begin with a top-level mission statement and develop down into an awareness of what technology means to the business and the way it should be organized. At its most fundamental level this framework is defined by the company's design configuration and the artefacts by which competitive advantage is obtained.

An obvious way to explain this theme is through the concept of a technology strategy paradigm. Dosi has suggested that technologies have paradigmatic qualities as do the natural sciences, and defines a technological paradigm as a ' "model" and a "pattern" of solution of *selected* technological problems, based on *selected* principles derived from the natural sciences and on *selected* material technologies' (original emphasis, Dosi 1982: 152). Such a paradigm indicates fruitful directions for technological change, defines some ideas of progress and has a powerful exclusion effect on the imagination of engineers and organizations. Similar ideas, referring more or less explicitly to Kuhnian paradigms can be found in other literatures. Thus Constant writes of the normal technology of a community of practitioners, a framework which shapes the incremental steps by which a technology is developed (Constant

1984). Similarly, Wojick has used the concept of evaluation policies, that set of decision-making procedures which defines the conceptual framework (administrative, social and economic as well as technological) within which technology is applied to the solution of problems (Wojick 1979).

A strategy paradigm defines a framework for conjecturing the future development of the business by suggesting appropriate directions in which the technology of the business can be developed. It provides the framework for hypothesis formation and testing and structures the accumulation of skills and knowledge by defining the ways in which problems are to be solved. It is a framework by which the business explores its technological and market environment. Such a framework has to be discovered; the company has to learn what is its paradigm if it is to compete successfully over the long term. Ultimately it is strategic paradigms which compete since they are the frameworks which make rival firms more or less creative.

Several important implications follow from this paradigm perspective. Paradigms are creative but they are also selective, they exert a powerful exclusion effect with respect to hypotheses which are not compatible with the prevailing view. As they develop they progressively limit the interpretive horizon of the business, affecting its ability to digest information coming from its environment. In some cases this can prove quite fatal through an inability to comprehend the significance of a different, superior design configuration articulated by a rival firm (Henderson and Clark 1990, Cooper and Schendal 1976). A further dimension of the paradigm is its organizational specificity. The business unit has to organize scientific and technological disciplines in an appropriate way and focus them on generating the required competence with respect to revealed technological performance. The strategic paradigm is a framework which conditions the internal selection environment of the firm, and firms differ in revealed performance in part because of differences in strategic paradigm. Unlike a scientific paradigm or a technological tradition, a strategic paradigm only requires consensus within the business unit, a consensus which, as we have seen in our case studies, is embodied in the decision-making structures of the organization in three crucial respects: (1) with respect to the determination of the options constituting the technological agenda, (2) with respect to the choice of options from that agenda and (3) with respect to the mode of implementation of the selected options. The strategic paradigm is a framework for non-empty, creative decision. It contains 'models' of the business unit's modes of interaction with its external selection environment, and it generates the particular puzzles which drive technological development. It also generates the exemplary or standard procedures for problem solving within the strategy. Thus the strategy paradigm determines the nature of the business unit as an experimental machine and reflects the decisions of its top competent team (Eliasson 1988). 'What kinds of experiments will be conducted by what methods, over what time frame, and with what resource commitment to internal or external activity?' are the central strategic questions. Experimentation is in this sense a method for exploration of the chosen design configuration. Differences in the long-run competitive performance of firms we argue are inextricably related with their strategic paradigms. Unless the internal selection mechanisms generate hypothesis and experiments consistent with the external selection environment, the business unit cannot expect to enjoy sustainable competitive advantage.

At this point it is relevant to make a distinction between good and bad paradigms. A good paradigm is progressive, it continually suggests new products, improvements to existing products and cost-reducing process innovations which are subsequently demonstrated to be profitable – the hypothesis is confirmed. It provides a basis for keeping ahead of competitors, it is proactive not reactive and each development suggests new steps for the business. By contrast a bad paradigm is limited to suggesting more of the same with an increasing emphasis on minor technical improvement. The good paradigm acts as a stimulus to experimentation and promotes the identification and discussion of novel business opportunities which build the core technology of the business. How good a paradigm proves to be in generating a sequence of profitable innovations will depend to a considerable extent on the underpinning technological design configuration. In some configurations, the routes to improvement are tightly specified and produce cumulative sequences of incremental innovations. Other configurations are more open and capable of supporting a wide range of products and processes consistent with the underlying design principles (Wheelwright and Clark 1992). Paradigms are intended to promote innovation but innovation within agreed channels. Clearly, however, the design configuration alone is not enough. The vision and awareness of the top management team in exploring the configuration and matching it with market opportunities is of equal importance. This is partly a matter of organization but, more significantly, it is a matter of the individuals who form the top management team.

On the basis of our own studies a number of tests can be proposed to distinguish good from bad paradigms. A good paradigm is reflected in a longer time scale for the strategic process and an emphasis on the continued development of the business through open-ended processes of learning. Failure of a hypothesis is perceived to generate valuable information. There is a recognition that the company must interact closely with external sources of knowledge relating to markets as well as technology. Finally, the internal organization of the agenda creation and selection process reflects the ways in which technological and market information is actually accumulated.

Of course, no paradigm remains indefinitely progressive, and any company needs to be aware of the dangers of conceptual lock-in and the increasing inability to read changes in the technological and market environment. It is all too easy for facts and concepts to be 'transmuted and rendered impotent in order to retain older patterns of thought' (Trivers 1981).

4.5 CONCLUDING REMARKS

In this brief chapter we have been able only to sketch the outlines of our view that strategies may be fruitfully interpreted as paradigms. To the extent that we are correct in this view, it follows that firms would benefit considerably from a clear understanding of the structure and logic of their own paradigm, which may only be imperfectly perceived. From this would come an enhanced sensitivity to changes in the external competitive environment and an awareness of how the current set of organizational structures contributes to or limits strategic vision and the analysis of business policy. Conceptual tools for mapping technology in terms of artefacts, and internal and external knowledge bases, will be of considerable value in this regard (Metcalfe and Gibbons 1989, Boden 1991). Similarly the concepts which philosophers and historians of science and technology employ will prove to be of great value. We have not touched on the contrast between Kuhnian paradigms and Lakatosian research programmes (Metcalfe and Boden 1991) or the notion of the crises which lead firms to change a paradigm. Equally we have not explored the problems which arise when the paradigm of a business unit becomes incompatible with the paradigm of its corporate parent. These are properly matters for further investigation, reflecting the theme that the competitive advantages firms develop reflect the worlds that those firms imagine.

NOTE

1 The companies which participated in the study were Pilkingtons plc, ICI Seeds Division and ICI Pharmaceutical Division, Lucas Industries Automotive Division and Rolls Royce New Business Ventures Division. We are grateful to all these firms for the time they put at our disposal in the conduct of the study. Because of limited space this paper draws directly on the cases of Lucas Industries plc and Pilkingtons plc. A restructuring at Rolls Royce plc prevented the completion of their case study. The case studies were completed by March 1991. Further accounts of all the case studies are provided in Metcalfe and Boden (1992). We draw particular attention to the important book by Loasby (1991) which develops views similar to those expressed here. We thank our colleagues in PREST, particularly Hugh Cameron, Denis Loveridge, Luke Georghiou and Christine Tiler, and also Rod Coombs and Albert Richards at UMIST. Any errors remain, of course, the responsibility of the authors.

REFERENCES

Arrow, K. J. (1984) *The Limits of Organisation*, New York: W. W. Norton.

Boden, M. (1991) 'The identification of technology priorities: a review', mimeo, University of Manchester.

Burns, T. and Stalker, T. M. (1961) *The Management of Innovation*, London: Tavistock Press.

Clark, J. M. (1961) *Competition as a Dynamic Process*, Washington DC: Brookings Institute.

Constant, E. W. (1980) *The Origins of the Turbojet Revolution*, Baltimore: Johns Hopkins University Press.

— (1984) 'Communities and hierarchies: structure in the practice of sciences and technology', in R. Laudan (ed.) *The Nature of Technological Knowledge: Are Models of Scientific Change Relevant?* Dordrecht: Reiter.

Cooper, A. C. and Schendl, D. (1976) 'Strategic response to competitive threats', *Business Horizons*, February pp. 61–69.

Dosi, G. (1982) 'Technological paradigms and technological trajectories', *Research Policy* 11: 147–62.

Eliasson G. (1988) 'The Firm as a competent team' , IUI Working Paper, Stockholm.

Grindley, P. (1992) 'Managing technology: organizing for competitive advantage', this volume.

Hayek, F. (1948) 'The meaning of competition', in *Individualism and Economic Order*, Chicago University Press.

Henderson R. and Clark K. (1990) 'Architectural Innovation: the reconfiguration of existing product technologies and the failure of established firms', *Administrative Science Quarterly* 35: 27–48.

Hughes, T. P. (1983) *Networks of Power*, Baltimore: Johns Hopkins University Press.

Jacob, F. (1982) *The Possible and the Actual*, University of Washington Press.

Kelly, G. A. (1964) 'The language of hypothesis: man's psychological instrument', *Journal of Individual Psychology* 20: 137–52.

Loasby, B. J. (1991) *Equilibrium and Evolution: An Exploration of Connecting Principles in Economics*, Manchester University Press.

Laudan, R. (1984) 'Cognitive change in science and technology', in R. Laudan (ed.) *The Nature of Technological Knowledge: Are Models of Scientific Change Relevant?* Dordrecht: Reiter.

Layton, E. (1974) 'Technology as knowledge', *Technology and Culture*, 15: 31–41.

Metcalfe, J. S. and Boden, M. (1991) 'Innovation strategy and the epistemic connection', *Journal of Scientific and Industrial Research* 50: 707–17.

—— (1992) 'Conjectures, refutations and the dynamics of capitalism', mimeo, University of Manchester.

Metcalfe, J. S. and Gibbóns, M. (1989) 'Technology, variety and organisation', in R. Rosenbloom and R. Burgleman (eds), *Research in Technological Innovation, Management and Policy*, vol. 4, New York: JAI Press.

Morgan, B. (1987) *Images of Organisation*, London: Sage.

Newman, W. H., Hogan, J. P. and Hegarty, W. H. (1989) *Strategy*, Chicago: South Western Publishing Co.

Pavitt, K. (1987) 'On the nature of technology', mimeo, SPRU, University of Sussex.

Pelikan, P. (1989) 'Evolution, economic, competence and the market for corporate control', *Journal of Economic Behaviour and Organisation* 12: 279–303.

Porter, M. (1985) *Competitive Advantage*, New York: Free Press.

Quinn, J. B. (1985) 'Managing innovation: controlled chaos' in J. B. Quinn, H. Mintzberg and R. M. James (eds), *The Strategy Process*, Prentice Hall International: 627–37.

Ramanathan, K. (1990) 'Management of technology: issues of management skill and effectiveness', *International Journal of Technology Management* 5: 409–22.

Rosenberg, N. (1983) *Inside the Black Box*, Cambridge University Press.

Sahal, D. (1981) *Patterns of Technological Innovation*, Chichester: Wiley.

Schumpeter J. A. (1942) *Capitalism, Socialism and Democracy*, New York: McGraw Hill.

Stacey, G. S. and Ashton, W. B. (1990) 'A structural approach to corporate technology strategy', *International Journal of Technology Management* 5: 389–408.

Swann, P. and Gill, J. (1992) 'The speed of technological change and development of market structures', Chapter 10.

Teece, D. J., Pisano, G. and Shuen, A. (1990) 'Firm capabilities, resources and the concept of strategy', mimeo, University of California, Berkeley.

Trivers, R. (1981) 'Sociology and politics', in E. White (ed.) *Sociobiology and Human Politics*, Lexington, Mass.

Wheelwright, S. C. and Clark, K. B. (1992), 'Creating Project Plans to Focus Produce Development', *Harvard Business Review*, March/April.

Vincenti, W. (1990) *What Engineers Know and How They Know It*, Baltimore: Johns Hopkins University Press.

Wojick, D. (1979) 'The structure of technological revolutions', in G. Bugliarello and D. B. Doner (eds) *The History and Philosophy of Technology*, Chicago: University of Illinois Press.

5 Supplier-user relationships and the management of expertise in computer systems development

Janette Webb and David Cleary

5.1 INTRODUCTION

This study explores the dynamics of buying and selling computer technologies, at a time when conventional managerial divisions of labour are being renegotiated and organizational hierarchies are themselves the focus of change. The empirical work reported is a summary of some of the findings from a project which explored the nexus of relationships between suppliers and their customers. It was argued that the management of such relationships is an important factor in the take-up and use of new technologies. In particular, it is one means by which suppliers gather feedback for product innovation, and users learn about new products, make purchasing decisions and construct plans for implementation.

Our main aim was to examine the ways in which firms manage supply chain relationships. Whereas much earlier research has focused on the firm as the unit of analysis, we concentrated on the interface between two or more businesses, situating the firm in its market context. We sought to analyse the business structures contrived to manage the qualitative uncertainties generated by the product development and technology acquisition cycles. The roles of technical experts and senior and middle managers, as interest groups in the firm hierarchy and as agents directing significant capital investments, provided the substance of the research. The technologies studied were high-value products developed by specialist suppliers in the computing and instrumentation sectors for application to production and quality control processes or to be used as specialist tools for industrial research, product development and testing.

The user–supplier relationship and the evolving market for computing products

Computer-based technologies are increasingly seen as integral to the success of many businesses. They are regarded as having a direct impact on such recognized determinants of competitiveness as productivity, efficiency and unit labour costs. At the same time, the development of appropriate systems and the specification of user requirements have become critical areas for 'expert management'. Many firms, centrally concerned with computer technologies as suppliers or users, are also exploring ways in which proactive management of the supply chain may provide significant sources of shared expertise for new developments. From an academic perspective, Clark and Staunton set out a prospectus for an approach to innovation studies which sees innovation as embodied not just in equipment, but in the combining of technology, social organization and knowledge (Clark and Staunton 1990). This means moving beyond the firm as the unit of analysis to examine relationships between suppliers and users of new technologies. It allows us to explore the role of users in shaping innovations (Fleck 1988) and to analyse the ability (or inability) of expert groups in one firm to identify, and integrate, external sources of expertise relevant to their business. The concept of expertise is a useful tool in such analyses, because it highlights the need to focus on the social relations involved in designing the technology, making the system work, using it and adapting it, and perhaps discarding it.

The groups involved include engineers, sales managers, end-users, consultants, finance directors, specialist buyers and so on. They may be employed by different organizations, linked by supply relationships. Such market exchanges may also be mediated by outside experts from advisory, educational and other government or financial support agencies. The different groups will not have equivalent status and skills, hence the social relations between them and the creation of a range of structural solutions to manage the transactions between them is of particular interest.

In the last forty years, the increasing involvement of managers in information technology (IT) purchasing decisions, together with the maturing of computing products and markets, has led to marked changes in the sales strategies used by suppliers. Although the market is too multi-layered for generalizations to be easy, it is certainly the case that since the 1950s function has on the whole gradually been losing out to application as the most important determinant of purchasing decisions. Managers tend to be considerably more in control of IT purchases in the 1990s than they were in the 1950s and 1960s, as one would expect in a market where the balance of knowledge has shifted in favour of users (Friedman and Cornford 1989). The result has been considerable change in the type of technologies most favoured by the market-place and in the rhetoric of selling. The increasing focus on applications has been reflected, in broad terms, in the growth of distributed computing, where the most pressing technical issues are to do with compatibility. Suppliers are trying to reshape their organization to make themselves more responsive to customers and aim to sell services and systems which solve business problems rather than 'hi-tech' products.

Managing expertise in organizations

Expertise is defined, for our purposes, as the expression of intertwined power relations, formal knowledge and experience-based know-how. The treatment of expertise as socially defined allows us to focus on the creation and dissolution of technical specialisms and the shaping of divisions within management. The management of change is treated as a political process, not simply a functional problem about finding the objectively correct solution to the division of tasks and distribution of resources. The fact that expertise is socially constructed and changing over time makes its management extremely problematic. All firms, however well established, have to anticipate and manage change. They operate under conditions of uncertainty: patterns of demand change over time in ways that firms can rarely fully control, technologies evolve or are displaced by successive innovations, the availability and market price of particular skills changes, established competitors alter their product lines and marketing strategies, new competitors may enter the market and there will be fluctuations in the wider economy. The general level of business activity is conditioned by macro-economic variables, such as commodity prices and interest rates, themselves dependent on political events and social trends.

The most important function of specialized knowledge and procedures within the firm is to minimize the uncertainties that attend each stage of the production process, as well as the external uncertainties that come into play once the product (and/or the service) is released onto the market. The supplier has to resolve uncertainties about the development, marketing and manufacturing of products to set time scales and budgets, and generate reliable estimates of how many will sell, at what price. A parallel set of processes can be described in the user firms who comprise the market for computer systems suppliers. Here expertise is needed to manage the interface with suppliers; expert groups play a key role in internal systems development, negotiating budgets and contracts, controlling costs and timetables, and making the systems run.

One of the underlying concerns of systems development in both user and supplier organizations is to 'build bridges' between the knowledge specialisms of different groups and to draw on and integrate the tacit and contingent knowledge located within groups in order to make new systems work. If we treat the relationship between the shape of computer systems and the distribution of expertise as simply a 'technical problem' for management, concerned with resourcing the business, it is possible to outline a number of hypothetical structural solutions which might be devised. Dyerson and Roper (1991) provide examples of these exercises in new systems development. The 'working party' or project team is probably the most common device used to manage the integration of the different sources of expertise and know-how necessary to the establishment of the system. In the successful examples, such as the computerization of PAYE, senior management used project teams to integrate the technical and project management expertise of external consultants with the internal understandings of system requirements and programming capabilities. Other structural devices include the incorporation, or secondment, of technical specialists to business departments, or *vice versa*, the secondment of end-users to technical groups. Some end-users may also begin to occupy new specialist quasi-technical roles, mediating between departments, senior managers and development engineers. It often seems to be women who fulfil these transitional roles, perhaps because of a facility for dealing with people and, tied up with this, the perception that they do not threaten the underlying male status quo (Tierney and Williams 1990). There may also be new elite groups of specialists, who are treated as a 'flexible resource' to be allocated to projects at the behest of senior management, or specialists may be hived off to separate or subsidiary companies. Joint, or collaborative, ventures between firms, may be experimented with, to the extent that they are perceived to limit the risk involved in investing in new technical directions. All of these, and other structures, may be supported (or undermined) by different reward and incentive schemes and different detailed divisions of labour between specialisms.

The above discussion would suggest that managing the combination of new technologies and expertise, in suppliers or users, is simply a matter of finding a rational structural solution to fit the organization for an era of continuous change. Let us muddy the water by putting power relations firmly in the centre. The switch in perspective means that expertise has to be seen not just as a business resource to be rationally allocated to tasks but also as a source of power and status. The management of expertise, within and across firm boundaries, is likely to be highly charged when issues of status and power underlie the negotiation and development of new products or systems.

5.2 THE PROJECT

The central objective of the project was to relate organization structures to style of contractual relationship between the main institutional actors. This allowed us to examine some of the means by which firms manage qualitative, as opposed to quantitative, uncertainties. For our purposes, organizations are regarded as creating different types of structures to locate and manage such uncertainties.

The style of contract between suppliers and users was characterized as varying along a dimension from adversarial to collaborative (Walton and McKersie 1965). The adversarial method of contract formulation is based on a zero-sum notion of profits and costs. It could be described as 'market mediated': typical of arrangements for the buying-in of products or processes which are well defined and understood. It requires the user organization to have resolved qualitative uncertainties internally (user needs and problems would be predefined and suppliers would have matched these with solutions). The only remaining uncertainty is the price of the good and the adversarial mode is well-adapted to such quantitative flexibility. This kind of relationship can also prevail in circumstances where the applications of a new technology are uncertain but the user firm has been able to resolve the uncertainties about applications internally (e.g. through the ability of specialist technical functions to provide solutions). The organization must, however, have internal structures capable of managing this uncertainty (such as technical skills, people able to articulate user needs and the ability to combine these into workable solutions). In contrast, the firm may choose to manage the uncertainties externally by collaboration with suppliers. The degree to which problems may be resolved by externalizing them is varied. In theory the whole task could be devolved to consultants, but at the cost of loss of control and greater financial expenditure for the user organization and a failure to develop in-house capabilities. More typically, a collaborative approach is likely to be adopted, requiring a problem-solving model of contracting, the creation of trust between institutional actors, joint participation and the objective of mutual benefits and rewards.

The structural dimension of the model is derived from the work of Burns and Stalker (1961) and was used to characterize the division of labour and managerial style in firms in terms of the organic/ mechanistic continuum. The mechanistic system is deemed to be appropriate for an organization which uses an unchanging technology and operates in relatively stable markets. It relies on specialized differentiation of functional tasks, hierarchical structures of control and vertical chains of formal authority; it tends to create barriers between functions and obedience to superiors is expected. The organic system, deemed appropriate to changing conditions and the requirements of innovation, relies on continual adjustment of the individual task through interaction with others, commitment to the concern beyond any technical job definition and a network structure of control, with no reliance on a supreme authority, but on expert knowledge. Burns and Stalker's study of the electronics industry, although over twenty years old, remains influential because of its insights into management processes. Much of the work claiming to build on their model of organization in fact adopts a functionalist perspective on the firm and fails to comprehend the sociological dimension of their analysis. Thus contingency theory, exemplified by Hull in a study of the relationships between R & D performance and organization structure, asserts that maximizing firm performance depends on obtaining the best fit between environment and internal structure (Hull 1988). In fact Burns and Stalker show why firms *fail* to manage the strategic matching of structure, environment and resources. They argue that organizations are plural structures, containing political and status systems as well as technical and commercial procedures. Thus actual organization structures are dependent on the relative strength of informal political systems and the relative capacity of senior management to interpret the environment and implement appropriate change. The attempt to develop an organic structure is therefore personally costly and frequently unsuccessful.

The more prescriptive aspects of Burns and Stalker's analysis are currently finding favour in mainstream management literature. In a period of widespread questioning of conventional 'expert' solutions to problems of efficiency and profitability, the taken-for-granted bases of managerial authority are also being held up for scrutiny, both by employers and their senior-manager agents and by competing expert groups, looking to improve the career chances of their own specialism. The last decade has seen the proliferation of books exhorting managers to change their ways from being planners who 'do things right' to becoming entrepreneurs who enthusiastically embrace the need to ask questions about whether they are doing the right things (Peters and Waterman 1982, Peters 1987, Waterman 1988). The common concern of these books is to convince managers of the need for continuous change and renewal in organizations. The emphasis is on 'flexibility' and the use of initiative at all levels. Boundaries between specialisms or between managers and managed or between organizations are meant to be dissolved, so that the only driving force is between a group and its 'customer' (internal or external). Teamwork is the core, but the composition of teams is continually changing, as task requirements change. As Wood points out, the prescriptions are thin on how to effect the detail of the proposed revolution and are even weaker on politics (Wood 1989). They are only loosely connected to social science. They do however reflect on, and contribute to, a broadly based shift in thinking about how organizations should be run and the business ideology of the manager's role. Our assumption therefore was that the broad distinctions between mechanistic and organic structures would be understood by managers and would form part of any restructuring initiatives concerned with the creation of responsiveness to the market.

Research design and methodology

The conceptual framework was examined by means of a broadly ethnographic methodology. The main fieldwork for the project was provided by three firms, two large multinationals and one medium-sized company. A programme of intensive interviewing was carried out in each of these, generating a number of case studies of specific technology acquisitions and/or new product developments. Some interviews were carried out in other firms, linked to the main companies by virtue of the supply-chain relationship. The main period of data gathering was from October 1988 to October 1990.

The most important research tool was the semi-structured interview. In each case a schedule of questions was drawn up beforehand, which served as the framework for the interview. These typically lasted between forty-five minutes and an hour and a half. The interview schedule was a point of departure rather than an end in itself: the objective was to allow the interviewee as much freedom as possible to define what was relevant to the line of questioning. Since we wanted to analyse the informal and the tacit aspects of user-supplier relations, as well as the more public face of contracting, semi-structured interviewing was the most appropriate technique. When requested by interviewees, copies of the schedule were forwarded to them prior to the interview. All interviews were tape-recorded, and fully transcribed. These were then sent to interviewees for comments and correction.

Those interviewed ranged from senior management to shop-floor personnel, but there was a strong bias towards middle and senior managers, technical experts involved in product development and R & D, and sales representatives. We were successful in gaining privileged access to one field work site, where a piece of action research on the product development process was conducted. The fieldwork was carried out with the product development group of a disk-drive manufacturer, and concerned the role of suppliers and customers in the development process. A high level of observation was possible, including shadowing the product development manager, attending project meetings, and being able to follow transactions as they unfolded. We provided feedback to the firm with the objective of contributing to planned changes in the management of product development.

The case-study firms

The three central firms, and the main technologies or acquisitions associated with them, were as follows.

Scottish Drinks plc

Nineteen managers, technical experts, and shop-floor supervisors were interviewed. Particular attention was paid to the organizational history of relationships between the engineering function, R & D lab and a newly created information services function set up after a 1986 takeover. A considerable body of material was obtained on the wide-ranging reforms that followed the takeover, when an attempt was made to pull a collection of largely autonomous brand-name companies into a single business unit. The fieldwork centred on the attempted standardization of systems acquisition and development, the role played by the information services function and the management of external suppliers. In particular, we examined specific purchases, both retrospectively and in real time, to look at the relationship between the acquisition of new systems and organizational restructuring. Current technology policies were assessed in the light of the preoccupation of senior managers with using particular information technologies as an instrument of organizational change. We looked in detail at the part external relationships played in these changes. For example the supplier portfolio changed from a collaborative, long-term relationship with a single major supplier to a more confrontational set of relationships with a number of competing suppliers; there was a project to centralize supply-chain management by means of IT systems, and business policy aimed to increase the use of external sources of expertise (consultants, supplier personnel, etc.) rather than growing all systems expertise internally. These issues were examined specifically in relation to the following technical acquisitions:

- An automatic process control system for a distillery, which formed the pilot for a common process control system.
- A laboratory analysis management information system for R & D.
- An automated plant maintenance system for a distillery, again forming a pilot for a common system.
- A financial management system for the head office, which formed the pilot for the introduction of common financial systems across the company.

Telewave Electronics plc

The second central study was the Scottish division of a US multinational corporation, Telewave Electronics (TE). It houses a regional sales team dealing in TE computer systems products and a specialized sales team concentrating on instrumentation. The division manufactures high-technology instrumentation test and measurement systems and has in-house R & D and marketing teams. Interviewing was carried out in each of these business units. The seventeen interviews carried out with TE personnel were evenly split between R & D, sales and marketing staff. Two additional interviews took place in a TE computer systems sales office in England. Detailed work was done on the organizational history of the plant, the changing pattern of relationships between sales, marketing and R & D departments, the product development cycle, sales strategies, relationships with users, and the nature and effectiveness of feedback loops designed to channel user experiences into product development. This work involved the detailed reconstruction of the development history of specific products and product enhancements, the collecting of material on particular user relationships where we also had accounts from the user side, such as Defence Electronics and Scottish Drinks, and detailed work on the development of collaborative sales strategies.

Midas plc

Midas is a computer disk-drive manufacturer based in the United Kingdom, with some development facilities in the United States and its main manufacturing in the Far East. The UK engineering manager was prepared to allow a shadowing exercise, and access to product development meetings and development engineers was agreed. Thirty-two interviews were carried out with Midas engineers and managers, including all of the product development engineers based in the United Kingdom. For a period of four months Janette Webb shadowed the engineering manager for one day a week. Ongoing product developments, which were three different types of disk-drive, were accompanied longitudinally during this period, and past product developments were reconstructed. Particular attention was paid to the management of expertise in electronic engineering, and the question of how the technical parameters of product development were set. The relationships between Midas and its suppliers and main customers were examined. Midas is a designated supplier to a major work-station manufacturer that was taken over by Telewave Electronics during the fieldwork period.

In addition to these firms, a number of others provided supplementary detail on supplier-user relations. First, material was collected on the organization of sales, marketing and product development in Defence Electronics (DE) telecommunications operating division. DE is an important, long-standing customer for TE. We were therefore able to gain some insight into this highly specialized supplier-user relationship. Second, interviews were carried out with the sales representative, project manager and general manager of Taylor Instruments/Combustion Engineering. This company supplied the automatic process control equipment to Scottish Drinks. A body of general material on relationships with users and the organization of sales was also collected. Third, material concerned with the organization of sales and marketing, and relationships with users was collected from Honeywell Bull (as it was then called). Bull was the established, long-term supplier of computer systems to Scottish Drinks, prior to takeover.

Apart from the case studies, contextual and documentary material was gathered from industry conferences and interviews with people well placed to give a strategic overview of the computer supply industry and the problems faced by users. They included trainers and consultants, representatives from DTI and Scottish Enterprise, local government, technology transfer institutes, and academics.

5.3 DISCUSSION

User–supplier relations and the market for computing products

Overall the project demonstrated the perceived importance to management of links between users and suppliers in the development of computer products and in the satisfactory purchase and integration of computer systems. Managers were commonly aware that, on the product development side, users had vital insights into new technical directions, and on the systems purchasing side, suppliers had vital expertise about the integration of the systems into the business. In both cases there is underlying recognition that the uncertainty involved in developing and using computer systems means that part of what is bought and sold is intangible know-how about the artefacts. Some managers were also aware that know-how can be traded informally, to mutual advantage, if the parties can develop a satisfactory relationship governed by a degree of trust. This awareness was typically accompanied by a business policy which asserted that all relevant expertise could no longer be developed and maintained in-house, because of the associated costs. It was therefore recognized that structures for collaboration with external sources of expertise needed to be put in place, without losing control of costs on the one hand and the initiative for subsequent developments on the other.

Suppliers and users were able to characterize relationships in the supply chain in terms of the range from adversarial to collaborative, but 'pure' forms of either were generally absent. The fieldwork took place in the context of the growing advocacy, by policy and practitioner communities, of 'partnership' or collaborative relationships with suppliers as a means of improving business efficiency and effectiveness. All of the firms were aware of this debate and were in general espousing a similar philosophy. In practice our informants also recognized however that they were inevitably engaged in a 'mixed-motive' relationship: integrative bargaining might be necessary to solve problems, but there was always a distributive aspect to the exchange, where relative costs and benefits are calculated. Both users and suppliers generally sought, through a collaborative rhetoric, to engage in 'attitudinal structuring' (Walton and McKersie 1965) in order to increase the subjective, non-quantitative, utilities to be gained from the contract. Thus users might argue that the supplier will benefit in terms of future product innovations, or gain in 'reputation' if the system is of a high quality, while suppliers might promise the transfer of intangible systems expertise and the resolution of certain business problems. By definition there is always an element of distrust in such relationships, but if firms can manage such distrust, such that it is limited to the formal, institutional level, negotiators may develop relatively close personal relationships and be able to engage in constructive systems development.

As in any negotiation, both sides constructed images of the other which informed their subsequent interactions. In terms of computer systems, users had rules of thumb which characterized the differential approach of the suppliers. They were particularly concerned with the extent to which suppliers were able to explain and demonstrate their products effectively, as opposed to simply having sophisticated technology which users had to have the skills to discover for themselves. They also characterized suppliers in terms of their responsiveness to customers, their ability to provide appropriately skilled people, both technically and socially, to work with the users in project management, their apparent orientations to the customer (narrowly instrumental as opposed to genuinely collaborative) and the extent to which they tended to 'over-promise' in order to win a contract.

Suppliers also categorized users not just in terms of the estimated size of the account but also in terms of their ability to manage technology acquisition, and hence suppliers, effectively. In general the 'hard negotiators', such as the head of Information Services in Scottish Drinks, who were willing to be intensively involved in discussing the system requirements and giving access to a range of end-users, were regarded as more effective by suppliers. Those who operated a more formal committee structure, which was used to generate an internal system specification and predefined list of necessary features for suppliers to measure their systems against, were regarded as less effective. The former is a more open-ended means of defining the system, allowing for uncertainty in the process, and anticipating a degree of collaboration over system definition with prospective suppliers. The latter may seek to be formally democratic, representative of user interests and tends to assume that all uncertainties can be resolved internally, before decisions are made about suppliers. Suppliers not surprisingly wanted early involvement in the process and argued that overly formal procedures were likely to result in poorer systems development if the applications of the technology are themselves uncertain. This may in part be a valid argument if the formal procedures obscure internal political processes within the user which tend to result in a powerful interest group being able to manipulate the outcome to its own ends. It is also of course a reflection of the supplier's vested interest in 'building themselves in with the bricks', as one TE sales rep put it, hence making them difficult to dislodge.

Suppliers operating in a very competitive market are eager to become knowledgeable about the user's business in order to appear indispensable as a source of relevant expertise. To facilitate this they are developing a consultative, 'user-oriented' approach to selling, where priority is given to the building up of stable, long-term relationships with users. In these terms, computer systems are seen not so much as 'boxes', material combinations of hardware and software, but as 'information engineering', devices which through the streamlining of information flows and production processes 'add value' to the balance sheet of the user. Thus, selling a system, from the supplier's viewpoint, involves a more interventionist strategy than obtained in the past: the supplier tries to position its salesforce and technical experts as a source of expertise, prepared to work together with the user to implement systems and monitor performance after installation. From the user viewpoint, this supplier strategy is treated with a degree of scepticism: it may be perceived as self-interested manipulation, designed to conceal the fact that as the computer systems market matures, there is an increasing lack of differentiation in products between suppliers. A systems acquisition remains a transaction between a user and a supplier in a competitive market-place, not a loving relationship founded on mutual advantage, as the rhetoric of consultative selling might assert.

The communication of technology requirements and capacities

between suppliers and users is generally mediated by technical experts. We examined their roles in negotiating the process and rate of implementation and setting the evaluation criteria for success in relation to financial and non-financial indicators. These negotiations tended to be evaluated as less successful by both sides in cases where the espoused business philosophies and management structures were incompatible and hence the relevant technical experts met with potentially contradictory agendas. In particular, those suppliers who were trying to adopt a consultative approach to systems development were most obstructed by a user firm with a traditional functionally specialized structure, with DP in a separate department, potentially threatened by the suppliers' attempts to deal directly with finance directors and end-users as well as, if not instead of, themselves.

There appears to be a paradox in relation to the continuum between adversarial and collaborative styles of contracting. The 'traditional' engineer-engineer approach to buying and selling computing and instrumentation systems, which was observed for example in the TE-Ferranti relationship and in the Scottish Drinks-Honeywell Bull case, was dependent on long-standing interpersonal collaboration, with institutionalized 'distrust' located functionally in the buying department and/or with specialist negotiators. The emerging approach, observed in Scottish Drinks' vendor management strategy, is dependent on more outwardly 'adversarial' relations, combined with more active collaboration in system specification and integration. The latter is harder work for suppliers, who are striving to differentiate themselves as providers of business solutions, as the systems 'hardware' becomes less of a differentiating factor. It requires a more elaborated division of expert labour on both sides and less tacit acceptance of a systems' worth, just because familiar Joe Bloggs is selling it. Those sales reps, or account managers as they preferred to be called, working with a customer who treats them as a qualified vendor, admitted that they worked less hard for the customer than they did on those accounts where they were in constant competition with other suppliers for the business.

The emerging style of integrative/collaborative relationships between user and supplier can, from the user's point of view, be classified under five headings:

- *Forced collaboration*. This is where users have no option but to set up a collaborative relationship with a supplier because there is no alternative source of supply for a particular technology (observed in the Midas case).

- *Collaboration as intervention.* Here, in contrast with forced collaboration, it is the customer rather than the supplier who holds the whip-hand. This occurs where the supplier is prepared to allow the user to intervene at all levels in the company and is characteristic of the active supply-chain management prescribed by organizational philosophies like JIT and TQC. A less extreme example is where a very large customer, such as a leading multinational, is afforded special organizational privileges by suppliers prepared to do almost anything to retain it as a customer (observed in relation to the interventionist approach of Midas customers to its production engineering and development processes, and reported by Taylor Instruments as the approach to their largest potential customers).
- *Mediated collaborations.* This is where a collaboration is mediated by a third party, such as consultants or a public-sector agency. Third parties can mediate not just in resolving disputes, but in the wider sense of providing an institutional medium within which user and supplier can communicate. Mediated collaboration is particularly associated with the setting of formal technical standards, tendering and project management.
- *Strategic collaboration.* This is where collaboration takes place between an evenly matched supplier and user because both perceive some strategic advantages in doing so. It takes the form of each involving the other to some extent in business planning, especially in relation to product development, and more or less formalized exchanges between senior management. The exact form collaboration takes is shaped by the tension between suppliers pushing for further integration, since closer partnership makes it less likely the user will shift to competitors, and users wishing to keep the relationship more open-ended, in order to avoid over-dependence on a particular supplier (observed in relation to the development of data-base management tools in Scottish Drinks).
- *Inertial collaboration.* Where collaboration is historically well established in a technically complex area, and where commercial ties are reinforced by long-standing personal relationships between gate-keepers in both user and supplier, it can become difficult for the user to imagine dealing with other suppliers. Inertial collaboration is associated with the most conservative industrial sectors, such as heavy engineering and defence

contracting (reported in the case of DE-TE and Scottish Drinks-Honeywell Bull).

The case studies led us to conclude that there is, at senior management level, an attempt to replace inertial forms of collaboration with the more proactive forms, albeit there is likely to be a gap between the espoused policy and its actual use. This occurs in part because such changes pose a threat to established interest groups in the firm hierarchy. Thus some DP professionals have a career built around their close relationship with one systems' supplier; conversely, the suppliers struggle to maintain the privileged relationship with the customer. Suppliers, however, recognizing the writing on the wall, were trying to bypass the traditional DP gatekeepers, by seeking direct contact at director level, thus excluding the DP representatives from a controlling role.

All forms of integrative/collaborative contracting were irreducibly mixed-motive in character. They were managed best by a structural division of labour which facilitates good interpersonal relationships between user and supplier representatives, while locating the distributive aspects of the contract formally with a different specialist group who negotiate over price. The preferred structure for the integrative aspects of the system development typically took the form of a relatively long-term project management team where members are enabled to combine the contingent know-how based in the user's organization with the system-specific technical knowledge of the suppliers. This suited both the supplier, who gains inside knowledge of the customer's business and is able to manage expectations about the level of system performance, and senior-management levels in the user who felt they had a greater degree of control over the conduct of the supplier in the delivery of a working system. Such a structure may work against the interests of the established DP professionals, since it sought to import technical expertise, rather than developing it internally, and may include a wider range of user department representatives than had been the case in the past. The mediatory role of the systems professionals was thus weakened.

The above discussion of collaborative contracting presupposes the capacity for analytic, open management and relative trust. Continuing engagement between users and suppliers not only requires technical expertise on both sides but is personally costly, particularly in a historical context of distrust and defensiveness. Senior management plays a significant role in facilitating the development of skilled negotiators and in facing up to the disruption entailed. We observed a determining limit to collaborative/integrative contracting where the 'partners' are very unequal (described above as forced collaboration), as in the relationship between Midas and a supplier of a high-tech, expensive sub-assembly. Despite a long-term history of supply, with considerable exchange of technical expertise over product development, and friendships between the development engineers on both sides, the supplier was able to dictate terms, because of Midas's weak financial state, its dependence on the expertise of the supplier for certain aspects of product development, and the ability therefore of the supplier to determine the progress of internal development timetables.

The role of user-feedback in product development

Suppliers of computing technology regarded major customers as a valuable source of expertise for product innovation. Thus strategic collaboration was perceived to have pay-offs in the longer term for product development in the supplier. This was observed in relationships between Scottish Drinks and its suppliers, and in relationships between TE and its customers, and Midas and its customers. The most effective feedback loops channelling user experience into product development were often informal, and were effective precisely because they were not directly controlled through a functional hierarchy. They can be contrasted with formal feedback loops, such as the market intelligence gathered by marketing departments, or the monitoring of fault reports. We classed informal feedback loops into three types:

- *Professional networks* consist of peer relationships that grow out of the institutional framework of trade associations, conferences and magazines. These are often important recruitment channels, with technical experts engaged on the strength of word-of-mouth recommendations by peers.
- *Friendship networks* can transmit user experiences in a particularly raw and uncensored form, as well as serving a variety of other functions.
- *Commercial networks* are based on specific business transactions and the process of replying to tender documents. Over time, it is through response to documents from users that many product developers build up their conceptions of 'what the market wants'.

All three of these networks are extremely flexible and can carry a wide range of information, from rumour and insider accounts of the performance of particular companies, to detailed technical information, as they presuppose shared technical expertise and a common technical vocabulary.

It follows that defining good practice in building user experience into product development cycles is more problematic than is commonly assumed. As a matter of course, what the user wants is not monolithic, and is often either technically impossible or, from the point of view of the supplier, illogical. When users are allowed to dictate the terms of product development to suppliers, rather than enter into a technical dialogue with them, development engineers regard the result as a wish-list of features or performance improvements. When these are pursued without any consideration of technical constraints – as was largely true of Midas, where product development was driven by the marketing manager's perceptions of user wishes – the results can be disastrous. Senior managers therefore need to facilitate the informal feedback loops, bringing together user and supplier personnel by, for example, encouraging active participation in professional associations, user groups, and other related forums. Equally, in product development cycles managers ideally hold the ring in a dialogue between R & D engineers and the marketing and sales force in most direct contact with users, rather than privilege the views of one over the other. Undue weight given to R & D can result in products being manufactured before markets for them are defined. Undue weight given to marketing and sales in product development can result in engineers being forced to work to unrealistic technical parameters to which they have no commitment. The dilemma, from a management perspective, and observed most sharply in the Midas case, is the perceived conflict between technical excellence and commercial success. How is it possible to create a structure which controls costs and timetables, while enabling technical innovation and informal contact between user and supplier expertise? The fear was that striving for improvements in design would mean losing control over budgets and timetables. The temptation is then to put in place what appear to be instrumental controls to filter user feedback, and hence contain this aspect of development within a standard framework. Paradoxically it seems, as in the Midas case, this can act to the detriment of technical innovation and therefore damage commercial success (Webb 1992).

The main conclusion reached here is that attempts to formalize and routinize feedback by locating it with a specialist function can undermine informal direct sources of feedback, used by development engineers to gain technical insights. It is a matter of facilitation rather than formalization – in particular, a little direct feedback was perceived by engineers as more valuable than a lot of indirect, interpreted and filtered feedback.

Changing definitions of the IT expert

The getting, cultivation and deployment of expertise pose crucial questions for managers, all of which are at the heart of 'business strategy' and the conditioning of relationships between firms. The result of the tension between function and application in computing markets is that there is a striking lack of consensus when it comes to the management of expertise. Function and application provide mutually exclusive axes along which it is possible to order notions of expertise and define 'experts'. Those definitions which stress function over application are a sub-set of the wider and historically well-established classification of the expert as scientist, a person initiated via higher education and workplace training into a body of specialized knowledge and practices. Unlike other definitions, which stress flexibility and the capacity to absorb and act upon a range of different kinds of information, expertise is defined as such precisely because it is highly specialized, difficult to combine with other branches of knowledge and comes encoded in a technical vocabulary which is impenetrable to non-initiates. Specialist knowledge is divided up into a large number of precisely defined fields, separated by disciplinary boundaries. According to this model, experts are defined as people working with a narrow but extremely detailed focus, in jobs which are highly segmented and have very clear boundaries. Outsiders, even those with a grounding in technical issues such as this project manager in Scottish Drinks, think of function-based expertise as 'technical' and therefore something of a mystery to outsiders. Depending on the circumstances, this can give it a certain glamorous mystique or provoke deep suspicion and hostility:

> I tended always to take the view that you don't interfere with the technical side; you've got technicians to solve those [problems]. From a business point of view you know what you want to get out, you know what you want to put in, and as long as you are able to explain, this is what I want out, you can let them get on with the mechanics of it. . . . I've been almost

taking it as the black box syndrome, seeing what goes in and what comes out and then understanding how it manipulates what's inside, but not getting too involved in the programming and the technical side.

As they seek to manage supply-chain relationships proactively and turn the company to face the market, however, senior managers are seeking to reject 'black box' constructions of expertise in favour of managerial, applications-based doctrines. Where the 'black box' notion of expertise stressed specialization, an opposing school of thought, represented among contemporary managers in this study, stresses 'flexibility' and 'providing a service to the business' over depth of specialist knowledge, and refers to 'old-style' technical specialists disparagingly as 'techies'. This managerial definition of expertise is, quite literally, more business-like. Expertise in technical function is seen as less important than expertise in managing applications to provide efficient information services across the business, which deliver both the horizontal flow of information necessary for controlling operations and the vertical flow necessary for management decision-making. This in turn depends on stressing the expert's capacity to absorb a wide range of information of different types – not just 'engineering' or even 'scientific' information, but information to do with the full range of company operations – and to monitor relevant external variables (level of demand, economic indicators, technical trends, etc.). This redefinition of the 'computer systems expert' is encapsulated in the following comment by a Scottish Drinks manager in the process of radically restructuring what he regarded as outmoded skills within his company:

I emphasized to everybody . . . there's a tremendous opportunity here to make these people, to turn them from sixties- or seventies-based DP [data processing] professionals into eighties, nineties information systems professionals. So first of all it's in their interest, financially and in terms of the market-place, to be *au fait* with the state-of-the-art tools, whatever they are. It's also in our interests because it's the only way we can realistically hope to keep on top of that MIS [management information systems] circuit. . . . So I've given them the commitment that I'll reskill and redevelop as long as they recognize that they've got to change.

This 'expert' is a generalist rather than a specialist, a jack of all trades rather than master of one or two, capable of extracting the information most relevant to management decisions from a mass of operational detail, and then making both everyday operational decisions and longer-term 'strategic' analyses.

Organization structure and the management of new technology

As anticipated, attempts to change the character and deployment of expertise were associated with a wider debate about the structure of the firm and its appropriateness for the perceived business environment. The case studies allow us to cast new light on Burns and Stalker's distinction between organic and mechanistic structures. Managers in the firms studied conceived of organizational change as proceeding along a technical/entrepreneurial axis. The ideal-typical features, representing the extremes of such a continuum, are described in Table 5.1. The technical organization is defined along similar lines to Burns and Stalker's concept of the 'mechanistic', but the entrepreneurial organization is more than 'organic'. The entrepreneurial organization was defined as the most

Table 5.1 The technical–entrepreneurial spectrum

	Technical	*Entrepreneurial*
Management structure	hierarchical decentralized autonomous departments	hierarchical centralized corporate control
Work relations	authoritarian rigid job boundaries high segmentation class-ridden	egalitarian fluid job boundaries low segmentation meritocratic
Third party relationships	stable long-term collaborative low competition	unstable short-term confrontational high competition
Technical policy	aspires to autonomy high IT capacity function prime factor in IT acquisition	contracts out many technical functions low but targeted IT capacity compatibility prime factor in IT acquisition
Management of expertise	segregated 'techie' 'scientist' specialist	integrated 'techie' is insult provider of business service generalist

desirable and economically effective, because the elements, detailed in Table 5.1, were believed to increase competitiveness.

The technical organization, in contrast, was regarded as increasingly outdated, and assumed to be in decline. This has implications for the management of expertise and user-supplier relationships. In the technical organization the objective is to cultivate and control expertise internally, and technical experts enjoy considerable autonomy but are relatively excluded from top management and control over business policy. The scientist/engineer is located in a specialist function, operating within a prescribed remit. Supplier relationships tend towards the long-term, inertial form of collaboration. Entrepreneurial companies, in contrast, regard expertise as a strategic resource which needs to be integrated across the business rather than compartmentalized into a black-box function. Selected expertise is likely to be bought in, retaining and developing in-house technical capacity only in areas regarded as essential. Technical experts are expected to be part of a 'business team' providing a service by working with managers, rather than operating autonomously. The engineer is no longer viewed as lone scientist but as a mediator between users and systems, acting as internal change agent, able to identify and develop 'strategic opportunities' with management and through external collaboration with other technical specialists. Instead of being a location of segmented specialized knowledge, the engineer is meant to become a business-minded generalist, sharing knowledge with management and responsive to senior management objectives. The *laissez-faire* style of management which gave relatively high levels of professional autonomy to experts, is replaced by managed autonomy, in exchange for a greater say in business policy at board level and an enhanced internal labour market via the management hierarchy.

Uncertainty is located and managed differently in the technical as opposed to the entrepreneurial organization. In the technical organization, it is located with particular expert functions (e.g. DP or R & D), or centralized at senior-management level. In the entrepreneurial organization a key concern of management is the analysis and control of uncertainty along the supply chain from product development to systems acquisition. The aim is to use specialist knowledge to minimize uncertainties at each stage of production and to apply expertise to the reduction of uncertainty about external market conditions and customers. The control of uncertainty is seen as synonymous with the management of expertise. Uncertainty is regarded as the norm, requiring continuing involvement at all levels. Expertise is the resource for identifying and analysing business opportunities, and the market is treated as a resource rather than as a problem.

Although the technical-entrepreneurial spectrum is essentially ethnographic reportage, it does have theoretical implications. The most far-reaching is the implication that radical organizational change is possible without radical change in market or economic indicators. For example, Scottish Drinks is a company that during the fieldwork period was undergoing deep-rooted and extremely traumatic organizational reform. A consequence of the takeover was the attempt by new senior managers to force Scottish Drinks from a technical to an entrepreneurial model. Throughout this time there was no structural change in the markets Scottish Drinks operated within, and economic indicators remained within fairly stable limits. The technical-entrepreneurial spectrum, in short, acted as an ideological charter underlying organizational change, which took place independently from market and economic change. Almost all theories of organizational change at the level of the firm assume some kind of fit between economic change and/or market conditions and organizational structure. We would argue that there is no direct relationship between supposed objective sectoral characteristics and strategic innovation by the firm. The analysis of strategic transitions therefore requires a sociological dimension:

> corporate actors seek rules for successful competition, but the definition of these and their subsequent implementation depends on social organization and authority relations in the firm. Internal struggles for power and conflicts of interest between corporate and divisional management affect the interpretation of market characteristics and competition and enacted strategy, in turn affecting profitability and perceived market characteristics.
>
> (Webb and Dawson 1991: 203)

5.4 CONCLUSION: THE ORGANIZATION POLITICS OF MANAGEMENT AND EXPERTISE

The espoused shift towards less functionally divided, more entrepreneurial structures, integrated by means of distributed computing systems, reflects attempts by senior management to criticize existing functional divisions. In the case-study firms this process was driven by management reorganization at the top. It was therefore never uncontentious nor lacking in contradictions.

Expertise is embedded in management control structures. Its deployment is therefore fundamentally concerned with power relations between and within management specialisms and skilled labour (i.e. it is not freely exchanged and developed). The allocation of resources to different specialisms becomes a key political issue. The changes are not merely threatening to the traditional technical functions however, but also pose a threat to conventional management control systems, in particular management's historical control over knowledge. In the 'brave new world' of management, computer technologies are treated as part of the necessary raw materials or tools for continuous innovation. In the more utopian forms of this thinking, the technology is itself a key means of breaking down barriers and, in particular, of reversing management's progressive control over information (Zuboff 1988). The reward for the demise of management hegemony is supposedly the renaissance of the organization and increased profitability.

Many of the prescriptions about fitting organization structure to new concepts of business management, expertise and computer systems are concerned with replacing functionalist hierarchy with the entrepreneurial style of organization. Our own work, and that of Burns and Stalker (1961), demonstrates that such structures are, however, not only threatening to established technical elites but are also highly threatening to existing functional managers. The entrepreneurial organization requires specialist managers, in the control structure, and 'professionals', in occupational niches, to integrate their different types of knowledge. The specialists may, depending on the terms, see this as an opportunity to gain the privileges of managerial status, or feel threatened because they may lose sole control over 'their' knowledge. Many middle managers are likely to suspect their own long-term demise if they, in turn, are unable to demonstrate some exclusive skill. In the ideology of the entrepreneurial firm, the manager can no longer rely on management by dictat. The role becomes one of co-ordinating different sources of expertise, with open access to shared information. Authority is derived from the exercise of recognized skills, not formal status. For most managers this offers a considerable threat to their identity, especially if they feel that their own relevant knowledge is inadequate. Such managers may retreat into defensiveness, giving contradictory signals to their subordinates and inhibiting the very changes they were meant to facilitate.

For both user and supplier, in the cases studied, the development of computer systems and technologies was not a textbook model of rational management, because it symbolized not only business development but also affected the status, career opportunities and future work lives of those involved. Not only do managers have to be educated in the techniques of supply-chain management, they also need to become astute negotiators of social relationships within and between firms.

NOTE

Case studies referred to are derived from real firms, but names have been fictionalized to preserve the anonymity of informants.

REFERENCES

Burns, T. and Stalker, G. (1961) *The Management of Innovation*, London: Macmillan.

Clark, P. and Staunton, N. (1990) *Innovation in Technology and Organisation*, London: Routledge.

Dyerson, R. and Roper, M. (1991) 'When expertise becomes know-how: the management of IT projects in financial services', *Technology Project Paper* 11, London Business School.

Fleck, J. (1988) 'Innofusion or diffusation?' Edinburgh University, Business Studies Dept, Working Paper Series.

Friedman, A. L. and Cornford, D. S. (1989) *Computer Systems Development*, Chichester: Wiley.

Hull, F. (1988) 'Inventions from R & D: organisational designs for effective research performance', *Sociology* 22: 393–415.

Peters, T. and Waterman, R. (1982) *In Search of Excellence*, New York: Harper & Row.

Peters, T. (1987) *Thriving on Chaos*, Basingstoke: Macmillan.

Tierney, M. and Williams, R. (1990) 'The problems of blackboxing technologies: what happens when the black box meets forty shades of grey?' Edinburgh University Research Centre for Social Sciences, Working Paper.

Walton, R. E. and McKersie, R. B. (1965) *A Behavioural Theory of Labor Negotiations*, New York: McGraw Hill.

Waterman, R. H. (1988) *The Renewal Factor: Building and Maintaining Your Company's Competitive Edge*, London: Bantam Press.

Webb, J. (1992) 'The mismanagement of innovation', *Sociology* 26: 471–92.

Webb, J. and Dawson, P. (1991) 'Measure for measure: strategic change in and electronic instruments corporation', *Journal of Management Studies* 28: 191–206.

Wood, S. (1989) 'New wave management?' *Work, Employment and Society* 3: 379–402.

Zuboff, S. (1988) *In the Age of the Smart Machine*, New York: Heinemann.

Part II
Skills and expertise in the workforce

6 New technologies, skills shortages and training strategies

Paul D. Foley, H. Doug Watts and Brenda Wilson

INTRODUCTION

Skill shortages in a nation's workforce can act as a barrier to the introduction of new technologies and lead to a reduction of a nation's competitiveness. There is sufficient evidence to suggest that skill shortages, in a general sense, have constrained technological advance in the United Kingdom (ESRC 1988). Throughout the 1980s and early 1990s the need to enhance the skill base of the UK workforce was seen as an important policy objective and, in the corporate context, Grindley (Ch. 1) and Kay and Willman (Ch. 2) stress that for the innovative organization the learning and building of core skills in both the technical and business areas is one of the key features necessary for the effective management and development of the firm. Yet the relationships between the introduction of new technology, skills shortages and training are not fully understood. This account reports on one of only two projects within the New Technology and Firm Initiative to focus specifically upon labour market questions.

The skilled workforce associated with new technologies can be divided broadly into three groups. These are professional scientists/ engineers (see Chapter 7), technicians and craft workers. The first group tend to operate within a national labour market and move throughout the United Kingdom when searching for employment. The other two groups operate predominantly within a local labour market and confine their job search to their home area; this applies particularly to craft workers and may be especially pertinent to labour markets outside the South-East, where long journeys to work are less readily acceptable. Our interest in this chapter falls on the craft workers and a concern with the relationships between new technology, skills shortages and training strategies for craft workers within local labour markets.

Although the focus of discussion is at the local level, it is of relevance to questions of national economic performance, since craft skill shortages in particular local labour markets can hold back the overall rate of the introduction of new technology in the nation as a whole. Thus local issues are of direct relevance to national policies of new technology. Similarly, since questions of craft skill shortages associated with new technology have to be addressed (at least in part) at the local level, the debate is also of direct relevance to those involved with technology, skills and training matters at the local level. Indeed, a basic knowledge of the role of skills shortages and their effects on the introduction of new technology will allow us to make suggestions as to how the diffusion of new technologies within local labour markets might be speeded up to meet national policy objectives of technological advance and increased competitive advantage.

New technology can be associated with new products (and, often, new industries), new processes or a combination of both. Considerable research has been undertaken on industries producing new high-technology products so the emphasis here is on the introduction of new process technology into traditional industries. Government statistics show that at the present time, despite the attention devoted to hi-tech industry, the vast majority of employment in manufacturing (almost 80 per cent) lies outside the 'hi-tech' sectors (Butchart 1987).

This chapter investigates the introduction of new process technology into traditional industries in a local labour market, and it is divided into three main sections. The first explores some of the implications of skill shortages and training matters for the introduction of new technology. The second and major section explores the empirical evidence relating to four key questions:

● What are the new technologies operating within a particular local labour market?
● How important are labour factors in the selection and operation of the new technologies?
● What kinds of skill shortages exist in firms using new technologies?
● How have firms responded to such shortages in their training strategies?

The third and final section is concerned with technology policy in the context of skills shortages and training issues. Overall, the prime objective of this chapter is to advance understanding of the impact of skills shortages and training upon the initiation of new technologies in firms and to provide an input into discussions of technology policy at both local and national level.

6.1 NEW TECHNOLOGY, SKILLS AND TRAINING

New process technology

Throughout the 1980s new process technology has been associated with the use of micro-electronics. By 1987, 59 per cent of UK manufacturing establishments were using micro-electronics in their production processes; by contrast, examples of other new technologies were less obvious. Only 17 per cent of establishments were using fibre-optics in processing, 11 per cent were using new materials and a mere 5 per cent biotechnology. Programmable logic controllers (PLC) and computer numerically controlled (CNC) machine tools were the forms of micro-electronic equipment found most widely as part of new process technology (Northcott and Walling 1988).

These national patterns are not necessarily replicated in each local area. Regional differences in the behaviour of firms have been highlighted in other chapters (Chs 3 and 9). Similarly, there is a difference between regions (such as South-West England and Scotland) in the proportion of establishments using new technologies. Not only are there differences between regions, but the regional patterns vary with the technologies, as Figure 6.1 indicates. Of course, some of these differences arise because of variations in the extent to which individual industries can use new technologies and regions with larger numbers of industries in which new technologies can be used will have a higher proportion of users than regions with a dominance of industries for which many new technologies are inappropriate. Nevertheless, studies published in the mid 1980s examining regional patterns within individual industrial sectors showed that some regions were using more new technology than others (Thwaites 1982), a picture confirmed, at least for CNC machines, by O'Farrell and Oakey (1992).

Just as each region shows a deviation from the national norm, so too each local labour market within a region will have its own characteristics. Sub-regional data on the use of new technology are not available and there exists only anecdotal information about the

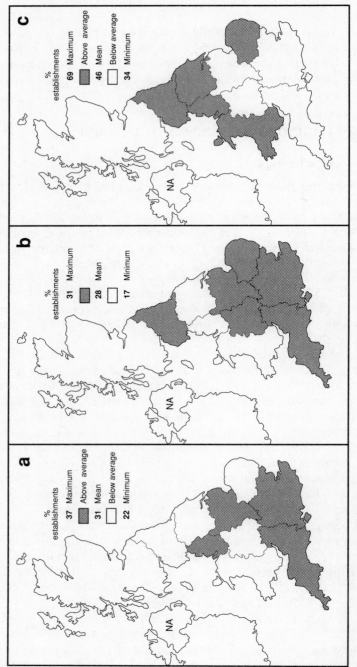

Figure 6.1 New process technology in the British regions, 1987. (a) CAD Work Stations (b) CNC Machine Tools (c) Programmable Logic Controllers

Source: Foley, Watts and Wilson (1992a)

nature of the technology used in geographical units smaller than a region. These tend to confirm the existence of variations in the use of new process technology between local labour markets in a specific region. Clearly, some regions and local labour markets are adopting new technologies at a slower rate than other regions and other local labour markets and, in aggregate, are slowing down the rate at which new technology is utilized in British manufacturing industry.

Craft skills shortages

Any potential impact of craft skills shortages on the use of new technology in a particular local labour market must be seen in perspective, and regional variations in the use of new process technology cannot be seen as a simple response to regional variations in the availability of workers with craft skills.

Geographical variations in the use of new process technologies can occur for a number of reasons. Attention has already been drawn to the difference between industries in their suitability for new technology. Another important reason for variation may be that since most new process technology arises from the manufacturers of process equipment rather than through development internal to an establishment (Thwaites 1983: 42), there may be time lags in diffusion to other areas (industries or firms); a point explored elsewhere by Stoneman and Karshenas (see Ch. 8). Firms developing new process technologies may be slow in spreading their supply and maintenance network from the original region (or industrial sector) and other regions may lack support facilities for new technologies. Other research suggests that establishments with R & D facilities and those which belong to larger organizations are most likely to introduce new technology (Harris 1988). The overall situation is summed up in the view that the 'ability of established centres of production to respond to the opportunities offered by new technology . . . is different given their inherited firm structures, managerial abilities, *labour market conditions* and relations with dominant markets' (Gibbs 1987: 318, emphasis added).

Of particular interest here are the labour market conditions affecting craft workers. Indeed, it can be suggested that the availability of craft skills in a local labour market can interact with the introduction of new technology in two ways:

• A shortage of craft skills may encourage the introduction of new technology to overcome the skill shortage.

- A shortage of craft skills may discourage the use of new technology because of the perceived lack of trained staff. This distinction has not been made clearly in the past in the discussion of skills shortage issues.

Training

Recruitment difficulties are often reported by firms. Frequently, the skills may exist within the local labour market, but individuals are not drawn out of that market because of poor working conditions, the image of an industry, the attractions of alternative jobs or low pay. In the late 1980s some firms experiencing craft-level shortages resorted to improvements in pay and conditions to attract skilled labour (Northcott and Walling 1988). The primary alternative to buying in the skills is to train and to develop corporate training strategies to complement the introduction of new technologies.

A dependence on recruitment to meet the demand for craft skills will increase the firm's dependence on the characteristics of the labour markets from which the recruits are drawn. Admittedly, recruitment of workers with the appropriate skills reduces a firm's training costs, but there are risks in new employees whose stability and loyalty have not been established. Training of existing employees means that the experience and abilities of trainees are well known before training begins. A responsibility to employees should further encourage training of existing staff as the new technology may be replacing jobs whose occupants may be suitable for internal training initiatives.

The mix of recruitment and training strategies may vary from labour market to labour market and from firm to firm (Training Agency 1989: 41). Training may be the only strategy available where the appropriate skills do not exist in the local labour market. Training of existing employees is, in part, a reflection of poor levels of training provision characteristic of the labour market outside the firm (Hendry 1990: 35), but employer-led training may be problematic. Employers may attempt to meet skills shortages in the simplest and most immediate ways (Totterdill 1990: 119–20). If short term training is the chosen solution it is likely to be narrowly focused upon specific job needs. Further, since the commitment of British firms to training is not high, anything other than basic or minimal training may be seen as expendable when profits are squeezed.

It is clear questions concerning the interrelationships between new technology, craft skills and training are best explored in the local context within which craft skills are usually marketed. Although the establishments will often be part of large multi-locational organizations, the plants themselves will be constrained by the characteristics of the local labour market in which they operate. Significantly, perhaps, plants which are part of larger organizations, have more autonomy over labour and training issues than over many other aspects of business behaviour.

6.2 TECHNOLOGY, SKILLS, TRAINING AND LOCALITY

Industries and new process technologies

Evidence was drawn from the Sheffield local labour market which, in terms of its current population size, is the third largest local administration in England and has much in common with the other large English provincial cities. Like all of them employment is dominated by the service sectors (mainly, distribution, hotels and 'other services', such as public administration, hospitals and education) and, like all of them, one of the three manufacturing divisions of the official classification of economic activities is amongst the top three economic activities in the city. However, whereas Leeds, Manchester and Birmingham have an important 'other manufacturing' category, the major manufacturing division in Sheffield, Newcastle and Liverpool is metal goods/vehicle manufacture. It is within this latter division that research was concentrated, overlapping into the metal manufacturing division because the boundaries between the two divisions were difficult to identify in practice.

A preliminary investigation of the new technology, skills and training issues across all sectors of the local Sheffield economy (also funded by ESRC as an introductory stage of the main study reported here) will be found in Foley, Watts and Wilson (1990 and 1992b).

In the main investigation of firms in traditional industries the sectors for detailed examination were selected from three two-digit industries identified by the UK Standard Industrial Classification (22 metal manufacturing, 31 mechanical engineering, 32 other metal industries). It should be noted that Bosworth and Wilson (Ch. 7) show that industries in the metal products group (to which these sectors belong) employed more new technologies than a comparator group based on the other manufacturing sectors. The selected industries accounted for about 65 per cent of the Sheffield manufacturing workforce in the late 1980s. A survey of firms operating medium and large plants (more than 100 employees) within these industries was carried out between mid 1990 and mid 1991. Where firms had multiple sites within Sheffield the largest establishment (in employment) was the subject of investigation.

The majority of firms (74 per cent) co-operated with the enquiry and the final data set included forty-nine establishments operated by fifty-two firms. Although three firms appear twice in the data (operating different establishments) their establishments had a considerable degree of autonomy and the terms firm and establishment are used as synonyms in the discussion below. The distribution of respondents across SIC categories did not differ significantly from that of the total number of firms in the initial sample. In some instances the number of establishments with particular characteristics or problems were small and in these cases the evidence should be treated in a cautious manner. It should be noted that because of the low number of non-users of new technology it was not possible to investigate the extent to which users of new technology differed from non-users and thus it is difficult to identify the extent to which the users of new technology have distinctive problems. Nevertheless, the establishments included in the survey employed over 11,000 workers (one-third of the employees in the relevant sectors), and it seems reasonable to argue that the results should be representative of the relationship between new process technology, skills and training in traditional metal-based industries operating in large establishments in a local labour market.

Some data at national level are reported in Northcott and Walling (1988, referred to below as the 1987 survey, reflecting the year in which their interviews were carried out) and they provide some useful comparative data for the more localized information on which this chapter is based. It is recognized that there is a three-year gap between the two studies. A further national comparator is provided by data on output change in the engineering industry. The average increase in output over the three years preceding the survey in the respondent firms was 17.8 per cent; for the UK engineering industry as a whole it was 18.0 per cent (Central Statistical Office, 1991).

The results of this enquiry do, of course, relate to the specific time period during which the interview programme was undertaken (April 1990 to April 1991). However, the questionnaire placed events within a particular time sequence and questions were asked both about past behaviour (usually up to three years earlier) and about expected patterns. Tests for trends within the period of the interview programme showed that there was no change during the twelve-month survey period in the proportion of firms with recruitment difficulties nor in the proportion of firms expecting to have difficulties in filling vacancies over the next year. Towards the end of the survey period firms were becoming less concerned about filling vacancies in three years time; whereas two-thirds expected difficulties to continue at the beginning of the survey, at the end of the survey period two-thirds expected to have no problems in three years time. The recognition that labour problems might ease in the future, evident in the later stages of the survey, may well reflect the steady rise in unemployment levels during the survey period. However, the overall pattern of stability in the results during the survey suggests that the information analysed below presents an accurate picture of the situation in the early 1990s.

New technology was defined in terms of new to the establishment. This definition is used primarily because interest lies in the fact that a particular piece of technology is more advanced than the previous system in use in the particular organization being investigated. As Clark observes, it is in this way that 'newness is socially defined in relation to its use by an organization . . . compared with past practise'. (Clark 1989: 5). The emphasis in this chapter is very much upon 'local innovation', the introduction of a technology into an establishment, rather than upon 'global innovation' which relates to the first use of a process technology in the United Kingdom or, indeed, the world. Like Stoneman and Karshenas (Ch. 8) this research is driven by the belief that it is the use of new technology rather than the generation of new technology that improves economic performance.

Although the main interest of the study was in traditional industries, no less than 85 per cent of the establishments used new technology in their production process; this is a rather higher level than that found in the 1987 survey (Northcott and Walling 1988) where 72 per cent of establishments manufacturing metal goods used micro-electronics in the production process. This higher figure may of course reflect the fact that over half the Sheffield establishments (56 per cent) had introduced an item of new technology into their manufacturing operations in the last three years. The failure to introduce new technology within the last three years (by 42 per cent of the Sheffield establishments) may simply reflect the fact that the establishments were already users of new technology by the mid 1980s. Nevertheless, 15 per cent of establishments were not using new technology, including one where new technology had been stripped out following takeover and second-hand older technology reintroduced.

The nature of the new technologies used in one-fifth or more of these establishments is shown in Table 6.1. The technologies were dominated by CNC machines (found in over half of new technology using establishments) and automatic test and calibration equipment (present in two-fifths of the establishments). There was strong evidence of the use of the 'newer' new technologies such as robots in a significant minority of establishments. The significance of robots in this listing may reflect their suitability for the hostile environments associated with the metals industries. There were also a number of specialist technologies outside these more general categories, such as a gas extraction furnace (special steels) and vibrator finishing (cutlery).

Table 6.1 New-technology users: technologies in use, 1990–1

Application	Establishments	
	n	%
CNC	25	57
Automatic test and calibration equipment	19	43
Specialist technologies	16	36
Robots	12	27
JIT	12	27
CAD	12	27

Source: Interview schedule.   *n* = 44

Selecting a new technology

The introduction of a new technology may denote major changes within an establishment and may be a particular challenge, with uncertain outcomes for the firm, its skills and its training strategies. In this section attention is concentrated upon those twenty-nine establishments that had introduced new technology into the manufacturing process over the last three years. The technologies included CAD/CAM, CAD, CNC and robots (each of similar importance in being adopted in a tenth or more of the establishments) and a number of specialist technologies including a vacuum induction degassing furnace (reported to be one of only two in the world).

The impact of a particular new technology will be influenced by the extent to which it represents a marked break with the past. In three-quarters of the establishments surveyed the most recently introduced significant new technology represented a radical new development for the firm and only in a quarter of cases did it represent incremental change. For most firms, the radical nature of the new technology introduced over the last three years presented a considerable challenge and a high degree of uncertainty, although only one quarter of those introducing new technology reported that it was the first major investment in new technology that they had made.

An interesting question concerns the extent to which the introduction of the new technologies was encouraged, or constrained, by labour considerations and, particularly, the characteristics of the local labour market. Analysis of the decision to select a new technology was not central to this investigation, but it was important as it allows the role of workforce and labour market characteristics to be seen in perspective. Lonie, Nixon and Collison (Ch. 12) note that skilled labour shortages were just one of seven major constraints on the introduction of new technology.

To measure the significance of labour considerations firms were asked which factors had had an influence upon the introduction of the last item of new technology. In each case, firms were asked to respond to a prepared list of factors. The opportunity to suggest other unlisted factors was offered but rarely taken up. The factors influencing the introduction of new technology emerged quite clearly. At the time of the survey an important influence was availability of finance, cited as a factor by two-thirds of the firms (Table 6.2). It is interesting to note that Goodacre *et al* (Ch. 13) identify shortage of funds as the most important factor acting as a constraint on R & D activity. Cost of finance was also important but only to just under half of the firms. This particular result is, of course, strongly influenced by the period during which the data were collected. Not all industries/firms can adapt as easily to new

Table 6.2 Factors influencing a decision to introduce new technology

Constraints	Establishments*	
	n	%
Available finance	18	67
Nature of product	15	55
Nature of production process	13	49
Cost of finance	12	46
Skill shortages	6	22

Source: Interview schedule. $n = 27$ (2 missing cases)

* Establishments introducing new technology in last three years.

technologies and therefore, not surprisingly, both the nature of the product and the nature of the production process influenced the decision in half the cases. At the bottom of the list of the five major factors comes expected skills shortages arising either from within the firm or from within the labour market in which it operated; a factor influencing just under one-fifth of the firms.

The observation that availability of finance is a more important factor than skills shortages is rather different from that found by the 1987 survey. Although the 1987 survey and the present one agree that availability of finance is important, the 1987 survey argued that for 51 per cent of the firms lack of people with micro-electronics expertise was a major disadvantage of using micro-electronics and thus a much greater emphasis was placed on skills shortages.

Not only do questions relating to skills and training have little input into the decision to introduce new technology, in less than half the firms did the introduction of new technology have an important effect on skills and training issues. Not surprisingly, in assessing the effects of the introduction of new technology, firms place emphasis on its advantages in increasing competitiveness, output, productivity and product quality (Table 6.3).

Table 6.3 Main effects of last item of new technology

Effect	Establishments*	
	n	%
Increased		
Competitiveness	20	69
Output	19	66
Productivity	18	62
Product quality	17	59
Enhanced possibility new products	15	52
Saving on materials wastage	15	52
New work organization	15	52

Source: Interview schedule.   *n* = 29

* Establishments introducing new technology in last three years.

Although labour issues are neither dominant in the decision to introduce a new technology nor important to the majority of firms as an outcome of the introduction of new technology, they are sufficiently prevalent to justify the inclusion of skills and training issues in any exploration of the relationships between new technology and the firm.

Skills shortages

Whereas in the examination of the decision to introduce new technology it was necessary to focus on firms introducing a new form of process technology in the recent past, skills shortages may be experienced by any of the users of new technology. It will be recalled that forty-four of the establishments (85 per cent) saw themselves as users of new technology. The most striking finding is that despite considerable publicity given to questions of skills shortages of all types less than one-half of the establishments using new technology had experienced skills shortages. In total 39 per cent of the new technology users were experiencing skill shortages.

Disaggregating the skill shortages according to twelve broad occupational groups, the most frequently reported shortage was that of skilled craft workers experienced by 30 per cent of the establishments using new technology (Table 6.4). It was argued earlier that the higher-level jobs (professional/administrative and engineer/technologist) are sought within national labour markets, and so it is only the skills shortages associated with craft workers which are of direct relevance to this discussion of local labour market issues. Indeed, the dominance of craft skill shortages, sought predominantly within local labour markets, illustrates the importance of the local perspective on new technology and skills adopted in this chapter.

Table 6.4 New-technology users: hard-to-fill occupations

Occupation	Establishments	
	n	%
Crafts people	13	30
Administrative staff	7	16
Professional scientists and engineers	6	14
Managerial	5	11
Operatives	5	11

Source: Interview schedule.   *n* = 44

It is possible to tie these skills shortages directly to the application of new technology. Firms were asked to specify the particular types of job that had fallen vacant over the last three years and then to indicate whether or not a shortage of skills had had any impact upon attempts to fill them. In this exercise forty-one different jobs were identified by firms. Exploring the difficulties associated with each job it was clear that skill shortages linked specifically to new technology were cited as a difficulty in only a small minority of cases. Shortages relating to traditional skills were of major significance. It would appear that in discussing the relationships between new technology and skills shortages, shortages of traditional skills are conflated with shortages tied to the specific skills needed by new technology.

The very small proportion of establishments with shortages of skills specifically related to new technologies (presumably those with expertise in micro-electronics) appears to contrast with the findings of the 1987 survey. In 1987, 21 per cent of the respondents in the metal goods sector (the closest parallel to the establishments in our data set) would have liked more people with specific micro-electronics skills, but most of these firms reported that this either presented no problems or had only presented problems in the past. However, it was interesting to note that, like this study, only a very small proportion of respondents had problems in finding micro-electronic skills at the time the survey took place.

To a certain extent the information on past skills shortages is only of historic interest. The long-term future of the local economy and the adoption of new technology by local establishments can be influenced by firms perceptions of future labour market conditions. Looking a year ahead, shortages associated with traditional skills were expected to decline in importance but, in the longer term, most firms were concerned about potential shortages of traditional skills rather than the skills associated with the newer technologies.

Further insight into the relationships between new technologies and skills shortages can be achieved by looking at the experience of firms adopting new technology within the last three years, rather than at all users of new technology considered above. The effects of the introduction of new technology on the demand for skilled labour appear to balance themselves out within this particular labour market. One-quarter of the establishments introducing new technology over the last three years found that they were using smaller numbers of skilled workers whereas an exactly similar proportion reported that they were using greater numbers of skilled workers. Certainly amongst those firms that found they needed to employ a larger number of skilled workers because of the introduction of new technology, only a small number felt this had created a skills shortage. In other cases, the adoption of new technology had permitted the firm to avoid a skills shortage, and this had been achieved by employing fewer skilled workers once the new technology was in place. This highlights one of the relationships between skills shortages and the introduction of new technology noted in Section 6.1.

The evidence of skills shortages may in fact underestimate the real level of skill shortages in the local labour market as the data may reflect adjustment by establishments to the characteristics of the local labour market. It is possible that such adjustment could take the form of a reluctance to introduce new technology. Nearly one-fifth of the establishments argued that skills shortages were restricting plans to use further new technology within the establishment. This is a confirmation of the second relationship between new technology and skills shortages noted earlier in section 6.1. It would appear that simply counting those vacancies which are hard to fill, underestimates skills shortages by excluding vacancies which would have existed if the new technologies had been adopted more widely.

Training

Two methods exist to avoid skills shortages associated with the introduction of new technology. The first and negative response noted above is not to adopt new technology. The second is to overcome skills shortages by introducing training programmes. Training programmes induced by new technology form part of total training programmes within an establishment and they have to be viewed in the overall training context. It is this overall training which is considered first as a precursor to a more detailed discussion of training associated with new technology.

Certainly, all establishments using new technologies were involved in training but this may exaggerate the level of commitment because of the statutory training requirements associated with health and safety issues. Table 6.5 shows that despite the 100 per cent commitment to training, there was a large variation in the

Table 6.5 New-technology users: staff trained per year

% of staff trained	Establishments	
	n	%
5–10	10	24
11–20	12	28
21–49	8	19
50–74	5	12
75 and over	7	17

Source: Interview schedule.　　　　　　　　　　　　　*n* = 42

percentage of the workforce trained in any one year. One-half of the establishments using new technology trained 20 per cent or less but a quarter did train 50 per cent or more.

Within these training programmes an important distinction can be drawn between in-house training and training provided off-site by other training organizations (Table 6.6). In-house training was dominated by on-the-job training used by all establishments, and by off-the-job training on site which was used by virtually all the establishments. Outside consultants brought on site were used by three-quarters of the establishments suggesting a lack of training expertise within the firm itself. It is perhaps worth noting that the high levels of training on site may, in part, be a reflection of the selection of large establishments for detailed analysis.

Table 6.6 New-technology users: main forms of training

Training	Establishments	
	n	%
On-site		
On-the-job	44	100
Off-job – by firm	40	90
– by consultants	34	77
Off-site		
Educational establishments	40	90
Training boards	29	65
Supplier	27	61
Trade-union course	24	54

Source: Interview schedule.   *n* = 44

Off-site training was dominated by the use of local educational institutions (used by 90 per cent of the establishments). Two-thirds of the establishments used training provided by an Industrial Training Board. The salience of the Training Board reflects the important role of the EITB in the engineering industry and the particularly high reputation among employers enjoyed by the Sheffield EITB Skill Centre (now known as Entra Sheffield Training Centre). Almost as important was the provision of training by suppliers. The significance of supplier-user relationships are explored in some detail by Webb and Cleary (see Ch. 5). The only other form of training used by more than half the establishments was courses provided by trade unions.

This overview of the nature of training activities within establishments using new technology provides a useful background for a review of the impact of new technology on training.

Amongst all users of new technology 75 per cent of the establishments had altered their training requirements as a result of the introduction of new process technologies (Table 6.7) and just over half of those changes had taken place within the last three years. Two-thirds of the establishments had altered their training to provide more specific training; more specific training being training directed at specific skills rather than generic training covering a job title. It might, in the case of a CNC setter-operator, refer to programming skills. Not surprisingly, new technology was also felt to require higher-calibre training which had been introduced in almost half of the establishments changing their training patterns. This higher-calibre training might involve a switch from on-the-job training to formal training courses. Nearly a third of the establishments had introduced more extensive training whereby staff normally omitted from all but the most perfunctory type of training were drawn into a formal programme so that a greater percentage of the workforce was trained. Finally, one-fifth had started a training programme.

Table 6.7 Impact of new technology on training

	n	%
Impact of new technology on all new technology users (n = 44)		
Changed training	33	75
No change/missing value	11	25
Nature of change in training (n = 33)		
More specific training	23	70
Higher calibre training	15	45
More extensive training	10	30
Started training programme	7	21
Impact of last item of new technology introduced (n = 29)		
Training costs increased	10	34
Training exceeded in-house capacity	10	34
Necessitated introduction of training strategy	7	24

Source: Interview schedule.

Turning to the experience of establishments which had introduced new technology in the last three years, it was possible to identify clear training impacts arising from the introduction of new technology. In around one-third of the cases training costs increased and training needs exceeded in-house capacity. In one-quarter of the cases, the use of new technology necessitated the introduction of a training strategy for the first time.

The reason for adopting a local labour market perspective on the relationship between new technology, skills and training is that there is a potential link between a firm's labour requirements and the labour market in which it operates. The strong dependence on local educational establishments has already been commented upon. A closer examination of the firms that have used local training provision, indicates that they are happy with the quality of training for new technology which is provided locally. Only two firms said a particular form of training was provided locally but was inadequate, and only three firms found that, although training for new technology was available locally, difficulties with timing, location or course level make it impractical to use it.

Nevertheless, some gaps were thought to exist in the provision of local training. One-third of the firms identified a training gap; a surprisingly high figure as the 1987 survey found that only 7 per cent of respondents reported that particular training courses were wanted but were difficult to find. The higher proportion of firms reporting an absence of the necessary courses reveals either a genuine deficiency in local training supply for new process technology or a failure to communicate the local availability of courses to the relevant personnel in the local firms. However, it must also be acknowledged that many firms recognize that local providers could not realistically be expected to meet their own firm's ideal requirements.

The diversity of changes in training as a result of the introduction of new technology perhaps go some way towards explaining why craft skill shortages affect less than half the establishments using new technologies. Nevertheless, the extensive training needs resulting from the introduction of new technology suggest that this is an area in which there may be significant policy implications to encourage the introduction and use of new technology throughout the United Kingdom.

6.3 POLICY ISSUES

Perhaps the most important policy issue to emerge from the analysis is that, at the local level, skill shortages appear to play a secondary role to financial factors in the adoption of new process technology. Thus policies aimed at easing the availability and cost of capital should perhaps be a first policy priority at national level. Stimulating the development of local capital markets may be of little relevance to larger establishments since many are part of major multi-locational organizations and thus will seek funds for capital investment from their parent companies or they have access, by virtue of their size, from a wider capital market.

A second important issue is that labour is not the major factor in holding back the introduction of new technology. It should also be noted that shortages of craft skills appear to affect less than half the establishments. Even if these skills shortages are removed the overall effects on the take-up and use of new technology are likely to be limited. Nevertheless, policies related to training for new technology at the local level need to be explored. Unlike capital investment, which tends to be controlled from outside the local area, most of the multi-locational firms in this study offer individual establishments a high degree of autonomy in training matters. No less than 77 per cent of externally owned establishments were able to control their own training strategy and 80 per cent were able to control their own training budget. Local control over training allows firms to respond to local training initiatives.

Local policies focused upon training can be targeted either directly at the firms operating in a specific local labour market or at the local training providers. An employment policy to encourage the take-up of new technology and/or greater utilization of new technology within firms already using it, needs to be targeted on firms (as trainers and users of new technology) and at external training providers in both the public and private sectors. Removal of barriers preventing the full utilization of labour resources within a local labour market must necessarily include a training strategy which is not only cost effective but also related to local needs.

A dilemma in policy terms is that since only a third of new technology users experience craft skill shortages, across-the-board training initiatives may, in fact, waste resources. Such inefficiency can arise by providing training not needed by the large proportion of establishments with no recruitment or training difficulties. Indeed, training may be misplaced unless clear markets for that labour have been established. Not only can unmarketable trained potential employees waste resources, it may also raise undue expectations among the newly trained.

The implications at the local level is that training for local needs has to be targeted very carefully indeed. Constraining local training co-ordinators, such as the TECs, to activities dictated by national government is not the way forward. Ideally, TECs need virement to pick and choose from national and local initiatives to meet the needs of their areas. Detailed locally focused schemes may provide a more effective use of limited financial resources than spending on generalized national schemes that may not meet local requirements. A flexible mix of training strategies to meet local requirements for skilled employees is essential.

The evidence shows clearly that in introducing new technologies firms underestimate training needs, they frequently find their in-house provision inadequate and are often required to rethink their training strategies. Clearly, it is important for firms to realize the problems this underestimation may present. Yet at the same time it should be stressed that the problems presented are not insurmountable. Offers to assist with training programmes have to be carefully worded to ensure that an emphasis on the training demands experienced by users of new technology does not deter firms from introducing new technology. Aggressive marketing of training activities may deter some firms from adopting new technology because of the high training needs associated with the use of new technology.

6.4 CONCLUSION

It is worth recalling that the evidence upon which this chapter is based is drawn from traditional metal-based manufacturing industries and is focused specifically on new technology, skills and training issues arising from larger plants. Although small plants are numerically more prevalent, the smaller number of large plants tend to account for the majority of employees in manufacturing. Although evidence is drawn from one local labour market, this labour market does not differ markedly from that of other major provincial urban areas. However, it should be recognized that many of the new technologies are well established ones rather than those at the leading edge of new technology.

New technologies introduced over the last three years are associated predominantly with micro-electronics and include robots, CAD and CAD/CAM. These supplemented new technologies already in place such as CNC machines and various forms of automatic test and calibration equipment.

Skills shortages associated with craft workers appear to have affected a significant number of establishments using new technology but, seen in context, labour-related issues were in second place to financial constraints. Nevertheless, it is difficult to control the financial environment within which the firms are operating (mainly because it reflects national and international trends) and it can be argued it may be more effective to focus policies on skills and training issues which can be manipulated, at least in part, at local level.

The clearly identified skill shortages were related mainly to traditional skills but a shortage of skills related specifically to new technologies were found in a small number of cases. Training needs were increased considerably by the introduction of new technology, but there still appeared to be gaps in training provision. In the context of craft skills a major policy implication is that local training co-ordinators (such as TECs) need to identify new technology induced training needs very carefully and perhaps be allowed larger discretionary budgets to target training more effectively. Only through carefully targeted training to overcome skills shortages will the labour-related barriers to the introduction of new technology be removed and thus enhance the take up of new technology at local level. By removing rigidities in the local labour markets the overall national utilization of new technology should rise and the overall competitiveness of British industry increase.

REFERENCES

Butchard, R. L. (1987) 'A new UK definition of high technology industries', *Economic Trends* 400: 82–9.

Central Statistical Office (1991) *Economic Trends* 454 (August).

ESRC (1988) *New Technology and the Firm Initiative*, Bid Document, Swindon: ESRC.

Foley, P., Watts, H. D. and Wilson, B. (1990) 'New technology, skills shortages and company training strategies', *Skills Bulletin* 14: 20–1.

—, — and — (1992a) 'Introducing new processes technologies: implications for local employment policies', *Geoforum* 23: 61–72.

—, — and — (1992b) 'Local perspectives on new process technology and employment', *New Technology, Work and Employment* 7: 125–35.

Gibbs, D. C. (1987) 'Technology and the clothing industry', *Area* 19: 313–20.

Harris, R. I. D. (1988) 'Technological change and regional development in the UK: evidence from the SPRU database on innovations', *Regional Studies* 22: 361–73.

Hendry, C. (1990) *Training in Britain: Employers' Perspectives on Human Resources*, London: HMSO.

Northcott, J. and Walling, A. (1988) *The Impact of Microelectronics: Diffusion, Benefits and Problems of British Industry*, London: Policy Studies Institute.

O'Farrell, P. N. and Oakey, R. P. (1992) 'Regional variation in the adoption of computer-numerically controlled machine tools of small engineering firms: a multi-variate analysis', *Environment and Planning A*, 24: 887–902.

Peck, J. A. and Lloyd, P. E. (1989) 'Conceptualising processes of skill change: a local labour market approach', G. J. R. Linge and G. A. van der Knapp (eds) *Labour, Environment and Industrial Change*, London: Croom Helm.

Thwaites, A. (1983) 'The employment implications of technological change in a regional context', A. Gillespie (ed.) *Technological Change and Regional Development*, London: Pion.

Thwaites, A. (1982) 'Some evidence of regional variations in the introduction and diffusion, of industrial products and processes within British manufacturing industry', *Regional Studies* 16: 371–81.

Totterdill, P. (1990) 'Technology, the labour process and markets: industrial policy and the organisation of work', *Local Economy* 5: 119–28.

Training Agency (1989) *Training in Britain: A Study of Funding Activity and Attitudes*, London: HMSO.

7 Qualified scientists and engineers and economic performance

Derek Bosworth and Rob Wilson

7.1 BACKGROUND

Qualified scientists and engineers have long been recognized as crucial to the existence of a successful manufacturing industry. Fears about various aspects of the role of professional scientists and engineers (PSEs) within the British economy have been voiced for almost as long as there has been a factory system. Problems were recorded and debated as early as the Playfair Report (Lyon 1852). The issues were hotly debated again at the time of the Finniston Report (Finniston 1980). Discussion over the last decade has tended to focus on the results of international comparisons of the quality of training and the availability of skills, for example, between Britain and Germany.

In the main, these comparisons have generally concluded that the output of people with degree and sub-degree qualifications in engineering in Britain is broadly comparable with other countries (Department of Employment 1987: 603). Further support for this view seems to have been given by other, more detailed, mainly international comparative case-study work, which indicated that the problems probably stemmed from inadequate training at intermediate skill levels (Prais 1990). While the focus of research has undoubtedly shifted towards lower-level skills, it is not at all certain that all of the questions regarding the higher-level skills have been adequately answered.

A report by the Engineering Council, written in response to the Department of Employment article, came to very different conclusions about the comparative position of professional engineering skills in Britain and Japan (Engineering Council 1988). It argues that the original comparisons significantly underestimated the output of Level 5 engineers (as it omitted individuals from Japanese

Special Training Schools). In addition, much higher proportions of Japanese students study both mathematics and technology subjects to age 18 than in Britain (*ibid.:* 15). More importantly, the report differs not only about the numbers of professional engineers being trained but also the quality; in Japan, it appears that the most able and most highly motivated students enter university engineering schools (*ibid.:* 16). This is, in part, a reflection of the relative status of engineering as a profession, as well as the importance attached to engineering as a wealth creating activity (Hutton and Lawrence 1981).

It has been argued, for example, that in many other countries, such as France, Germany and Japan, PSEs appear to play a more active role in the strategic decision-making of companies than in the UK (Engineering Council 1987: 16). Indeed, the Engineering Council report suggests that Japanese engineers are better trained for such a role than engineers in the United Kingdom (*ibid.:* 16). There is certainly some evidence to support the hypothesis that UK management has been relatively poorly qualified, and the qualifications which are held have tended to be in accountancy and finance rather than science or technology (Crocket and Elias 1983, Bosworth and Jacobs 1989). On the other hand, it should be noted that the British engineer/manager has much more to contend with than their German counterpart: the low-status of industry, neglect of the engineering dimension (historically at least), greater problems of industrial relations (Lawrence 1980 and 1982).

In 1989, for example, according to data from the *Labour Force Survey*, less than 20 per cent of corporate managers and administrators had a degree or equivalent qualification, while the figure for managers and proprietors of small businesses was below 6 per cent (Bosworth and Wilson 1991). Only about one-third of corporate managers and administrators with a first or higher degree had qualifications in science and technology; about the same proportion were qualified in social sciences (including accountancy and finance). The trends in qualifications over time are mapped out elsewhere (Bosworth 1992). Directly comparable data are not available for the United Kingdom's main competitors, but anecdotal evidence suggests that those with science and engineering qualifications play a much greater role in management in France, Germany and Japan.

7.2 AIMS AND METHODOLOGY

Given this background, the present study of the *Role of Scientists and Engineers in the Process of Technological Change* was funded under the ESRC/DTI New Technologies and the Firm Initiative, with supplementary funding from the Engineering Industry Training Board (now the Engineering Training Authority).

This project has attempted to establish differences in the extent to which companies employ professional scientists and engineers, including their roles and responsibilities, and to investigate the likely consequences of such differences for the performance of companies. Put at their crudest, the underlying hypotheses tested are, first, whether key characteristics in terms of company and industry structure can explain differences in the use and deployment of PSEs across companies and, second, whether companies employing greater numbers of scientists and engineers in roles involving higher levels of responsibility perform measurably better or worse than other companies with fewer such people or employing them in lower-level jobs. The latter can be crudely stated as, other things being equal, do 'engineering led' companies out-perform 'accounting and finance led' companies in some dynamic sense? This is, of course, an over-simplification. As the work by LBS shows, the link between innovation and commercial success is far from straightforward (see Grindley, Ch. 2. of this volume). Nevertheless, this basic dichotomy forms a useful device for examining the role of PSEs in the process of technological change and international competition.

In order to examine these issues a conceptual framework is required. At the present stage, such a framework is necessarily fairly eclectic in nature. The processes with which the project is trying to grapple are, by their very nature, very complex. It is not obvious that they can necessarily be expressed in a simple, mathematically rigorous form. Nevertheless, one objective of the project is to collect quantitative data which could be subjected to econometric analysis. This implies the need for at least the rudiments of a mathematical model, linking the employment of PSEs to the characteristics of the company and its subsequent performance.

In order to test these and related hypotheses, two related sets of data have been assembled. First, using telephone survey techniques, a sample of over 700 companies were interviewed. This provides a unique database that will be the subject of future interrogation using multivariate techniques. Second, a number of in-depth case studies were carried out, including a small number of foreign companies. The rationale for the former was that the micro company database would enable generalizations of the role of PSEs within the UK economy. The rationale for the latter was that case studies would help to reveal some of the more complex interrelationships, feedbacks and unmeasurable factors (such as individual personalities) involved, given that the complexities of the real world are often very difficult to model quantitatively, especially where there are long and uncertain time lags.

The present chapter has deliberately been kept short and so it cannot provide a detailed description of the results of the project to date; this can be found elsewhere (Bosworth *et al.* 1992). Indeed, the chapter cannot even provide a complete summary because the project is still under way and a number of loose ends remain to be tied up. However, it should give the reader a flavour of the issues with which the project has tried to grapple, and an overview of the quantitative and qualitative evidence that has been collected in order to test the various hypotheses outlined above.

7.3 CONCEPTUAL MODEL

The underlying conceptual model developed during the course of this project has two principal, related strands. The first relates to the nature of firms' reactions to competitive shocks. The second deals with proactive investment in higher-level skills as part of a company strategy towards human resource development.

The first dimension of the model has been developed from research initiated under the ESRC-funded pilot study for the New Technologies and the Firm Initiative (Bosworth *et al.* 1990). It is essentially in the Schumpeterian tradition of industrial economics, emphasizing structure, conduct and performance. In its simplest form the model suggests a dichotomous choice for companies faced by increasing levels of competition. The first is the 'low-value-added route', linked to cost reductions arising from labour-saving changes including deskilling, sub-contracting and casualization of the workforce. This route does not generally imply that the firm will invest in new plant and machinery; in the extreme, the company makes existing assets 'sweat'. The alternative is the 'high-value-added route', linked to quality improvements, training, skill improvement and longer tenure of employment. In the extreme, it involves new product design and improvement, as well as investments in plant and machinery.

In terms of the two stylized extremes, the dichotomous economic model clearly indicates that the non-innovative, cost-saving, alternative is a cul-de-sac leading to more intensive competition with other low-cost producers, often from the Third World. The high-technology route, linked to new product development, is, by contrast, 'open ended', with more opportunities for 'niche markets' and higher levels of monopoly power arising from product differentiation. While the model links the firm's preferences regarding the route to the firm's size and to the nature and quality of its management and skills of its workforce, it also recognizes that the extent to which the two alternative approaches are observed in practice will also depend on the degree to which the 'short termism' of the stock market becomes an economic imperative which governs the operation and choices of companies.

The second part of the model views the recruitment and subsequent employment of graduates and, in particular, PSEs as a form of investment by the firm. Employers report a range of advantages and disadvantages of employing graduates (Rigg *et al.* 1990, Bosworth and Wilson 1991). Amongst recruiters, specific knowledge and high levels of skills stand out as the most important qualities. However, many other factors are emphasized, including greater speed of learning, higher motivation, greater analytical skills, communication skills, leadership potential, adaptability and initiative.

The second element of the model that underpins the present research, therefore, is the notion that the demand for PSEs is only partly a response to the imperatives of current demand and may only be loosely connected with the current production activities or output of the company. Much of their day-to-day activity will be concerned with output next week, next month, next year or even the next decade. The most obvious example is the employment of PSEs in research and development activities, where the rewards may not be reaped for many years, but to some extent the argument applies to all of the functional areas of the firm, from marketing to general management.

It has been recognized in earlier work that the employment of graduates is a form of investment in human capital (Rigg *et al.* 1990, Bosworth and Wilson 1991). Employers of graduates generally report that they take considerably longer to be effective than other types of recruit and they are prepared to allow more initial training in order to gain the full benefits from employing them. According to the PSI/IER survey (Elias and Rigg 1991), new graduates took an average of one working year to become fully effective in private-sector companies. They received, on average, eighteen days of formal training during this first year, but larger firms provided almost twice as much training as smaller companies. These findings again confirm that many firms see new graduates as a long-term investment in key employees rather than as highly-qualified staff who simply make a larger contribution to the current level of output.

The key implication is that in so far as the firm employs PSEs in dynamic functions, the employment of highly qualified labour, such as professional scientists and engineers, should be treated as an investment activity by the company. The costs of PSEs are incurred by the firm from day one of their employment, but the returns are only obtained over the longer term. In economic parlance, the marginal cost of PSEs exceeds the marginal revenue product in the early years, but this inequality is reversed in later years because then current output levels will be related not just to the labour input at that time but to labour inputs from previous years. This phenomenon has been partly recognized in discussion of on-the-job training (Becker 1964, Mincer 1962). The present analysis extends this by emphasizing that the firm's investment in human capital extends beyond formal, on-the-job training. Much of the day-to-day activity of many qualified people can be regarded as contributing to future rather than current output. As with the analysis of on-the-job training, this type of activity can therefore be regarded as an investment by the company in future output. The key conclusion of this kind of analysis is that firms will pay such personnel more than their marginal revenue product in the short term, but hope to gain when their marginal contribution exceeds their pay in later years.

The two strands of the model can be linked together in so far as professional scientists and engineers may respond quite differently to the challenges posed by competitive shocks. PSEs may look for scientific and engineering solutions, thereby taking a longer-term view in determining the routes which companies follow. In this way, a central tenet of the research is that scientists and engineers play a key role in the process of product improvement, technological change, productivity and economic growth. This role extends beyond the more obvious areas concerned with research and development into various other functional activities within the firm, including production, marketing and general management.

To characterize, crudely, the first, non-innovative, 'cost saving' route might be seen as a 'finance and accounting' reaction to competitive pressure, while the second route can be regarded as an 'engineering led' response. It seemed likely that 'finance and accounting led' companies would tend towards the former route, while 'engineering led' companies would have an inherent inclination to consider the latter. It should be noted that these are extreme positions. However, to some degree the same arguments appear to be relevant to a comparison between, say, cost-saving innovations through the introduction of new process technology (i.e. *via* 'off-the-shelf' investments) and product improving technology that requires in-house R & D skills. On the other hand, case-study work reveals that firms that become committed to process change as a long-term strategy, also develop skills and interests that lead to product developments (Stoneman, Bosworth and Gibbons 1992a and 1992b). Thus, 'off-the-shelf', high-technology process innovations may be a mechanism which allows companies to bridge the gap between the vicious circle of disinvestment and the virtuous circle linked with product innovation and improvement.

7.4 FORMAL MODEL

The real world in which companies operate is a highly complex one with multiple interactions and feedbacks. In order to operationalize the general conceptual model, it is necessary to simplify the various links and relationships. As a first step in this process, a recursive system has been developed which is described in detail elsewhere (Bosworth and Wilson 1991).

The starting point is equations explaining the structure of the board of directors, including the characteristics of the managing director (MD). All board members, although the MD in particular, are important as they offer leadership, define the goals of the firm and take decisions which are (presumably) consistent with those goals. There is a large and still growing literature on various aspects of leadership including the causes and consequences of entrepreneurship (Kirby 1990, Sinclair 1990, Blanchflower and Oswald 1991). The board structure is argued to be determined by a number of variables reflecting market structure and firm organization. These variables include the product area of the company, its size, the degree of market concentration, organizational structure of the firm (i.e. foreign versus domestic owned, independent versus group and single versus multi-site), including the position of the company within the group hierarchy.

Such a model of the determinants of the structure of the board is clearly only a starting point for the analysis of management. Other aspects of the New Technologies and the Firm programme throw more light on these issues. The core study, for example, investigates the links between the economic performance of the firm in technology to the nature of organizational relationships and, in particular, the effectiveness of different organizational architectures in producing and exploiting new technologies (see Grindley, Ch. 2 of this volume). Management itself is under considerable pressure for change as the movement from functional hierarchies to more entrepreneurial style organization gathers momentum (see Webb and Cleary, Ch. 5 of this volume). It is also clear that innovative activity interrelates with market structure; technical change can be concentrating or de-concentrating (see Swann and Gill, Ch. 10 of this volume).

The goals of the company are argued to be determined by the background of the MD and the structure and discipline areas of the board of directors. In addition, however, the same MD and board might set different goals depending on the particular product market environment and the organizational structure of the company. A clear implication is that, in principle, the adoption of different goals can be expected to lead to different firm performance, other things being equal. In practice, whether such differences materialize in practice will depend on the way in which the goals are operationalized. Existing evidence, for example, suggests that more sophisticated capital budgeting techniques do not lead to improved firm performance in the long run (Klammer 1972, Haka *et al.* 1985). A number of goals are distinguished in the survey including those of maximizing market share, maximizing profits, minimizing costs and so on.

In turn, it is argued that the employment structure of the company will depend on the goals of the firm, the composition and background of the board, the nature of the product market and organizational structure. Clearly, direct production jobs will be closely related to the technology of the production processes associated with each product and, therefore, industry. In addition, however, it is expected that firms which adopt longer-term, more dynamic goals may require a somewhat different mix of labour (i.e. more qualified and more highly skilled).

The fourth relationship explores the linkages between technological change and the variables outlined above. Technological change is measured by the use of, and therefore the recent introduction of, advanced technologies, including CNC (Stoneman and

Karshenas, Ch. 2 of this volume). This approach provides a fairly natural extension of the traditional structure-conduct-performance representations of the Schumpeterian model. The specification now explicitly includes the goals of the firm. The study by Lonie and Nixon, for example, argues that corporate strategy (and the fundamental beliefs of top management which underpin it) are a dominant influence on investment in new technology (see Ch. 12). It also includes the employment structure of the enterprise, which will determine the ability of the firm to operationalize its dynamic goals. Skill availability and its links with innovation are dealt with in other parts of the initiative (see Foley *et al.*, Ch. 6 of this volume).

Finally, the economic performance of the enterprise is related to the use of advanced technologies (i.e. the level and area of recent innovative activity), employment structure (i.e. the use of highly qualified persons and the level of skills in the company), the goals of the company, board structure and so on. Economic performance is measured in a variety of ways, including improvements in market share, growth in real profits and growth in real turnover. The key point that is emphasized is that current performance is related not just to current levels of employment of scientists and engineers but to their involvement, at various different levels, in the past.

In subsequent econometric work it is hoped to explore the relative strengths of the various relationships and links set out above, and to isolate the key feedbacks. Note that some right-hand-side variables will appear in more than one equation: for example, firm size features in each of the stages outlined above. This variable can have both direct and indirect effects: for example, firm size may be related to company performance directly but also indirectly through its impact on technology, employment structure, and so on, which also appear in the explanation of firm performance via the earlier relationships.

The analysis of the data to date, however, has been much more limited, concentrating on descriptive statistics, bivariate analysis and some preliminary multivariate analysis. The discussion in the following section focuses on a number of key findings from this preliminary analysis.

7.5 COMPANY SIZE AND PERFORMANCE STRUCTURE

Structure of the board and MD's background

The structure of the board varies considerably across industries. In the engineering sector, for example, about 36 per cent of boards in the sample have no graduates, compared with 35 per cent in other manufacturing, 40 per cent in the primary and construction sector and 44 per cent in services. Thus manufacturing companies are somewhat more likely to have graduates on the board than non-manufacturing companies. This result is reinforced by the fact that about 13 per cent of engineering sector companies have wholly graduate boards, compared with only 5 per cent in other manufacturing and an overall average for all industries and services of only 10 per cent.

Perhaps not surprisingly, the result relating to the engineering sector also applies in the case of the proportion of PSEs on the board, given the importance of engineering for this occupational group. Only 44 per cent of engineering companies do not have a scientist or engineer on the board (note that this percentage must be greater than or equal to the percentage of companies with graduates). The figure for engineering is again the highest of any of the broad sectors distinguished here and can be compared with 72 per cent of service-sector companies which do not have PSEs on the board. By implication, these figures demonstrate that one of the key variables thought to influence the performance of UK companies varies significantly across sectors.

A further dimension of interest is the background of the company MD. In the unweighted sample (in which engineering is over-represented) there are 148 MDs with an engineering or technology background out of a total of 706 (21 per cent). Even allowing for the fact that the majority of these are located in the engineering sector (96 out of 148), engineers and technologists are still well represented in the total, but there are major differences across sectors. While 35.5 per cent of MDs in engineering companies have a science or engineering background, only 11 per cent of MDs in other manufacturing and 13.5 per cent of those in services are so qualified. Surprisingly, perhaps, the engineering sector has the lowest proportion of MDs with a science background amongst the broad sectors distinguished here. The results within engineering also reveal some interesting differences. Electronics, for example, has a higher than average share of 'self-made' MDs (i.e. with no formal qualifications), while motor vehicles and aerospace tend to have a much higher proportion from an engineering and technology background.

MDs with a social science background are the largest group numerically, even given the over-representation of engineering within the total sample. This group accounts for 156 of the 706 MDs (22 per cent of the total). In practice, the group is dominated by business and finance which, with 131 MDs, is only slightly smaller than the engineering and technology group. Interestingly, 19 per cent of engineering companies have MDs with a social science background, which is still quite high. As might be expected, this group is more extensively represented outside of the engineering sector than MDs with an engineering and technology background. Some 24 per cent of MDs in the primary and construction sector have a social-science background, compared to 19 per cent in engineering, 18 per cent in other manufacturing and 29 per cent in services.

The third largest group was that designated as 'self-made', with no particular background formal qualifications or experience distinguished. Out of 706 MDs, 144 were allocated to this group (about 20 per cent of the total). Some 27 per cent of MDs in the primary and construction sector are in this 'self-made' category, compared with 25 per cent of MDs in the service sector, 23 per cent in other manufacturing and only 15 per cent in engineering. Thus the proportion of 'self-made' MDs is significantly lower in engineering than in other manufacturing (or in all other industries and services).

The data also show significant differences in the composition of the board and the background of MDs across different sizes of companies. As might be expected, the proportion of graduates on the board increases with company size. The proportion of PSEs also appears to be a function of firm size (although the proportion is lower for the largest size-category than the medium size-category, which probably reflects differences in the underlying industrial distribution of firms of different sizes). In the same way, it is possible to illustrate how size is related to the background of the MD. In firms of less than 100 employees, 19 per cent of MDs have an engineering and technology background; this rises to 24 per cent amongst firms of between 100 and 999 employees, but only 17 per cent amongst largest firm sizes (over 1,000 employees). The comparative results for individuals with a social-science background are 19 per cent amongst the smallest firms; 21 per cent for the middle size-range; but 33 per cent amongst the largest firms. The 'self-made' group show the opposite pattern with 27 per cent of MDs falling in this category amongst the smallest firms; 16 per cent in the intermediate firm-size group; and only 12 per cent amongst the largest firm-size group. Not surprisingly, small firms have a high percentage of those from a 'self-made' background.

Detailed analysis suggests many contrasts, depending upon various other aspects of the company structure: domestic versus foreign ownership; whether the company is an independent or part of a group; and whether the company is based on a single site or multiple site. Foreign firms seem more likely to have a higher percentage of graduates and PSEs on the board. Being part of a group reveals a similar pattern. Multi-site companies appear to be associated with a higher proportion of graduates on the board (but not PSEs).

The results also indicate (not surprisingly perhaps) that the MD is much less likely to be 'self-made' if the firm is foreign owned. This is much more likely, however, if the company is independent and, to a lesser extent, if it operates on a single site. Other differences are less clear-cut. In the case of UK-owned companies, 21 per cent report having an MD with an engineering background, compared with 19 per cent of foreign-owned companies. About 22 per cent of UK companies have an MD with a social-science background (again, largely dominated by business and finance) compared with 25 per cent of foreign owned. This almost certainly reflects the difference in the extent of UK-based manufacturing activity between the two types of firm.

The data also indicate the differences between independent companies as opposed to those that form part of a group. On average, independents will be smaller that those that are part of a group and this can be expected to influence the background of the MD. In practice, the importance of engineering and technical backgrounds is about the same for the two groups; about 20 per cent of independents had MDs with an engineering or technological background compared with 21 per cent of those forming part of a group. About 20 per cent of independents had MDs with a social-science background, compared with 24 per cent of group members. Where the distinction shows through most clearly, however, is the case of 'self-made' MDs, associated with 29 per cent of independents and only 14 per cent of group members. It seems fairly clear that companies which are part of a larger group are more likely to select individuals with specific expertise, with evidence of a preference for social-science skills (probably business-related and communicative skills) over other types.

The same kinds of caveat apply in the case of the single site versus multi-site results. Single site firms are more likely, for example, to be smaller, independent companies. About 24 per cent of single-site companies have an MD with an engineering or technological background, compared with 20 per cent of the multi-site companies. Again, it appears likely that other 'skills' (such as business-related and communication) are selected in multi-plant operations. In practice, the difference is slight; 21 per cent of individuals in single-site companies have a social-science background, compared with 24 per cent of multi-site companies. On the other hand, as might be expected, the proportion of 'self-made' individuals is considerably smaller in multi-site companies. In practice, while this result is confirmed, the differences are not enormous: just under 19 per cent of MDs fall into the 'self-made' category in multi-site companies, compared with just over 22 per cent in single-site companies.

It is perhaps to be expected that foreign-owned companies will tend to be professionally managed, often by individuals selected for their specific expertise; about 23 per cent of UK companies had 'self-made' managers, compared with only 10 per cent of foreign-owned companies.

Any conclusions drawn about the distinction between domestic and foreign-owned UK companies should be treated with some caution. The foreign-owned units may be materially different in nature to their UK counterparts; for example, production activities may be relatively less important and distribution may be more important. In addition, if the over-sampling of engineering companies affects the UK-owned sample differently than the foreign, then the comparisons will again be affected. Both of these problems might well affect the proportion of engineers in particular. Twenty-three per cent of the sample is foreign owned and, although this amounts to 131 companies, and when this group is broken down further, sample numbers can be quite small.

Company goals

Setting goals does not of course ensure that they will be achieved. The state of the market within which the company operates and the quality of its management, workforce, technology and capital equipment, will together determine how the company performs and whether its goals are achieved. A major aim of the project was to establish the relative importance of these various elements. However, this requires quite sophisticated multivariate analysis, which has yet to be completed. In addition, while the following discussion outlines the main goals, at this stage it does not explore the extent to which such goals are similar or different in content.

Preliminary analysis suggests that the structure of the board and the background of the MD may significantly affect the goals the company sets. In particular, the presence of graduates or PSEs on the board appears, *ceteris paribus*, to make it more likely that the company will have formulated clear goals and that these goals will entail either maximizing market share and/or the growth of the company. Likewise, the background of the MD seems to be important. Having an MD with an engineering or technology background as opposed to, say, being 'self-made' has the effect of influencing the company to maximize profits or sales. Finally, having an MD with a business and finance background has a similar impact, although the emphasis is now more on the maximization of market share and/or profits than MDs with, say, an engineering or technology background.

Investment appraisal methods were not at the heart of the present research project. The main questionnaire surveys and case studies were largely undertaken with the personnel or overall managers of the companies. However, subsequent case-study work reveals an essential tension between the engineering-driven desire for new technology and the accountants' need to quantify the benefits of the new technology.

Earlier work had already thrown light on the linkages between the employment of graduates and the planning horizon of firms (Rigg *et al.* 1990, Bosworth and Wilson 1991). The direction of cause and effect cannot be determined from this information, but it is clear that larger companies and employers in the public sector have longer planning horizons (two to three years) than smaller firms (less than six months). Given that the employment of graduates can itself be regarded as an investment (as shown above), it is hardly surprising to find that it is firms with a longer planning horizon which are more likely to employ them; on the other hand, graduates will themselves bring a longer-term view of the costs and benefits of various activities associated with longer planning horizons.

In the case studies, in which this issue was investigated in detail, the subsidiary's own accountants worked in combination with the engineers to produce a proposal for approval by others at a higher level in the hierarchy. On the other hand, the proposals were couched in terms of easily quantifiable benefits from increases in capacity and cost and savings. In practice, some of the more important *ex post* benefits were associated with what, at the time of the decision, were regarded as more qualitative factors that could not be quantified in terms of the company's formal accounting procedures. However, *ex post*, these more qualitative dimensions proved to be of considerable importance to the success of the innovation. The unaccounted benefits far exceeded the unaccounted costs and, by implication, had such factors been taken into account in the original calculations, such firms would have been more likely to have undertaken the investment and, overall, the level of investment would have been higher.

There are some unanswered questions here. The first of these is how the appraisal rules and guidelines are set and whether these differ between companies which can be described as 'engineering led' and those which are 'finance and accounting led'. The second is the appropriateness of such rules across different companies within a group and the potential, for example, for conflict between, say, a 'cash-rich' subsidiary and a 'cash-scarce' parent. It is hoped that such issues will form the subject of future research.

Employment of PSEs

Of the 700-plus companies surveyed, just under 40 per cent employed no graduates, while almost 60 per cent employed no PSEs. The sector and size of the company appear to be key factors determining these dimensions of employment. For the great majority of companies that employed such personnel, graduates and/or PSEs only accounted for a small proportion of their total employment (less than 5 per cent). On the other hand, a small proportion (usually quite small) of specialized companies (whose main activity is focused on research and development of a particular new product) have a significantly higher proportion of PSEs.

The relationship between company size and the number of graduates and PSEs is not as simple as might be supposed (Bosworth and Wilson 1991). The probability of a company reporting no graduates falls significantly from the 1–99 to the 1,000-plus size-category. The proportion of companies reporting between 1 per cent and 4 per cent density of graduates rises significantly with firm size. On the other hand, the highest densities of graduates are found amongst smaller, presumably high-technology or knowledge-based, companies. An almost identical pattern emerges in the case of PSEs, although obviously the proportion of companies with no PSEs is higher for all firm sizes, and there are relatively fewer small companies which exhibit very high densities of PSEs.

It is often argued that the United Kingdom is becoming an 'assembly' nation because an increasing proportion of UK manufacturing companies are becoming foreign owned. The argument relies on the assumption that 'higher-level activities' such as research, design and development are undertaken in the parent company's home country. By implication, high-level activities are being exported, leaving lower level, 'assembly' activities within the United Kingdom.

The present results provide no evidence to support this hypothesis, although it is fair to say that we have a number of reservations about the results available to date. These reservations are worth stating prior to presenting the results as a precautionary note. R & D is widely defined in the questionnaire and does not only cover activities covered by, say, the Frascati Manual (OECD 1975). In addition, R & D is likely to be more closely associated with larger independents and with groups of companies. It should be noted, however, that the questions attempted to elicit information about R & D within the company rather than the group.

The results indicate that the proportion of companies reporting an R & D department is significantly higher for foreign-owned than for UK-owned companies. Some of the companies in our sample report undertaking R & D activities without the aid of graduates or PSEs. This is certainly possible, even in engineering where we found examples in the case-study work of individuals without degrees undertaking work in the R & D area. The survey evidence also shows that the proportion of companies with graduates in R & D is far higher amongst foreign-owned companies. The same finding is also true of the proportion of companies with PSEs employed in R & D. Thus an important result is that there is no evidence that the growth of foreign ownership has reduced the R & D intensity of UK companies. This result is not just a feature of the R & D function, it appears to hold across the company as a whole; foreign-owned companies are more likely to report employing graduates than UK-owned companies, and the same is true of PSEs.

Clearly these results require confirmation using multivariate analysis, holding other things constant such as sector, company size and so on. At this stage, however, we do not expect this finding to change greatly. The findings to date do not support the hypothesis that the shift to foreign ownership is 'de-skilling'; if anything, the opposite appears to be true.

Two other aspects of company structure were investigated, independent versus group and single versus multi-site companies. Clearly there is a strong link between these two dimensions which shows up in the similarity between the two sets of results. The results indicate that group members and multi-site companies both report significantly higher amounts of R & D and employment of graduates and PSEs in R & D than independents and single-site companies. Again this finding is not restricted to the R & D function but applies throughout the company as a whole.

Technological performance

While a considerable amount of multivariate analysis remains to be undertaken, it is possible to report some work which has already been completed on the topic of the analysis of technological performance. One section of the original questionnaire obtained information about the different types of technologies which the company uses. Companies were asked which of nine different technologies they used, and were allowed to specify any additional technologies not listed as an open-ended question.

One simple piece of analysis simply counted up the number of technologies that the firm reported using. This can be regarded as an index of the technological activity of the firm. It was recognized from the start that this would only be a very crude indicator as the technologies covered can be very different both in type and their 'closeness' to the technological frontier. Nevertheless, clear evidence was found of systematic links between the technology index and a variety of right-hand-side variables.

Other things being equal, there were significant differences between industries, with the metal-products group significantly more likely to employ more technologies than the base group (other manufacturing), and construction likely to employ significantly lower numbers of the technologies than the base group. Thus these two industries formed the two extremes. These results are consistent with the fact that some of the technologies (such as CNC machines) are more relevant to some types of production than to others.

The size and nature of companies were particularly important determinants of the number of technologies in use. Larger firms were significantly more likely to employ a larger number of these technologies than their smaller counterparts. Foreign ownership was another key determinant, with UK-owned companies likely to use a significantly smaller number of the technologies than their foreign-owned counterparts in the United Kingdom. Their negative signs within the multivariate equation suggested that a company which was an independent, based on a single site and UK owned, would employ a significantly lower number of technologies.

Another group of variables that plays a significant role concerns the employment of highly qualified persons. Of these variables, the presence of individuals with a degree on the board had a positive influence on the number of technologies, but the presence of highly qualified individuals with a science and technology qualification is also highly significant in the explanation of the technology index. The existence of an R & D department also had a significant positive effect on the number of technologies employed, confirming earlier links in the literature between formal R & D activities and the extent of innovation activity. A variety of other variables, including the structure of the workforce, will be tested in subsequent empirical estimates.

Finally, some preliminary tests have been carried out to explore the issue of self-selection: do firms which appear in the sub-sample that employs at least one of the technologies have unobserved characteristics that make them more likely to employ a higher rather than a lower number of the specified technologies? Some evidence was obtained by means of a two-stage sample selection bias correction procedure (Heckman 1977) that this was the case. In practice, however, the associated bias coefficient, although positive, was not significantly different from zero. However, the lack of significance of this variable probably stems from the wide range of technologies specified, with only a very small proportion of companies not employing at least one of them.

Economic performance

Links between the background of the MD and the structure of the board and *actual* performance have, to date, been investigated by means of simple cross-tabulations; confirmation will require more sophisticated multivariate analysis. In practice, most firms report improvements in their market share, real profits and turnover over the preceding five years. Nevertheless, there is some evidence that the proportion of firms reporting improvements increases with the number of graduates on the board. However, nothing can be said at this stage about the direction of causality. The links between performance and the proportion of PSEs on the board or the corresponding proportion of individuals with a technical background are less clear-cut.

The results appear to indicate that performance is much better amongst companies with an MD from a science background, although this is based on a very small part of the sample. The ratio of higher to lower market share for managers with an engineering and technology background is 6.2 (i.e. just over 6 : 1). This compares with a somewhat higher figure of 6.3 for those with a social science background and 6.7 for the 'self-made' group. The corresponding results for the growth in profits (i.e. were profits higher or lower than five years ago) show that the ratio of higher to lower for MDs with an engineering and technological background is 2.8, compared with 3.6 for those with a social-science background. The figure for the 'self-made' group, on the other hand, was only 2.4. Finally, the ratio of higher to lower turnover is 6.6 for MDs from an engineering and technology background, compared with 3.4 for firms whose MDs have a social-science background and 5.3 for the 'self-made' group. The results appear to confirm the hypothesis that MDs with an engineering and technology background place greater emphasis on growth than on profits *vis-à-vis* other types of managers.

A preliminary analysis of the link between performance and the use of highly qualified personnel generally, and PSEs in particular, reveals some notable differences. The employment of graduates and PSEs in the R & D department is associated with a statistically significant higher proportion of companies that report higher profits, greater turnover and/or improved market share. However, from this preliminary analysis there does not appear to be a simple relationship between performance and the shares of such groups within total employment. Nevertheless, companies where employment of such categories forms over 20 per cent of the total appear to perform significantly better than those which have none.

There may, of course, be a number of factors which influence both the structure of employment and company performance. It is clear, for example, that structural factors, such as whether the company is foreign owned or not, whether it is independent or part of a group, and whether it is a single- or multi-plant operation, all have important influences.

Generally speaking, foreign-owned companies appear to employ greater proportions of graduates and PSEs, are more likely to have introduced new technologies in recent years and are more likely to have been involved in market restructuring activities (such as the introduction of new products). These things all appear to be associated with improvements in company performance. In particular, development of new products, general restructuring and the introduction of new technology to deal with both administration and production are all correlated with improved performance in terms of profit, market share and turnover.

Being part of a group or part of a multi-plant operation shows similar benefits. Many of these factors may be linked to other characteristics of the company such as size and product type. The purpose of the multivariate analysis which is currently under way will be to disentangle the separate influences of the various factors. However, these preliminary results appear to suggest that the intensity of use of qualified personnel is at least one of the important factors influencing company performance and that the presence of highly qualified scientists and engineers, both in general and on the board of directors, has an important effect on both company goals and performance.

7.6 CONCLUSIONS

The results so far suggest that there are statistically significant links between the deployment of highly qualified personnel, their role in strategic management of the company and dynamic economic performance. These relationships are complex, being influenced by the proportions of highly qualified people employed, by the ways in which they are utilized and the extent to which they are given responsibility and real power in the decision-making processes of companies.

ACKNOWLEDGEMENTS

This paper reports a number of results from a project on the Role of Scientists and Engineers in the Process of Technological Change, which was funded by ESRC under the New Technologies and the Firm Initiative. The authors are grateful to ESRC for their support. Thanks are also due to Paul Taylor, Wayne Thomas and Ruth Hermitage for their assistance in collecting and collating the data. Jackie Lewis was involved in various elements of the case study work. We would also like to thank the other research teams on the New Technologies and the Firm Initiative for their helpful comments, particularly Peter Swann and Paul Stoneman. Maureen Garcia typed the manuscript with her usual efficiency. Responsibility for any remaining errors lie solely with the authors.

REFERENCES

Becker, G. S. (1964) *Human Capital: A Theoretical and Empirical Analysis, with Special Reference to Education*, Princeton: Princeton University Press.

Blanchflower, D. G. and Oswald, A. J. (1991) 'What makes an entrepreneur?' Applied Economics Discussion Paper Series, No. 125, Institute of Economics and Statistics, Oxford.

Bosworth, D. L. (1992) *Professional Occupations*, in R. M. Lindley and R. A. Wilson (eds) *Review of the Economy and Employment, 1991: Occupational Studies Part 1*, Institute for Employment Research, Coventry: University of Warwick.

Bosworth, D. L. and Jacobs, C. (1989) 'Barriers to growth in small innovatory firms: management attitudes, behaviour and abilities', in S. Metcalf *et al.* (eds) *Barriers to Growth in Small Firms*, London: Routledge.

Bosworth, D. L. and Wilson, R. A. (1991) 'Role of scientists and engineers in the process of technological change', paper presented to the Royal Aeronautical Society Conference, London.

Bosworth, D. L., Lewis, J. A. and Jacobs, C. (1990) *Shared Facilities and the Innovating Firm*, Aldershot: Avebury Press.

Bosworth, D. L., Wilson, R. A. and Taylor, P. (1992) *Technological Change: The Role of Scientists and Engineers*, Aldershot: Avebury Press.

Crocket, G. and Elias, P. (1983) 'British managers: a study of their education, training, mobility and earnings', *British Journal of Industrial Relations* 22: 39–46.

Department of Employment (1987) 'Higher education output in engineering: international comparisons', *Employment Gazette*, London: HMSO.

Engineering Council (1988) *A Comparison of the Statistics of Engineering Education: Japan and the United Kingdom*, London: Engineering Council.

Finniston, Sir M. (Chairman) (1980) *Engineering Our Future*, Report of the Committee of Inquiry into the Engineering Profession, Cmnd 7794, London: HMSO.

Haka, S. F., Gordon, L. A. and Pinches, G. E. (1985) 'Sophisticated capital budgeting selection techniques and firm performance', *The Accounting Review* 60(4): 651–69.

Heckman, J. J. (1977) 'Sample selection bias as a specification error', *Econometrica* 47(1): 153–62.

Hutton, S. P. and Lawrence, P. A. (1981) *German Engineers: The Autonomy of a Profession*, Oxford: Oxford University Press.

Kirby, D. A. (1990) 'Entrepreneurship research in the UK: a review of the literature', Occasional Paper No. 9059, Durham University Business School, Durham.

Klammer, T. P. (1972) 'Empirical evidence of the adoption of sophisticated capital budgeting techniques', *Journal of Business*, July, 387–97.

Lawrence, P. A. (1980) *Managers and Management in West Germany*, London: Croom Helm.

—— (1982) 'Culture and Ingenuity', *Human and Environmental Studies Journal* 1(1): 67–73.

Mincer, J. (1962) 'On-the-job training: costs, returns and some implications', *Journal of Political Economy*, Supplement.

OECD (1975) *The Measurement of Scientific and Technical Activities: Proposed Standard Practice for Surveys of Research and Experimental Development* (Frascati Manual), Paris: OECD.

Lyon, Baron Playfair (1852) *On Technical Education*, Edinburgh (quoted in Sir M. Finniston, *Engineering Our Future*, Report of the Committee of Inquiry into the Engineering Profession, Cmnd 7794, London: HMSO.

Prais, F. (ed.) (1990) *Productivity, Education and Training*, London: National Institute for Economic and Social Research.

Rigg, M., Elias, P., White, M. and S. Johnson, S. (1990) *An Overview of the Demand for Graduates*, Policy Studies Institute/Institute for Employment Research, London: HMSO.

Sinclair, A. (1990) 'Archetypes of leadership', Working Paper No. 11, June, Graduate School of Management, University of Melbourne, Melbourne.

Stoneman, P., Bosworth, D. and Gibbons, A. (1992a) *A Charter for Manufacturing*, London: Machine Tool Technologies Association.

—— (1992b) *Investment, Productivity and Competitiveness in UK Manufacturing Industry*, Research Report, Institute for Employment Research, Coventry: University of Warwick.

Part III

Markets and consumers

8 The diffusion of new technology: extensions to theory and evidence

Paul Stoneman and Massoud Karshenas

8.1 INTRODUCTION

In this chapter we report upon results deriving from a research project entitled, 'Explorations into the Theory, Empirics and Policy of Technological Diffusion', funded as part of the ESRC Research Initiative on New Technologies and the Firm. The research itself is driven by the belief that it is the use of new technology rather than the generation of new technology that improves economic performance. It will make little difference to either a firm's competitiveness or profits, or to an economy's productivity and output if new technologies generated by the R & D process are not used by firms. Moreover, many of the technologies that firms will wish to use will not be self-generated but will come from other firms and industries (or in many cases even from overseas). In such circumstances it is at least as important (if not more important) to have some understanding of the process of adoption of new technologies as it is to understand the generation of such technologies. This chapter is thus about the use or adoption of new technologies.

The process of adoption of new technologies is known as the diffusion process. The framework that was in our minds when undertaking the research was a simple one. With respect to new process technologies we think of one industry supplying new technology embodied in a specific capital good and firms in another industry or industries making decisions as to whether to install that technology. With respect to new product technologies we have a similar conception except that the potential buyers are households. It is fair to state that not all technological decisions will fit this framework but it is a beneficial starting point.

To prepare the ground, it is useful to begin with a number of 'stylized facts', which in essence are just observed empirical regularities. Among such stylized facts relating to the diffusion process are the following.

- The spread of a new technology across its potential market takes time, often a considerable period of time.
- The rate of take-up of technologies, and the final level of use of technologies, differ across countries.
- The rate of take-up also differs across technologies and implicitly, as different technologies are appropriate for different industries, across industries.
- A plot of the use of technology against time most frequently generates an S-shaped, or sigmoid, diffusion curve.

This last observation merits some further explanation. One may measure the extent of diffusion in a number of ways. For new process technologies one may talk of individual firms and measure 'intra-firm diffusion' by the proportion of a firm's output produced using a new technology, or the proportion of its capital goods that is of the new type (e.g. the proportion of total locomotive stock that is diesel as opposed to steam). One may also talk of 'inter-firm diffusion' and measure diffusion by the proportion of firms in an industry or sector using a new technology at greater than some base level. One may even talk at the economy-wide level and measure diffusion by the proportion of capital goods that are of the new type. Whichever level is looked at, however, if the generic measure is called 'market penetration' and this is plotted against time, it is common to observe that the plot has an S-shape. This basically means that diffusion starts off at a slow pace, and then speeds up, but after some point the process slows down again with the level of market penetration tending to some asymptote.

The observations on the diffusion of new process technologies are mirrored in observations on new product technologies. If one plots the proportion of households owning a new consumer durable against time then it is common to observe that the plot is S-shaped.

To illustrate such stylized facts, in the following three tables some data on the diffusion of new process technologies is presented. Table 8.1 contains raw data on the use of robots in different countries. Table 8.2 contains data on the take up of different technologies in different countries, and Table 8.3 contains data on the take up of a number of different technologies in the United States. In Figure 8.1 a diffusion curve mapping out the spread of use of CNC machine tools in the United Kingdom is plotted that neatly illustrates the S-shape referred to above.

Table 8.1 Stock of robots 1974–84

	1974	*1984*
Italy	90	2,700
France	n/a	3,380
Germany	130	6,600
Japan	1,000	64,657
USA	1,200	13,000
UK	50	2,623

Source: Edquist and Jacobsson 1988, 56.

Table 8.2 The diffusion of technologies

Innovation	*% of output produced using new technology*	*Years from own date of innovation*		
		UK	*West Germany*	*Sweden*
Special presses (Paper-making)	10	3	2	2
Tunnel kilns (Brick-making)	10	n/a	2	8
Basic oxygen process (Steel)	20	5	8	9
Gibberalic acid (Brewing)	50	4	n/a	3
Continuous casting (Steel)	1	6	9	3
Shuttleless looms (Textiles)	2	6	6	9
Automatic transfer Lines (vehicles)	30	10	1	2

Source: Nabseth and Ray 1974, 17.

Given the observations above, the literature on technological diffusion is concerned with trying to answer the following questions:

- Why does diffusion take time and why does the diffusion curve show an S-shape?
- Why do some technologies diffuse faster than others?
- Why do some industries diffuse technology faster than others?
- Why do some countries diffuse technologies faster than others?
- Why do some firms or households adopt new technology before others, or what is the same question, why are some firms and households early adopters and some firms and households late adopters?

Table 8.3 Diffusion indicators, United States

Innovation	No. of years taken for half of potential adopters to acquire
Industrial robot	12
NCMT	5
Diesel locomotives	9
Centralized traffic control	14
Car retarders	13
Continuous wide-strip mill	8
By-product coke oven	15
Continuous annealing	13
Shuttle car	5
Trackless mobile loader	6
Continuous mining machine	3
Tin container	1
High-speed bottle filler	6
Pallet loading machine	5

Source: Mansfield 1989.

In fact answers to all these questions can be derived if one can understand the basic driving forces behind the diffusion phenomenon. From a basic understanding of the phenomenon predictions will follow: for process technologies, predictions are derivable regarding which firms in which countries and which industries will adopt early or late (and also some predictions as to at what date particular firms will adopt), and for new product technologies, predictions on which households will adopt early and late and so on. In fact from knowledge of the basic driving forces one may provide a rationale as to why diffusion follows an S-shaped curve and also what the determinants are of the parameters of that curve.

In the rest of this chapter these basic questions are addressed. The chapter proceeds on two levels. First, the diffusion of a new process technology (specifically computer numerically controlled machine tools) across firms in the engineering sector in the United Kingdom is explored. Second, the diffusion of a new product technology (specifically colour television) across households in the United Kingdom is analysed. In both cases an attempt is first made to illustrate the state of our current knowledge relating to the diffusion of new technology and then the contribution deriving from the research undertaken in this project is detailed. This forms Sections 8.2 and 8.3 of the chapter. (The research in this project also included work on both theory and policy but we will not report upon those results here). Conclusions are detailed in Section 8.4.

In the main body of this chapter technical details are kept to a minimum. There are two technical appendices that cover this material. Throughout the main body of the chapter explicit references to the academic literature are also kept to a minimum; however, full reference to the literature can be found in Karshenas and Stoneman (1990, 1992a, 1992b) which also contain much more of the background technical material. In the technical appendices references are included. In various ways, many of the other papers in this book also relate to the diffusion phenomenon. Those by Cleary and Webb (Ch. 5), Lonie and Nixon (Ch. 12), Foley, Watts and Wilson (Ch. 6), and Cawson, Haddon and Miles (Ch. 11) are most relevant.

8.2 THE DIFFUSION OF NEW PROCESS TECHNOLOGY

There is a growing body of theory attempting to explain the basic driving forces behind the diffusion of new process technologies. The prime purpose of the research reported upon here has been to explore which of these approaches have empirical support and which approaches do not have empirical support. There are four basic approaches to diffusion analysis in the literature:

- *The information and learning or 'epidemic' approach*. This approach argues that those firms who have not adopted a technology at a particular point in time either do not know of the technology, or are uncertain of the performance of the technology, or consider that the technology is too uncertain and thus too risky to adopt at that time. The theory also suggests that as use of the technology does extend this usage will generate information that will either extend the knowledge of the technology or reduce its uncertainty and riskiness and this will lead to further use.

- *Differences between firms or the 'rank' approach*. This approach argues that potential adopters of new technology differ from one another and at a moment in time only those firms for whom it is profitable (or more correctly most profitable) to adopt the technology at that moment in time will adopt. The non-adopters do not find it profitable to adopt. Thus a technology may have economies of scale and at a moment in time it may only be profitable for large firms to adopt it. As time proceeds, it is argued, the cost of acquiring the technology will fall and, as it does so, non-users will find it profitable to become users. It is possible to extend this analysis to allow that because the cost of the technology is falling firms may delay adoption until the price has fallen.

- *Competitive interaction or the 'stock'-based approach.* This approach argues that as firms adopt new technology, the market price for the products they produce will fall. As it does so, the benefit to be obtained from new technology will also fall. Given the cost of acquiring new technology, the non-adopters would not be able to adopt the new technology and make a profit. However, as time goes on the cost of acquisition will fall, and it then becomes profitable for more firms to adopt, and thus diffusion proceeds.

- *Pre-emption or 'order'-based approach.* This approach argues that there may be benefits from adopting first, perhaps arising from obtaining better geographic locations, better market positions, pre-empting the limited pool of skilled labour or from first-mover advantages more generally defined. Adoption is then considered to be a race, and the prize obtained depends upon one's position in the race. Given the cost of acquiring new technology, it may only be profitable for the nth ranked adopter to acquire, and thus non-adopters are the ones who are lower in the adoption order and do not find it profitable to adopt. However, as time goes on and the cost of acquisition falls, it will be profitable for the $n + 1$th or $n + 2$th to adopt, and so diffusion proceeds.

To explore the empirical validity of the four approaches outlined above the diffusion of computer numerically controlled (CNC) machine tools in the United Kingdom was investigated. We are particularly grateful to Alfred Thwaites and Neil Alderman of CURDS at the University of Newcastle upon Tyne for providing us with their data on this phenomenon. CURDS surveyed in 1981 and 1986 all identified establishments in UK manufacturing in the engineering and metal-working industries (see Thwaites *et al.* 1982). The questionnaire enquired into the date of adoption by the establishments of several different technologies of which CNC was selected for the present study. Using the data from the 1981 survey yielded observations on 1,056 establishments for which the date of adoption (if any) was known.

In Figure 8.1 some indication of the pattern of adoption that can be observed in the data is illustrated. It is worth stating that the

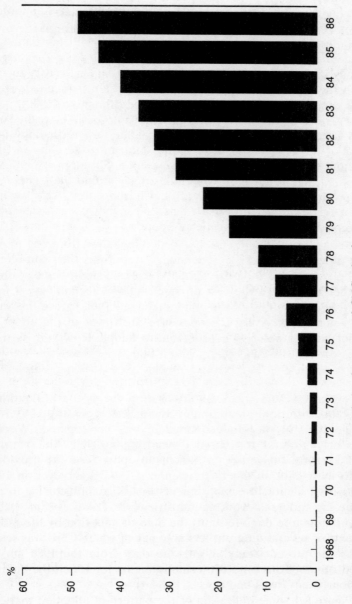

Figure 8.1 Diffusion curve: cumulative frequency of CNC adoptions

data can be looked at in a number of different ways and one can see different starting dates and speeds of adoption across industries, regions and types of firms, exactly as one would expect, although this is not shown in the figure.

The next stage was to attempt to see how far this data was consistent with the theoretical hypotheses above. The actual methods used are detailed in the Technical Appendix 8.1. In this section the procedure is paraphrased rather than detailed. Further details can also be found in Karshenas and Stoneman (1990).

If the rank approach to diffusion has some basis in reality one would expect to find that as the price of the new technology falls so use of the technology will expand, and moreover, those firms for whom the technology is most profitable will adopt it first. We argue that large firms in growing industries will find the technology most profitable, and thus these firms will adopt first. This we find to be so. The approach also predicts that if the cost of acquisition is expected to fall, this will delay adoption. We found this to be the case. Thus there is considerable support for the rank-based approach.

The stock-based approach argues that as more firms adopt, it is less profitable for other firms to adopt. Thus for a given cost of acquisition one would expect that a non-adopter is less likely to adopt if many other firms have adopted. We did not find this to be the case and thus there is little support for this approach.

The order-based approach implies that if a firm expects other firms to adopt quickly, it will try to adopt early (other things being equal), for a delay will mean it goes further down the adoption order and thus makes lower returns. We did not find, however, that (expected) fast adoption by others had this effect and thus there is little support for this view.

Finally, the epidemic approach would argue that diffusion would proceed even if prices did not fall or any other changes occurred. This we find to be the case.

Thus, overall, for the example of numerically controlled machine tools in the United Kingdom, the two main driving forces in the diffusion process are found to be differences between firms and information and learning (or rank and epidemic effects). In particular, large firms in growing industries will be early adopters, and as the cost of acquisition of the technology falls, usage will extend to smaller firms in less fast growing industries. However, even if the cost of acquisition did not fall, the process of learning would lead to more extensive use. It was also found that if the cost of acquisition is expected to fall, then this can delay adoption of technology.

8.3 THE DIFFUSION OF NEW PRODUCT TECHNOLOGY

The literature on the diffusion of new product technologies is in many ways less sophisticated than that on the diffusion of new process technologies. The dominant approach in the literature has been one related to the information and learning or epidemic approach detailed in the section on process technologies above. There has been some work built upon the heterogeneity of potential adopters (or the rank approach) but this has been limited. The game-theoretic approaches (stock- and order-based approaches), however, have not been pursued in this context and in any case are probably not relevant to consumer decisions.

The majority of the literature on product diffusion is probably located in marketing rather than in economics, and marketing has particularly concentrated on the epidemic approach. For the purposes of this section it is useful to give more detail on this approach to the analysis of diffusion. The epidemic approach likens the process of adoption of new technology to the spread of a disease.

Assume a community with a number of persons susceptible to a new infection, N, a number of already infected people S, and a constant rate of infection β (i.e. β = probability of contracting the infection after a contact is made). Under the assumption of a homogeneously mixing population, it is plausible to assume that the probability for a susceptible to meet an infected person and contract the disease in a small time interval dt is $\beta(S/N)$. In a population of $(N-S)$ susceptibles the average number of infections in a small time interval dt would therefore be:

$$dS = \beta \ \frac{S}{N} \ (N-S)dt \tag{1}$$

Integrating this equation gives a simple deterministic logistic curve for the spread of the epidemic as a single-valued function of time. The empirical results of fitting the logistic or epidemic-type models to data on product diffusion have not been entirely satisfactory. The following problems have been observed in the empirical case studies. First, the fit of the model varies from one case to another. While a particular curve fits the data for certain new products adequately, it performs poorly with respect to others.

Further, it is often noted that different growth curves with different properties and divergent forecasts fit a particular set of data equally well. Second, the parameter estimates often show wrong sign or magnitude compared to what theory would suggest. Third, forecasting performance varies widely across different products, and sometimes the calculation of the forecast error is too complicated and not reported. As has been pointed out in a series of recent papers, some of these problems arise from the stochastic specification of the models and the estimation methods used, but our approach is to look again at the basic theory underlying the epidemic story.

The following assumptions are made in the above derivation of the simple logistic growth curve: (1) infection spreads through contact between the members of the community, and it is not sufficiently serious for cases to be withdrawn from circulation by isolation or death, (2) each infected individual has the same chance of coming into contact with a susceptible member of the community independently of the age of his infection or his location and (3) no case becomes clear of infection during the course of the epidemic. These assumptions are additional to the assumption that β is the same for different individuals, that is individuals are equally susceptible to the infection once a contact is made.

The analogy often made between the spread of epidemics and the diffusion of a new technology or product is either based on the learning processes involved in the use of new technology and its transmission through human contact, with the 'infection' being information, or based on pressures of social emulation and competition.

In a most important contribution Bass (1969) partially modifies the assumption that the diffusion process takes place as an endogenous learning process within a homogeneous population. Bass distinguishes between two homogeneous groups: the innovators, who are not subject to social emulation or endogenous learning, and the imitators, for whom the diffusion process mainly takes the epidemic form discussed above. This gives rise to a positively skewed logistic curve which has become influential in the marketing literature. Different interpretations of the Bass model have appeared in this literature. For example, one may attribute the exogenous part of the Bass model to promotional advertising, and the endogenous part to 'word of mouth'. However, it has been argued that the model originally formulated by Bass does not abandon the assumption of a homogeneous population as is commonly maintained in the literature that followed it, but rather, it distinguishes between the endogenous and exogenous influences at work in the process of adoption in a homogeneous population. This has led to the setting-up of a logistic model which explicitly distinguishes between the innovators and imitators in the population. It is interesting to note that, in empirical studies, either based on the Bass model or on its reformulation, the exogenous factor turns out to play an insignificant role in the diffusion process. In our view this may result from the *a priori* assumption of a dominant endogenous growth factor in these models; in the interaction between the endogenous and exogenous factors it is the endogenous element which in the long run would have the dominant influence.

To explore this further, in our research we constructed a new model. To illustrate the basis of this, consider the standard logistic model as separating the acquisition decision into two parts. The first is that information spreading or the pressures of social emulation generate a 'desire to acquire', and second is that some proportion of this is converted to actual acquisition decisions through β, the probability of acquisition (contracting the infection) once the 'desire to acquire' (contact) has been established. In the new model proposed here two basic changes to the standard model are made.

First we allow for β to be a function of economic variables rather than being taken as a fixed parameter. As the empirical study below refers to a consumer durable, colour televisions, we consider β to be a function of disposable income (YD), the price of colour televisions (P) and credit conditions (CRED). In addition our model differs from much of the other empirical work on diffusion in that we incorporate economic factors directly into the model rather than using a two-stage procedure and as a result allow β to vary *over time* as a result of variations in income, the price of colour televisions and credit conditions.

The second modification to the standard epidemic model that we introduce is to respecify the nature of the learning or emulation process. The respecification allows for the standard logistic as a special case. The reason for doing this is that, as we noted above, a major weakness of the standard epidemic, logistic or Bass type models is that they, *a priori*, assume that endogenous factors throughout the diffusion process remain dominant in the learning or emulation process. It is more plausible, however, to set up a more general model which could test this proposition (even though it may after all turn out to be correct under certain circumstances). This objective is met by the new model through dropping some of the restrictive assumptions of the simple epidemic model.

One assumption which has an important bearing on the behaviour of the simple epidemic model, and does not seem to be plausible in the case of the diffusion of new products, is that of a homogeneously mixing population. It is more reasonable to assume that each individual has contact with only a limited number of individuals in the society, and therefore his or her direct influence in terms of social emulation and/or learning gradually wears off as his or her immediate contacts adopt the new product. In addition, with the existence of exogenous sources of information and learning, one would also expect the effect of endogenous learning through personal contact to gradually wear off as the news about the existence and the qualities of the new product become common knowledge.

The new model was tested on data on the spread of colour television ownership in the United Kingdom. The details and the results are added as Technical Appendix 8.2. The results were encouraging and certainly superior to other types of epidemic models used in the literature with which we made comparison. Our results indicate that endogenous forces only played a small role in the diffusion of colour televisions and the exogenous forces played a much larger role. This contrasts completely with the basic assumptions of the simple epidemic and Bass models. In addition, we found that the model gave parameter estimates that reflected theoretical predictions. In all therefore our findings confirmed the superiority of the new model.

8.4 CONCLUSIONS

The research that we have reported on above largely concerns the development and testing of models that purport to explain the forces that drive the diffusion phenomenon. In the text we have illustrated that our study of process technologies has thrown considerable doubt on the validity of game theoretic based diffusion models, although the rank effect and epidemic based models do capture some of the essence of the diffusion process. In the study of colour televisions we have illustrated that the epidemic-type models are useful but considerable modifications to the simple models are required if they are to be very useful in explaining real-world diffusion phenomena.

Given our approach and our results it would seem to be important to explain why it matters as to which theoretical approach is relevant and which is not. There is, of course, the academic argument that understanding is important in its own right, but some further justification can be provided. One justification is that for the purposes of government policy such insights are crucial. Take for example the case of a new process technology. If information spreading is the driving force behind the diffusion of new technology then a government policy to stimulate information spreading would be desirable, practical and effective in increasing the use of new technology. If the other theories were right, however, then such a policy would neither be necessary nor work. If the other explanations hold, then they basically say that the firms that have not at a moment in time adopted a new technology have not done so because it is not profitable for them to adopt. If one has a belief in the operation of markets this would lead one to conclude that a government policy to speed up the use of technology is not desirable or necessary unless there is some market failure in the system. If there were such a failure then some subsidy policy might be necessary or some policy to release constraints on scarce resources might be desirable. This is not the place to go into the full implications of this work for government policy, but this should make clear that a major benefit of this sort of work is the spin-off in terms of designing policies.

The second rationale for undertaking this type of work is that what is basically being undertaken is a study of the intertemporal demand for a new product or process. This implies that one spin-off from this work could be a greater understanding for firms as to how the market for their new products will develop over time – that is, there is a positive benefit from this type of work for the forecasting of future product demand. A follow-on from this would be some insight into how firms' intertemporal pricing and advertising policy may be optimized in the face of the pattern of intertemporal demand. Thus what may at first sight to be a matter of pure or curiosity driven research does have quite explicit practical uses.

TECHNICAL APPENDIX 8.1: THE DIFFUSION OF A NEW PROCESS

Consider a new technology that a firm can acquire by purchase of a new capital good. Define $h_{ij}(t)$ as the hazard rate for firm i in industry j in time t, i.e. the probability that firm i in industry j will adopt the new technology in time t given that it had not already adopted by time $t-1$.

In Karshenas and Stoneman (1990), a theoretical model is constructed that enables us to write (dropping j subscripts) that

$$h_i(t) = h_0(t).J(r(t)P(t),\ K(t),\ C_i,\ p(t),\ (a_0 + a_1C_i + a_2K(t))\frac{k(t)}{r(t)} \quad (A1.1)$$

Where $h_0(t)$ = baseline hazard
$r(t)$ = interest rate
$P(t)$ = price of the new capital good in time t
$K(t)$ = number of adopters in industry j at time t
C_i = vector of firm characteristics
$p(t) = P(t + 1) - P(t)$
$k(t) = K(t + 1) - K(t)$

Equation (A1.1) is written more succinctly as (A1.2)

$$h(t,X|\beta) = h_0(t)\ \exp\{X'\beta\} \quad (A1.2)$$

where X incorporates $rP(t)$, $K(t)$, C_i, $p(t)$, $k(t)$, and cross product terms.

In the section below we proceed to estimate equation (A1.2). The following restrictions on the coefficients of the model are suggested by the theory. The coefficient, including cross product terms, on $k(t)$ is indicative of the order effect. In the presence of an order effect this coefficient should be significantly greater than zero. The coefficient on $K(t)$ reflects both the stock and order effects. If both exist then the coefficient on $K(t)$ should be significantly less than zero. The coefficients on the elements of C_i are indicative of the rank effect, and in the presence of such an effect the coefficients should be significantly different from zero. The baseline hazard reflects epidemic forces and in the presence of epidemic effects the baseline hazard should show a positive duration dependence.

We thus consider that (1) if the coefficient on $k(t)$ is significantly greater than zero and the coefficient on $K(t)$ is significantly less than zero then the hypothesis that there are both stock and order effects cannot be rejected, (2) if the coefficient on $k(t)$ is not significantly greater than zero, but the coefficient on $K(t)$ is significantly less than zero then the hypothesis of there being an order effect can be rejected, but the hypothesis that there is a stock effect cannot be rejected and (3) if the coefficient on $k(t)$ is significantly greater than zero, but the coefficient on $K(t)$ is not significantly less than zero, then the hypothesis of there being a stock effect cannot be accepted, but the hypothesis that there is an order effect cannot be rejected. We view this latter situation as providing weak support for the order hypothesis. In addition, if the baseline hazard shows a positive time dependence then the hypothesis of an epidemic effect cannot be rejected; if the expectation terms $p(t)$ and $k(t)$ carry significant positive coefficients then the hypothesis that acquisition decisions are not myopic cannot be rejected; and finally, if the elements of C_i carry significant coefficients then the hypothesis of rank effects cannot be rejected.

The variables included in the rank effect have thus far been implicitly referred to as the vector C_i. We need to be more specific about these variables at this stage prior to moving to estimation. There are of course numerous firm-specific factors influencing the adoption decision, some of which may not be even observable or quantifiable. The factors which will be considered below are those which in the literature are believed to exert a systematic influence on the adoption decision – the unsystematic random factors being absorbed in the residual, that is, the base line hazard.

Our data set is on the basis of establishments and we treat each establishment as an individual firm. The factors related to the rank effect which we have been able to include in the model are the following:

- Size of the Firm (SIZE)
- Growth of Output (GY)
- Date of Establishment (EDATE)
- Research and Development Expenditure (R & D)
- Corporate Status of the Establishment (STATUS)
- Concentration Ration (CRATIO)

Estimation and results

One may estimate the model as specified assuming a non-parametric baseline hazard. However, since we are interested in testing the time dependence of the baseline hazard and also as the computational costs of estimating the non-parametric model was found to be prohibitive, we decided that it was more appropriate to estimate a parametric version of the model. Time dependence of the baseline hazard was first tested by estimating a proportional hazard model assuming a Weibull distribution of adoption time, which takes the form:

$$h(t;X(t),\beta,\alpha) = \alpha t^{(\alpha-1)} \exp\{\beta_0 + X'(t)\beta\} \qquad (A1.3)$$

where the time subscript on X is indicative of the fact that some of our explanatory variables are time dependent. With $\alpha = 1$ this model is transformed to a model with constant hazard, that is one with exponential distribution of adoption time. With $\alpha > 1$ the model suggests positive duration dependence of adoption time which as we discussed above is indicative of the existence of epidemic effects.

Various elements of the vector $X(t)$, such as adoption precedence variables K_t and k_t, ouput growth and concentration ratio, are industry specific. It is plausible to assume that the epidemic effects as captured by the baseline hazard would also be industry specific. Even if there is *a priori* reason to suggest the contrary, still it is desirable to be able to test this proposition in a general model with industry-specific epidemic effects. We therefore estimate the following more general Weibull model with industry-specific baseline hazard:

$$h_j(t;X(t),\beta,\alpha_j) = \alpha_j t^{(\alpha_j-1)} \exp\{\beta_{0j} + X'(t)\beta\} \qquad (A1.4)$$

where subscript j indicates industrial specificity of the baseline hazard or epidemic effects. Clearly the model with homogeneous baseline hazard is a special case of this model with $\alpha_j = \alpha_k$ and $\beta_{0j} = \beta_{0k}$ for all j and k.

The maximum likelihood estimates of the parameters of the Exponential and Weibull models with industry-specific baseline hazards are shown in Table 8.4 in which time-dependent variables carry a t subscript. Since one of the aims of the model is to test the importance of epidemic effects, in estimating the model we dropped adopters in the first period in each industry from the sample which reduced the sample size from 1,056 to 1,041. As can be seen the likelihood ratio test for industry-specific baseline hazard rejects the hypothesis of aggregate epidemic effects in favour of industry

Table 8.4 Maximum likelihood estimates of the Exponential and Weibull models

Coefficient	Variable	Exponential model	Weibull model	
α_1	TIME	—	1.8443	(0.6086)
α_2	TIME	—	1.0274	(0.7049)
α_3	TIME	—	1.6791	(0.6210)
α_4	TIME	—	2.8534	(0.6612)†
α_5	TIME	—	2.1120	(0.7682)
α_6	TIME	—	2.1174	(0.5765)*
α_7	TIME	—	3.7242	(2.2146)
α_8	TIME	—	3.3413	(0.8347)†
α_9	TIME	—	1.8581	(0.4745)†

β_{01}	CONSTANT	-4.5205	(1.0719)†	-5.1788	(1.4948)†
β_{02}	CONSTANT	-5.1291	(1.1092)†	-3.8722	(1.5439)*
β_{03}	CONSTANT	-3.1888	(1.0461)†	-3.3933	(1.2256)†
β_{04}	CONSTANT	-4.3820	(1.0931)†	-6.0950	(1.4714)†
β_{05}	CONSTANT	-3.7481	(1.0962)†	-5.1931	(1.8167)†
β_{06}	CONSTANT	-7.8031	(1.3428)†	-8.8598	(1.4446)†
β_{07}	CONSTANT	-2.7395	(1.0612)†	-7.7088	(4.5282)
β_{08}	CONSTANT	-2.9994	(1.0524)†	-4.7861	(1.4895)†
β_{09}	CONSTANT	-3.3459	(1.2935)†	-4.3003	(1.5332)†
β_1	K_t	0.2053	(0.0208)†	0.1793	(0.0286)†
β_2	K_t/r_t	0.7030	(0.1602)†	0.6204	(0.1922)†
β_3	SIZE	0.0620	(0.0198)†	0.0637	(0.0244)†
β_4	GY_t	0.3233	(0.0843)†	0.3433	(0.0832)†
β_5	r_tP_t	-0.0092	(0.0037)*	-0.0099	(0.0049)†
β_6	ρ_t	0.0306	(0.0150)*	0.0324	(0.0144)†
β_7	R&D	-0.0003	(0.0054)	-0.0013	(0.0059)
β_8	EDATE	-0.0071	(0.0082)	-0.0055	(0.0084)
β_9	STATUS	0.5475	(0.4874)	0.5849	(0.5043)
β_{10}	CRATIO	0.0105	(0.0178)	0.0088	(0.0177)

Cross Product Terms

β_{11}	$K_t . [k_t/r_t]$	-0.1998	(0.0562)†	-0.1954	(0.0476)†
β_{12}	SIZE . $[k_t/r_t]$	0.0010	(0.0562)	-0.0094	(0.0614)
β_{13}	$GY_t . [k_t/r_t]$	0.8025	(0.2356)†	0.7538	(0.2420)†
β_{14}	R & D . $[k_t/r_t]$	-0.0051	(0.0142)	-0.0031	(0.0147)
β_{15}	EDATE . $[k_t/r_t]$	0.0077	(0.0156)	0.0078	(0.0156)
β_{16}	STATUS . $[k_t/r_t]$	-0.5543	(0.9668)	-0.6043	(0.9584)
β_{17}	CRATIO . $[k_t/r_t]$	-0.0060	(0.0302)	-0.0034	(0.0322)

Log likelihood	-631.1	-613.7
No. of Observations	1,041	1,041

Likelihood ratio test for industry-specific baseline hazard: ($\alpha_1 = \alpha_2 = \alpha_3 \ldots = \alpha_9$ & $\beta_{01} = \beta_{02} = \beta_{03} \ldots = \beta_{09}$)	153.2 $(\chi^2_{.99}(8)=20.1)$	179.6 $(\chi^2_{.99}(16)=32.0)$

Likelihood ratio test for the significance of epidemic effects: ($\alpha_1 = \alpha_2 = \alpha_3 \ldots = \alpha_9 = 1$) 34.8 $(\chi^2_{.99}(9)=21.7)$

Likelihood ratio test for the existence of order effects: ($\beta_2 = \beta_{11} = \beta_{12} = \beta_{13} = \beta_{14} = \beta_{15} = \beta_{16} = \beta_{17} = 0$)	180.0 $(\chi^2_{.99}(8)=20.1)$	89.4 $(\chi^2_{.99}(8)=20.1)$

Figures in parentheses refer to the asymptotic standard error of coefficient estimates.
* Significant at the 0.05 level (in the case of α's significantly greater than 1 at the 0.05 level).
† Significant at the 0.01 level (in the case of α's significantly greater than 1 at the 0.01 level).

specific epidemic effects. We shall therefore discuss the results only for the heterogeneous or industry-specific baseline hazard case.

The parameter vector β remains stable in moving from the Exponential to the Weibull model, though the likelihood ratio test for the significance of epidemic effects rejects the Exponential model in favour of the Weibull model. The coefficient α_j in the Weibull model is significantly greater than one in the case of four industries, suggesting positive duration dependence of adoption probabilities. This, however, does not necessarily imply that the remaining five industries do not exhibit epidemic effects in technology diffusion. As we shall see below, epidemic effects in the case of the latter industries seem to have been captured by a positive stock effect.

A notable aspect of the results is that the coefficient on K_t though statistically significant has the opposite sign to that predicted by the game-theoretic order and stock-effects models. This does not, however, necessarily indicate the absence of stock effects in diffusion. It is in fact difficult to empirically distinguish between the negative effect of adoption precedence assumed by game-theoretic models and its positive epidemic effects. By allowing a time-varying baseline hazard to capture some of the epidemic effects we attempted to make the negative stock effects empirically more visible. However, the evidence suggests that even if such negative stock effects exist they are by far outweighed by the positive effects of adoption precedence as suggested by epidemic theories.

Order effects are primarily reflected in the coefficient of k_t inclusive of the interaction terms. As the likelihood ratio test for the existence of order effects shows, there is evidence of significant influence of k_t on the diffusion process. It should be noted that with the inclusion of the interaction terms the sign of the order effect coefficient varies between establishments and over time. Evaluated for the Weibull model, and at values prevailing at the adoption time/censoring time for the time varying covariates, this coefficient turned out to be negative in the case of 1,037 out of 1,041 total number of establishments, with a mean value of -5.65. In other words, as in the case of stock effect, the order effect coefficient seems to be significant but with the wrong sign.

Size of establishment which has traditionally played an important role in the probit type or rank-oriented models has a significant and positive effect on the adoption probability, in conformity with the *a priori* predictions of theory and with other empirical studies. As can be seen the date of establishment has no significant effect on adoption probability, implying that, allowing for all other firm characteristics, new firms do not appear to have a higher adoption probability than old firms. Output growth, on the other hand has a positive and significant coefficient, suggesting that periods of market expansion correspond to faster rates of adoption of new technology.

The coefficient of the technology price variable is also significant and has the correct sign. The highly significant and positive coefficient of the expected change in price variable (p_t), which is also in conformity with the predictions of theory, suggests that the myopic type models, as used, for example, by Hannan and McDowell (1984), may be seriously misspecified.

As can be seen from the table, the other establishment-specific characteristics, R & D and corporate STATUS, do not seem to exert a significant influence on the speed of adoption, nor does concentration.

In terms of the rank, stock, order, and epidemic effects it appears that the pattern of CNC adoption in the United Kingdom indicates the existence of rank and epidemic effects, but provides little support for the stock and order effects suggested by the game-theoretic models.

TECHNICAL APPENDIX 8.2: THE DIFFUSION OF A NEW PRODUCT TECHNOLOGY

To pursue the ideas detailed in the text we distinguish at each point of time between three subsets of the total population (or total maximum adopters) N in the following way: the number of owners of the new product at time t who continue to be instrumental in social emulation or learning (X); the number of owners at time t who no longer contribute to the diffusion of the new product (Y); and the number of non-adopters who are 'susceptible' at time $t(Z)$, such that $N = X + Y + Z$. As before we define $S = X + Y$ as the total number of owners at time t. The non-homogenous mixing is catered for by assuming that only X and not S influences learning and emulation. In addition, we allow for exogenous factors to influence learning and emulation by incorporating an external growth factor q in the learning or emulation process. Specifically we have that:

$$\frac{dS}{dt} = \beta(q + X/N)Z = \beta(Nq + S - Y)(N - S)/N \qquad (A2.1)$$

To complete the model we specify that the number of 'influential owners' X will 'depreciate' over time according to (A2.2)

$$\frac{dY}{dt} = \alpha X = \alpha(S - Y) \tag{A2.2}$$

where α is the coefficient of decay of the 'active' adopters. Equations (A2.1) and (A2.2) may be manipulated to yield

$$\Delta S_t = \beta[Nq + S_{t-1} - a \sum_{i=0}^{t-1} (1 - \alpha)^i S_{t-i-1})](N - S_{t-1})/N \tag{A2.2}$$

This is a general distributed lag model which reproduces the simple logistic model with $\alpha = 0$ and $q = 0$, the Bass model with $\alpha = 0$ and $q > 0$, and a degenerate diffusion case with $q = 0$ and $a \geqslant \beta$. It is thus an encompassing model which allows for the testing of those restrictions which are in the existing literature usually imposed on diffusion models on *a priori* grounds.

For the purposes of estimation the following equation is used:

$$\Delta S_t = \beta_t[q + S_{t-1} - Y_{t-1}(\alpha)](1 - S_{t-1}) \tag{A2.3}$$

$$\text{where } Y_{t-1}(\alpha) \equiv \alpha \sum_{i=0}^{t-1} (1 - \alpha)^i S_{t-i-1}$$

where the ownership level S is shown as a ratio of saturation level N which is taken as fixed in this formulation. In the empirical model only the β parameter is considered to be a variable function of economic variables, while both q and the saturation-level parameters are fixed.

For television ownership, the study below, we have assumed the saturation level to be equal to the total number of households in each period, which seems plausible given that in the early 1980s more that 80 per cent of households owned colour televisions. We nevertheless consider the sensitivity of the model to the assumed saturation level by allowing it to equal a fraction Θ of the number of households and then varying the value of Θ in the following version of equation (A2.3) by increments between 0.8 and 1.0:

$$\Delta S_t = \beta_t[\Theta q + S_{t-1} - Y_{t-1}(\alpha)](\Theta - S_{t-1})/\Theta \tag{A2.4}$$

where the ownership level S_t is shown as a proportion of total number of households and Θ is the ratio of saturation level to the number of households.

To take care of the possibility that the variance of S_t changes as the saturation level is approached, we propose to estimate the following transformation of the model:

$$(\Theta \Delta S_t/(\Theta - S_{t-1})) = \beta_t(\Theta q + S_{t-1} - Y_{t-1})(\alpha)) + u_t \quad (A2.5)$$

where u_t is assumed to be an iid($0, o^2$) error term.

The model was applied to the date for colour television ownership in the United Kingdom over the 1968–86 period. Quarterly figures for colour television ownership were collected on the basis of monthly licence figures published in the *Monthly Digest of Statistics*. To overcome seasonality we have estimated the model in four-quarter lag difference, using a four-quarter moving average transformation of the quarterly stock data. Denoting the original data series by K_t, we applied the following linear filter, $S_t = (1/4)(1 + L + L^2 = L^3)K_t$ which gives $\Delta S_t = \Delta^4 K_t$. The model was estimated in terms of ΔS_t and S_t. The economic variables included in the model as determinants of β were, the retail price of colour television (P) (deflated by the general retail price index), real personal disposable income (YD), and a proxy for credit conditions (CRED). The quarterly price variable was lagged four periods to safeguard against possible simultaneity bias arising from the interaction between demand and price. The income variable was also lagged one period. The hire purchase deposit was taken as a proxy for the credit conditions variable (the other relevant variable, that is, the maximum repayment period, is highly correlated with the hire purchase deposit and hence is not included). The credit variable is meant to reflect the effects of liquidity constraints on consumer demand.

The model was estimated both in the form shown in equation (A2.5) with $\Theta = 1$, and in log transform form. As the latter showed slightly better results we report here only the results from the log-transformed model. Incorporating the relevant economic variables in the β coefficient (assuming constant elasticities):

$$\beta_t = a_0 P_{t-4}^{\alpha_1} YD_{t-1}^{\alpha_2}.CRED_t^{\alpha_3}$$

and taking logs from both sides of equation (A2.5) gives equation (A2.6) which is the final form used for estimation:

$$LS_t = a_0 + a_1 P_{t-4} + a_2 YD_{t-1} + a_3 CRED_t$$
$$+ Log(q + W_{t-1}(\alpha)) + u_t \quad (A2.6)$$

where for brevity Log $(\Delta S_t/(1 - S_{t-1}))$ is denoted by LS_t and

$(S_{t-1} - Y_{t-1}(\alpha))$ by $W_{t-1}(\alpha)$. On theoretical grounds we expect the following coefficient signs: $a_1 \geqslant 0$, $a_2 \geqslant 0$, $a_3 \geqslant 0$, and $q \geqslant 0$.

The above equation was estimated by Non-linear Least Squares (NLS), which, adding the assumption of normality of the error term replicates the results from Maximum Likelihood estimation. Though the data series start from 1968 Q1, the equation was estimated for a sample of sixty-seven quarterly observations, from 1970 Q1 to 1986 Q3. The starting point of 1970 Q1 was chosen because colour transmissions up to the fourth quarter of 1969 were confined to BBC 2, and in any case the licence figures for those early years may not accurately reflect colour TV ownership. A grid seach was conducted for the value of α which minimized the standard error of regression (or assuming normality of errors maximized the likelihood function), and $\alpha = 1.2$ was chosen as the optimum value. The estimated equation for the value of $\alpha = 1.2$ was:

$$LS_t = 4.17 - 0.801P_{t-4} + 0.981YD_{t-1} - 0.359CRED_t$$
$$\quad\;\, (5.10) \quad (-8.16) \quad\;\;\; (1.86) \quad\quad\quad (-2.18)$$

$$+ \; Log(0.0011 + W_{t-1}(1.2)) \quad\quad\quad\quad\quad\quad\quad (A2.7)$$
$$\quad\;\; (4.18)$$

$$T = 67, \quad R^2 = 0.937, \quad \sigma' = 0.1540, \quad LL = 32.8,$$

$$F,AR1 = 1.58, \; F,AR4 = 1.45, \; F,Hetr = 0.089, \; Z1 = 0.933$$
$$\quad\;\; [4.0] \quad\quad\quad\;\; [2.35] \quad\quad\quad\quad [4.0] \quad\quad\quad [5.99]$$

The asymptotic t ratios of the coefficient estimates are given in brackets. As can be seen, all of the coefficients have the correct sign and they are all statistically significant at the 5 per cent significance level. In addition, a number of other test statistics are provided for testing the overall goodness of fit and the adequacy of the underlying error assumptions of the model. R^2 is the multiple correlation coefficient adjusted for the degrees of freedom, σ' is the asymptotic standard error of regression, and LL is the maximized value of log likelihood function. F,AR1 and F,AR4 are the asymptotic F test statistics for first order and joint first to fourth order serial correlation of residuals.

One of the interesting results of the above estimate is the relatively high value of α, 1.2. This implies that the epidemic or endogenous growth factor was not very important in the diffusion process. This is a perfectly plausible result in the case of colour television ownership, for by 1968 the majority of the households already owned monochrome TV sets and were familiar with the qualities of the new product in terms of TV programmes and so on. Furthermore, colour television transmission in the United Kingdom had a relatively late arrival – by 1968 colour TV ownership was already widespread in the United States. It seems natural therefore that the endogenous learning processes through the epidemic mechanisms would play only a small role in the diffusion of colour television (one may note that Horsky 1990 has a similar finding).

We next proceeded to test the appropriateness of the assumption that the ultimate saturation level was the total number of households. For this purpose we replaced the dependent variable by the new variable $Log(\Theta S_t/\Theta - S_{t-1}))$ and after transferring $Log(\Theta/(\Theta - S_{t-1}))$ to the right-hand side of the equation, estimated the parameter Θ together with other parameters by NLS. The estimated value of Θ was 0.9 which was significantly different from 1.0. To test the sensitivity of this result to the assumption of $\alpha = 1.2$ we conducted a new grid search for the value of α. The outcome was that the values of $\alpha = 1.2$ and $\Theta = 0.9$ were optimum. Since it was found that the parameter estimates of the model do not significantly change by setting $\Theta = 0.9$, and as the maximum LL values were relatively close, it was decided that the value of $\Theta = 1.0$ was appropriate. A more thorough estimation procedure, of course, may require modelling of the saturation level in terms of economic variables.

Equation (A2.6) was re-estimated over the 1970–80, 1970–82, 1970–83, and 1970–84 sub-periods by NLS in order to test the structural stability and predictive power of the model. The coefficient estimates remain fairly stable over the different sample periods. The Chow tests for structural stability do not reject the hypothesis of structural stability for any of the sample periods.

REFERENCES

Bass, F. (1969) 'A new product growth model for consumer durables', *Management Science* 15, 215–27.

Cohen, W. M. and Levinthal, D. A. (1989) 'Innovation and learning: the two faces of R & D', *The Economic Journal* 99, 569–96.

Cox, D. R. (1972) 'Regression models and life tables' (with discussion), *Journal of the Royal Statistical Society*, Series B, 34, 187–220.

Davies, S. (1979) *The Diffusion of Process Innovations*, Cambridge University Press.

Edquist, C. and Jacobsson, S. (1988) *Flexible Automation: The Global Diffusion of New Technology in the Engineering Industry*, Blackwell: Oxford.

Hannan, T. H. and McDowell, J. M. (1984) 'The determinants of technology adoption: the case of the banking firm', *RAND Journal of Economics* 15(3), 328–35.

Karshenas, M. and Stoneman, P. (1990) 'Rank, stock, order and epidemic effects in the diffusion of new process technologies: an empirical model', Warwick Economic Research Papers, no. 356, June, University of Warwick.

—— and —— (1992a) 'A flexible model of technological diffusion incorporating economic factors with an application to the spread of colour television ownership in the UK', *Journal of Forecasting*, 11(7): 577–602.

—— and —— (1992b) 'The empirics of technological diffusion', in P. Stoneman (ed.) *The Handbook of the Economics of Innovation and Technological Change*, Oxford: Blackwell.

Mansfield, E. (1989) 'Industrial robots in Japan and the USA', *Research Policy* 18: 183–92.

Nabseth, L. and Ray, G. F. (1974) *The Diffusion of New Industrial Processes: An International Study*, Cambridge University Press.

Quirmbach, H. C. (1986) 'The diffusion of new technology and the market for an innovation', *RAND Journal of Economics* 17(1): 33–47.

Reinganum, J. F. (1981) 'Market structure and the diffusion of new technology', *Bell Journal of Economics* 12: 618–24.

Thwaites, A. T., Gibbs, D. C. and Edwards, A. (1982) 'Inter-regional diffusion of production innovations in Great Britain', Final Report to the DTI and EC, CURDS, University of Newcastle upon Tyne.

9 Product marketing and sales in high-technology small firms

Ray P. Oakey, Sarah Y. Cooper and Janet Biggar

9.1 BACKGROUND TO THE COMPLETED RESEARCH

This research into marketing in high-technology small firms was stimulated by the conclusions of other work into these types of enterprises, performed over the past ten years. In particular, in assessing the policy implications of previous pieces of analytical work (Oakey 1984, Oakey *et al.* 1988), consideration repeatedly focused on *how* the performance of existing high-technology small firms might be improved. It was frequently noted that overall growth in these firms was not impressive, either at the aggregate level or through the emergence of *individual* small firms that experience rapid growth (Oakey and Rothwell 1986, Oakey 1991). The experiences of Acorn Computers and Inmos have shown that independence is often sacrificed for investment cash to ensure survival (Fleck and Garnsey 1987), partly caused by the short-term attitude of many British investment institutions towards capital invested in manufacturing enterprises. Thus, high-technology small firms that might have grown to be the 'flag ship' enterprises of high-technology sectors in Britain, frequently become branches of foreign multi-national firms. It would appear that any policy prescriptions directed at improving growth performance beyond the currently observed level should address themselves to the root cause of this indifferent performance.

A possible cause of the unimpressive growth noted in high-technology small firms in the above studies can be generally attributed to a high level of management *introspection*, also noted by other research into high technology small firms (Rothwell and Zegveld 1982). This inward-looking attitude to innovation and growth emphasizes the reduction of any risks associated with the different stages of the innovation process (discussed in Section 9.2 below).

Examples of such introspection include, for example, the infrequent use of substantial technical links with external research collaborators, rendering the establishment of licensing or joint-venture arrangements very rare events. In addition, while a consistently noted low level of external investment capital involvement must partly result from high interest rates over the past ten years, the high level of reliance on internal profits as a major source of investment is also caused by a strong aversion to any external involvement with lending institutions (see Lonie and Nixon, Ch. 12 of this volume). Finally, while there are many other minor examples of introspection, perhaps the most damaging act of introversion is the frequent *total* abandonment of marketing in favour of a satisficing reliance on unsolicited orders (for evidence of all these features, see Oakey *et al.* 1988).

In view of this evidence of introspection, and the need to improve the overall performance of high-technology small firms, the fundamental objective of this research was to test the assertion that a more *proactive* approach by agencies offering external assistance would improve the performance of introspective enterprises. The rationale for a more proactive approach was based on the observation that *both* the assistance providing agencies and the potential high-technology small firm recipients of aid, were fundamentally reactive in nature. Even the currently professionally advertised Department of Trade and Industry 'Enterprise Initiative' remains reactive in that it mainly depends for success on introspective firms *coming forward* to access assistance of unknown value. The proactive approach is based on the principle that, if an agency is serious about the problem in question, and the solutions it offers, then assistance should be *delivered* into the high-technology small firm by individuals acting as *active* providers of the assistance packages on offer. While it might seem perverse to 'promote' free advice and assistance, it could also be argued that the future growth and prosperity of Britain's high-technology industry cannot be entrusted to risk-averse businessmen, who are also frequently *prevented* from accessing assistance because they are over-burdened by the day-to-day running of small firms.

However, the advocation of a more proactive approach to the delivery of policy to small firms may be criticized on (at least) two major grounds. First, it has been argued that the managers of small firms would view the offer of a more proactive service as an unwanted intrusion that consequently would be resisted. Second, others have argued that such a labour-intensive form of assistance would be prohibitively expensive, in which the benefits achieved through proaction would be massively outweighed by the costs. Without evidence to the contrary, advocates of a more proactive system have found these assertions difficult to refute. Thus research was initiated to test the hypothesis that a more proactive approach would be both achievable, *and* of good cost-benefit. Moreover, the frequent contact with industrialists implicit in such a 'hands on' approach to policy delivery provided an ideal opportunity for the performance of a more conventional academic study into the practice of marketing in high-technology small firms. Marketing was chosen as a primary focus for study because previous research had indicated that this was an area frequently neglected by high-technology small firms, suggesting that there was clear scope for improvement (Oakey *et al.* 1988). Further, marketing was considered a valid topic of study for research concerned with the problems of innovation and growth in high-technology small firms, since marketing is a final integral part of the total innovation process.

9.2 INNOVATION AND MARKETING IN HIGH-TECHNOLOGY SMALL FIRMS

Before proceeding with a description of the methodological and analytical approaches of this completed research, it is of contextual value to elaborate slightly on the relationship between marketing and innovation, since its position as a final act in the product innovation process, and special features that are specific to marketing, render this activity a likely candidate to be starved of resources. Figure 9.1 offers a visual depiction of a *total* product life-cycle in which marketing costs are incorporated into a simplified model of costs and revenues concerning a product innovation. The model highlights the point when active marketing is required as often being concurrent with the stage at which the firm is under *maximum* financial stress, at the end of a period of R & D for which no return from sales has yet been obtained. Thus, while many aggressive product-based high-technology small firms may in principle accept the value of a strong marketing input as part of their total innovation effort, lack of capital at the end of the innovation process may well ensure that marketing is either inadequately performed or totally neglected.

The above assertions do not imply that there are no special skills associated with marketing. A major problem for many small firms

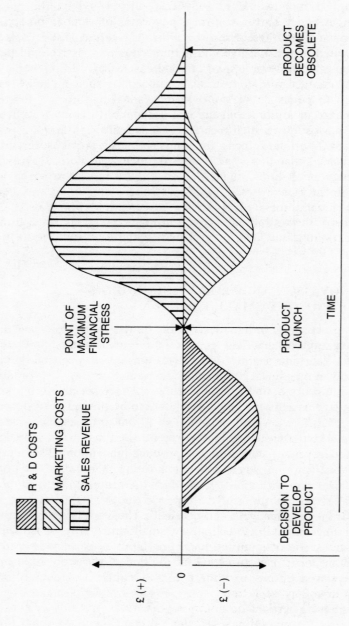

Figure 9.1 A complete product life-cycle model

is that technical entrepreneurs may well attempt, through a rapid 'changing of hats' to fill the role of chief researcher, production engineer, salesman and accountant, at relevant points in the product development cycle. While the strength of this approach is that a number of jobs are performed for the cost of one salary, the practice is often a suboptimal situation in which all four roles are performed poorly, due to lack of specialist skills and time. In view of its late stage in the product cycle, marketing is often the part of the process to suffer most from this over-ambitious allocation of meagre resources. Most established high-technology small firms would benefit from a small full-time marketing department, in order both to use specialist skills to increase sales, *and* to provide technical intelligence feedback to the R & D department on the performance of existing products, and on the future needs of customers. The key contextual point in considering Figure 9.1 is that the incorporation of marketing into the product life-cycle is not intended to imply that the specialist skills at various points in the process are irrelevant. Rather, Figure 9.1 suggests that *all* these skills must be effectively employed in sequence if *optimal* benefit is to be achieved from a cycle of innovation. In this sense the strength of the innovation 'chain' is dependent upon its weakest link, which often tends to be marketing.

A final reason why marketing might be omitted from the total innovation cycle is that, unlike R & D and production, marketing is not an *essential* prerequisite of the innovation process. While new products cannot emerge without investment in R & D and production, marketing can be avoided by a reliance on unsolicited orders from customers. In many forms of high-technology production, 'acceptable sales' can be achieved through a few advertisements in technical journals and 'word of mouth'. However, while the resultant level of sales may be 'acceptable' to the owners of small firms in the short term, sudden recessions in particular sectors may render such marketing provisions inadequate, and they certainly do not achieve the level of sales possible. In many high-technology small firms, a satisficer attitude appears to be in operation among managements in which the best returns on product development costs are not achieved, due to a concentration on adequate rather than *maximum* sales. Although it must be accepted that the maximum is never possible to define in terms of a hard target sales figure, it is certainly viable as a *principle*, and as an indication of a positive approach to sales.

9.3 RESEARCH OBJECTIVES AND METHODOLOGY

This research had three major objectives. First, as a basis for the detailed observation of marketing behaviour, firms included in the study were examined to determine the extent of their marketing effort in terms of methods of selling, exports and other measures of commitment or sophistication. It was originally intended that the establishment of a series of 'datum' levels of activity at the outset of the project might enable the impact of subsequent proactive marketing assistance to be detected when assistance programmes were concluded. This was to be achieved by the division of the survey population of sixty small Scientific Instruments and Electronics firms of less than 200 workers into thirty firms to receive assistance, and a further thirty firms (matched in terms of age, size and productive activity) to act as a control.

Although a substantial amount of success was achieved in the individual assistance programmes in a number of cases (discussed in detail below), experience of the *feasible* levels of marketing success stemming from the research suggested that any impact achieved would be overwhelmed by the wider economic factors which influence a firm's performance (e.g. level of demand in the economy). Thus the research design was modified to use the previously planned sixty start and end of survey interviews as contextual time-series measures of the changing conduciveness of the marketing environment for the high-technology small firms of the survey, providing a general context in which later detailed investigations might be set. With regard to the measurement of the success of proactive assistance programmes, these are accounted below, together with a crude estimate of the total expenditure of resources deployed in producing the results achieved.

Second, as intimated above, a major objective of the research was concerned with an attempt to promote the sales of thirty product-based and subcontract high-technology small firms equally divided between the planning regions of South East England and Scotland. These firms were selected by a stratified sampling method to ensure equal proportions of firms according to age, size and product/subcontract-based activity in the two study regions. The assistance involved the agreement of appropriate programmes of assistance with all these aided firms. Although individual projects varied slightly, depending on agreed target markets, the assistance generally involved a questionnaire/mailshot survey of potential customers which sought in a neutral, academic manner to invite potential customers to consider the enclosed literature on the assisted firm's product or service, with a view to either purchase *and/or* making suggestions on how the product or service might be improved. Thus the design fulfilled two functions of value to assisted firms, constituting an attempt to sell, followed by a brief market research survey. As mentioned in the introductory part of this chapter, the results of the proactive section survey provide hard evidence on which the success of this part of the research may be judged from a cost-benefit viewpoint.

The third major objective of the research was, as noted in discussion of the questionnaire/mailshot, to provide the assisted firm with a brief paper on the respondent's perceptions of the product or service promoted by the research team. While in a number of specific instances the comments of potential customers provided information of direct and substantial importance to assist firms (e.g. on technical problems with the product or process), the 485 returns from potential customer firms to the thirty programmes of assistance, when amalgamated, produced a valuable data set on the overall marketing problems of high-technology small firms. Thus, while the firm-specific evidence has provided detailed information of relevance to individual survey firms, suggesting modification to future marketing strategies, these data, when aggregated, create a robust picture of general marketing bottlenecks. Such barriers will be useful points of departure during discussion of possible ameliorative government policy aimed at the improvement of marketing in such firms in the conclusion of this chapter.

9.4 RESEARCH RESULTS

In keeping with the division of the research objectives into the three main themes noted above, the results of the study will also follow this pattern. Thus a brief analysis of changes in the performance of the sixty survey firms over time will be followed by a presentation of the results of attempts to promote sales, while a discussion of results from the market survey of potential customer evaluations will conclude the empirical section of this chapter.

The growth or decline of study firms over the survey period

The following presentation of key growth or decline indicators for the survey firms provides a useful contextual insight in to the overall fortunes of these high-technology enterprises over the two-year study period from 1988 to 1990. In particular, these measures of growth can be compared in the conclusion of this paper with the marketing behaviour of firms at both national and regional levels. However, any assertion of a direct link between marketing behaviour and performance must be heavily qualified by the observation, made at other points in this paper, that other major macro-economic forces may play a larger part in determining the performance of firms at national and regional levels (e.g. demand in the economy).

An initial indication of growth is employment change over the two-year study period, by study region. Perhaps the most significant general trend to note is the substantial proportion of firms at a national level which suffered a decline in employment. Indeed, 50.9 per cent of survey participants experienced a decline in their workforces, with 18 per cent recording a fall of over 25 per cent. However, although there is no statistically significant regional variation, Scottish firms performed marginally better, both in terms of lower proportions in the 'job loss' categories and higher proportions in the 'job gain' groupings. An overall interpretation of these employment change results suggested that the now acknowledged recession in British manufacturing industry may have influenced the performance of survey firms. Both the substantial decline in employment in the two regions, and the slightly worse figures in the South East of England, suggest that the current recession, and its acknowledged delayed spread outward from the South East, may be a major cause of these patterns of results. Thus, the value of these results on performance may lie, not in their establishment of a link between marketing and growth, but more realistically, in determining the conduciveness of the economic climate in which more aggressive marketing may, or may not, take place.

Confirmation of the poor growth performance of survey firms over the past two years is provided by changes in turnover. Again, virtually half of survey enterprises (i.e. 44 per cent) experienced a decline in turnover over the study period. Indeed, these figures are very similar to the employment data discussed above in that Scottish firms performed marginally better than their South Eastern counterparts, with 46 per cent of their total number in the 20 per cent and over growth category, compared with 25 per cent of South Eastern firms. These small regional differences notwithstanding, statistics on employment and turnover suggest that the growing recession may be producing a poor overall performance in survey firms. These combined data suggest that the proactive assistance part of this research has taken place in an economic climate that has progress-ively worsened as the projects have been initiated throughout late 1989 and 1990. These circumstances must have produced a partial impact on the level of success achieved by the proactive effort. Indeed, at a specific level, it is interesting to note that the slightly better growth performance of Scottish firms concurs with the greater success enjoyed by the assistance programmes in this region.

Moreover, the final performance variable presented in this section continues to indicate a slightly superior Scottish performance. An enhanced performance by the Scottish survey firms was noted with regard to export sales over the two-year study period, when com-pared with their South Eastern counterparts. In particular, while 39 per cent of the Scottish group of firms increased export sales by 20 per cent and over, the equivalent figure for South East England was 6 per cent. In addition, five of the six firms exporting for the first time during the survey period were located in Scotland. These results support the analysis of later passages of this chapter which use other evidence to argue that Scottish firms, due to a smaller local market, may be more inclined to look further afield for cus-tomers, which would clearly include an export orientation.

The results of attempts to promote the sales of survey firms

As previously mentioned, each of the thirty firms that had been stratified and sampled by age, size and subcontract/product-based orientation were approached in order to agree a target market for the mailshot/questionnaire surveys. The research team made no attempt to dictate the type of target market agreed, since the assisted firm was deemed most able to identify the best potential market in terms of cost-benefit. While there was no imposed upper limit to the level of assistance offered by the research team, the final number of mailshot/questionnaires sent out was dependent on the *quality* of the identified population of potential customers. If a large population of prospective customers with strong sales potential was identified, the survey was consequently large. Conversely, in other cases, the survey size was determined by a limited number of potential customers in the particular sector or geographical area concerned. Thus, although the average size of survey involved sev-enty-six questionnaires, the range was as high as 253 mailings, and as low as thirty-two potential customers. In each case, detailed desk research was performed to identify *relevant* potential customers. For example, one firm identified the United States university market as a target, which resulted in the compilation of a list of 189 universities with relevant departments, from which a possible purchase might occur. Generally, surveys for product-based firms were larger since there were frequently a limited number of potential new customers for subcontractor firms in their local area where transactions were economically and logistically viable. Such a limitation mainly stemmed from a reluctance of most subcontractors to sell to non-local customers (i.e. beyond a thirty-mile radius). This was particularly true in the printed circuit board industry, where regular customer contact is a very important part of the service, and ease of frequent contact clearly decreases with distance.

Table 9.1 summarizes the main results of the assistance programmes. Each of the 2,294 questionnaire mailshots was dispatched to prospective customers, together with relevant sales literature. Considerable goodwill was encountered from the assisted firms throughout, sometimes involving secretarial assistance concerning the compilation of target lists, the mailing costs of the survey, and the provision of frequently expensive sales literature (e.g. one firm provided 253 brochures at a cost of £4 each). The 485 returned questionnaires represented an overall response rate of 21 per cent which is a reasonable level of response to this rather unusual survey, especially since they were not 'chased up' by means of repeat mailing or telephone calling. Respondents were asked to read the enclosed sales literature, comment on their intention regarding purchase, *and* (where appropriate) indicate how the product, service or clarity of sales literature on offer might be improved to better meet their requirements. Respondents who clearly indicated that they did not intend to purchase the goods or services on offer were asked to state why the items advertised were not suitable. This enabled firms that did not achieve sales as a result of our efforts to gain some return for their participation in the survey. Finally, all respondents were asked to suggest new areas into which the assisted firm might diversify in the future. The questionnaire was deliberately restricted to a small number of questions in order to secure a reasonable response rate.

In summarizing the aggregate results on the attempt to promote sales, it must be emphasized that one important feature of a proactive project of this type has been the longer than expected period over which customer reaction continues to occur. In the conventional social-science research project involving questionnaire-based research, data are collected, analysed and then written up. In the context of this project, the 'results' continued to occur months after

Table 9.1 Summary of results from assistance programmes

	South East product-based		South East service-based		Scotland product-based		Scotland service-based		Total	
	n	%	n	%	n	%	n	%	n	%
Questionnaires sent out	1,036		188		496		574		2,294	
Questionnaires returned (% response rate)	197	(19)	28	(15)	132	(26)	128	(22)	485	(21)
Information kept on file	123		14		77		58		272	
No purchase at any time	63		13		30		32		138	
Will enquire	8		1		15		9		33	
Intend to purchase	2		0		1		22		25	
Confirmed orders	3		1		6		7		17	

the original finish date of the project (i.e. 31 August 1990) – later extended to 31 August 1991. Indeed, perhaps the most significant general principle learnt by the research team during the proactive part of the research is that selling is, in many cases, a far more protracted exercise than envisaged in the original research proposal to ESRC. For example, a wide range of purchasing behaviours extend from the period between first contact and final purchase, including the custom of tendering in subcontract areas of business, annual purchasing rounds by customers (e.g. especially in the public sector) and the common tendency only to purchase products when a sudden need arises. This trend is particularly relevant to the Scientific Instruments sector, where the purchase of a new instrument is often prompted by a sudden fault or need (e.g. gas detection equipment). Put simply, varying levels of both need and funds, often make ordering a protracted business. This is reflected in the fact that orders continue to be received for the products of assisted firms from the recipients of the mailshots.

The evidence in the lower part of Table 9.1 on the success of the proactive efforts of the research team strongly reflects the long-term nature of marketing in practice. While a majority 272 (56 per cent) of the respondent firms indicated that the product or service on offer was relevant, and that they intended to keep the survey literature on file for future reference, thirty-three firms (7 per cent) were intending to make further enquiries with a view to purchase, twenty-five firms (5 per cent) had an intention to purchase in the near future, and seventeen firms (4 per cent) purchased goods or services. The degree to which these figures represent success or failure is difficult to judge. The substantial variation in the degree of intent suggests that the current level of 'hard' sales might increase in the future. However, it is also true that the current level of success has been achieved through a substantial amount of liaison on the part of the research team between sellers and potential customers. In many instances, the introspective and reactive attitude towards marketing noted above as being important in earlier work (Oakey *et al.* 1988), continued in a number of cases *after* the assisted firm had been notified of a potential customer's interest. Indeed, it should be noted that the seventeen purchases of products or services occurred in only six of the thirty assisted firms. In two cases the firms achieving orders had high-quality gas-measurement and thermal-imaging products on offer, while a third, a subcontract firm, was successful largely through the extremely vigorous selling efforts of the owner. It should also be noted that *most of* these successes were achieved in Scotland, which is an initial indication of a number of strong regional variations that will be augmented by later analysis.

Confirmed orders amounted to £24,880 in value by January 1992. In terms of the cost-benefit to this proactive research, it is estimated that the approximate total labour and other resources devoted to operationalizing the complete programme was £18,762. However, this sum does not include the overheads that would be inevitable if a full-time agency was promoting such marketing assistance. Clearly, any further orders would improve the benefit side of the equation, while the potential customer evaluations analysed in the following section can be legitimately added to the output of the proactive effort. However, any additional sales achieved as a result of modifying marketing behaviour in response to the findings of the potential customer evaluations would be a long-term gain, beyond the capacity of this research to measure. Estimating a price for the potential customer evaluations undertaken would be a very difficult exercise. Any additional cost of this approach to the overall survey was negligible since it was paid for by the product promotion mailshot. It would seem reasonable to assume that a consultant would charge at least £1,000 per firm for the individual reports produced by the research team which, must be worth at least £30,000. A more detailed evaluation of the value of this proactive approach is reserved for the conclusion of this chapter, where the relevance of these qualitative and quantitative results will be discussed in the light of *all* the research results.

An analysis of customer evaluations

This section of the chapter presents a number of interesting trends which have emerged from the postal self-completion questionnaire that accompanied the sales promotion mailshot and sales literature. The evidence is grouped into two major categories derived from the characteristics of assisted firms. The relatively large population size of 485 responses produces a number of results with strong statistical significance. The major themes analysed below are the 'product or service status' and 'location of the assisted survey firms'.

The product or service status of survey firms

A fundamental reason for the balancing of the survey sample to ensure roughly equal numbers of product and service-based firms was the anticipation that both marketing and resultant customers would vary between these two activity types. For example, previous research has indicated that subcontractors in high-technology industries tend to be locally orientated (e.g. printed circuit-board making) (Oakey 1984) and maintain fewer customers, won on a contract-tender basis. Product-based firms, conversely, typically maintain widespread markets and usually possess some form of marketing capacity to stimulate orders for their products.

This difference in customer base is immediately apparent. While service-based firms received 95 per cent of their survey replies from other industrial companies, product-based firms obtained substantial returns from universities, polytechnics and other research organizations (21 per cent) and public-sector organizations (22 per cent). While it is readily acknowledged that this pattern of response must reflect the total population of target customers agreed for the mailshot with assisted firms, it remains a reasonably accurate guide to the types of customer these two categories of high-technology firm would generally target for marketing purposes. The main implication of this evidence is that subcontract firms generally offer very specialist services to a sectorally more narrow group of industrial customers where, due to the common practice of tendering, price margins are also narrow. Again, the printed circuit-board industry is a good example of this phenomenon.

The suggested greater spatial diversity of customers in product-based firms is confirmed by the location of respondents to the mailshot survey questionnaire with respect to assisted firms. Product-based firms recorded a 61 per cent level of response from the rest of the United Kingdom (beyond a 99-mile radius), compared with 36 per cent of service-based firms. Moreover, the greater degree to which firms responding to the service-based firm mailshots were situated locally is confirmed by the 35 per cent of respondents that were less than thirty miles away from the plant, when compared with 12 per cent for product-based firms. These combined results on customer diversity and location support the assertion that subcontract firms tend to maintain a smaller, more specialist core of customers within a smaller geographical area, when compared with product-based firms. These sectoral and locational trends concur with specific impressions gained at individual project-level during the assistance programme.

Although not part of any general pattern of results, evidence on pricing is included here since it differs between service- and product-based firms for reasons suggested above. The most common form of pricing for subcontract firms is the tendering system, which tends to negate the setting of a selling price for most of these firms. Since most subcontract prices are agreed by tender *before* the work is performed, the low level of respondents mentioning 'no price included' in the sales literature for this group of firms is explained by its irrelevance to this form of transaction. However, while price lists are *very important* for those firms manufacturing discrete products, a majority of product-based firms did not provide a price list to accompany their sales literature. Indeed, thirty-nine (12 per cent) or the respondents to the product-based firm part of the mailshot survey complained that the product was difficult to evaluate because its price was not stated. It is possible that this minority of respondents are only a small proportion of potential customers for whom this omission was very irksome, since in only two of the eighteen product-based projects was a product price included in the literature. In the case of exports and 'one-off' bespoke work, pricing may be difficult, due to fluctuating exchange rates and the varying costs of specialized customer requirements respectively. However, in a number of cases, the failure to include a current price list may render a very competitive product of little interest to a potential customer, due to his resultant inability to judge whether the product on offer represents good value for money. It should be remembered that sales literature is all the evidence of a product's worth that will be seen by potential customers, *if* the literature is poor or poorly presented. Moreover, a lax attitude towards the quality of sales literature was confirmed in a number of survey cases, when sales literature provided by assisted firms appeared rather 'old fashioned', of poor quality and with no price list.

Another ramification of the product/service dichotomy with which this section of the analysis is concerned is the frequency with which goods or services were required by potential customer firms. In general terms, the greater difficulty experienced by product-based firms in presenting their products to customers at an *appropriate* moment is confirmed by survey results. Although the *level* of demand for the services of subcontract firms may vary, there is frequently a continuous market for goods and/or services provided at a competitive price. If the printed circuit-board example is again cited, there is a generally constant need from relevant large firms for circuit boards. Survey responses confirmed this assertion by indicating that a statistically significant *lower* proportion of the replies, received by subcontract service-based firms to the market survey, indicated that their service was 'relevant but not currently needed', than the 55 per cent of responses received by product-based firms. Such difference is accounted for by the fact that product-based firms tend to offer products with a very specific function (e.g. gas analyser or pressure transducer), implying that if the potential customer does not require these specialized items at the time of survey, the 'relevant but not currently needed' response will be more prevalent in replies to product-based firms. This trend is also supported by the observation that there was a much higher level of intention to purchase for the service-based group of firms (18 per cent) than for their product-based counterparts (1 per cent). Moreover, a substantially larger 62 per cent of replies to product-based firms contained the 'retain information on file' response, compared with the 45 per cent level in service-based firm respondents.

These data suggest a number of issues for policy consideration regarding the differing marketing requirements of product and service-based firms. In particular, the market demand for the services of subcontract firms tends to be constant, and when these markets have been won they can become a constant source of business to favoured firms who often then benefit from the inertia associated with the 'better the devil you know' syndrome. However, not only are the markets of product-based firms more sectorally and geographically spread as noted above, but demand for products is rarely constant, and is characterized by 'windows of opportunity' when potential customers are unlikely to respond favourably to a single sales effort, due to intermittent need. This reality, in turn, implies that selling in product-based firms must be, predominantly, a long-term exercise involving repeated physical or telephone calls to ensure that those firms interested enough to 'retain information on file' do make a purchase *when* the need arises.

The location of assisted survey firms

Previous evidence on the success of the proactive element on this research has suggested that notable regional differences may exist in the data collected. These differences might be expected, given that the initial design of the research sought to contrast the highly prosperous South East of England with the peripheral planning region of Scotland. However, it might be conversely expected that some of the potential differences would be mitigated by the known presence of a substantial core of high-technology industry in Scotland's 'Silicon Glen'. None the less, the main advantage of South-

East England has proved in the past to lie, less in its *proportionate* superiority of entrepreneurship and management performance in individual firms, judged on a one-to-one basis (Oakey 1984), but on the comparatively larger *absolute* size and level of sophistication of the high-technology industrial base in this region. This is a particularly important point with regard to marketing since such a critical mass of high-technology production means that South-Eastern firms are often able to sell most of their output *intra-regionally*, and gain a number of economies as a result.

The above argument is supported by a number of sharp regional differences. In particular, while 31 per cent of the clients of the South-East survey assisted firms were 'universities, polytechnics and research organizations', the equivalent figure for Scotland was 3 per cent. The respondent customers of the Scottish firms were much more heavily concentrated in the public sector, especially the health service. The observation that one-third of the responses to the South-East market survey were from research organizations or universities further confirms the frequently noted concentration of *both* public and private research organizations in this region (Buswell *et al.* 1985). Geographical differences were apparent in these data since South-Eastern firms received fewer customer responses from within thirty miles of the plant when compared with their Scottish counterparts. However, the proportion of respondent customers in the 30 to 99-mile radius grouping was over double that of Scotland. Significantly, in the 'other UK' category, the Scottish proportion was again higher than their South-Eastern counterparts. This pattern of results must, at least in part, reflect the above noted absolute size of the South-East region, *both* in terms of numbers of producers *and* geographical area. The pattern for Scotland, together with experience gained during the compilation of lists of target firms, suggests that once the local customers (within thirty miles) have been exhausted, assisted firms were forced to move to a national level to identify potential customers. In the South East, however, it is certainly true for product-based firms, that a business based in London would expect to find potential customers up to, and marginally beyond, the planning region boundary (e.g. in the Cambridge area).

The following set of results presents data that might initially appear contradictory, but on closer examination do conform to the above regional trends noted for marketing behaviour and experience gained through working with individual firms in the two study regions. Perhaps the most interesting data to emerge from the customer response part of the study is that almost half of the suggestions for improvements in the advertised product related to improvements in its technical specification (i.e. thirty-seven out of eighty-four). Interestingly, almost double the number of responses in this category at twenty-three, were to assisted Scottish firms, compared with fourteen to their South-Eastern counterparts. Thus, this initial evidence on customer appraisal *suggests* that, South-Eastern firms may experience fewer problems with the quality or applicability of their products or services.

However, a different pattern of regional results emerges when marketing *effort* is analysed. Almost twice as many South-Eastern respondent customers complained of a lack of prices in sales literature, when compared with respondents to Scottish firms. Moreover, this pattern of significant regional difference is supported by further evidence on 'poorly presented literature' and 'lack of technical detail', where these minority responses with 'problems' were significantly biased in favour of the customers of South-Eastern assisted firms. An overall summary of these data might conclude that there is some evidence that, although the South Eastern assisted firms might have experienced less trouble with the acceptability of product or service quality, Scottish firms appeared to be more efficient in their marketing methods. An important theme for consideration in the conclusions below is the possibility that, due to their obvious peripherality, Scottish firms are frequently instilled with the need to market their products more aggressively, to the English market or abroad if they are to survive and grow. This assertion of a more aggressive marketing performance is also supported by previous evidence from the proactive part of the study on actual sales, in which *most* were achieved by Scottish firms (see Table 9.1).

A summary of all the above results might argue that South-Eastern firms may be rather lazy in their approach to marketing due to the existence of a large *intra-regional* market for their goods or services 'on their doorstep'. Indeed, this lax attitude may partly explain the generally less impressive growth performance of the survey firms of this region, when compared with Scotland (see Section 4.1, pp. 83–89). All these results will be considered in terms of possible policy implications in the following conclusions.

9.5 CONCLUSIONS AND RECOMMENDATIONS

At a general level, the previously observed lack of marketing provision noted in earlier investigations by this research team has been confirmed by the individual assistance programmes devised for firms within the proactive part of the study. Close interaction with individual marketing staff, which cannot be achieved by a single interview visit, indicates that, in many cases, a number of marketing projects could have been attempted. This is particularly true when foreign markets are considered, and also where national markets, with good potential, have not been penetrated by survey firms. Both anecdotal conversations with personal contacts in high-technology small firms and the substantial level of customer interest from respondent firms evident in Table 9.1, confirm that there is much scope for continued marketing assistance and subsequent improvement in the assisted firms.

Another pervasive feature of the proactive survey was the general poor quality and information content of much of the sales literature provided by assisted firms. While in a number of cases the assistance programme conveniently coincided with the production of bright new sales literature, in many other instances a request for sales literature prompted a search of drawers or cupboards to unearth material that looked, from quality of artwork and 'wear and tear' viewpoints, to be in desperate need of revision. The introspection of firms towards marketing was subtly reflected in a frequent lack of concern for the quality of the sales literature in general, and in the provision of price lists in particular. The most extreme form of introspection was represented by those assisted firms which were reluctant to build on the mailshot/questionnaire survey with follow-up contacts of the potential customers expressing an interest in the promoted product or service. Indeed, the three most successful survey firms all buttressed our efforts with systematic sales effort to the targeted firms. Unfortunately, these were the exceptions rather than the rule, and the reactive attitude which relied on unsolicited orders continued in an attitude to our proactive survey in many firms who 'waited for things to happen'. However these observations are not intended to imply that proactive assistance is pointless, but suggest that a greater effort than was possible during this study will be needed to help ensure the *maximization* of results in terms of sales.

The regional results were of interest, partly because evidence suggested that the products and services of the South East attracted marginally less criticism, and in the manner in which Scottish firms appeared more proficient at marketing their output. The generally impressive performance of Scottish firms, both in the market survey and the proactive programme was encouraging, and must partly stem from a realistic evaluation of the need to market vigorously to survive in a region on the periphery of Britain and Europe. None the less, these results should not be interpreted in the Scottish case as evidence of a satisfactory level of marketing. In both South-East England and Scotland there remains much scope for increased sales. The motive to increase sales in South-East England and other British regions could be part of a strategy to increase exports and reduce balance-of-payments problems, while in the development regions increasing sales could be seen as a means of preserving and expanding the small stock of high-technology small firms.

A further general trend in the data presented in this chapter is both the greater sales potential and degree of difficulty associated with marketing in product-based firms. The fluctuating needs of customers, widely spread markets at home and abroad, and the frequent dearth of capital for marketing after R & D and production have been achieved, often ensure that marketing is erratic and under-resourced. However, there is little doubt that a number of these product-based firms have great potential for rapid sales growth. While service firms are often locally orientated, involving the simple linking of producer with customer within the local area, selling products is a much more difficult task in sectoral and geographical terms. However, the substantially higher potential financial gains associated with high-technology product sales is enhanced by the observation that the specialist nature of products, and the wide geographical spread of many customers ensures that problems of 'additionality' are avoided, since unlike subcontractors it is less likely that product-based firms will poach each others markets within the regional or national economy.

In conclusion, it is argued that this modest study has produced substantial benefits to a number of the assisted firms, both in terms of the marketing effort and the customer evaluation survey. It is clear from all the above evidence that there is considerable scope for the provision of marketing assistance to high-technology small firms on a substantial and regular basis. Assistance with marketing could be a normal producer service to such firms in a similar manner to accounting and other specialist skills. However, it is unfortunate that the potential for this service remains substantially underdeveloped. In common with most services to the firm, the rationale for the purchase of external expertise rests on the twin motives of insufficient 'in-house' time and/or expertise. In the marketing context, there is considerable scope for a new agency to liaise between firms and potential customers and perform a number of the tasks attempted in this research, together with other services. While this suggestion might be deemed intervention, it could also be judged as a corrective mechanism to repair market failure. However, political ideology need not confuse this issue since, while government agencies might be involved in the initiation of such bodies, they would probably be more successful as self-sustaining private-sector bodies, once formed. For a fee or commission as appropriate, a range of services might be offered to high-technology small firms including:

- Assistance with the accessing of existing government aid to domestic and export marketing.
- Direct assistance in the selling of products to new customers at home and abroad.
- Assistance with the establishment of links with agents and distributors overseas.
- The provision of specialized market surveys.

While it is acknowledged that many of these services are wholly or partly provided by existing agencies, the novelty of the proposed agency would be that the service would be personally *delivered* into the firm and provided as a complete marketing package, mainly on a commission basis. This study has indicated that there would be substantial interest and goodwill shown by small-firm owners to such a service and the downstream sales growth of *existing* proven products would combine to produce beneficial effects for both national and regional economies. There was no evidence in this study of any resistance to the assistance provided which suggests that such an agency would be very welcome. Indeed, a number of assisted firms have asked when we intend to perform our next mailshot for them! In a number of ways this study has been experimental in its methodology. The research not only depended on enlisting the initial support of respondents within firms, common in a normal questionaire-based study, but also on the continued interaction with thirty firms over a two-year period. In methodological terms, the research can be generally judged a success, although the nature of this proactive effort has ensured that the reducing impact of our work continues to register. The results of this research will contribute to conceptualizations that form the basis for continuing work on the *complete* innovation cycle in high-technology small firms performed by the authors.

REFERENCES

Buswell, R., Easterbrook, R. P. and Morphet, C. S. (1985) 'Geography, regions and research activity: the case of the United Kingdom', in A. T. Thwaites and R. P. Oakey (eds) *The Regional Economic Impact of Technological Change*, London: Pinter.

Fleck, V. and Garnsey, E. W. (1987) 'Strategy and internal constraints in a high technology firm: the management of growth at Acorn Computers', Research Paper No. 2/87, Department of Engineering, Cambridge University.

Oakey, R. P. (1984) *High Technology Small Firms*, London: Pinter.

Oakey, R. P. and Rothwell, R. (1986) 'The contribution of high technology small firms to regional employment growth', in A. Amin and J. Goddard (eds) *Technological Change and Industrial Restructuring*, London: Allen & Unwin.

Oakey, R. P., Rothwell, R. and Cooper, S. Y. (1988) *The Management of Innovation in High Technology Small Firms*, London: Pinter.

Oakey, R. P. (1991) 'High technology small firms: their potential for rapid industrial growth', *International Small Business Journal* 9, (4): 30–42.

Rothwell, R. and Zegveld, W. (1982) *Innovation and Small and Medium Sized Firms*, London: Pinter.

10 The speed of technology change and the development of market structure: semiconductors, PC software and biotechnology

Peter Swann and Jas Gill

10.1 INTRODUCTION

This chapter summarizes a project that has examined the relationship between the speed and predictability of technology change and the development of market structure – that is, the number and sizes of participating firms. It summarizes five case studies taken from rapidly changing markets. Inevitably, this chapter can only present a brief overview of the case studies and conceptual framework, and these are set out in more detail in Swann and Gill (forthcoming).

While the relationship between innovation and market structure has been studied extensively by economists and other social scientists, the literature is inconclusive about whether rapid technology change will lead to greater or lesser concentration. In this chapter it is argued that a given technological path or trajectory with a given speed and direction of technology change may lead to a variety of outcomes in the market. The market outcome will depend critically on how far the actual path that emerges is consistent with the technological 'visions' of the principal participants. If, for example, the technology takes a radical departure, inconsistent with the visions and plans of existing market leaders, then the result will be deconcentrating – at least in the short to medium term. If, alternatively, the technology accelerates along a generally recognized and well-anticipated path, then the result will be concentrating – even if there is some realignment in the league table of market leaders. (This latter phenomenon is sometimes called *turbulence* in market share.) The chapter illustrates these arguments with three cases from the semiconductor industry, one from PC applications software and one from biotechnology.

10.2 MOTIVATION

The link between rapid technology change and market structure is not a simple one. Simple econometric studies tend to be inconclusive, with case studies and theoretical analysis indicating why this should be. Two contrasting arguments emerge from cases and theoretical analysis. First, that incumbent market leaders accelerate the pace of technology change to throw off the competition and to sustain market leadership. Second, that radical innovations which are incompatible with the existing market leaders' technology strategy are a severe challenge to those incumbents, and can present a market opportunity to small firms of greater organizational flexibility – for example, start-up firms. Without an analytical structure that can differentiate between these two cases, it is clear why the macro-relationship is inconclusive.

It is important of course not to romanticize the role of small firms in high-technology industries. For example, the work of Pavitt and Patel shows that large firms account for the lion's share of patents in high-technology industries (e.g. Pavitt and Patel 1991).[1] Moreover, if a league table is constructed showing the proportion of all patents in an industry due to large firms, the electronics industry is placed near the top. Moreover, to take an example within the electronics industry, production of memory chips is now so capital intensive that only a handful of global producers are active at the leading edge of that technology.

Yet those familiar with the history of the electronics industry – particularly from 1970 to 1980 – will know that it is the (then) small start-up firms such as Intel and Zilog (now far from small) whose radical innovations had such a critical impact on the subsequent development of the industry. Indeed, one of the most telling aspects of that history is how (with one or two exceptions) the semiconductor market leaders of the late 1960s did not make such a success of the microprocessor era (see the first case study in Section 10.4). Such phases may perhaps be atypical, and these start-ups would need to grow rapidly (either organically or by seeking a 'parent') to sustain the market advantage offered by their radical innovation. Nevertheless, they do illustrate the potential for radical innovation to be deconcentrating – even if only temporarily.

Another, and very well-known example of this is the emergence of the PC. The first PCs produced in the mid 1970s may have been essentially hobbyist machines, but with the entry (in particular) of the Apple II, it became clear that the PC was more than just a hobbyist market. The established computer manufactures had been slow to enter this part of the market, which lead to the popular image of IBM's core business being threatened by a company that had been set up in a garage five years earlier.

To introduce the PC, IBM had to set up a special design team that was outside the IBM core structure. This team could develop a distinct vision of where computer technology was going, with minimal intervention from the rest of the company, and consequently could complete the PC project very quickly.[2] Xerox, on the other hand, had already developed much of the PC technology at its PARC research centre, but it has been suggested that PARC's vision was rather different from the guiding institutional vision (Smith and Alexander 1988) and Xerox did not make the most of their technological lead.[3]

Some theoretical economic perspectives suggest the opposite result, including for example the analysis of patent races.[4] The winner of a first race may not be in a hurry to start the second race (which he may lose). But speaking loosely, the monopolist stands to lose more if market structure changes to a duopoly than the entrant stands to win, so that there is a tendency for the monopolist to invest most in winning the patent race, and hence a tendency towards persistent dominance. Such analyses tend to assume away the organizational difficulties illustrated above in the IBM and Xerox cases: if it cannot be developed in house, buy it in. But if persistent dominance leads to a deeply mechanistic organizational structure (in the sense of Burns and Stalker 1961),[5] the persistent monopolist may be too slow to respond to the possibilities offered by radical innovations outside its current vision.

It is apparent therefore that to clarify the macro-relation between rapid technology change and market structure it is necessary to place each within an historical or 'life-cycle' context, and Section 10.3 describes a model that does this.

10.3 ANALYTICAL COMPONENTS

This section will argue that the effects of technology change on the relative performance of firms of different types will depend on the organizational structures of firms, the extent to which the technology path is compatible with the firm's strategic vision for its technology, and the extent to which that vision is (and has to be) embodied in organizational structure. The section starts, however, by distinguishing two different concentrating and deconcentrating tendencies, that will be used throughout the rest of the paper.[6]

Two aspects of concentration and deconcentration

In what follows, we distinguish two conceptually distinct concentrating tendencies, both of which have a counterpart deconcentrating trend. They are: (1) movements in the four-firm (or generally, *n* firm) concentration ratio and (2) the concept of *turbulence*, or *disruption* (to be defined below). These will be summarized in Table 10.1, but first they need some introduction.

Most of the discussion of trends in industrial concentration looks at movements in the concentration ratio; that is the combined market share of the largest three or four firms. An industry or market shows an increase in concentration, by this measure, if the four-firm concentration ratio increases – or, conversely, a decline in concentration if the ratio decreases.

An increase in this ratio may mean that the shares of the firms that are already the largest increase their market shares even further. *Alternatively*, it may be that existing market leaders have been displaced by one or more newcomers. Even if concentration increases (by the concentration ratio), there may be a deconcentrating tendency that leads to a change in the league table of market shares. This is the concept of turbulence (Audretsch 1992), or disruption. A natural measure of disruption or turbulence is the proportion of the market that changes hands in a given period. This is calculated simply by adding up the gains of each of the firms who increase market share during that period. The sum of gains must be equal (and opposite) to the sum of losses, since market shares sum to 100 per cent.

An increase in the concentration ratio may be accompanied by either no change (consolidation) or some change (disruption, or turbulence) in the league table. On the other hand, a decrease in the concentration ratio *cannot* be accompanied by consolidation in the shares of existing market leaders. Either the top four remain the top four, in which case their combined market share must fall, or else they don't, in which case their combined market share must fall even further.

The semiconductor market gives a striking example of turbulence which does little to change the aggregate concentration ratio. There was very little movement in the four firm concentration from 1972 to 1986, while disruption (the extent of market share changing hands) ran at around 15 per cent over each two-year period from 1972–4 to 1984–6.

Table 10.1 summarizes the possible combinations of these two trends.

Table 10.1 Concentrating effects: possible combinations

	Concentration ratio	Current market leaders' shares	Comments
A (+ +)	Rise	Consolidate	End of PLC; innovation well anticipated by large incumbent or fast-growing pioneer
B (+ −)	Rise	Erode	Shift to low-cost competition (e.g. in memory market)
C (− −)	Fall	Erode	Early phase of sub-market

In the discussion that follows, we refer to the two-character summary of each outcome (+ +, − −, and so on). In some cases, the '+' or '−' is replaced by an '=', meaning that there is no change in that aspect of concentration.

These measures can be applied to overall markets: what, for example, is the effect of the microprocessor on concentration in the semiconductor market as a whole? Alternatively, they can be applied to specific sub-markets: what is the history of concentrating trends in the microprocessor sub-market following its inception? The histories will be rather different from these two perspectives – as will be made clear in Section 10.4.

Technological and market visions, trajectories or paradigms

We return now to the conceptual framework guiding our case studies. In what follows, the terms 'visions', 'trajectories' or 'paradigms', mean more or less the same things. Moreover, there is not intended to be any deterministic content to the word 'trajectory'. This is not an exogenous and predetermined (if unknown) path that the technology and market is bound to follow; rather it is the leading vision within any organization of where the technology and the market for that technology is going and what therefore that organization must be prepared for. Different organizations will have different visions, and none of them will necessarily be 'right' in the sense of having a complete and accurate picture of the way the technology and market actually develops. Chapter 4 of this book, by Metcalfe and Boden, develops the idea of a strategic paradigm in much more detail.

What is important here is that the vision defines the range of technological and market outcomes for which the organization can be prepared. If the actual path of the technology strays too far from a company's vision, then that company may only be able to follow at a cost or time disadvantage. In such circumstances, and where most firms' visions have turned out to be incorrect, small organic firms may be at an advantage. Conversely, when a large organization finds that the vision is accurate, that organization will be well placed to take advantage of economies of scale that arise from having an organizational structure designed to cater for that vision.

Visions can be updated, of course, but that is not unproblematic at the level of the organization, as firms become accustomed to organizational routines (Nelson and Winter 1982), and visions become embodied in corporate or organizational structure (Metcalfe and Boden, Ch. 4 of this volume). To change the vision and in a manner that will allow the economies of scale to be exploited, requires a corresponding change in organizational routines and structure.

Of course, this inertia is not necessarily inefficient. On the contrary, when the vision is correct, the mechanistic structure is a source of economies of scale. When a technology settles down, so that its path can be foreseen, it is firms of this type that will have an advantage. The organic structure is more or less an irrelevance at that stage. But when the technology is at an early stage, and trajectories are hard to predict, the organic structure will be able to adapt more readily to follow the emergent path.

From technology change to change in market structure: A summary

To summarize, the effects of technology change on the relative performance of firms of different types will depend on the organizational structures of firms, the extent to which the technology path is compatible with the firm's strategic vision for its technology, and the extent to which that vision is (and has to be) embodied in organizational structure.

How, then, does this interact with market structure? At one level, it would take a complete catalogue of information on participants, their corporate structures and visions to work through the implications for changes in market shares. It could be argued that without that catalogue, it is not possible to know the effects on individual firms, and still less the net effect on market structure. We shall argue, however, that certain patterns will be discernible in the absence of the catalogue.

In particular, when technology change follows an unexpected path, the smaller organizations – particularly the small start-up firms – have an advantage and from the perspective of the total market for that technology, the effect on market structure is deconcentrating and disruptive $(--)$. When the path is getting better understood, a number of the medium-sized incumbents may be able to switch path effectively, but at the level of the market for the technology as a whole, the effect on structure is still type $(--)$.

Shake-out in the later stages of the product life-cycle means that there is very likely to be an increase in concentration. This may be $(++)$, but can also be $(+-)$. Who is shaken out? In the memory cases, one common occurrence is that the higher-cost technology leaders exit from a market when it starts to mature, and then move up to the next generation of product. Occasionally in that market, the leaders at the late stage of the product life-cycle are the low-cost producers, some of whom may be late entrants who did not have a position of market leadership in the early maturity phase of the life cycle. In that case, type $(+-)$ occurs: growing concentration but with further disruption to the market league table.

The outcome observed will depend on whether the market under consideration is for a product with *network externalities* – that is, where the value of the product depends as much on the *network* of supporting products, services and expertise around the product, as on the *intrinsic quality* of the product – Cawson *et al.* (Ch. 11 of this volume) also consider products of this sort. In such cases, the late stages of the product life cycle are likely to see reconcentration of type $(++)$, rather than $(+-)$.

Interconnections

Swann (1992) presents a simulation model that integrates the various effects described above. The key elements are these. Any organizational structure reflects (implicitly) a technological vision. If the actual technology trajectory is in line with the vision, then larger firms (or incumbents) can exploit static and dynamic economies of scale to increase market share, and change is concentrating (eventually of form $++$). If the actual trajectory is not in line with the vision, mechanistically structured firms suffer 'off-trajectory' costs, which put them at a disadvantage to the organic firm, and means that radical change incompatible with a vision is deconcentrating $(--)$ at the level of the industry. The new sub-market starts concentrated, but will deconcentrate as followers enter $(--)$.

The eventual outcome depends on how quickly the various firms' organizational structures can adapt to the new vision required for the new trajectory. If this is a slow process, then the dynamic scale economies (and network effects) accrue primarily to the smaller organic firms, and deconcentration persists in the overall market even if reconcentration $(++)$ occurs in the sub-market. If, however, this readjustment is fast then the large organization's superior scale economies may allow it to catch up again. If so, we observe reconcentration in the overall market $(++)$, and reconcentration $(+-)$ in the sub-market.

The simulation model frequently generates outcomes where small organic firms play a key role in the early phase of a radical change in technology, but when the trajectory is better predicted, the large firms tend to take over again. The large firms may not take over if the network effects are so strong that the small pioneer remains the market leader throughout – and becomes big in the process $(+-$ in the overall market). An example of this is the microprocessor case, where Intel was never caught up by any of the pre-microprocessor market leaders in integrated circuit (IC) technologies.

The model also explores the advantages and disadvantages that can accrue to the divisionalized firm. In the model, each division has a different but very specific vision and domain: they are not encouraged to pass outside that domain. Sometimes in the simulations, this divisionalized firm can enjoy an advantage because an unpredictable trajectory is followed by these different divisions – with one division responsible for some of the innovations and another responsible for others. Thus, for example, in the microprocessor case, a components division might be responsible for some innovations (in high-performance microprocessors) and a system division for others (in single-chip microcomputers). These benefits are, however, contingent on learning economies (and network effects) passing from one division to another; or in other words, they depend on the *absorptive capacity* of the multidivisional firm (Cohen and Levinthal 1990). (See also Chapter 2 of this volume, by Grindley, for a discussion of this issue.) Without that, the multidivisional structure does not cope so well with an unstable environment.

10.4 CASES

There are five cases summarized here: microprocessors, memory chips, standard logic, PC applications software, and a biotechnology product (HIV diagnostics). These are discussed in more detail in Swann and Gill (forthcoming).

Microprocessors

The microprocessor case study (Swann 1990b) illustrates three main issues. First, it represents a radical innovation, incompatible with most incumbent's visions of the future, and consequently presented a severe challenge for those incumbents. Of the integrated circuit (IC) market leaders in the late 1960s, only Motorola had much success with the microprocessor. From the beginning, the most successful firm was Intel, started in 1968, who was a small player before they first introduced the microprocessor. From the viewpoint of the integrated circuit market, therefore, the introduction of the microprocessor was a clear case of $(--)$, although as noted above the four-firm concentration ratio in the semiconductor market changed little in the 1970s, so it could alternatively be classed as type $(=-)$.

By the mid 1970s the microprocessor vision was becoming widely accepted, and most major semiconductor companies had attempted to enter that market. Did this mean that the original incumbents were able to regain the advantage? Our study suggests that for one incumbent (Motorola) the answer was 'yes', while for many others, the answer was 'less so'. It was the new firm Intel which best articulated the continuation of the microprocessor vision, and this they did in a very public fashion; their sequence of product introductions matched this fairly accurately. Motorola's vision and that of Zilog (a spin-off from Intel) followed that of Intel fairly closely, and these companies were successful in the microprocessor market. Motorola's microprocessors were perhaps never quite as successful as those of Intel, but they maintained a market position second only to Intel for most of the period we studied (1973–88). Zilog's Z80 is probably the best-selling microprocessor of all time (apart from four bit single-chip computers).

On the other hand the apparent visions of some other firms were not so convincingly set out, and the sequence of product introductions was altogether more confusing as the manufacturers overshot in their early product introductions and had to 'double-back' to fill gaps in their product line. So while a large number of firms entered the eight-bit microprocessor market, many fewer entered the sixteen-bit race, and even less the 32-bit race.

In short, then, the convergence of the technology trajectory onto the Intel vision did ultimately lead to reconcentration in the sub-market for microprocessors, and this was reconcentration of the type $(++)$ in that sub-market. Conversely, the initial deconcentrating effect of the microprocessor on the IC market as a whole was of type $(--)$, and did not get reversed to $(++)$ in that total market, as the market leaders of the 1960s never really recaptured their leading positions.

That said, however, the summary of the case given above is an over-simplification in two important regards. First, the phenomenon of *second sourcing* (where firms produce direct copies of a particular design under licence) is very important in microprocessors. There appear to be marked deconcentrating trends that result from the growth of entrants producing second-source products only, and it is arguable that these are not really deconcentrating. The arguments above really apply to own-design production only, where second-source production has been omitted.

Second, the success of Intel was not simply attributable to a well-articulated and accurate vision. It was at least in part the result of Intel's strategy of rapidly expanding the network of supporting products and services around their microprocessors. Moreover, the success of Intel microprocessors was helped considerably by the decision of IBM to base its PC around the Intel 8088 eight/sixteen-bit product. Yet that decision should not be seen as exogenous. It was in turn a reflection of Intel's support network, the feedback they obtained through their marketing and distribution networks, and equally their clearly articulated vision of the future for the microprocessor. Bandwagon effects (including the custom of IBM) exhibit obvious positive feedback.

Memories

The memory market case-study (Gill 1990a) exhibits different deconcentrating and concentrating trends from the microprocessor market, and this is not perhaps surprising since the vision is a much simpler one and has been well accepted amongst most producers from the beginning. Moore's Law stated that the number of components per chip had doubled each year and this could be expected to continue.[7] Later it was recognized that the growth rate must tail off a bit, but exponential growth in the number of components per chip could still be expected. In the context of the memory market, this meant that the 16K dynamic RAM (DRAM) would be replaced by the 64K dynamic RAM (DRAM), and that in turn by the 256K DRAM, and so on. Within a particular product category, there would be improvements in the speed and power consumption of the device, but these possibilities would be exhausted quite quickly.

The first DRAM to market in large numbers (4K DRAM) was first introduced by Intel just before its microprocessor, and indeed the two devices would be used together. Yet it was never such a radical innovation on its own terms as the microprocessor, and market leaders in semiconductors before the introduction of the 4K DRAM were for the most part reasonably successful at entering the memory market. Memory was not (at first) as disruptive an influence on the semiconductor market as the microprocessor.

Within the sub-market for any size of memory chip (e.g. 4K), the inevitable deconcentration $(--)$ would follow as new entrants joined the pioneers. But in the early days the other parameters of the product were being improved, and so long as this happened, the rate of decline of concentration was fairly slow. When, however, these improvements in other parameters stopped, more widespread entry would take place, and the deconcentrating effects $(--)$ would be more marked. Towards the end of the life cycle for that particular chip size, reconcentration would be observed, but this would often be of the form $(+-)$ as those remaining in the market at the end would not necessarily be the market leaders at an earlier stage.

This may seem at odds with the argument that rapid change along a well-recognized trajectory (consistent with most firm's visions) is concentrating towards the early incumbents. On closer inspection, however, it is not. During the reconcentrating phase, many of the higher-cost technology leaders exit from the market for that particular chip size, and move up to the next generation (i.e. from 4K to 16K, etc.). This sub-market would be in the introductory phase of its product life-cycle, but soon it would enter the growth phase as it made the earlier generation obsolete for many users. In short by moving up to the next generation at a judicious moment the technology leading pioneer could maintain market share while abandoning the declining market to low-cost competition, often from the newly industrializing countries (NICs) of South-East Asia, but also from Europe.

In short, as the technology trajectory sped from 4K to 16K to 64K, and so on, the early pioneers (Intel and Fujitsu, for example) managed to maintain their market leadership. Viewed across all memory sub-markets, therefore, the long-term effect on concentration is no worse than $(==)$, and sometimes $(++)$.

The memory market, moreover, is perhaps the most striking example of the third concentrating effect – namely, the marked increase in size of the key players. Many commentators would observe that this is simply the result of the ever-increasing capital intensity of memory production. Against that background concentration more or less has to be $(++)$ or $(+-)$.

But this answer is incomplete: *why* has production become ever more capital intensive? It is not, surely, a purely exogenous phenomenon. And why is it more marked in memories than elsewhere? The answer must have something to do with the clarity of the vision of the future for this technology. Against that background, memory manufacturers were confident to invest in ever more capital-intensive (and perhaps in the short term short-term inflexible) production technologies. Had the technological vision been less clear or less confidently held, manufacturers would have been more cautious, and the degree of capital intensity would not have grown so fast.

Standard logic

Standard logic (see Gill 1990b) is the precursor to the microprocessor approach to circuit design. As such it is an old technology, dating to the early 1960s. While the integrated circuit was considered quite a radical idea in the earliest days, the trajectory it has followed since has been fairly straightforward – except in one important respect. The two main aspects of technology change have been, first, the improving speed and power performance of the circuit technologies from which standard logic building-blocks were made and, second, the expanding range of these building-blocks made possible by the continuing miniaturization of components and consequent increase in functionality per chip. This has been the vision and the reality for most of the history of standard logic.

The one area in which the vision was blurred (or at least conflicting visions were held), and accordingly the one respect in which the trajectory has not been straightforward is in the underlying semiconductor technology used to make these building-blocks. One of the earliest integrated circuit technologies, transistor transistor logic (TTL), is still the market leader today, albeit in a much upgraded version. In the market for TTL building blocks, the effect of steady technology change as described above has been very near to (==), and on occasions mildly (++). The market has shown consistently high and stable concentration ratios, and the level of disruption or turbulence is remarkably small (see Gill 1990b).

But amongst the other technologies – most of which have not been particularly successful – one (CMOS) has emerged as a serious challenger to TTL. CMOS is radically different from TTL in its speed/power trade-off, and in its method of production. When the two sub-markets (TTL and CMOS) are grouped together, CMOS is seen to have a deconcentrating effect on the market (− −), because the firms who have been most successful in TTL have not for the most part been so successful in CMOS (and *vice versa*).

Again, this story is something of an over-simplification. As with the microprocessor, standard logic components are not used on their own, but rather they are assembled into a network of chips. Having the same network feature as the microprocessor, we would expect them to be subject to concentrating trends of the (++) type in the latter stages of a product life-cycle. In fact, the product ranges of different manufacturers may overlap to a significant degree, in the sense that there are standard building-blocks that can be obtained from more than one manufacturer. For that reason a network can be assembled using the products of more than one manufacturer, and the concentrating effect of network externalities would not be as high as in the microprocessor case.

PC applications software

The case study of PC applications software (Swann 1991) illustrates two of the polar opposites discussed above. Rapid incremental change of a fairly predictable sort – the sequence of upgrades (including the incorporation of rivals' innovations into the product) to a particular software package – tends to be steadily concentrating (++). Indeed, the standard economic model of *de facto* standards (with upgrades) seems to apply rather well to this incremental change (see Swann and Shurmer 1991). As the software trade press frequently observes, much software innovation is of this sort.

But there have been more radical software innovations, so radical indeed, they spawn new software categories – so that some users start to replace general-purpose ubiquitous tools with more special-ized purpose-designed software tools. This sort of innovation tends to be much more deconcentrating (− −). Indeed, some observers have suggested that in the software market a particularly deconcentrating rule applies: 'A firms' best product is its *first* one'.[8] If that is so – and we discuss below whether the rule is a plausible one – then a market leader in segment A (say) can never expect the same success in another market segment as it has enjoyed in A. Taken literally this must mean *either* that market segments for new software categories must be less concentrated than earlier market segments (which seems inplausible as the *de facto* standard process is a strong force for concentration); *or* that a new entrant will be the market leader in a new market segment.

But why should a firm's best product be its *first* one? The argument is in three steps. Some users tend to use a number of software products together, so that material is passed to and fro between one package and another (see Lamaison 1991). A successful product in one segment will have a certain 'look and feel' and the wise producer will seek to ensure that his offerings in other segments have a similar 'look and feel' so that the buyer of suites of programs is likely to buy them all from one source. While the producer is wise to exploit these network externalities (and switching costs), it does mean that they run the risk of applying a user interface originally designed for one environment to another environment, for which it is less suitable. In short, the producer of a market leader in segment A is so constrained in their user interface that they have to settle for a second-best design for market segment B (viewed as a stand-alone product), and hence they will not achieve such market success with that second product.

It may be asked whether the network externalities to the market leader in segment A don't more than offset the design constraint on the product from segment B? And if they don't, why does the producer let himself be constrained? The answer is that in the short to medium term these network effects *do* provide offsetting benefits; in the long term the design constraint becomes more and more serious. Yet incumbents dare not distance themselves from their existing network in the short term. These observations introduce some interesting dynamics into the economics of software production.

Our case study examined the market leaders in twenty-seven software categories. We found that relatively few firms were placed first in more than one market segment. Moreover, some of the market leaders are very small and young firms. More generally, concentration across the group of software markets was much less than would be expected. Moreover, the evidence suggests that correlation in leadership of different market segments is less than might be expected. All this suggests that the introduction of new software categories tends to be deconcentrating (− −).

Biotechnology: HIV diagnostics

This case study (Gill 1990c) concerns HIV (human immune-deficiency virus) diagnostics − that is, diagnostic kits used to mass screen blood donors for antibodies to HIV. As these are products used to perform tests, some of their technical characteristics are straightforward: sensitivity (the probability of a true positive test result conditional on obtaining a positive test result); specificity (the probability of a negative test result conditional on the patient not having the disease). In addition to cost, other important character-istics of the diagnostic kit include its speed of operation, ease of use and its shelf life.

Technology change in the period of study can be mapped in terms of these key characteristics, but also in two other ways. There have been three generations of diagnostic kit, which produce the antigen required for the diagnostic in three different ways. Second, there has been some progress in extending the scope of kits, so that the range of virus strains detected is increased.

The conclusion is that technology improvement *within* a particular generation of technology takes place for only a short period (about six months), and has relatively little influence on market structure. Indeed, during that period of improvement within a generation, there is still net entry and slightly falling concentration, but rela-tively little market share disruption. If this within-generation improvement has any effect at all, it acts to consolidate existing market structure (+ +).

The more important competitive influence on market structure is, we argue, the effect of changes from one generation to the next. The new generations rapidly make the products of earlier generations obsolete, and those firms successful in the market for one generation do not always find success with the next generation. In this sense, the between-generation shifts in technology are some-what disruptive, even if overall concentration stays very high (+ −). Having said that, the levels of disruption observed are (at the firm level) low compared to those observed in some of the semiconduc-tor cases.

Throughout the period studied, large firms were responsible for most of the new product introductions, and were the pioneers in ongoing developments (e.g. in the automation of tests). The implication for this study would be that none of the innovations described were radical enough to shake up market structure and generate significant deconcentration.

For an industry that is sometimes claimed to be very similar to semiconductors, this conclusion is a surprising one. But the implication is that the industries are not after all that similar. Perhaps the main reason for this is the different regulatory environments in the two industries. Semiconductor products have shorter development times and can even be marketed (up to a point) *before* they are ready – by the procedure of pre-announcements. This hardly applies to diagnostic kits, or more generally to pharmaceutical products, which have long lead times and whose marketing is subject to much tighter regulations. Many have observed that this is perhaps the main obstacle to the long-term survival of the small firm in biotechnology.

10.5 SUMMARY AND CONCLUSIONS

The main purpose of this study was to explore how the effects of technology change on market structure could depend on the speed, direction and, most of all, the predictability of that technology change. The underlying hypothesis has been that the effect of a given technology path depends on whether it is consistent with widely held 'visions of the future' of the technology. If it is, then large incumbents will be best placed to exploit economies of scale and consolidate their market share, and the net effect is concentrating. If not, then there is an opening (temporarily at least) for small, often start-up, firms to enter this new market, and the outcome is deconcentrating. The study has explored the theoretical and empirical support for this hypothesis.

The theoretical analysis has been summarized in a very flexible simulation model. The simulation model frequently generates outcomes where small organic firms play a key role in the early phase of a radical change in technology, but when the trajectory is better predicted, the large firms tend to take over again, unless the network effects are so strong that the small pioneer remains the market leader throughout – and becomes big in the process (+− in the overall market).

The case studies are of three sorts. First in microprocessors the radical innovation was deconcentrating and disruptive (−−) from the perspective of the total IC market, and where the pioneer was never displaced by earlier (pre-microprocessor) incumbents.

Ultimately the pioneer's market share started to rise again and from the perspective of the sub-market the effect was concentrating and non-disruptive ($++$).

Second, in semiconductor memories, rapid technology change between generations was concentrating ($++$) from the perspective of the overall market, though within a generation of the technology, ($+-$) would be observed at the end of its product life-cycle.

Third, and in contrast to semiconductor memories, in standard logic steady and predictable technology change within a generation served to consolidate market structure ($++$), while the introduction of CMOS (a totally different technology to the original TTL) was disruptive and deconcentrating ($--$). A similar story applies in software, where incremental innovations were typically predictable and served to increase concentration, while the appearance of new software categories seems to be deconcentrating. The biotechnology case studied (HIV diagnostic) is somewhat similar to the last two except that there is very little firm-level disruption in this market.

But while the case studies are of different forms, the support for our central hypothesis is still there. Rapid technology change of a predictable and well-anticipated form can be concentrating – for as long as it cannot be copied. Rapid technology change that is more radical, and less predictable, can by contrast be deconcentrating and disruptive, even if only temporarily.

The broad policy implication of these findings is this. It seems that even in capital-intensive industries subject to economies of scale, radical innovations can still be contrived which offer a temporary advantage to the smaller firm, and without such firms such radical innovations may take place more slowly (if they happen at all). The frequency of these openings may be low (and very low in some industries), and moreover it may be declining as large firms develop organizational structures exhibiting flexible specialization.[9] Nevertheless, they still exist, and infrequent as they may be, their economic significance is out of proportion to their frequency.

NOTES

1 It can be argued that the importance of patenting varies over the product life-cycle, and many of the important innovations identified in our studies, do not derive directly from a patent.
2 See for example, Editorial on the IBM PC, *Byte* January 1982, p. 6.
3 Similar stories are told of how difficult the leading manufacturers of carriages found it to compete effectively in the market for cars – and, *mutatis mutandis*, of difficulties faced by leading manufacturers of pens

in the market for biros, slide-rules in the market for calculators, and radio valves in the market for semiconductors.

4 Dasgupta and Stiglitz (1980) was one of the first papers in a large literature suggesting tendencies towards persistent dominance. On the analysis of patent races, see Harris and Vickers (1985).

5 The concepts of 'competence-destroying' and 'competence-enhancing' technology change (Tushman and Anderson, 1986) and the concept of 'organizational routines' (Nelson and Winter 1982) are very useful here. See Kay and Willman (Ch. 1 of this volume) for a review of some of these concepts, and also Webb and Cleary (Ch. 5 of this volume). A summary of how this literature informs our analysis is also given in Swann (1992).

6 One other aspect of changing industrial structure is the rise of joint ventures in such industries. This is not addressed here, but see Chapter 15 of this book (Georghiou and Barker).

7 This law was first articulated by G. Moore in 1964. See Noyce (1977).

8 I am grateful to Tom Prusa for this insight.

9 Blair (1972), by contrast, argues that the broad trend of innovation since the 1940s has been deconcentrating rather than concentrating, and Geroski and Pomroy (1990) find support for this too.

REFERENCES

Audretsch, D. (1992) 'The technological regime and market evolution: the new learning', *Economics of Innovation and New Technology* 2(1): 27–36.

Blair, J. M. (1972) *Economic Concentration: Structure, Behaviour and Public Policy*, New York: Harcourt Brace Jovanovich.

Burns, T. and Stalker, G. (1961) *The Management of Innovation*, London: Tavistock.

Byte (1982) Editorial on IBM PC, January 1982, p. 6.

Cohen, W. M. and Levinthal, D. A. (1990) 'Absorptive capacity: a new perspective on learning and innovation', *Administrative Science Quarterly* 35(1): 128–52.

Dasgupta, P. and Stiglitz, J. E. (1980) 'Uncertainty, industrial structure and the speed of R & D', *Bell Journal of Economics* 11: 1–28.

Geroski, P. A. and Pomroy, R. (1990) 'Innovation and evolution of market structure', *Journal of Industrial Economics* 38(3): 299–314.

Gill, J. (1990a) 'The speed of technology change and the development of market structure: memories', Brunel University, CRICT Discussion Paper.

—— (1990b) 'The speed of technology change and the development of market structure: standard logic', Brunel University, CRICT Discussion Paper.

—— (1990c) 'The speed of technology change and the development of market structure: Biotechnology (HIV Diagnostics)', Brunel University, CRICT Discussion Paper.

Harris, C. and Vickers, J. (1985) 'Patent races and the persistence of monopoly', *Journal of Industrial Economics* 33: 461–81.

Lamaison, H. (1991) 'Standards in PC software – questionnaire report', CRICT, Brunel University, unpublished paper.

Nelson, R. R. and Winter, S. G. (1982) *An Evolutionary Theory of Economic Change*, Cambridge, Mass: Harvard University Press.

Noyce, R. (1977) 'Microelectronics', *Scientific American* 237(3): 62–9.

Patel, P. and Pavitt, K. (1991) 'Large firms in the production of the world's technology: an important case of non-globalization', *Journal of International Business Studies* 22: 1–21.

Smith, D. K. and Alexander, R. C. (1988) *Fumbling the Future*, New York: Morrow.

Swann, P. (1990a) 'The speed of technology change and the development of market structure: theoretical issues', Brunel University, CRICT Discussion Paper.

—— (1990b) 'The speed of technology change and the development of market structure: Microprocessors', Brunel University, CRICT Discussion Paper.

—— (1992) 'The speed of technology change and the development of market structure: PC applications software', unpublished paper, London Business School.

—— (1992) 'Rapid technology change, "technological visions", corporate organization and market structure', *Economics of Innovation and New Technology* 2(1):3–25.

Swann, P. and Shurmer, M. (1991) 'Preannouncements, vertical quality competition, network externalities and de facto standards in the PC spreadsheet software market', Brunel University, Economics Discussion Paper.

Swann, P. and Gill, J. (forthcoming) *Corporate Vision and Rapid Technological Change: The Evolution of Market Structure*, London: Routledge.

Tushman, M. L. and Anderson, P. (1986) 'Technological discontinuities and organizational environments', *Administrative Science Quarterly* 31(3): 439–65.

11 The heart of where the home is

The innovation process in consumer IT products

Alan Cawson, Leslie Haddon and Ian Miles

11.1 INTRODUCTION

This chapter reports on a project which examined the process whereby products based on new information technologies are developed for the consumer market. By looking in some detail at innovation in three representative product areas, we sought to show how a range of possible product configurations which is made possible by advances in technology is narrowed down into specific product ideas and designs. We found it useful to refer to this range of possibilities as 'product space', within which several different kinds of products may be marketed (see also Miles, Cawson and Haddon 1992).

One of the aspects of product innovation that interests us is how information about consumer preferences and wishes is built into the process, given that with radically new innovations it is impossible to ask consumers directly. It seems to us that innovation is a complex interaction between 'technology push' and 'market pull' factors, and that various proxies for the market are employed during the development process, one of which is the understanding of the market success or failure of past products.

To explore this, we chose to study three kinds of product which have not yet been commercialized, so that at the time we were conducting our interviews we could observe the range of factors which goes into final product design prior to market launch. The three case studies are as follows.

Electronic messaging

Electronic messaging embraces a number of different products and services through which individual users can communicate from the home. One type (electronic mail or E-Mail) consists of screen-based communication through the use of modems attached to personal computers. Messages are sent over the public switched telecommunications network (PSTN), and held by the service providers (usually in a central mainframe computer) for access by the recipient, who logs onto the system from his or her personal computer. Another important kind of electronic messaging comprises facsimile transmission (fax), again through the PSTN, but in this case the modem is built into the product, rather than being sold to microcomputer owners as a peripheral device. Messages are sent directly from machine to machine, and are read in paper form rather than on a screen. Both of these different types of messaging have given rise to competing products with the same product space. They are both examples of *network-dependent technologies*, which face a critical-mass problem in their introduction. The utility of the product to any one user depends upon the number of other users connected to the network: a single modem or a single fax machine has zero utility, unlike, say, a microwave oven, which is just as useful to the user whether there is one or a million other users.

Home automation

The product space for home automation arises from technological possibilities opened up by the incorporation of microprocessor devices into domestic appliances ('white goods') and audio-visual products ('brown goods'). The connection of such devices onto a network within the home allows them to be controlled remotely, and linked together. In addition, the home network can be interfaced to the external telecommunications network, so that appliances can be controlled from outside the home. The principal applications concern energy management (control of heating and energy-hungry appliances such as washing machines and dishwashers), home security (alarms and remote sensing of intruders), entertainment (audio and video distributed through the home) and practical aids for the disabled and/or elderly. The successful interfacing of such a wide range of appliances requires the acceptance of common standards and protocols, where there are a number of competing systems. Home automation is another example of a network-dependent technology, but of a different kind. Here the network adds to the utility of the product, but does not define it. The problem for producers is that of convincing potential users that the extra value created by networking is worth the premium price of the individual appliances together with the cost of buying or installing the network.

Interactive compact-disk-based multimedia

Compact disks, which provide near-perfect digital sound, have proved to be one of the most successful consumer products of the 1980s. The two companies which hold the patents on CD technology, and which agreed common standards in advance of the launch of any consumer products, are Philips and Sony. In the process of defining CD-Audio as a consumer product, it became apparent to them that optical-disk digital technology opens up further product spaces for different kinds of applications. CD-ROM (CD-Read Only Memory) stores the equivalent of some 150 books on a single disk, and has found many applications in the publishing industry. CD-I (CD-Interactive) combines text, still and moving video images, computer graphics and sound, on a single disk which, unlike conventional television or video, can be accessed interactively rather than in linear form. All these CD-based technologies have in common that the 'product' combines hardware (the player) and software (the programme material). Such *software-dependent technologies* require the co-ordination of hardware and software production in order for a market to be developed. CD-I raises more complex problems for software production than did CD-Audio or CD-ROM, since an existing stock of software (music or books) cannot readily or simply be converted to the new medium. In this case innovation is just as importantly about the creation and marketing of software as about hardware. Since the CD-I standards were published in 1987 a number of competing, or potentially competing, products have been announced, which will put different firms, or coalitions of firms, in competition with Philips and Sony in the consumer market.

In this chapter we develop a dynamic model of the innovation process, which we use to explore what we think are the most important features of the three cases.

11.2 THE INNOVATION PROCESS

In none of our case studies can we identify the 'invention' of the product as a discrete event which can be detached from other events. Each of the products in some way depends on a 'cluster' or 'constellation' (Freeman and Perez 1988: 46–7) of innovations rather than a single invention, and a single firm can at the same time be involved at various different stages of innovation in related products. The engineers at Philips, who were exploring the applications of the laser in the 1960s, worked for a company which was at the same time introducing a major change in the product design of the tape recorder: the shift from reel-to-reel to the compact cassette. That 'product' was maturing, but changing through important incremental innovation (i.e. the storage technology for the tape), at precisely the same time that very early research was started on what was to become the radical innovation of the compact disk. The management of innovation in a very large company like Philips is a complicated organizational problem of linking innovative processes at very different stages, but which may come together at a later stage in competing or complementary products. Coupled to that is the problem – perennially acute for Philips – of moving from the laboratory to the market, from the domain of the engineer and the designer onto the agenda of the marketers.[1]

Innovation is also iterative, in the sense that experience is constantly being fed into the process, both of past products and of early generations of the product itself. In all three of our case studies, designers were influenced by the experience of the home computer boom of the 1980s, but the design teams read this experience in very different ways.[2] The early pioneers of electronic mail saw the spread of home computers as indicative of the potential of a much wider market, and tended to accept uncritically the scenarios of the ubiquitous multi-purpose home computer drawn by their manufacturers. By contrast, the designers of CD-I and its competitor, CDTV, sought to distance their products as far as possible from the home computer and position them as enhanced television rather than a computer. In the case of home automation, the home computer was one influence among many. Some designers saw the home computer as the heart of a home system, but others based their ideas on different precursors such as existing home security devices.

While it is important for product designers to track past products and use successful examples to try to 'position' new products, the lessons that can be read from past products are by no means unambiguous and can be uncertain where the use of the products is likely to involve quite different patterns of behaviour on the part of consumers. The outstanding success of audio compact disks led Philips designers to want to recapture some of that process with CD-I, but whereas audio CDs provided a perceptibly better means of doing something with which consumers were already familiar (i.e. listening to recorded music), interactive CD requires the user to adopt a very different kind of relationship to the television from that familiar from passive viewers. Producers' confidence in the potential of interactive CD was in part based on their reading of another successful past product – the infra-red remote control device – from which they took the view that consumers would want to exercise much more control over their television.

The experience of past innovation and the process of invention gives rise to what we can call a 'technological understanding' about the potential applications of new technologies. It is within this understanding that the idea of the 'product space' develops – that is, the cluster of applications of a particular family of technologies. Firms may be confident that there is a 'product space' for a particular technology, but much less confident about what particular product configurations are likely to be successful within that space. Thus our case studies of electronic messaging, home automation and interactive multimedia are examples not of products but of product spaces within which we can expect different products to be designed, often in direct competition to each other.

The bare elements of our conception of the innovation process are captured in Figure 11.1, in which product design is seen as only one stage in a cycle which is constantly repeated as products are marketed and the results are fed back into the process. The combination of invention and the experience of past innovation can also lead to 'technological misunderstanding' when the experience of past products is misinterpreted. The difference between understanding and misunderstanding for consumer products is tested in the market-place, and there is no suggestion here that technology is 'good' or 'bad' for such judgements lie outside the scope of our study. The criterion at work is market success. Thus from within the product space there arise different possibilities for configuring products, and from these one or more is launched into the market.[3] However, we do not treat 'the market' as an external omniscient referee sitting in judgement on product success and failure. We see it instead as a set of information flows between producers and consumers in which successful producers listen and learn from as well as speak to consumers.

Treating the market in this way reminds us that information does not stop flowing at the point of sale, and that a great deal of information relevant to innovative success can be gained by monitoring the experience of consumers in *using* products. This is

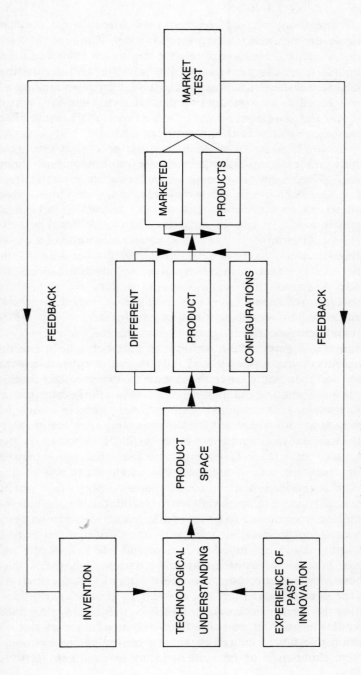

Figure 11.1 The elements of the innovation process for consumer products

especially important because consumers will often use products in ways which are not anticipated by producers – a process that we call 'post-purchase innovation'.[4] The home computer was originally conceived as a general-purpose machine which could be put to a variety of uses in the home, from cataloguing recipes and maintaining home accounts to word processing and games playing, and it was thought that this would give it more mass-market appeal than early games consoles which were restricted to a single application. In use, however, some of these more fanciful applications were discarded, and games playing became the most important single application. Eventually home computers were reconfigured to stress their dominant application, and games-only computer consoles such as Nintendo made a successful reappearance. An entirely new range of home computers specifically configured for word processing was launched by Amstrad with its PCW machines; the range was built at a cost sufficiently low for it to be able to compete against electric typewriters rather than the existing array of (professional) word processors (Thomas 1990). This example should alert us to the point that important innovations can occur at any stage in the cycle, and can consist of reconfigurations of existing technology rather than technological breakthroughs.

In Figure 11.2 we put some flesh on the bare bones of the model by representing the knowledge and skills that different actors bring to the process. In some cases the nature of the product space is such that skills and competences – what Teece (1987) calls 'complementary assets' – are required which are not available within the firm (sometimes not within *any* single firm), and a variety of inter-firm alliances and joint ventures may be required to bring together the necessary expertise. In the case of the interactive compact disk, where the success of the product was known to require the simultaneous production of hardware and software, this problem was especially acute. The development of interactive multimedia software involves bringing together the design and production skills of a range of professionals working in quite different industries, such as computer programmers and audio and video producers and designers. Philips did not have sufficient expertise in-house, and so set up two joint-venture companies in the United States, American Interactive Media and Optimage, in order to gain access to these skills. The problem of software production was also compounded by the reluctance of other firms to invest in advance of market launch: a familiar 'chicken and egg' problem where a large installed base of machines is a prerequisite for firms to invest in software

production, and an extensive software catalogue is needed to persuade consumers to invest in the hardware. In the case of CD-I,
Philips has attempted to solve this problem by investing itself in
software production, and subsidizing other firms to produce software titles in order to offset some of their risk.

The balance of the contribution of the different actors involved
in the 'whole product' varies considerably between firms, but also
between different product spaces within the scope of the same firm.
Philips is a major player in both home automation and interactive
multimedia, but it has organized the innovative effort in these
product areas in very different ways. In both cases the original
product space was understood as 'IT in the Home' so that its home
automation products and CD-I were configurations within the same
space. Later on, however, as the technologies developed and
market conditions changed, interactive compact-disk based multimedia was identified as a product space in its own right and
detached from home automation. Philips management at main
board level identified CD-I as an important product for the future
of the company, and in effect put home automation onto a back
burner. A separate organizational structure was created – Philips
Interactive Media Systems – better to co-ordinate the complex tasks
involved in launching CD-I.[5] In many ways home automation is yet
more complex, involving as it does the co-ordination of efforts from
an even more heterogeneous range of actors such as house-builders
and public-sector utilities.

The various actors represented in Figure 11.2 draw their knowledge and experience from different sources. What we have been
concerned to do in our research is to probe how systematic this
knowledge base is, and how far it incorporates information about
consumer markets and consumer behaviour. How far is the definition of the product space itself, as well as the design paradigms
of the consumer products within it, based on producer perceptions
of consumers, and how far on evidence taken directly from consumers? What we have found is that firms place a good deal of
reliance on tacit knowledge accumulated by producers. The use of
systematic theories (e.g. in marketing and consumer psychology) is
more than offset by unsystematic experiential knowledge gleaned
from a wider community of actors which meets at industry conferences and exhibitions, or in trade associations, or is passed on by
trade and professional journals.[6] Such knowledge is not necessarily
'inferior' to the use of systematic theories, since we have reason to
question the real-world relevance of some of those theories, for

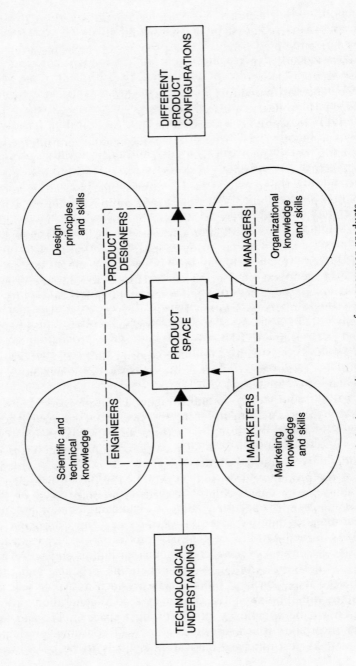

Figure 11.2 A firm-centred model of the innovation process for consumer products

example, the life-style approaches used by marketers in segmenting potential markets (Zablocki and Kantner 1976). What seems to be important is whether and how such knowledge is tested. Japanese consumer electronic companies seem not to employ conventional market research techniques at all; indeed, the president of the Sony Corporation rejects them explicitly as having no relevance to new technology products (Morita 1988). But what many of them do, successfully, is operate a very rigorous process of testing prototype products both with users and early purchasers, and it is the results of such empirical tests which feed back into the innovation process.

The firms in our case studies do use some systematic techniques for pre-market tests, for example focus groups to tease out consumer reactions to both the product space and to possible or probable product configurations. User reaction to electronic messaging, home automation and interactive multimedia has been tested and will continue to be tested. The difference, at least at first sight, and without the benefit of first-hand research in Japan, seems to be that in Europe such techniques are used *before* product launches, whereas in Japan they are used extensively after test marketing to early adopters where the final designs for the eventual mass market products are not yet fixed. Early purchasers are offered prototypes at prices which reflect estimates of later mass-production costs, rather than development costs. If the market tests and monitoring of consumer reaction are favourable, then the firms ramp up mass production very quickly. If not, the products disappear even more quickly back into the labs. In Europe 'the launch' is a major event, with pre-publicity and often major advertising effort. In Japan new product prototypes appear in the major Tokyo consumer electronics stores without pre-publicity, and 'the launch' takes place later when the probability of final success is higher.

The pattern of innovation in electronic IT products for the home suggests that one of the consequences of the shortening of the product life-cycle is the near continuous launching of new product configurations within the same product space. The estimation of producers of the 'shelf life' of their new products is reduced as each successive generation of products is launched. Philips engineers, for example, know that CD-I is a first-generation product, and that even before it is launched, other producers such as Apple will be competing with Philips in the design of second-generation prototypes. Given the complexity of the product space in IT, and the level of uncertainty which surrounds all new IT consumer products, we think that post-purchase innovation is likely to be of growing importance, especially as the distinction between 'professional' and 'consumer' IT products is becoming more and more blurred.[7] Products now used in the home offer power and functionality which only a few years ago was available only to professionals. We should not be surprised if the imagination of millions of consumers surpasses that of a small number of professionals. The next generation of interactive multimedia products which is based on recordable CD technology will offer almost unlimited scope for innovative usage, and opportunities for small businesses in much the same way as independent video rental stores helped to shape the pattern of how VCRs were used.

Thus Figures 11.1 and 11.2 should be read as a rough guide to a complex set of processes. It is a task-related representation of innovation rather than one which builds on product characteristics or firm or industry characteristics. To that extent it is very general, and useful in so far as it can help us to identify commonalities and differences within more concrete processes of innovation. The next section of this chapter attempts to do this for our three case studies. It examines the specific nature of the general concepts like 'technological understanding' as revealed in the innovation process for specific technologies. It will not be applied exhaustively but will be used to identify some of the more important issues in consumer innovation in IT.

11.3 INNOVATION STREAMS, STANDARDS AND THE DEFINITION OF 'PRODUCT SPACE'

Interactive multimedia, home automation and electronic messaging are all technologies which may have an impact on the mass consumer market in the 1990s. If we look at the technological heritage of these potential consumer products we can identify the confluence, and then sometimes the separation, of a number of innovation streams, including those flowing from what we may call 'heartland technologies'. The specific technology that is common to our three cases, and beyond them common to IT in general, is the microprocessor. All of our cases use, and indeed depend on microprocessor technology, for their potential in the domestic market. Although fax technology dates back to the nineteenth century, until the 1980s it was a 'professional' technology with very restricted applications, especially in the newspaper industry. The respecification of the product as an everyday 'personal' technology, easy to use and affordable for the home, would not have been possible without the microprocessor. Likewise E-Mail originated amongst professional computer users, but with the diffusion of cheap microcomputers and modems into the home, it became possible to offer E-Mail as a consumer product.

The two heartland technologies which are the most important for our case studies are the microprocessor and the laser. It is the application of these which has created and helped to shape the product space for the new domestic ITs we have studied. Neither of these technologies completely redefined the product space, since the new products are sub-sets of more general forms of communication which have been developing for a very long time. They did, however, allow for a radical reshaping of the products, and through this open up the possibility of their being incorporated into mass-market consumer products.

Other innovation streams are also significant for our cases. For example, electronic messaging had its origins in the use to which large mainframe computers were put, and the development of networking through terminals attached to mainframes. Once computers were connected to the telephone network through modems, the possibility arose for the network operators to offer remote computing power, in the form of retrieval of information from central data bases, to domestic telephone subscribers via a link to the domestic television. But it was the microprocessor which permitted cheap computing power to become available to personal users, and opened up a product space for alternative forms of messaging (e.g. bulletin boards) not dependent on large central mainframes. Further the coupling of the modem to facsimile technology as a computer peripheral enabled a different form of electronic messaging, through the medium of paper as well as electronic pulses, to appear as a competitor to earlier forms of E-Mail. Such confluences of major and minor innovation streams shift the understandings of the product space, as well as change the identity of competing products and the nature of the competition between them. Again we find that the vision of E-Mail in the home begins with the simple idea of users leaving messages for each other in a central mailbox, but then becomes more complex and more uncertain as parallel technologies are fed into the process. The separate fax machine appears as a potential home product and competitor to E-Mail, and subsequently the fax card for the PC is developed.

This process, whereby parallel innovation streams cross each other to modify the technological characteristics of products, and perhaps open up new product spaces, does take place within particular institutions which have quite different kinds of interests and approaches which affect the way in which innovations are embodied in product design and marketing strategies. The most important difference we have noted in our research is that between firms which sell predominantly to consumer markets, and those with institutional and public-sector customers. The different approaches can be illustrated by contrasting approaches to the issue of setting standards.

Where, on the one hand, products are developed in the context of the consumer electronics industry, and the target market is seen as predominantly made up of households, then inter-product competition gives rise to *de facto* standards around the characteristics (and often patents) of the successful product. In the consumer video market, for example, a long process of competition led to the emergence of VHS and the eclipse of the competing Betamax and V2000 formats. But with further innovation, especially in camcorders, a successor format battle is currently being waged between VHS and Super-VHS in one 'camp' and 8mm and Hi–8 in another. This battle was only the latest in a long line stretching back through cassette versus eight-track tape technology to drum and disc phonographs. *De facto* standards setting can be extremely expensive for the loser and provides an incentive to collaborate in setting standards before market launch, as was successfully done between Philips and Sony with CD-Audio, and is being attempted with CD-I. Pre-market standardization such as was achieved with CD products is, however, relatively rare, and does not mean that the same firms will extend the process to other products. Both Philips and Sony have developed competing recordable digital audio technologies – the Philips Digital Compact Cassette and the Sony Mini-Disk despite over ten years of collaboration over CD.

Where, on the other hand, the innovation stream, runs through public-sector institutions and public markets, it is more likely that there will be a common interest in either collaboration towards defining *de facto* standards or institutional pressures for the definition of *de jure* standards through public standards bodies such as the International Standards Organization (ISO) or Cenelec.

The home automation case demonstrates this process very well. Since it is a network technology, both within the home, and connecting the home to the outside world through telephone or television cables, the various actors can quickly perceive the benefits of early moves towards common standards so that the different products of different manufacturers will all work with each other.

Individual manufacturers do not themselves make the whole range of home automation products, but the fact that their products can be connected to those of other manufacturers adds value to their products. In so far as telecoms network operators and public utilities are involved, the latter, for example, in mains-borne signalling technology, there is a predisposition towards agreed *de jure* standards in advance of mass-market launch. Leading firms have been involved in European collaborative Eureka and subsequently Esprit projects which have had the definition of common standards as their prime objective. But the process, which once again seemed relatively uncomplicated in its early stages, became more complex as parallel developments occurred in telephony, especially the development of the Integrated Services Digital Network (ISDN) pioneered by the public-networks operators. A network technology for inside the home, like Philips' Digital Data Bus (D2B), is greatly affected by ISDN technology, and at the very least engineers have to develop interface technology and interface standards to allow communication to flow between the two networks. The result is a familiar story: technology takes much longer to introduce than we originally expected.

The expected diffusion paths for E-Mail into the home have been complicated by the development of the low-cost personal fax. Likewise, Philips and Sony expected that the CD-I standard that they had agreed in 1986 would lead to the early launch of CD-I as a consumer product. However, parallel technological progress in digital video compression by the RCA Sarnoff Research Laboratories, and the announcement of Digital Video Interactive (DVI) by RCA in 1987, forced Philips and Sony to reconfigure CD-I to include full-screen full-motion video for the consumer product. Parallel work on digital video compression for the motion picture industry and the telecoms industry has put compression technology into the institutional domain where *de jure* standards are critical. The result has been a further delay in the launch of CD-I whilst the ISO considers draft proposals, including CD-I, for a common standard for video compression which is expected by 1992. Even before its launch as a professional product, the new owners of DVI, Intel, have been forced to adopt a new video compression technology in order to keep abreast of technical change. The longer the delay, the more likely it becomes that competing products will be launched and yet another format battle joined. The advantage of such battles, however, is that they avoid the danger of prescribing the future course of the innovation process through non-market-sensitive collective decisions.

11.4 FROM 'INVENTION' TO 'PRODUCT SPACE'

We have suggested that there are major and minor innovation streams, which can divide and join in unexpected ways. It has been a constant feature of innovation that technologies developed in one context are applied imaginatively – sometimes through the genius of a single individual – to areas quite unrelated to their origins. Entirely new industries such as semiconductors and biotechnology have arisen through *spin-offs* from existing technologies. At a more-modest level, the application of laser technology to recording sound and pictures onto an optical disk was one such spin-off. In order to turn this into a marketable product, complementary innovations in both materials and processes were required, as was the further development of microprocessor and integrated-circuit technology. But the definition of the product space, as well as the process of configuring the first products, took place against the realization that the designing of appropriate applications software was going to be crucial to the success of the product. This software could not be created using existing skills and firms; new kinds of integration were required for multimedia design. Work on the software infrastructure led Philips to a series of international joint ventures, and to a considerable investment over a period of several years before any return could be expected from the consumer market.

In contrast to CD-I, home automation has been a *spun-together* technology, in which quite separate innovation streams came together to create the potential for home automation products. Innovation in domestic electrical technology, mains-borne signalling, building materials, audio-visual networking and local area computer networking offered potential for interlinkages. The tendency to control electrical appliances through built-in microprocessors offered the potential for their being linked together via a network and controlled remotely. Here the product space was deeply influenced by technological possibilities in many cases derived independently of any systematic understanding of consumer needs or demands. But in Britain, under the auspices of a quasi-governmental body (NEDO), some consumer research was undertaken which helped producers to see how they might configure products. In this case, however, the range of players and the variety of configurations is enormous, and the boundaries of the product space are less clear than for interactive multimedia. Different combinations of actors, such as the Esprit group and the Home of the Future consortium, represent different kinds of firms, and they tend to define the product space in different ways. Smaller hardware firms can identify market niches (e.g. in products for the disabled) and develop products within the space that can be marketed independently but may later be adapted as standards are set.

Electronic mail to the home via the telephone network is a classic example of a technological solution in search of a problem, and can be described as *technology-focused* product space. In Britain Prestel was devised using available computer technology to get more revenue from the networks, but its introduction pre-dated both the home computer and the development of more user-friendly man-machine interfaces. Thus in its original form it used a keypad, a modem and a television, and its marketing was based on the (unresearched) concept of there being an unfulfilled consumer demand for general information held in computer databases. The interpersonal electronic messaging was added to the system later on, when the means of accessing Prestel had become the personal computer. Its diffusion into the home was largely restricted to home computer hobbyists, and assisted by the development of cheap modems for Sinclair machines.

The potential of E-Mail for a wider consumer market remains uncertain, especially in the face of advances in personal fax technology made by Japanese consumer electronics and office equipment suppliers. Their ease of use and familiarity suggest a much greater potential for people working at home, but perhaps later more generally as a consumer product. Both examples of electronic messaging illustrate the more general proposition that the boundaries between consumer and professional products and technologies are continuing to become more blurred. Domestic fax is more clearly *demand-focused*, its diffusion more observable through signs and letterheads, and its user interface is less complex and more familiar.

11.5 FIRMS IN THE INNOVATION PROCESS

Within firms and inter-firm networks we have identified the key actors as engineers, product designers, marketers and line managers. Their numbers, designations and distribution within the firm varies considerably according to the type of firm and the nature of the technology.

CD-I involves as core partners three of the world's biggest consumer electronics companies and a major manufacturer of microprocessors and integrated circuits. Its early development was engineer-driven; indeed, the original two core partners, Philips and Sony, have long been regarded as innovators and pioneers of new technology with very large corporate R & D centres. Philips experienced some difficulty in securing an organizational home for CD-I development within the corporate structure once the basic R & D was completed and the product development phase in progress. For many years Philips had twin hierarchies of engineers and commercial managers at each level of the company, and its multinational operations were composed of a loose federation of semi-autonomous national organizations. During the lifetime of CD development, Philips has attempted to move to a product division structure across its entire field of activity. CD-Audio player manufacture was established in a single vast plant in Belgium to serve the global market. With CD-I, however, the more complex relationship between hardware and software, and the overlap between professional and consumer markets, has meant that the company has found it difficult to establish secure boundaries. Traditional interdivisional rivalries between telecommunications and consumer electronics, and between consumer-oriented divisions and business systems, confused the innovation strategy for CD-I and led to the reorganization of divisional boundaries. The variety of skills required for software development led Philips to try to manage a number of different groups of creative professionals in computer software and the audio-visual industries with whom their line managers had little experience of dealing. The web of joint ventures that made up American Interactive Media proved expensive to operate and difficult to control. The eventual solution may well be that Philips goes even further than it has already gone in relaxing its attempt to control software development and enforce quality standards. In 1990 Philips went into the red for the first time in its 99-year history, and simply cannot afford to carry all the costs of developing the software infrastructure.

Home automation reflects some of the same diversity of skills and professional communities, but unlike CD the number of firms involved in hardware development is large and the number includes many medium-sized and small firms. Many of these firms combine the tasks of R & D, product design, line management and marketing. It is for this reason, as well as for the standards issue discussed above, that formal and informal means of collaboration have been embraced. However, it is clear that many of these smaller firms feel excluded from the processes at work in Eureka and Esprit, and the large firms appear to benefit disproportionately from the public money distributed through such programmes. The experience of home automation shows how difficult it is to manage inter-firm collaboration in a way which is seen to be just by those firms excluded from formal participation. An as yet unresolved issue for Esprit is that of what happens when the phase of 'pre-competitive collaboration' ends, and the phase of fierce inter-firm competition in the market-place is supposed to begin. It will only become a pressing issue, however, if specific products appear from the collective effort which promise to achieve a substantial market. The market potential analysed in consultants' reports has yet to be tested.

Electronic mail presents another variation in terms of firms and industry structures. The network is managed by a very strong firm (BT) with a smaller competitor (Mercury), and both have already launched E-Mail services aimed at both professional and small business/residential markets. Other providers will include cable TV operators and a number of other organizations (including British Rail) about to be licensed by the government to offer competing services to those of BT and Mercury. All of these new players will investigate the provision of domestic E-Mail alongside smaller firms which offer services over BT or Mercury (or soon, other) networks. The different versions of product configuration for domestic electronic messaging tend to include the same hardy perennials like home banking and home shopping, none of which has yet proved to be a mass market proposition. Fax may offer a more perceptible cost and efficiency advantage over the postal services, especially as the number of users increases beyond the critical-mass threshold, which has yet to happen in the consumer market for E-Mail. Compared to E-Mail, fax is easy to use and does not require keyboard skills. The suppliers of fax equipment are major Japanese consumer electronics firms with a wealth of experience of responding to consumer demand. By contrast E-Mail providers are new service operators targeting niche markets, or BT (which lacks experience of selling in a competitive market directly to consumers).

11.6 FROM INVENTION TO INNOVATION: THE MARKET TEST

Successful innovation in consumer products can only occur when a product or a technology finds buyers. There are several examples, such as the V2000 VCR, where the 'better' technology has failed and the 'inferior' technology has succeeded. All of our case studies come from the field of consumer electronics and involve technologies where there is unlikely to be a substantial amount of public purchasing. In addition, the technology cannot usually be argued to have strategic implications for national economic or defence security, which might justify public subsidies. The test of successful innovation in these product spaces is almost entirely a market test.

In such cases the advertising and marketing effort is an important determinant of success, and the winning firms are likely to be those where marketing criteria are built in to the innovation process at all stages, and not simply at the final stage after products are designed. Market intelligence can help to shape a product, and it is often innovative configurations of existing technologies, rather than sallies into novel product spaces, which provide substantial rewards. The radio/cassette combination, twin-deck cassette players, and, above all the Sony Walkman, are examples of imaginative reconfigurations of 'maturing' products. Such innovation can take place in software as well as hardware, and it is likely that we will see existing audio-visual material creatively 'reworked' to provide quite new interactive programming. In CD-I hardware we will see lap-top and hand-held players, as well as a spate of attempts to provide combinations of CD-I with existing audio-visual products like CTV and VCR. As we have seen with VCRs, the development of a standard leads suppliers to differentiate their offerings from those of their competitors by way of adding more and more features. The advent of recordable CD in the 1990s will add the further dimension of post-purchase innovation on the part of users which will greatly shape the social impact of the technology.

Home automation provides the most scope within our chosen case studies for different product configurations, in part because of the much larger number and diversity of suppliers, which means that the product space is less densely populated. For the mass market, early indications suggest that, at least in Britain and the United States, home security will be an important initial application. But also significant, especially in offering opportunities to small firms, is the application of the technology to the needs of the elderly and the disabled, where public policies may well influence at least to some extent the direction of the market. However, such diversity leads to acute problems for suppliers of how to market home automation products, and how to give it a consistent (and non-threatening) image when many consumers express fears of being controlled by machines. Such problems suggest a slow and incremental build-up of the market, with as many failures as successes. Here the ability of suppliers to test prototypes and respond quickly to market signals may be a critical factor in determining which of the vast number of players accumulates a winning hand. The possibility of world standard products, like the fax machine, VCR and CD-Audio and eventually CD-I, is a remote one in home automation, given the sheer heterogeneity of consumer habits and tastes in most of the various application areas, and the mosaic of national regulations in areas such as building and public utilities.

11.7 CONCLUSION: INNOVATION AS A PROCESS

The emphasis in this chapter has been on seeing innovation as a dynamic and cyclical process which encompasses the sale of the products as well as their research, development and design. We have argued that the idea of the product space can be useful in highlighting the extent to which technological spin-offs and convergences present opportunities for new products, but by no means guarantee successful innovation. It is fortunately not our task to predict what successful products will arise from those examined in our case studies. We have given some considered views, however, on those factors which affect the boundaries of the product space and which affect the configuration of products within it. We have drawn particular attention to organizational factors within the firm, and in inter-firm collaboration. In consumer markets the important role of such organizational structures should be to collect and interpret data on market characteristics, and feed it continuously into the innovation process. We have commented on the weight put on anecdotal and indirect evidence of consumer preferences and behaviour, which arises in part because of the difficulties of applying standard market research techniques to radically new technologies. What could be done, but is rarely done in any serious way, would be to collect evidence in detail and in depth about the way in which consumers use technology in the home. It seems to us that a better appreciation of domestic life, and the role played within it by specific products, would help to identify specific needs around which firms could organize product design, and even allocate resources for research and development.

NOTES

1 For a discussion of the importance of firm structure (or 'architecture') in managing innovation, see the Chapters in this book by Grindley (Ch. 2) and by Kay and Willman (Ch. 1) and also Grindley (1991).
2 The experience of the innovation of the home computer is extensively documented in Haddon (1988).
3 This approach has a good deal in common with Teece's (1987) concept of design paradigms. For an application in telematics, see Thomas and Miles (1990).
4 Fleck (1990) also emphasizes the importance of user involvement in innovation in respect of industrial users.
5 Swann and Gill (Ch. 10 of this volume) refer to similar problems in the innovation of the Personal Computer which had different outcomes at IBM and Xerox.
6 Cleary and Webb (Ch. 5 of this volume) also draw attention to the role of 'informal networks' in transferring expertise between firms.
7 The VCR was a 'professional' innovation adapted for domestic use (Rosenbloom and Cusumano 1987); Digital Audio Tape (DAT) recorders were a 'consumer' innovation adopted by professional broadcasters.

REFERENCES

Fleck, J. (1990) 'The development of information-integration: beyond CIM?' Department of Business Studies, University of Edinburgh, Working Paper Series 90/2.
Freeman, C. and Perez, C (1988) 'Structural crises of adjustment, business cycles and investment behaviour', in G. Dost *et al* (eds) *Technical Change and Economic Theory*, London: Pinter.
Grindley, P. (1991) 'Turning technology into competitive advantage' *Business Strategy Review*, Spring: 35–48
Haddon, L. (1988) 'The roots and early history of the British home computer market', unpublished PhD thesis, Imperial College, University of London.
Miles, I., Cawson, A. and Haddon, L. (1992) 'The shape of things to consume', in R. Silverstone and E. Hirsch (eds) *Consuming Technologies*, London: Routledge.
Morita, A. (1987) *Made in Japan*, London: Fontana.
Rosenbloom, R. S. and Cusumano, M. A. (1987) 'Technological pioneering and competitive advantage: the birth of the VCR industry', *California Management Review* 21(4):51–76.
Teece, D. (1987) 'Capturing value from technological innovation', in B. Guile and H. Brooks (eds) *Technology and Global Industry*, Washington: National Academy Press.
Thomas, D. (1990) *Alan Sugar: The Amstrad Story*, London: Century.
Thomas, G. and Miles, I. (1990) *Telematics in Transition*, Harlow: Longmans.
Zablocki, B. D. and Kantner, R. M. (1976) 'The differentiation of lifestyles', *Annual Review of Sociology No. 2*, Palo Alto: Annual Reviews.

Part IV

Financing new technology

12 Internal and external financial constraints on investment in innovative technology

Alasdair Lonie, Bill Nixon and David Collison

12.1 INTRODUCTION

In-depth enquiries such as those recently conducted by the CBI (1991) and the House of Lords Select Committee on Science and Technology (1991) invariably report the existence of significant constraints on manufacturing investment in the United Kingdom. However, it is notoriously difficult to determine the relative importance of the plethora of constraints that are identified because of the complexity of the decision-making process and the heterogeneity of the company sector. In large companies the flow of formal and informal information across organizational levels and functions tends to make assessment of the dominant factors influencing the timing and level of investment relatively tentative. In smaller companies the lack of formalized procedures means that there is frequently no clear audit trail, particularly when decisions are taken by an owner-manager, seemingly almost entirely on the basis of intuition refined by many years of experience.

This chapter examines the relationship between strategy and financial appraisal, highlighting the entrepreneurial (or quasi-entrepreneurial) role of the 'project champion'; it draws heavily on case-study material and focuses on external as well as internal constraints on innovative investment. The study examined quantitative and qualitative data relating to the capital expenditure decisions of thirteen companies (ten in the United Kingdom and three in the United States) that had made significant investments in new technology. Three of the UK companies were launched by venture capital finance in the 1980s. In the case of one highly innovative company twenty years of data were examined. For a number of others nine years or less of data were analysed, the length of the analysis generally depending on the age of the company. All of these companies undertook most of the manufacturing/assembly work relating to their products. Our case studies represent both innovation and diffusion of technology. At least five of the companies in our study regularly generate products and processes that are new to the industry. In the case of the three large US manufacturers senior executives believed that with a corporate culture so devoted to innovational goals any inhibitions in this respect could only lead to disorientation in the workforce and adverse judgements by the capital market. One of our UK case-study companies had developed a product so radical that it is still not subject to serious commercial challenge twenty years after its inception. Others believe that they have an innovational advantage of two years or less over their closest competitors. But a number of the projects examined involved the application of well-established technologies to the development of new or improved products for markets with which the companies were already closely connected. The fact that in our selection of innovating companies medium-sized firms were under-represented is consistent with the finding of Pavitt, Robson and Townsend (1987) that innovation tends to be concentrated in large and small firms; in practice we tended to visit firms with a fairly high tolerance of academic investigators.

The conceptual basis of the approach

The authors approached the role of internal and external constraints by enquiring why our case-study companies were not prevented by external financial pressures or by internal control systems from engaging in what were frequently high-risk innovational expenditures.

This chapter's approach is fairly wide-ranging and considers corporate culture, strategy, organizational structure and systems – including financial controls. It also attempts to relate insights developed in the liquidity literature of the late 1950s and early 1960s to more modern analyses of capital structure, financial distress and capital rationing. However, the twin themes of our investigation have been, first, to identity the nature of any strategic override of financial controls and, second, to gain insight into the nature of a corporate culture that is committed to innovation and seemingly impervious to external financial pressures that inhibit more conventionally managed companies. Our analysis of the capital expenditure decision process is grounded in the contingency theory literatures on management, management information systems and accounting.

We adopted this approach because the open-systems perspective of these literatures recognizes the dynamics of the interacting variables that influence technology investment decisions and corporate performance.

12.2 INTERNAL CONSTRAINTS ON INNOVATIVE COMPANIES

Strategy and financial appraisal: innovation at risk?

The 1980s witnessed a number of important contributions to the long-running debate over whether management accounting practices needlessly curb decisions to invest in new technology. Several different schools of thought have been identified (Swann 1988), but perhaps no great injustice is done if we group the protagonists into two main categories. On the one hand, there are writers who have argued that cost-accounting practices have operated to stifle the creative vision of individuals who are well versed in the intricacies of the production process, 'people with a deep understanding of machine design, software engineering and manufacturing processes' (Hayes and Jaikumar 1988: 78). The case that capital budgeting procedures are biased against strategic and innovative investment has been cogently argued. Project appraisals are said to ignore the qualitative longitudinal benefits of many advanced technology projects destined to initiate an inter-temporal sequence of capital expenditures (see, for example, Hayes and Abernathy 1980, Hayes and Garvin 1982, Kaplan 1984). High discount rates based upon an exaggerated and inappropriate perception of risk were enshrined in accounting conventions which frustrated innovative investment (Lee 1987, McNair *et al.* 1988, Myers 1987). Biases arising from an inconsistent treatment of inflation or the scramble for resources in the firm's 'internal capital market' went uncorrected. Financial appraisal ignored the organizational or strategic context of investment decisions and neglected the behavioural response of rival firms in its calculations (Hopwood 1985, Kaplan 1986b, Finnie 1988, Scapens 1988, Bromwich and Bhimani 1989). These points were often made with evangelical fervour and in a manner which revealed a measure of contempt for the accounting profession – 'bean counters' (Halberstam 1987, Frey 1991). A speaker addressing a conference of production managers is, it is said, assured a warm round of applause if he includes a vituperative reference to the role of management accountants in his talk.

On the other hand, there are the finance specialists who have acknowledged the force of many of these objections but noted the lack of financial sophistication of much of the strategic planning literature and suggested that a good deal of the criticism levelled at project appraisal is more properly directed against widespread malpractices in capital budgeting which financial management experts are seeking to eliminate. Capital budgeting is capable of adopting a broad view by calculating the covariances of the estimated cash flows of different projects and a long view by utilizing the theory of options. Identification of intangible benefits will result in enhanced net present values (NPVs). At the same time if management are intent on pursuing a project for which a positive NPV cannot be generated on an acceptable set of assumptions and employing best-practice appraisal techniques, it is assuredly the responsibility of any finance department to seek clarification of the grounds for the project's acceptance and an explanation for an executive decision which is, on the face of it, not economically rational. These reservations may be far from contemptible. Schmookler (1966) noted that only one or two out of five radically innovative projects achieve a level of sales which yields a break-even return, a verdict with which today's venture capitalist would not necessarily disagree. Again, the comment of US banker, J.H. Arnold in 1986, that the most pessimistic scenarios many businessmen are prepared to contemplate often prove overoptimistic has equal validity when applied to the United Kingdom. The problem is often not only the large cash-flow forecasting errors associated with new processes and new products but also the fact that several years may elapse before a company can determine whether an innovation is likely to achieve sustained profitability (Beardsley and Mansfield 1978, Biggadike 1979).

There is a fast-growing literature on the problem of how corporate strategy and financial appraisal may be most effectively reconciled (Myers 1987, Marsh *et al.* 1988, Barwise *et al.* 1989, Pike and Dobbins 1986, Finnie 1988, Swann 1988, Kaplan 1989, Samuels *et al.* 1990, Carr *et al.* 1991). In general such approaches advocate the adoption of what Pavitt and Patel (1988) have termed 'a technologically dynamic' evaluation of capital expenditures which nevertheless remains true to the principles of financial appraisal. However, generalization is fraught with danger in this area. It has been suggested that, 'The use of threshold levels of capital expenditure beyond which senior or board level managerial approval is required creates a bias towards smaller projects with conventional technology and against Advanced Manufacturing Technology (AMT)' (Samuels *et al.* 1990: 170). This statement may well apply to firms which use orthodox financial appraisal techniques in an unimaginative fashion for all projects. For a number of our UK case-study companies the opposite appeared to be the case: the financial appraisal standards applied to small projects were often significantly higher than those applied to major projects, a phenomenon noted by Marc Ross in his 1986 study of the capital budgeting practices of twelve large US manufacturing companies (Ross found that the hurdle rates applied to small projects were, in extreme cases, four times as high as those applied to a large investment). In some of the innovative companies that we studied strict criteria – for example, insistence on a high positive cash flow in the first year of operation – were not applied to major projects; they were subjected to a detailed evaluation procedure which was different in kind[1]. But the difference in treatment was not, as Hayes and Jaikumar have suggested, tantamount to a desperate attempt by the chief executive to rescue the fortunes of his company from the dead hand of the management accountant; rather it was a systematic separation of crucial market-driven investment decisions from those that were much less vital to the survival of the company. Ho and Pike (1991) have noted that a characteristic response of UK companies to the risks associated with new technology investments is to give special priority to the project's degree of fit with company strategy. A survey of UK management attitudes to risk by Daing (1992) revealed that managers were often prepared to trade-off abandonment value and NPV.

Overcoming 'Myopia': the role of the champion

The temptation to generalize from a small number of case studies should be strongly resisted, yet it is almost axiomatic that a successful innovating company must be run by one or more people with entrepreneurial qualities as well as administrative skills. Although the importance of the entrepreneur to innovational ventures has been understood throughout history, the role of the product (or project) champion seems to have been highlighted only relatively recently. It has gained wide currency in certain circles in the United States, and Bell Atlantic launched a 'Champion programme' in 1989 (in one of the high-performance US firms that we visited a young self-confident individual was introduced to us by a senior executive as 'our project champion' in charge of steering an important new project through its development stage to commercial viability and mass production). The problem of finding men with the attributes of a 'champion' was strongly emphasized. Also, according to the senior manager whom we interviewed, 'Your product champions are either marketing or technical persons. You rarely have a financial person . . . because most of the things that we are doing tend to revolve around a specific product or technology going to market'.

References to project champions cropped up repeatedly in the oral evidence in the House of Lords report on innovation in manufacturing technology. The belief that radical innovational ventures require the impetus of someone with exceptional drive, imagination, powers of co-ordination and character has been a theme in the literature of corporate strategy for many years (Schon 1963, Zaleznik 1977, Quinn 1979, Maidique 1980, Peters and Waterman 1982, Tichy and Devanna 1986, Lonie *et al.* 1988, House of Lords, Select Committee on Science 1991). The most systematic investigation of the characteristics of the champion of innovation in manufacturing industry is perhaps that by Howell and Higgins (1990) in the course of which they interviewed over 150 'key' individuals associated with twenty-eight successful innovations in twenty-five large Canadian organizations. One feature which emerged from their study was that, because of their exceptional self-confidence, champions apparently believed that they could undertake high-risk ventures without placing their job security or personal reputations in jeopardy. Confidence in their own abilities, combined with unswerving belief in the value of their project, resulted in the most tenacious pursuit of a successful outcome without apparent pause for reflection about the consequences of failure.

A number of observations are relevant. First, in Chapter 12 of the *General Theory* which discusses long-term risk-taking, Keynes (1936) represented such behaviour as heroic rather than rational. However, an ability to inspire others with infectious excitement about their manufacturing vision may produce a team commitment which substantially diminishes the likelihood of failure. Second, since risk-taking is perceived to be an essential quality of management, the relentless drive of champions to achieve a success in the management of innovations identifies them as future candidates for top executive positions. Champions appear to believe that they can control probabilities, altering the actuarial risk of failure by exercising their special powers and persuading others to share their conviction (March and Shapira 1988). Third, according to Howell and Higgins, champions normally enjoy a large measure of autonomy in their area of special responsibility as a result of many years of hard-earned success in working with innovative projects. Their careers have often included wide-ranging experience in different divisions that results in a valuable cross-disciplinary perspective and a fertile response to new problems. The average champion had worked eighteen years with the company, building a reputation for unusual achievement in handling risky projects and generating commercially viable ideas. For such individuals sponsorship – so crucial to the implementation of many innovative projects (Lockett 1990) – is generally not a problem because their seniority enables them to generate and sustain project momentum in their own right.

Central to the concept of 'champion' is the notion that this person's drive towards commercial success should be supported rather than hampered by organizational and financial practices which constrain the day-to-day operations of the firm. In two of the US companies special teams were selected for new projects: positions on the team were advertised internally – and, if necessary, externally – and applicants were interviewed and carefully evaluated by reference to the skill requirements of the project. The resultant 'tiger team' (the phrase used by company Y) was therefore an elite squad with its special loyalties and commitment, its own budget and, in the case of company X, its own factory in the grounds of the company. The self-confidence of such units is often remarkable. In response to a question about the abandonment criteria relating to innovative projects the R & D manager of company Y said that they tried to avoid thinking about such things.

> 'We believe in innovation so much – the whole corporation is really built on miracles . . . and so when a project gets in trouble . . . boy have I got good people working to solve it . . . so I tend to hang on. You put your trust in the quality of your people . . . I know that with these people I can solve it and that will carry project after project.'

It follows that the role of the financial representative on such teams was minimal or passive after the project budget was assured. According to the R & D manager he had 'low horsepower' compared with the engineers and marketing people once the project was under way. In company X the finance director himself attended the initial project meeting to assure the team of its financial backing but was subsequently replaced at team conferences by one of his subordinates. The company X executive whom we interviewed put it this way:

'If you are going to champion a new undertaking . . . you have got to have [finance people] with you from day one, because they can become adversarial if they are not involved. We went through a transition in this company about five years ago when finance went from being traditional bean counters to being interactive players.'

And do they involve themselves in presentations and things like this to top management?

They are top management.[2]

In company Z the imperatives of the strategic plan were supreme at every stage, although financial targets were carefully monitored, as was true of all three US companies.

In the UK case-study companies that participated in our project, the chief executives who were primarily responsible for the innovating drive were often closely supported by other members of the management team (in some cases a buy-out or buy-out/buy-in team), including – and sometimes most particularly – the finance director. In general, the finance function either adapted to the strategic vision of the chief executive or was overridden, although smaller projects might be required to conform to a two-year payback and even show a substantial net cash flow in the first year of their operation. In most instances the successful innovating executives were, not unexpectedly, outstanding individuals who appeared to be well aware of their special talents and who had successfully surmounted severe financial pressure on at least one previous occasion.

The strategic override of financial constraints and the internal capital market

Six of our companies (especially the large US ones) undertook detailed investment appraisals that used several techniques and many sources of internal and external data. Among the UK companies the formal investment appraisal calculations and data ranged from the very extensive (company D) to what one managing director (MD) described as 'gut feel' (company B). When questioned more closely the MD explained that management accounting system (MAS) and capital investment appraisal techniques (CIAT) calculations were undertaken but had relatively little influence on the investment decision: 'Of course we did all those (discounted cash flow) calculations (for a major loan application); we did them again and again until they came up right'.

We encountered several instances of this type of healthy contempt for the integrity of standard techniques, whose applicability to the appraisal of innovative projects is inevitably not wholly satisfactory (Klammer *et al.* 1991), suggesting that accounting numbers and CIAT calculations are used as rationalizations for decisions that have already been made upon the basis of experience, or of opportunity-cost factors such as the consequences of not investing or of deferring expenditure which are not captured by conventional CIATs (cf. Carr *et al.* 1991). Yet all of these companies had experienced, and some were still experiencing, acute financial pressure; operations and expenditures that were perceived to be non-strategic were tightly controlled. In parallel with this tight control of operational activities and transactions we found a different approach to expenditure that was deemed to be of strategic significance. In practice strategic investments were subjected to much more detailed scrutiny than other forms of investment, but special rules applied.

Although the management of company E produced elaborate sales and cost projections for a major project, the decision to go ahead was made in the absence of an IRR or NPV calculation; however, by inference both were highly favourable. This willingness to treat strategic expenditure as a special case which required a degree of freedom from normal financial constraints continued in company E even when the parent company became much more financially oriented. However, this apparent indulgence of an expensive, innovative capital project became explicable upon closer examination. Abandonment of the project in the early years, when it was incurring negative cash flows and large accounting losses, would have entailed even greater short-term accounting losses and cash outlays. A more positive motivation for proceeding was the profit potential captured by a break-even chart that showed a huge contribution beyond a production capacity of about 20 per cent. If quality problems could be resolved, and a solution to these problems always seemed to be imminent, then the company's financial performance should become quite exceptional. In the case of company E there was nothing fundamentally wrong with the strategic logic of their decisions; the low emphasis that managers, even accountants, placed on capital investment appraisal analyses reflected the relatively high influence of factors that these analyses do not readily capture.

The pervasiveness of this low influence of the MAS on the technology-investment decisions in the companies in our study cannot be attributed to any inability on the part of the managers in question to explain their decisions in the language of finance. Factors which managers believed were relevant to the strategy-MAS relationship concerned the nature of the strategy (described in reactive, defensive, prospective or proactive terms) and their time horizons. A financial executive in company Y explained that the relatively low influence of the MAS on technology-investment decisions (which again contrasted sharply with the tight cost control of operations) did not mean that the imperatives of technology or the aspirations of engineers necessarily dominated finance:

> 'Engineers shape our strategy, but it is the nature of the strategy more than the people that is responsible for the apparent low influence of the finance role. The strategy is proactive, so data are inevitably softer than if you are pursuing a more reactive, follow-the-leader strategy.'

He also made the point that market leaders to not compete on price until the nearest competitors are closing in, by which stage 'You have obsolesced the product and all the development costs, and you are well down the experience curve. You don't need too many (overhead) apportionment bases or activity costings to guide decisions in this area'.

Another point made by this finance executive was that in capital-expenditure decisions which did not affect strategy, or were only very peripheral to it, financial analysis would dominate unless a project received a great deal of in-house sponsorship. Occasionally large projects were undertaken on the strength of very little financial analysis simply because the CEO 'wanted to work out something'.

A vice-president of company Y explained that the company's commitment to new product development was a dominating influence on the organizational arrangements and on how management information systems are used: 'Our organization, policies and management style are aimed at developing as many new products as possible. To achieve this long-term goal we are willing to accept some internal disorder and sacrifice immediate profits'. The vice-president in charge of planning in company Z is acutely aware of the potential conflict between the control function and the creativity that is needed to support strategy. Again, because new product and process development is perceived to be an activity of high strategic significance, the MAS influence is constrained:

'Our planning system (including the MAS) does an effective job of controlling and measuring our base operations . . . naturally in a firm like ours innovation and new business development are vital. At the very least I hope that the planning system does not stifle new ideas.'

Company Z maps technological trajectories for up to twenty years and has detailed financial plans for five years.

What emerges from our findings is that the emphasis which the companies in our study place on product and process innovation affects not only the use of the MAS but also the organizational arrangements for pursuing strategic objectives. Clearly these companies are unrepresentative when judged against the decline in real industrial investment in the United Kingdom in recent years and against the evidence that has been adduced to support claims of managerial short-termism.

Our evidence says something about the strategy-MAS relationship in the type of company described by Goold and Campbell (1987a, 1987b) as 'strategic planning/strategic control'; it says relatively little about the strategy-MAS interaction in which the dominant culture favours short investment paybacks,[3] and whose financial control system is exercised in such a way as to 'impose a more demanding and penetrating discipline than the capital market itself' (strong internal capital rationing). The findings of Webb and Cleary (Ch. 5 of this volume) that the key role of specialized knowledge and procedures within the firm is to minimize uncertainty at each stage of the production process helps to highlight the argument of Demirag and Tylecote (1992) that pressures in financial control companies 'segmentalize', increasing rather than diminishing asymmetries of information.

Strategy or terror? the risk of failing to invest

It is easy to conceptualize strategy as the intervening variable between the organization and the external environment, the means by which the firm decides to pursue perceived opportunities in which it has a comparative advantage and takes corrective action to compensate for those areas in which it has a comparative disadvantage. In practice, the position is not so clear, as the CEO of company Y explained: 'You're always scared you're not going to have the best products and not enough orders, so you have to design as if the whole world is after you. I don't know whether it's strategy or terror'. The managers of the three American companies (X, Y and Z) that we interviewed all believed that their company's survival and growth depended on a steady stream of new and improved products and processes; fast development time is also believed to be crucial.[4] The reasons for the technology investments of the UK companies are more disparate. However, none of them invested primarily to compete on price. Indeed, company C could not possibly have competed against established market leaders on price or won market share by producing a similar product at a lower price. Instead its managers invested more than they could finance from internal sources in R & D[5] in order to develop an electronic pump with unique attributes. The alternative to not investing for this company was to run it down, probably within two or three years, as the market for mechanical pumps contracted. Company B was in a similar position. With obsolete products and processes it might have continued for a few more years by scaling down its operations still further. An innovative director, who is a metallurgist, saw an opportunity to develop a new process that enabled the company to produce more precisely and faster to customer specifications while improving quality and productivity. He arranged a management-buyout and introduced the new process. The parent company of company E had a portfolio of 'sunset' businesses when it decided to diversify by investing in the production of an innovative product that also required a synthesis of three established technologies in a unique way.

The consequences of not investing which managers in several of our companies articulated was a powerful motive for doing so. This awareness that we encountered of inactivity or being late is not consistent with Kaplan's evidence:

> Most of the capital expenditure requests I have seen measure new investments against a *status quo* alternative of making no new investments – an alternative that usually assumes a continuation of current market share, selling price and costs. Experience shows, however, that the *status quo* rarely lasts.

> (Kaplan 1986a: 88)

This is not to suggest that Kaplan's claim does not have substance; our companies are not representative in so far as they were deliberately selected because they actually did invest in new technology. Neither does our evidence with regard to the reasons for investment suggest that all the companies in our study have the same strategic orientation. What these differences do however suggest is that generalizations do not apply here. Many companies, possibly some that fall into Kaplan's category, are presented with opportunities and threats similar to those that the managers in our companies faced; they may even face the same hierarchy of constraints. Yet they make different decisions.

Unsophisticated MAS and limitations on innovational investment

There appear to be five principal disadvantages of maintaining unsophisticated capital budgeting and management accounting practices, as is true of certain of our case-study participants which were committed to an ongoing programme of innovational investment. First, the capacity of such firms to tap relatively inexpensive external sources of finance is likely to be severely curtailed; merchant banks and specialist venture-capital finance companies normally lack the tolerance of sub-optimal accounting systems that is usually found in local bank managers and representatives of hire-purchase finance companies and require a clearly set-out business plan. Second, unsuitable overhead recovery systems for product costing may mean loss of profit in a number of ways, such as the underpricing of products or the cross-subsidization of one product line with another; in extreme cases managers may harbour quite erroneous notions about which activities are responsible for losses, resulting in the misdirecting of the productive efforts of the firm. Third, any consequent loss of profit limits managers' ability to finance planned expansion out of retained earnings or to borrow on the basis of the firm's track record. Fourth, the dangers of bias in judgement about investment expenditures are increased if it is not possible to audit the results of past decisions because the error-correction procedure is missing. As the studies of Kahneman and Tversky (1979) and Statman and Tyebjee (1985) have demonstrated, bias inevitably exists even in the most sophisticated of forecasting exercises. Fifth, when strategic factors are not explicit in the investment decision data, positive NPV projects may be rejected on the basis of a myopic technique such as payback.

MAS and its new simultaneous multiple environments

On the strength of our initial analysis it seems clear that the Contingency Theory (CT) studies undertaken up until now have failed to capture either all the major contingent variables (see Emmanuel *et al.* 1990) – except in a broad, generic, way – or the complexity of practice. This criticism applies with particular force to studies in the accounting/strategy area. To some extent these limitations reflect a 'research lag' and the rate of change in the business environment, which in turn is being driven in large part by technological innovation and an accelerating rate of knowledge diffusion.

Studies suggesting different types of competitive strategies (Porter 1985), strategic management styles (Goold and Campbell 1987a, 1987b), environments (Waterhouse and Tiessen 1978), cultures (Deal and Kennedy 1982), organizational forms and control systems (Mintzberg 1989) seem to oversimplify organizational reality, certainly in terms of the situations of the companies in our study.

Our analyses (inter and intra case studies) strongly suggest that the extant CT literature does not adequately reflect the fact that technology is allowing organizations to move closer to customization so that the market is becoming increasingly fragmented. We found that even a single-product company (which company E largely is) operates in several quite distinct markets; some of the overseas markets are different from each other and from the United Kingdom in terms of competition, customer expectations and requirements, distribution channels and wider social, economic, legal and political environments. However, even in the domestic market this essentially single product company operates in at least five distinct segments; the result is that the company has virtually as many competitive strategies. In most segments company E is fortunate in that it does not need to compete primarily on price, relying much more on the unique attributes of the product, but in some areas, even within the same segment, it competes fiercely on price. Apart from the crash that is taking place in the life cycle of most modern products, it is apparent from our studies that the notion of four strategies to correspond roughly with the four phases of the product life-cycle (PLC) – introduction, growth, maturity and decline – is too simplistic.

The large US computer manufacturer (company Y) simultaneously competes in an even greater array of disparate markets with their own quite different environments. None of the companies in our study invested in technology primarily to pursue a low-price strategy. This is not to imply that costs are unimportant; they are simply not a pivotal consideration in these technology-dependent companies. Indeed, the CEO of company Y said that, 'We will never compete on price' and its promotion consistently emphasizes product quality, established reputation, service and delivery. 'We have it now' has been a powerful marketing slogan in an industry where competitors often promote products still being developed – the technique of 'predatory preannouncement' designed to prevent existing customers from switching to other suppliers and to persuade those intending to purchase to wait a little longer (Farrell and Saloner 1986). The attempt of these companies to match their competitive strategies to their different markets is totally consistent with CT. The problem is that each strategy needs to be supported by an appropriate strategic management style, use of systems (perhaps even different systems) and structure.

The hierarchy of constraints

Within the dominant constraint of strategic management style (a product of disposition and culture[6]) we found a whole series of rotating constraints so that when one is elevated, another replaces it. The major constraints (their ranking has no special significance) that we encountered were:

- Finance
- Production knowledge
- Marketing expertise
- Market share
- Plant capacity
- Skilled labour
- Management expertise

The finance constraint is interesting because the authoritative evidence that in normal times internally-imposed financial constraints assume much greater importance for UK companies – both large and small – than external constraints imposed by the capital market (Wilson Committee 1980, Pike 1983, Scapens *et al.* 1982) does not at first sight appear consistent with our findings about small innovative companies. However, on closer inspection what seems to be internal rationing of funds sought for positive net present value projects may prove to be justified by top management's need to shape their investment programme to the strategic priorities of the firm. 'Internal rationing' may therefore be more aptly described as strategic management of financial resources.

Of special relevance for the future of innovational investment is the observation that the financial profiles of small, high-growth firms and bankrupt firms are very similar – in particular, they have in common low liquidity and high gearing (Ray and Hutchinson 1983, Hutchinson 1990, Lonie *et al.* 1990). What distinguishes one category from the other is their respective rates of profitability; sharply reduced profits in a squeeze may rapidly transform a small firm with high economic potential into an insolvent one. Apart from the external rationing constraints on vulnerable companies which are mentioned in the next section and considered in detail in Lonie *et al.* (1991), we found that investment in small firms in our study was constrained by the reluctance on the part of proprietors to seek outside equity because of the fear of loss of control and outside interference in their affairs. However, the founder of one of the companies in our study is an exception to this generalization. In 1957 he and his partner sold a 70 per cent share of the equity to a venture capital company. Today, he is still CEO and in 1989 the company made $1.1 billion profit after tax.

12.3 EXTERNAL CONSTRAINTS ON INNOVATIVE COMPANIES

High interest rates

The relevance of interest rates to innovative investment plans seems indisputable. A 3i telephone survey of 218 respondent companies conducted at the beginning of April 1990 indicated that high interest rates were mentioned almost twice as often as staff/skills shortages when respondents were asked to name the single most important obstacle to innovation (House of Lords Select Committee on Science 1991, vol. 2). The relative importance of internal and external constraints will obviously vary according to the austerity of the economic climate and other factors such as the corporate culture and perhaps the nature of the industry. As already noted in this chapter, the small innovative companies among our case studies generally ignored internal financial controls when they judged it to be in the long-term interests of the company. However, their aspirations were at times severely constrained by the pressures exerted by high interest rates and strong external rationing of funds.

We divided our relatively heterogeneous group of case-study companies into two categories – financially strong and financially vulnerable companies, a partition similar to but not quite identical with the division into large and small companies. We postulated that financially strong innovative companies would not normally be subject to any form of capital rationing or subject to liquidity constraints of any significance; nor would asymmetries of information between management and 'outside' equity holders or creditors normally be significant. Such companies would be much less affected by rises in interest rates, or by the maintenance of high interest rates, than the average business. In so far as the illiquidity generated by increases in interest rates created a disparity between the actual and the desired composition of the companies' assets and liabilities, managers would have little difficulty in adjusting balance sheet variables, such as outstanding bank loans or trade credit, until an acceptable structure was restored.

By contrast, financially vulnerable companies would be particularly sensitive to increases in interest rates and would tend to suffer exceptional financial pressure from a protracted spell of high rates. The illiquidity generated by the rises in interest rates would tend to create a balance-sheet disequilibrium which could not readily be eliminated. Companies might find themselves trapped in a position of high indebtedness and balance-sheet imbalance, discriminated against by banks and trade creditors and exploited by customers with superior financial strength and bargaining. Asymmetries of information and hence agency costs might be relatively high, particularly if a vulnerable company engaged in capital expenditure which involved technological innovation. Moreover, it seemed to us that important technological innovations frequently involved small and medium-sized companies in large external funding requirements, which represented another form of imbalance; if companies borrowed heavily then during the period when the companies' gearing ratios were exceptionally high, the dangers of a sharp increase in interest rates would be formidable until healthy cash flows permitted the companies to reduce loan commitments and return to a more acceptable balance-sheet structure. Innovational investment was in consequence likely to involve the smaller companies not only in possible technological and commercial risks but in potentially severe financial risks. On the other hand, if companies believed that innovation was essential to their survival, the price of innovating might be to have to endure greatly increased financial risks associated with high gearing levels. The larger the external funding needs of the company, the more likely would it be to encounter steeply rising marginal costs of finance. In other words, as perceived by company management, the cost (not the opportunity cost to shareholders but managers' subjective notion of cost (see Grabowski and Mueller 1972; Nickell 1978) of using retained earnings would be much lower than any other form of funding and the supply of funds schedule would be subject to sharp discontinuities as the company switched from preferred to less-preferred sources of funds (e.g. Trivoli and McDaniel 1987; Fazzari, Hubbard and Petersen 1988) perhaps finding in the case of equity finance that the costs were so prohibitive as to exclude the company from the market entirely.

The distinction between financially strong and financially vulnerable firms has relevance to the issue of R & D expenditure and innovational investment in the United Kingdom. According to the international comparison of R & D expenditure published by Bain & Company in July 1990 the problem of insufficient spending on R & D lies not with very large UK companies 'but with small to medium sized companies' (see also Pavitt *et al.* 1987); a US study cited by Bain suggested that small US firms (less than 500 employees) were roughly 50 per cent more innovative than large firms, causing Bain to draw the conclusion that 'there could be a large potential reservoir of innovation within small British companies' (Bain & Company 1990: 16). However, smaller companies are, as a rule, more vulnerable to 'squeeze' than larger companies and R & D, with its long-run speculative payoff, and innovational investment, with its relatively high-risk characteristics, are logical candidates in any exercise in retrenchment.

But the position is complicated by three factors. First, the economic cycles of companies may have a different rhythm from the general business cycle, because their domestic markets are dynamically different from the rest of the economy or because their main markets are overseas. Second, the strategic imperatives of a technology- or market-driven company may cause it to maintain its innovational priorities in spite of severe financial pressure. The CBI/Nat West *Innovation Trends Survey* (CBI 1991) indicates that in companies employing between 50 and 199 people the number increasing R & D product spending in 1990 and 1991 appears to be larger than those reducing expenditure. 'Financial control' companies (Goold and Campbell, 1987a, 1987b) are more likely to respond to cash-flow pressure by cutting risky investment than 'strategic planning' companies which adopt a more long-term perspective. The strategic management style therefore influences the way that managers respond to external pressures such as high interest rates (Demirag *et al.* 1990). Third, US evidence (Kahn 1989) and casual empiricism based on the UK investigation of the present chapter suggests that very substantial changes have taken place in the interest sensitivity of industries and companies in the course of the 1980s. The companies and industries which suffered the greatest contraction in the first half of the 1980s have presumably lost their most vulnerable elements and have taken precautions against future financial emergencies.

By and large we found that the characterization of vulnerable and strong companies was an accurate one. The executives of the large US companies whom we interviewed displayed impressive confidence that the capital market was on their side. As one graphically expressed it, 'If you are a financially strong company you can do what the hell you like, within reason.' The management of the two UK quoted case-study companies were more diffident about the responses of the equity market; the representative of the group which had experienced severe adverse share-price reactions in the past was, not surprisingly, particularly vexed by the fickleness of investors. The most extreme example of (self-imposed) capital rationing among our case studies was an engineering company with growth opportunities which financed its investment entirely from retained earnings and disdained an overdraft; all the equity of the company was in the hands of two directors. Most of the UK companies experienced financial pressure in certain years during the 1980s and two or three were in some danger of insolvency. For the smaller companies, as one would anticipate, relations with their local bank were extremely important. However, as two small independent private companies pointed out, insistence by institutional equity-holders on contractually agreed high dividends exerted very much the same kind of pressure on their cash flow as high interest costs.

Announcements of new technology investment: selective disclosure and the hierarchy of 'outsiders'

The capital market's reaction to company announcements about heavy investment in new technology is of major importance (Chaney *et al.* 1991). If the market decides, for example, that the financial strength of the company is insufficient to absorb the possible losses associated with a high-risk venture the share price of the company in question may fall sharply; on the other hand, if the market concludes that innovative investment is essential for the company's new and promising market strategy, the effect on share prices may be salutary. What is far from certain is that the positive net present value of the capital expenditure (as calculated by the company) will inevitably be impounded into share price.

It is appropriate to highlight one of the principal findings of questionnaire surveys of UK financial analysts and finance directors undertaken initially in 1988 (Al-Qudah *et al* 1991). One-third of the company respondents (67 out of 203 finance directors) limit disclosure of information about their capital expenditure intentions to one or more selected parties (e.g. their bankers, specialist investment analyst, unit trust manager and major shareholders), while over a quarter of respondent companies (57 out of 203) make no disclosure to any parties whatsoever. This variation in attitude and practice was mirrored in our own study: of the three large innovative US corporations which supplied information on this point, companies X and Z disclosed no specific technical information about their capital expenditure intentions, whether innovative or not – their fairly regular contacts with investment analysts normally related to matters of general results. By contrast, company Y, which is by far the largest of the three, claimed to disclose fairly detailed information about their investment in new technology, using all of the conventional channels, because the company's management perceive the impact of such information to have a 'very positive' effect on their share values and also because to fail to do so would be interpreted adversely by the market. The vice-president in charge of corporate planning in company Z, which has a highly diversified portfolio of projects, argued that 'it is *unlikely* that any single investment in new technology is sufficiently material to influence market value'. As the Al-Qudah survey of 203 UK companies reveals, the statement that capital expenditure information is unlikely to affect share values is the standard response of the non-disclosing company. Although the reason advanced by the vice-president of company Z is not necessarily invalid, his dismissal of any suggestion that the views of investment analysts about new technology employed by his company might influence share values confirms that Z is a company which prizes its proprietary information (this impression was confirmed by the fact that he courteously stonewalled virtually every question put to him about specific company practices in our two-hour interview). A senior executive of company X suggested in his response to our questionnaire that questions about the role of analysts were 'too complicated to address'. In discussion with us he explained that the most important factor was to have to account for company performance to a shareholder constituency every quarter. He complained about the short-term planning horizons of the shareholders of his company and stated that although places like Edinburgh, Glasgow and London were reputedly homes of many long-term investors, his recent experience suggested that they were no different in this respect from investors in the rest of the world. Once again company Y offered a very different perspective and argued that the views of analysts were so important that virtually continuous contact was desirable and that analysts should be given as much technical information about innovations as they wished.

Of the two UK public companies which explained their attitude to the disclosure of investment intentions, company F (the smaller of the two) believed that disclosure was worthwhile if investment in new technology represented a shift in company strategy or a change in company risk – as the survey of UK companies revealed, a very common, and sensible, retort – but company E suggested that the fickleness of the market warranted a 'very cautious' approach to a policy of disclosing investment in new technology. (Company E's recent adoption of a policy of greater openness about planned changes in strategy and related expenditures had received a setback shortly before our interview when the company's annual results were judged to be disappointing in relation to the preceding hype and share values declined sharply on the announcement of apparently healthy earnings.)

Finance specialists such as Brigham and Tapley (1985) have suggested that the argument that share values will rise by the size of the NPV only after the formal public announcement of capital expenditure may be a realistic portrayal of the market's reaction to news about 'smaller firms' or indeed 'neglected firms' (e.g. see Arbel and Strebel 1983). They further suggested that by the time 'most large, widely-followed firms' publicly announce capital expenditure plans the net present value of the project will already have been fully impounded into equity values. Al-Qudah *et al*'s study does not confirm Brigham and Tapley's plausible intuition, there is no significant variation in disclosure by size. Instead it highlights the importance of the propensity to disclose by companies and also documents the highly selective nature of such revelations, resulting in a strongly ordered hierarchy of company outsiders, the most favoured of whom are quasi-insiders, with corresponding inhibitions on market efficiency.

Disclosures of investment in new technology by private companies

One of the features of the replies to our questionnaire which the project team failed to anticipate was the importance that virtually every private company studied ascribed to communicating new techology-related expenditure information to *customers* and, in certain instances, to potential purchasers of the company. The fact that customers, among others, are important stakeholders in their suppliers' companies has only recently been acknowledged in the financial management literature (e.g. see Cornell and Shapiro 1987, Barton *et al.* 1989). Farrell and Saloner (1986) have stressed the crucial importance of timing in determining whether a new product supersedes the existing technology. The disclosure of investment in new technology in our case-study companies was therefore closely linked to the marketing strategy of the company and the timing of the announcement was likely to be determined by this strategy. In the case of small engineering companies such information generally referred not to processes of a novelty likely to astonish competitors but simply to the purchase of new, high-precision equipment that it was only common sense to mention to potential customers. One of the engineering firms (Company J) also emphasized the import-ance of an early announcement about new equipment to another group of stakeholders – the employees. New machines were, if possible, installed and put into operation on the day of their arrival.

12.4 CONCLUSION

Many factors within the organization influence the decision to invest in new technology. The dominant influence, however, is corporate strategy and the fundamental beliefs of top management which underpin it. When technology-based new product and process devel-opment is at the hub of corporate strategy, then financial controls fail to constrain investment in innovative technology. An integrated team approach that maintains consistency among strategy, organizational structure, systems and people reduces information asymmetry, alters perceptions of risk and exerts a crucial influence on the technology investment process.

The role of external constraints on genuinely innovative firms appears to be much more important for enterprises that are new or small, or have undertaken ambitious programmes of expansion which have further weakened an already fragile balance sheet and cash-flow position. The well-known start-up problems of innovative ventures are not examined in this chapter; instead some attempt is made to explain the implications of the severe financial pressures that new and innovative firms are liable to experience. The finding that made the most lasting impression on the writers was that the plans for innov-ative investment of certain small vulnerable case-study companies were not modified by cash-flow pressures. The corporate culture of these companies was so committed to innovation that the owner-managers were prepared to risk liquidation by continuing with their plans. Although investing in such high-risk enterprises may be hazardous, the nation can only benefit from the brio of the innovators who survive and prosper. The least the government can do is to display greater awareness that the cash-flow pressures unleashed by sustained high interest rate policies are highly discriminatory and, in the case of many small innovating firms, lethal.

ACKNOWLEDGEMENTS

The authors are grateful for the help they received in the preparation of this chapter from Professor G.A. Stout, Mr R.B. Steel, Mr D.M. Power, Dr R. Kouhy, Ms A.M. Mounsey, Mrs P.M. Shafe and Dr P. Swann.

NOTES

1 Klammer, Koch and Wilner (1991) reported that in six surveys conducted between 1965 and 1988 on large US firms, roughly 30 per cent of projects were exempted from normal evaluation techniques on grounds other than small size.
2 The UK case study by Carr *et al.* (1991), however, suggested that any questioning of the assumptions underlying strategic investment by financial executives tended to come too late to influence acceptability.
3 Corporate culture may be defined as the fundamental operating beliefs of top management.
4 This finding is consistent with the results of a survey of UK companies carried out by Little (1991) and with the US study of Chaney *et al.* (1991), which found that announcements of new products had a significant effect on share values, especially for technologically based enterprises such as computer, electrical equipment and appliance companies.
5 They did this by persuading the two external consultants undertaking the R & D to become directors and accept a share of the equity in lieu of consultancy fees.
6 Corporate culture and other factors which shape innovation in UK companies were examined in the paper, 'External performance pressures and innovation in the UK' by Demirag *et al.* delivered at the *European Workshop on External Pressures*, Sheffield, 11–12 October 1990, and in Demirag and Tylecote (1992).

REFERENCES

Al-Qudah, K. A., Walker, M. and Lonie, A. A. (1991) 'Evidence on the accessibility and perceived usefulness of information relating to the capital expenditure intentions of UK quoted companies', *Accounting and Business Research* 22 (85): 3–12.

Arbel, A. and Strebel, P. (1983) 'Pay attention to neglected firms,' *Journal of Portfolio Management* 9, (4): 37–42.

Arnold J. H. (1986) 'Assessing capital risk: you can't be too conservative', *Harvard Business Review* 64 (5): 113–21.

Bain & Company (1990) *Innovation in Britain Today*, London: Bain United Kingdom, Inc.

Barton, S. L., Hill, N. C. and Sundaram, S. (1989) 'An empirical test of stakeholder theory predictions of capital structure', *Financial Management* 18, (1) 36–44.

Barwise, T. P., Marsh, P. R. and Wensley, J. R. C. (1989) 'Must finance and strategy clash?' *Harvard Business Review* 67 (5): 85–90.

Biggadike, R. (1979) 'The risky business of innovation', *Harvard Business Review* 57 (3):103–11.

Beardsley, G. and Mansfield, E. (1978) 'A note on the accuracy of industrial forecasts of the profitability of new products', *Journal of Business* 51 (1): 127–35.

Brigham, E. F. and Tapley, T. C. (1985) 'Financial leverage and the use of the net present value criterion: a re-examination', *Financial Management* 14 (2): 48–52.

Bromwich, M. and Bhimani, A. (1989) *Management Accounting: Evolution not Revolution*, London: CIMA.

CBI(1991) *Innovation Trends Survey*, Issue 2, London: CBI Natwest Technology Unit.

Carr, C., Tomkins, C. and Bayliss, B. (1991) 'Strategic controllership: a case study approach', *Management Accounting Research* 2: 89–107.

Chaney, P. K., Devinney, T. M. and Winer, R. S. (1991) 'The impact of new product introductions on the market value of firms', *Journal of Business* 64 (4): 573–610.

Cornell, B. and Shapiro, A. C. (1987) 'Corporate stakeholders and corporate finance', *Financial Management* 16(1): 5–14.

Daing, N. I. (1992) 'Managerial responses to risk in capital budgeting under asymmetries of information', unpublished Ph.D. dissertation, University of Dundee.

Deal, T. E. and Kennedy A. A. (1982) *Corporate Cultures*, Reading, Ma: Addison-Wesley.

Demirag, I., Kirk-Smith, M., Morris, B. and Tylecote, A. (1990) 'External performance pressures and innovation in the UK', paper delivered at the European Workshop on External Pressures at Sheffield University, 11–12 October.

Demirag, I., and Tylecote, A. (1992) 'The effects of organizational culture, structure and market expectations on technological innovation: a hypothesis', *British Journal of Management* 3: 7–20.

Emmanuel, C., Otley, C . and Merchant, K. (1990) *Accounting for Management Control*, London: Chapman and Hall.

Fazzari, S. M., Hubbard, R. G. and Petersen, B. (1988) 'Financing constraints and corporate investment', *Brookings Papers on Economic Activity* 1: 141–206.

Farrell, J. and Saloner, G. (1986) 'Installed base and compatibility: innovation, product preannouncements and predation', *American Economic Review* 75 (5): 940–55.

Finnie, J. (1988) 'The role of financial appraisal in decisions to acquire advanced manufacturing technology', *Accounting and Business Research* 18(70): 133–40.

Frey, D. (1991) 'Learning the ropes: my life as a product champion', *Harvard Business Review* 69(5): 46–57.

Goold, M. and Campbell, A. (1987a) *Strategies and Styles*, Oxford: Blackwell.

—— and —— (1987b) 'Many best ways to make strategy', *Harvard Business Review* 65(6): 70–6.

Grabowski, H. G. and Mueller, D. C. (1972) 'Managerial and stockholder welfare models of firm expenditure', *The Review of Economics and Statistics* 54: 11–24.

Gray, R. H. (1985) *Accounting for R & D: A Review of Experiences with SSAP 13*, London: Institute of Chartered Accountants in England and Wales.

Halberstam, D. (1987) *The Reckoning*, London: Bloomsbury.

Hayes, R. H. and Abernathy, W. J. (1980) 'Managing our way to economic decline', *Harvard Business Review* 58(4): 67–77.

Hayes, R. H. and Garvin, D. A. (1982) 'Managing as if tomorrow mattered', *Harvard Business Review* 60(3): 70–9.

Hayes, R. H. and Jaikumar, R. (1988) 'Manufacturing crisis: new technologies, obsolete organizations', *Harvard Business Review* 66(5): 77–85.

Ho, S. S. M. and Pike, R. M. (1991) 'Risk analysis in capital budgeting contexts: simple and sophisticated', *Accounting and Business Research* 21(83): 227–38.

Hopwood, A. (1985) 'The growth of "worrying" about management accounting (a commentary on "accounting lag": the obsolescence of cost accounting systems by Kaplan, R.S.)', in K.B. Clark et al. (eds). *The Uneasy Alliance*, Cambridge, Mass.: Harvard Business School Press.

House of Lords Select Committee on Science and Technology (1991) *Innovation in Manufacturing Industry*, Vol. 1, *Report*; Vol. 2 *Oral Evidence*, London: HMSO.

Howell, J. and Higgins, C.A. (1990) 'Champions of change', *Business Quarterly* 19(2): 36.

Hutchinson, P. J. (1990) 'The effects of stage of development of the firm on accounting ratios and the implications for multivariate discriminatory techniques', paper delivered at the British Accounting Association Conference, Dundee, 4–6 April, 1–24.

Kahneman, D. and Tversky, A. (1979) 'Intuitive prediction: biases and corrective procedures', in S. Makridakis and S.C. Wheelright (eds) *TIMS Studies in Management Science*, volume 12, Amsterdam: North Holland/Elsevier.

Kaplan, R. S. (1984) 'Yesterday's accounting undermines production', *Harvard Business Review* 64(4): 95–101.

—— (1986a) 'Must CIM be justified by faith alone?' *Harvard Business Review* 86(2): 87–95.

—— (1986b) 'The role for empirical research in management accounting', *Accounting Organizations and Society* 4/5(11): 429–52.

Kahn, G. A. (1989) 'The changing interest sensitivity of the US economy', *Federal Reserve Bank of Kansas Economic Review*, November: 13–34.

Keynes, J. M. (1936) *The General Theory of Employment, Interest and Money*, London: Macmillan.

Klammer, T., Koch, B. and Wilner, N. (1991) 'Capital budgeting practices: a survey of corporate use', *Journal of Management Accounting Research* 3(3): 113–30.

Kreitner, R. (1989) *Management*, Boston, Mass: Houghton-Mifflin.

Lee, J. Y. (1989) *Managerial Accounting Changes for the 1990's*, Wokingham: Addison-Wesley.

Little, A. D. (1991) *Managing Consultants: Managing Rapid Technological Development*, London: A. D. Little, Managing Consultants.

Lockett, M. (1990) 'The factors behind successful technology innovation', in M. Wartner, W. Wobbe and P. Brodner (eds) *New Technology and Manufacturing Management*, Chichester, Wiley, Ch. 16.

Lonie, A. A., Nixon, W. A. and Grinyer, J. R. (1988) 'The dependence of innovation upon group support: a case study', *Review of Business and Economics* 4: 27–34.

Lonie, A. A., Power, D. M. and Sinclair, C. D. (1990) 'The discriminatory impact of interest rate changes on companies, industries and regions', *British Review of Economic Issues* 12(28): 79–106.

Lonie, A. A., Sinclair, C. D. and Power, D. M. (1991) 'Effects of interest rates on UK companies, recession myopia and the "short-termism" debate', Discussion Paper, Department of Accountancy and Business Finance, University of Dundee.

Maidique, M. A. (1980) 'Entrepreneurs, champions and technological innovation', *Sloan Management Review* 21(2): 59–76.

March, J. G. and Shapira, Z. (1988) 'Managerial perspectives on risk and risk taking', in J. G. March (ed.) *Decisions and Organizations*, Oxford, Blackwell.

Marsh, P. R., Larwise, T. P., Thomas, K. and Wensley, J. R. C. (1987) *Managing Strategic Investment Decisions in Large, Diversified Companies*, London: Centre for Business Strategies.

McNair, C. J. Mosconi, W. and Norrish, T. (1988) *Meeting the Technology Challenge Cost Accounting in the JIT Environment*, Montvale NJ: National Association of Accountants, Montvale.

Mintzberg, H. (1989) *Mintzberg on Management*, New York, Free Press.

Myers, S. C. (1987) 'Finance theory and financial strategy', *Midland Corporate Finance Journal* 5(1): 6–13.

Nickell, S. J. (1978) *The Investment Decisions of Firms*, Cambridge: James Nisbet and Cambridge University Press.

Nixon, W. A. and Lonie, A. A. (1990) 'Accounting for R & D: the need for change', *Accountancy* 105(1158): 90–1.

Otley, D. (1987) *Accounting Control and Organizational Behaviour*, London: Heinemann.

Pavitt, K., Robson, M. and Townsend, J. (1987) 'The size distribution of innovating firms in the UK: 1945–1983' *Journal of Industrial Economics* 35,(3): 297–316.

Pavitt, K. and Patel, P. (1988) 'The international distribution and determinants of technological activities', *Oxford Review of Economic Policy* 4,(4): 35–55.

Peters, T. J. and Waterman, R. H. (1982) *In Search of Excellence*, New York: Harper & Row.

Pike, R. H. (1983) 'The capital budgeting behaviour and corporate characteristics of capital-constrained firms', *Journal of Business Finance and Accounting* 10(4): 663–71.

Pike, R. H. and Dobbins, R. (1986) *Investment Decisions and Financial Strategy*, Oxford: Philip Allan.

Porter, M. E. (1985) *Competitive Advantage*, New York, Free Press.

—— (1987) 'From competitive advantage to corporate strategy', *Harvard Business Review* 65(3): 43–59.

Quinn, J. B. (1979) 'Technological innovation, entrepreneurship and strategy', *Sloan Management Review* 20(3): 19–30.

Ray, G. H. and Hutchinson, P. J. (1983) *The Financing and Financial Control of Small Enterprise Development*, Aldershot: Gower.

Ross, M. (1986) 'Capital budgeting practices of twelve large manufacturers', *Financial Management* 15(4): 15–22.

Samuels, J. M., Wilkes, F. M. and Brayshaw, R. E. (1990) *Management of Company Finance*, London: Chapman and Hall.

Scapens, R. W. (1988) 'Research into management accounting practice', *Management Accounting* (UK) 66(11): 26–8.

Scapens, R. W., Otley, D. T. and Lister, R. J. (1984) *Management Accounting, Organizational Theory and Capital Budgeting*, London, Macmillan.

Scapens, R. W., Sale, J. T. and Tikkas, P. A. (1982) *Financial Control of Divisional Capital Investment*, London, The Institute of Cost and Management Accountants.

Schmookler, J. (1966) *Invention and Economic Growth*, Cambridge, Mass: Harvard University Press.

Schon, D. A. (1963) 'Champions for radical new inventions'. *Harvard Business Review* 41(2): 77–86.

Statman, N. and Tyebjee, T. T. (1985) 'Optimistic capital budgeting forecasts: an experiment', *Financial Management* 14(3): 27–33.

Swann, K. (1988) 'Investment in AMT, a wider perspective,' *Production Engineer* 67(8): 50–3.

—— (1988) Investment in AMT a review', *Production Engineer* 67(9): 53–7.

Tichy, N. M. and Devanna, M. A. (1986) *The Transformational Leader*, Chichester: Wiley.

Trivoli, G. W. and McDaniel, W. R. (1987) 'Uncertainty, capital immobility and capital rationing in the investment decision', *Journal of Business Finance and Accounting* 14(2): 215–28.

Waterhouse, J. N. and Tiessen, P. (1981) 'A contingency framework for management accounting systems research', in R. H. Chenhall *et al. The Organisational Context of Management Accounting*, Marshfield, Ma: Pitman.

Wilson Committee (1980) *The Committee to Review the Functioning of Financial Institutions*, London: HMSO.

Zaleznik, A. (1977) 'Managers and leaders: are they different?', *Harvard Business Review* 55(3): 67–88.

13 Accounting for R & D costs

Does it matter? Perceptions of analysts and company management

Alan Goodacre, Rob Ball, Jim McGrath, Ken Pratt and Richard Thomas

13.1 INTRODUCTION

Low investment in research and development by UK companies has been cited as a contributory factor to the comparatively poor performance of UK industry. The reasons underlying this low R & D investment remain unclear, despite considerable discussion in both the financial and academic press. One argument blames the short-termism of the city whereby long-term considerations are eschewed in favour of quick returns. This may be reflected in a preference against investment in R & D with its attendant uncertainty and long-term nature. Another identifies 'managerial short-termism' as a key force behind poor investment in the UK (March 1990). It can also be hypothesized that the current required accounting treatment of R & D might contribute to the observed low level of R & D investment.

This research is concerned with the possible impact of current accounting treatment on investment in R & D. In particular, the chapter describes:

- experiments which sought to test whether the method of accounting for R & D is likely to have any impact on the valuation of companies by investment analysts, and also whether there is evidence of preference against investment in R & D, and
- a survey of the views of company management concerning R & D investment and the accounting treatment of R & D expenditure.

One of the general guiding principles which accountants have chosen to adopt requires benefits and costs to be matched as far as possible so that the net benefit (or cost) of undertaking a particular course of action can be assessed. Thus, if the benefits from undertaking R & D are expected to arise in future accounting periods the R & D costs should be carried forward, as an investment (asset), to be matched with these future benefits. However, another of the accountant's principles (conservatism) suggests that a 'cautious' approach should be taken both to income and asset measurement. The effect of this is to try to ensure that neither the profit nor the value of the organization shown on the balance sheet are ever overstated. The latter principle counsels the immediate writeoff of all R & D expenditure in view of the uncertainty in determining the magnitude and duration of the future benefits which might arise. This conflict between the two principles has provoked controversy over many years and concerning different issues; it is usually resolved in favour of 'conservatism'.

Consequently given that the returns from R & D are uncertain, the accountant's response is usually to assume that the R & D investment is 'worthless' and should therefore be treated as an expense in the period in which it is incurred and the R & D 'investment' does not appear at all on the balance sheet. In the United States this is the required treatment in the accounting standard on 'Accounting for R & D costs' (Statement of Financial Accounting Standards No. 2 [SFAS 2]). In the United Kingdom a slightly less conservative approach is allowed; the Statement of Standard Accounting Practice No. 13 (SSAP 13) requires all pure and applied research expenditure to be written off against profit immediately while development expenditure *may* be carried forward ('capitalized') and matched against future revenue as long as certain conditions, principally concerning expected economic viability, are met.

It is recognized by most accountants that some R & D expenditure is speculative with highly uncertain benefits; this should quite reasonably be treated as an immediate cost rather than an asset. However, there is considerable debate about whether *all* R & D costs should be treated in this way. Arguments in favour of the immediate expensing of R & D costs rely heavily on the conservatism principle, but it is also contended that, as far as the income statement is concerned, the amount charged by way of R & D expense will be quite similar whichever of the two methods is followed. If R & D expenditure is constant then the amount charged will be identical. In the more usual situation of rising nominal (if not real) expenditure the annual charge under capitalization and amortization will be lower as it will be the average of several previous year's expenditure. Proponents of the matching principle argue that expenditure on R & D is presumably undertaken by a firm in the expectation of future benefit, and as such this investment ought to be recognized on the balance sheet of the firm. They claim that 'a subjective estimate of the value is better than an arbitrary value of zero' (Drebin 1966).

An important feature of this conflict is that the cash-flows of the firm are totally unaffected by the accounting treatment. There are currently no hidden tax advantages relating to either treatment. The differences relate entirely to the financial situation of the firm as *reported* in their periodic financial statements. In a period of increasing R & D investment, the reported profit and balance-sheet assets are both higher for a firm which capitalizes some or all of its R & D expenditure.

Somewhat surprisingly, in the United Kingdom, companies generally choose not to capitalize development expenditure even when the conditions for capitalization in SSAP 13 are met. It is possible that this may be driven by a desire to please city analysts, with their expressed preference for expensing (Gray 1986), or perhaps the simplicity of avoiding the need to distinguish between development and research costs is attractive. Memories of the demise of Rolls Royce, which some associated with its policy of capitalizing development costs, also seem to persist.

The effect of the current accounting treatment in reducing reported profits and balance-sheet asset values could impact on R & D investment in several ways. If city sentiment responds to the lower profits with a lower share price, it may be more difficult for the company to raise equity finance, or at least, for equity finance to be more costly. It may also make the company more vulnerable to a hostile takeover bid, in which the bidder company attempts to benefit from the biddee's hidden assets. The reduced asset value may also lead to greater difficulties in raising loan finance as a result of restrictive covenants based on the balance-sheet value of company assets. Management may therefore feel pressure to reduce R & D expenditure to minimize the effect on the reported earnings and balance sheet. A similar but more direct pressure may be felt by management if their remuneration package is based on the reported profit of the company. This would be of increased significance in times of rapid management turnover, when managers' horizons and aspirations are more short term.

Part of the current research focused on smaller companies, often considered to be more innovative than larger concerns. Previous research in the United States has suggested that the R & D investment decisions made by managers in some smaller companies may have been affected by the required R & D accounting treatment.

Smaller companies do not often have a portfolio of investments at different stages of maturity, whereby the positive cash flows from more mature projects can be used to finance R & D. It has also been argued that providers of finance are likely to place greater emphasis on the financial statements as a source of information for smaller companies, given their shorter track record and the usual paucity of alternative sources. Thus smaller companies may be more vulnerable to misinterpretation of financial accounting information than larger ones. One of the purposes of the present research was to investigate whether UK company management, especially in smaller companies, felt constrained by the accounting treatment of R & D.

The concern that high R & D-intensive companies might be disadvantaged, in the financial markets, by the required accounting treatment of R & D was also of interest. This situation might result if investment analysts do not adequately compensate for the hidden R & D investment assets in such companies. Alternatively, if the markets, in some sense, prefer investment in assets less uncertain than R & D this may contribute to the unease expressed by company management. If either of these occurs, or even if company management (incorrectly) believe them to occur, it may have important consequences as far as the amount invested on R & D by UK industry is concerned.

13.2 PREVIOUS RESEARCH

There appears to have been little empirical research on accounting for R & D costs in the United Kingdom. Hope and Gray considered the development of the accounting standard for R & D in their discussion of the political nature of the standard setting process (Hope and Gray 1982). Gray also undertook a major review of Accounting for R & D under SSAP 13 for the Research Board of the ICAEW (Gray 1986). Several of his findings are of particular relevance to the present study:

- Analysts considered that R & D information was important for companies in 'high-tech' sectors.
- Analysts expressed a strong preference for disclosure of R & D expenditure – now required for large companies in SSAP 13 (revised).
- Analysts will tend to discriminate against companies spending

below the 'industry norm'. They will not positively discriminate in favour of those which spend over the norm.

• Analysts tend to prefer R & D to be written off and the majority will write back some or all of any deferred development costs.

Another survey considered the relationship between firm size, ownership and industrial concentration, and the method of managing R & D activities (Fisher and Lothian 1987).

In the United States the accounting standard on 'Accounting for R & D costs' (SFAS 2) was issued by the Financial Accounting Standards Board (FASB) in October 1974. Its major provision was that the costs of all R & D activities should be expensed in the year incurred. Prior to this, companies could freely choose how to account for R & D costs. Dukes and colleagues, in a study mainly of large firms, found no evidence that the introduction of SFAS 2 had any significant impact on the R & D expenditure decisions made by the firms (Dukes *et al*, 1980). In a similar study on forty-three smaller 'over the counter' (OTC) companies, Horwitz and Kolodny tested the impact of the standard on the amount and variability of R & D expenditure (Horwitz and Kolodny 1980). In direct contrast to Dukes *et al.*, they found a significant effect (reduction) in R & D expenditure following the introduction of SFAS 2. Managers of research-intensive firms, which were required to switch to expensing of R & D costs, perceived that their firms might be disadvantaged as a result of the change with respect to obtaining federal agency contact awards. Horwitz and Normolle examined this contention but found no evidence to support it (Horwitz and Normolle 1988). Elliot *et al.* attempted to reconcile the differences in these two conflicting studies (Elliot *et al.* 1984). They replicated the earlier studies and essentially confirmed the results already reported concluding that there appeared to be an association between SFAS 2 and reduced R & D expenditure for certain (mainly small) firms. However, they also extended the research to consider whether any degree of causality was involved. They found that, overall, the economic position of capitalizers was weak and that the decline in R & D could easily be attributed to this weakness, coupled with the generally unfavourable economic conditions of the period.

Dukes also examined the market response to the SFAS 2 requirement to expense R & D costs and found that the market was apparently able to recognize that although the reported accounting numbers changed, the change was merely one of allocation with no significant impact on the cash flows of the firm (Dukes 1976). These results are in line with some earlier research concerning market reaction to other accounting changes – for example, stock-flow assumptions LIFO versus FIFO (Sunder 1973, 1975). However, in their major review of market-based research, Lev and Ohlson considered that the evidence that investors can 'see through' the veil of alternative accounting treatments was somewhat mixed and cited various 'surprises'(Lev and Ohlson 1982).

Wilner and Birnberg provide a useful review of the literature on functional fixation in accounting which, on balance, seems to support the hypothesis that individual users of accounting information are unable to adjust their decisions for changes in accounting methods (Wilner and Birnberg 1986). Several studies are of particular relevance to the current project. Abdel-Khalik and Keller investigated the effects on portfolio investment decisions of a switch from FIFO to LIFO stock valuation, with sixty-one bank investment officers and security analysts as experimental subjects and found evidence of fixation. (Abdel-Khalik and Keller 1979).

Bank loan officers and a small number of financial analysts were the subjects in an experiment concerning accounting for computer software costs (McGee 1984). The main issue related to whether capitalization of costs should be an acceptable treatment. Financial data, based on the accounts of a major software manufacturing company, were constructed for two hypothetical companies: the first capitalized certain software costs; the second, identical in all other respects, expensed all software costs. McGee found that the bank loan officers reacted much more favourably towards the company which capitalized software costs; the analysts were less convergent in their opinions but still slightly favoured the capitalizing company as evidenced by the assignment of a higher stock price, on average.

Summary and implications

There seems to be some fairly weak evidence that the accounting treatment of R & D expenditure may have had an impact on levels of R & D spend. For this to be supportable, management decisions must be affected by an essentially cosmetic change in reported profits. This might arise if management's wealth is directly affected by reported profit, as it might be if part of management's remuneration package is linked to profit. Alternatively, if management *believe* that investors' views on the company will be affected by the alternative treatments of R & D costs then they may alter their R & D investment decisions to minimize this. The 'fault' lies with investors if their views on a company *are* affected by the accounting treatment of R & D; it lies with management if they are not. Prior research evidence as to whether investors are able to 'see through' different accounting treatments, which have no real cash-flow effect on the company, is somewhat inconclusive. Finally, the effect on reported balance-sheet assets might contribute towards a change in management decisions if this has a real impact on the company's ability to raise debt finance, as a result of loan covenant restrictions based on the reported balance-sheet value of assets.

The research project seeks to address the above issues. It is in two parts. The first considers 'external' (i.e. investor) perceptions of R & D accounting and investment, while the second investigates those of 'internal' constituents (i.e. management).

13.3 INVESTMENT ANALYSTS STUDY[1]

Objectives

In this part of the research two separate questions were asked:

- Is the valuation by investment analysts of a company's shares affected by the accounting treatment of R & D expenditure?
- Do investment analysts distinguish, in their valuation of a company, between investment in R & D or in plant and machinery?

Investment analysts were chosen as subjects, as representative investors. As professionals within the investment community, it was considered likely that they exert significant influence over the values placed on companies in the stock market. This is effected both through their traditional 'stockbroker' research role and influence on the opinion of both private and professional investors, and through their direct investment role as managers of large investment funds which control an increasingly large proportion of equity investment.

Research method

The controlled experiment methodology used here has been adopted in many accounting situations (e.g. Estes and Reimer 1979, Wilkins and Zimmer 1983, Schwan 1976). The method was considered appropriate as it enables the isolation of the specific factor being investigated. Additionally, consideration of hypothetical changes such as the full deferral of R & D costs, is possible with this approach. However, the main weakness of the method lies in the artificiality of the situation, within which the research subjects are asked to make decisions; their responses may differ when their performance in judging the desirability of investing in a company has some tangible pay-off. In the current research attempts were made to mimic a realistic decision situation both in terms of the materials presented to the analysts and in having a small monetary incentive.

Each research subject received a covering letter, details of the competition, a single-sheet questionnaire and a set of financial statements for *one* of three model companies. Respondents were asked to estimate the share price on 31 December 1989 and the earnings per share for the accounting periods ending 31 December 1989 and 1990.

Research material

A full set of financial statements, including notes, directors' report and chairman's statement was derived for a hypothetical small UK electronics company. It was considered important to include a complete, and convincingly presented, set of financial statements to match closely the data set which an analyst would normally use. The significant effort involved was necessary to avoid the extreme artificiality often criticized in experimental studies of this type. The electronics sector was chosen in view of the comparatively high R & D expenditure within the sector – that is 52 per cent of profit before tax and 6 per cent of turnover in 1988 (*Datastream*, 19 April 1989). The financial statements possessed features which were representative of a typical industry-average company, with narrative descriptions and information based on the accounts of one real company suitably adjusted to be appropriate for the results reported and to reduce the likelihood of recognition. In particular, the R & D expenditure was at the sector-average level and was written off immediately against profit. For brevity this company will be termed 'expenser'.

The assumed set of R & D expenditure was then remodelled on the basis that all of the expenditure was capitalized each year and then written off against profit over the anticipated life of the 'asset' which was taken to be (somewhat arbitrarily) four years. Although it can be argued that capitalization of all R & D expenditure is unrealistic, such an extreme view was necessary for reasonably differential effects to be observed in the income statement. This formed the basis of a second set of financial statements, termed 'Capitalizer'.

A third set of financial statements (termed 'Fixed-Asset Buyer') was constructed on the assumption that an amount equivalent to that spent on R & D in the first and second companies was instead spent on plant and equipment. A small amount of R & D spend was indicated in the accounts to negate the possibility that the firm was merely not disclosing expenditure on R & D.

One important assumption in the derivation of the accounts for the Fixed-Asset Buyer company was that the earnings generated from investment in plant and machinery would be similar to those generated from R & D investment. This assumption was adopted for two reasons. First, it was difficult to estimate the different level of return which might be expected on R & D investment and also how variable the return pattern might be. Second, leaving the historical earnings basically the same as for Expenser was more neutral. It allowed the analyst to impose his own views about returns to R & D without being prompted by historical results in the particular company suggesting higher/lower or more variable returns. Consequently the historical return on net assets and earnings per share (EPS) for the Fixed-Asset Buyer and the Expenser companies were very similar over the five years summarized in the financial statements.

Table 13.1 provides a summary of the important accounting differences arising in the three model companies.

Results

Requests were sent out to investment analysts in stockbrokers, banks, and other investment intermediaries.[2] These were divided equally between the three model companies. Of 1,027 mailings, 69 usable replies were received together with an additional 76 replies giving reasons for 'non-response', a 14 per cent overall response rate; A response rate of 16 per cent is implied when multiple requests to the same address are appropriately excluded. Although this appears low in percentage terms, it is thought to be reasonably representative in view of:

• the expectation that perhaps many of the Society of Investment Analysts (SIA) sample would not be directly involved in invest-

Table 13.1 Comparison of accounting information for the three model companies

	1988			1987			1986			1985			1984		
	(1)	(2)	(3)	(1)	(2)	(3)	(1)	(2)	(3)	(1)	(2)	(3)	(1)	(2)	(3)
Profit before tax (£000)	5794	6048	5875	5307	5658	5527	4334	4426	4329	4929	5545	5502	4046	4321	4321
Profit after tax (£000)	3720	3974	3712	3531	3882	3628	2709	2802	2672	2864	3480	3184	2052	2328	2201
Earnings per share (pence)	12.1	13.0	12.1	11.5	12.7	11.8	9.1	9.5	9.0	9.6	11.7	10.7	9.1	10.4	9.8
Shareholders funds (£000)	20108	24384	21970	18519	22638	20486	17047	20815	18917	16297	19972	18204	14096	17155	15683
Return on net assets (%)	28%	24%	26%	28%	25%	27%	25%	21%	22%	30%	27%	30%	28%	25%	27%

Notes:

(1) = Company which immediately expenses all R & D expenditure. (Expenser)

(2) = Company which capitalises all R & D expenditure and writes off the resulting asset over a four-year period. (Capitalizer)

(3) = Company which spends an equivalent amount, as both 1 and 2 above, but on plant and equipment. (Fixed-Asset Buyer)

ment analysis (only two replies were received out of 187 sent to
SIA members at personal addresses);
- the absolute size of response at sixty-nine is over twice as large
  as Gray obtained from an admittedly smaller number of requests
  (Gray 1986);
- the quality of response and respondents was high (i.e. experienced analysts with knowledge of small companies, or the electronics sector – see Table 13.2).
- responses were received from virtually all of the major investment research houses.

A summary of responses and respondents' experience is given in
Table 13.2. The average time which the analysts spent on the
exercise was 40 minutes within a range of 10 to 120 minutes. If
reliable, this encourages the belief that the task was given serious
consideration.

Table 13.2 Summary of responses

Number of usable responses:	*No.*
• Expenser	22
• Capitalizer	24
• Fixed-Asset Buyer	23
TOTAL	69
Directly involved in investment analysis within the last five years	61* (88%)
More than two years' experience in investment analysis	56 (81%)
Mean length of experience in investment analysis	4.5 years (approx.)
Directly involved, during the last five years, in analysis of:	
• electronics sector	36 (52)%
• small companies	41 (59%)
Mean rating of accounting knowledge (Scale: 1 = weak, 5 = strong)	3.5
Mean rating of knowledge of accounting for R & D (Scale: 1 = weak, 5 = strong)	2.7

Note:
* Of the eight without recent direct involvement in investment analysis, five had
'over five years' experience' in investment analysis.

Hypothesis A

The first question under consideration can be restated formally as a testable hypothesis:

A. The valuation of a company's shares by investment analysts is unaffected by the accounting treatment of R & D expenditure.

If this hypothesis holds, and analysts are able to 'see through' the essentially cosmetic effect of the change in accounting treatment between Expenser and Capitalizer, the mean share price of the two companies should be the same. The results are presented in Table 13.3. The mean share price estimates for the two companies were 171.3p (Expenser) and 170.7p (Capitalizer); these are not different at the 5 per cent significance level. Thus the null hypothesis cannot be rejected, and it can be concluded that the valuation by investment analysts, in aggregate, of the company's shares appears to be unaffected by the accounting treatment.

This result supports some previous market-based research (e.g. Dukes 1976) suggesting that investors, at least in aggregate, see through accounting differences and value companies appropriately. It also confirms similar experimental studies which have focused on different accounting issues such as the capitalization of leases (Wilkins and Zimmer 1983, Abdel-Khalik *et al.* 1978 and 1981) in which analysts and bankers have not been 'fooled' by different accounting treatments.

However, it is completely at odds with the McGee (1984) result, in which the company which capitalized software costs was favoured by bankers and by analysts. It is possible that sending both sets of data to each subject might account for the difference. This seems unlikely, since McGee obtained similar observations whether the bankers received one or both of the data sets. There is little reason intuitively to suggest why the US research subjects should respond differently from the UK ones. One explanation of the US analyst results might be that significant small sample bias is being observed, but this would still require the contention that US bankers are more easily 'fooled' than analysts.

In the absence of an expectation of a large reduction in R & D expenditure by the company, analysts should predict a lower EPS for Expenser than for Capitalizer, in view of the higher R & D charge relating to immediate write-off against profit of R & D costs. For both 1989 (and 1990) this was observed, with a mean EPS estimate of 13.2p (14.4p 1990) for Expenser compared to 13.7p

(14.7p) for Capitalizer. This lends some support to the view that a consensus forecast of EPS by analysts, would seem to make allowance for the different accounting treatments of R & D. Although the observed difference was not statistically significant the direction was appropriate. The magnitude of difference was less than might have been predicted on the basis of continuing constant growth of R & D expenditure by the company, but the full information on historical R & D was not available to the analysts in the financial statements. The size of EPS difference is consistent with analysts' expectation of some reduction in the growth of R & D spend in the next two years which is reasonable given the anticipated decline in the economy, with margins under pressure and high interest rates.

For 1989 it was possible to compute an implied price earnings (PE) ratio for each company. A 'rational' view of the capitalized R & D firm would suggest a lower PE ratio as a subjective adjustment for the slightly 'overstated' EPS resulting from the capitalization and lower expense in the profit and loss account.[3] This expectation is confirmed in the results, with a lower mean implied PE ratio for Capitalizer, though the difference is not significant at the 5 per cent level (Table 13.3).

Table 13.3 Analysts' mean estimates of valuation variables: Expenser versus Capitalizer

	Expenser (1) (pence)	Capitalizer (2) (pence)	Difference (pence) (2)–(1)
Share price	171.3 (5.5)	170.7 (6.0)	−0.6
EPS 1989	13.2 (0.2)	13.6 (0.2)	0.4
EPS 1990	14.4 (0.4)	14.7 (0.3)	0.3
Implied PE ratio 1989	12.9 (0.4)	12.4 (0.4)	−0.5

Notes:
Standard errors in parentheses.
Differences are not statistically significant, even at the 10% level.

(1) $n = 22$ except for EPS 1990 where $n = 21$
(2) $n = 24$ except for share price and implied PE ratio where $n = 23$

Hypothesis B

The second question concerned whether analysts distinguish between investment in R & D or in plant and machinery. This might be restated in a testable form as:

B. Investment in R & D is valued no less highly than investment in plant and machinery.

If this holds, the estimated share prices for Expenser and Fixed-Asset Buyer would be expected to be very similar, since both firms have the same total level of investment, and historically have achieved similar levels of earnings per share.

This was rejected at the 5 per cent significance level (see Table 13.4). The share price estimate of 158.0p for the Fixed-Asset Buyer was significantly *lower* than for Expenser (171.3p), a result which was initially surprising. It implies that not only did the analysts value R & D *no less highly* than investment in plant and equipment, they actually valued it *more* highly in the circumstances represented in the companies' accounts.

Table 13.4 Analysts' mean estimates of valuation variables: Expenser versus Fixed-Asset Buyer

	Expenser (1) (pence)	Fixed-Asset Buyer (2) (pence)	Difference (pence) (2)–(1)
Share price	171.3 (5.5)	158.0 (3.5)	−13.3*
EPS 1989	13.2 (0.2)	12.7 (0.2)	0.5*
EPS 1990	14.4 (0.4)	13.6 (0.4)	−0.8
Implied PE ratio 1989	12.9 (0.4)	12.5 (0.3)	−0.4

Notes:
Standard errors in parentheses.
* Difference is statistically significant at the 5% level.

(1) $n = 22$ except for EPS 1990 where $n = 21$
(2) $n = 23$

Observation of the EPS 1989 estimates and the implied PE ratio indicates that the lower share price for the Fixed-Asset Buyer results partly from an expectation of lower earnings and also from the application of a lower PE multiplier. The former seems to imply that investment in R & D is expected to generate higher earnings than investment in plant and equipment – in this particular industry, where maintaining competitiveness is thought by analysts to depend on innovation of products or processes, and on spending up to a certain 'appropriate' level on R & D (perhaps taken as the industry norm). Both views were frequently espoused by the respondents in support of their estimated earnings or share price, when asked open-endedly to comment on their assessment of the company.

The lower implied PE multiplier can be rationalized in two ways.

Either, contrary to popular belief, earnings from R & D investment are not considered more uncertain than those from Fixed-Asset Investment, or, perhaps more realistically, analysts are particularly suspicious of firms which 'underspend' on R & D, reflecting a view that earnings growth depends on innovation.

Conclusions

In summary it would appear that investment analysts:

- are able to see through different accounting treatments of R & D expenditure:
- do place value on what they perceive to be an appropriate level of R & D expenditure for a company. In particular, companies which spend less than this appropriate level are likely to be valued less highly. The project has not explored the valuation of companies which 'overspend' on R & D, but previous research suggests that analysts do not positively discriminate in favour of such companies (Gray 1986).

These results have interesting implications for policy makers. The accounting treatment of R & D does not appear to prejudice the valuation of companies by analysts, though disclosure of amounts spent or capitalized is, based on the comments received from the analysts, likely to be important. The latest revision to the R & D accounting standard (SSAP 13) for the first time required large companies to disclose R & D spend but did not change the conditions for capitalization of R & D costs. There is no evidence in this research to support the contention that allowing companies to capitalize more R & D costs would encourage analysts to look more favourably on R & D spenders; the raising of finance would probably not be improved by allowing the capitalization of R & D expenditure. However, the requirement to disclose information on the amount spent on R & D will be welcomed by analysts.

More generally the observation here that analysts, admittedly in aggregate and in contradiction with some other studies, appear able to react rationally to the different accounting treatments of R & D costs, would imply that disclosure adequacy is a more useful goal for accounting regulators than practice prescription.

Any claimed short-termism in the market does not seem to extend to analysts' views on R & D; the results do not support the view that 'the market' discriminates against long-term (R & D) investment, at least up to a level which is viewed by the market as appropriate (the industry 'norm'). Whether the current 'industry norm' is really sufficient to allow UK companies to become (or remain) competitive in world markets is open to considerable debate, but is not addressed in this research.

Limitations

Care should be taken in generalizing from these results. Only one particular industrial sector was investigated. The artificiality of the experimental method, even with attempts to reduce this, is obviously a weakness. Company profits throughout the period were fairly strong and it would be interesting to observe analysts' reaction to a company which continued to spend on R & D when profits were not so strong, or when losses were being reported.

13.4 COMPANY MANAGEMENT STUDY[4]

Objectives

The second part of the research sought to investigate whether small UK firms might be discouraged from investing in R & D as a result of the required accounting and disclosure treatment of R & D expenditure. Small high-technology firms were chosen in view of previous research which suggested that they may experience different, perhaps more acute, problems in raising finance and also (e.g. Horwitz and Kolodny 1980) that the requirement to expense research expenditure might have a greater impact on R & D investment decisions. Larger firms were included in the postal questionnaire for comparison purposes.

Research method

Although expensive to administer, structured interviews allow issues to be explored in depth, with elaboration on responses by participants. This approach was applied to a limited number of small companies. In order to cover a wider range of organizations and to compare the behaviour of small and large firms a postal questionnaire survey was also employed. This was constructed in the light of information collected in the structured interviews.

Sample companies for both parts of the study were selected from *Datastream* and the *Hambro Company Guide*. They were chosen from those industrial sectors with a high probability of significant

R & D activity in medium- and high-technology areas. Subjects for the structured interviews were restricted to executives in small companies in the Unlisted Securities Market (USM), the Third Market and the OTC market.

A target of thirty companies was set, and achieved, for the structured interviews. Companies were asked to provide a senior financial and senior technical official to be interviewed by the research team (although in practice on some occasions only one of these officers was available). For the postal questionnaire, 315 firms were contacted, from which sixty-one usable responses were received. Thirty companies were not involved in R & D or were untraceable, giving a response rate of 21 per cent. Although low, this response rate compares favourably with those obtained by Gray (1986) and Fisher and Lothian (1987).

In both structured interview and postal questionnaire the instrument was broken down into four sections: background details of the organization, background details of R & D activities, R & D budget details and accounting for R & D and its disclosure.

Results

Details of the organization

Sample companies were drawn from a range of industrial sectors of which the electronic and electrical engineering sector was predominant. Respondents were mainly senior technical and financial officers although some of the postal questionnaires were completed by other senior executives. A reasonably uniform geographical spread of participants was obtained with a slight bias towards London and the South East.

Postal questionnaire replies were evenly divided between 'small' companies[5] and 'medium and large' ones (termed 'large') as shown below. All but a small minority of the companies classified themselves as either medium or high-technology companies.

'Small' companies	27
'Large' companies	27
Unclassifiable	7
Total number of postal responses	61

The seven companies were unclassifiable either because the replies were anonymous, or because the companies were no longer separately identifiable on *Datastream*, probably because of take-overs.

Details of R & D activities

Since only development work that meets certain criteria can be capitalized under SSAP 13, it is of interest to obtain a breakdown of R & D expenditure between pure research, applied research and development. Results are given in Table 13.5. Spending is dominated by development work (particularly in the case of small companies). A minority of firms (both large and small) had difficulty in distinguishing between research and development expenditure. The sources of funding for the R & D work are shown in Table 13.6. These results clearly show that most R & D is financed from companies' own resources, though customers do provide a significant level of support for a minority of firms. Government funding is practically negligible. Most contributors suggested that external funding had a positive influence on R & D spending levels; firms would inject additional R & D funds of their own into projects which were externally supported.

Table 13.5 Breakdown between pure research, applied research and development

Size of Company	Average % of R & D expenditure			No. of firms
	Pure research	Applied research	Development	
Small	2%	14%	84%	57*
Large	7%	15%	78%	27

Note:
* For some measurements the result for 'structured interview' ($n = 30$) and postal survey ($n = 27$) small firms have been combined to give an overall small company sample size of 57.

Firms were also asked to identify constraints on R & D activity. Both large and small firms identified funds shortage as the most important factor, although skills availability was ranked a close second. This closely mirrors the results of the Foley *et al.* study concerning skills shortages, which is reported in Chapter 6 of this volume. Doubts about market size, ideas shortage and space shortage (in London and the South East) were also important.

R & D budget details

Factors which influence the R & D budget were investigated in order to assess the role which accounting policies might play. Respondents were asked to rank the importance of various factors

Table 13.6 Breakdown of funding sources for R & D

Source of funding	Structured interview (small firms)		Postal questionnaire					
			Small firms		Large firms		Unknown	
	No. using source	av. % for all firms	No. using source	av. % for all firms	No. using source	av. % for all firms	No. using source	av. % for all firms
Own resources	30	88%	26	62%	24	82%	6	87%
Government support	5	0.3%	4	8%	12	4.4%	2	1.7%
Customer contracts	11	12%	11	30%	13	14%	4	12%

on a scale from 1 (low importance) to 5 (high importance). Results obtained are shown in Table 13.7.

Table 13.7 Relative importance of different factors in constructing an R & D budget

| Factor | *Importance – mean response (rank)* | | |
	Structured interview	*Small firms (questionnaire)*	*Large firms (questionnaire)*
Value of future benefits	4.13 (1)	4.33 (1)	4.26 (1)
Detailed cost of project	3.57 (2)	3.35 (3)	3.74 (2)
No. of projects considered	2.82 (3)	3.19 (4)	3.00 (6)
Projected profit	2.67 (4)	3.81 (2)	3.51 (3)
Previous year R & D budget	2.37 (5)	2.78 (6)	3.30 (4)
Previous year's profit	2.30 (6)	3.15 (5)	3.15 (5)
Previous year's turnover	2.20 (7)	2.37 (7)	1.96 (8)
Competitors' R & D	1.50 (8)	1.67 (8)	2.04 (7)
Industry sector norm	1.32 (9)	1.30 (9)	1.56 (9)

As might be expected, for all companies the most significant factors were detailed costs of projects and perceived value of future benefits. Last year's budget appeared to be more important in large companies than in small ones. This is understandable if many of the large companies have reached a state of equilibrium and many of the small ones are still expanding. Previous year's profit and projected profit (which are influenced by R & D policy) were reasonably significant factors. The difference between structured interview and postal questionnaire responses is puzzling. A very interesting feature was that competitors' R & D spend or even the idea of an industry sector norm is generally ranked of low importance, particularly by small companies. This is in marked contrast to the first part of the current study which showed that these ideas are of considerable importance to analysts.

Bonus schemes for senior management may be important if they influence behaviour with respect to R & D. Both large and small companies indicated that bonus schemes were operated, with the majority of schemes being profit related. Thus there would appear to be built-in incentives to maintain short-term profits whether by cuts in R & D investment or by capitalization of R & D.

Replies relating to the management accounts in operation suggested that the majority of companies in the survey had sufficient knowledge of their R & D cost structures to be in a position to capitalize qualifying development expenditure.

R & D accounting policies

Questions were included to identify the policy each company adopted to account for qualifying development expenditure under SSAP 13, and the source of, and motivation for, the policy (Tables 13.8 and 13.9). Companies' reaction to hypothetical regimes in which *all* R & D is required to be expensed (as in the United States), or in which elements of *research* as well as development may be capitalized and amortized, was also explored.

Not unexpectedly, the predominant treatment was expensing of

Table 13.8 Accounting policy adopted

	Expense all R & D	Capitalize under SSAP 13			No answer
		Occasionally	Always	Total	
Small firms – structured interview	24 (80%)	2	4	6 (20%)	0
Small firms – questionnaire	21 (78%)	3	3	6 (22%)	0
Large firms – questionnaire	24 (89%)	1	1	2 (7%)	1 (4%)
Indeterminate size – questionnaire	7 (100%)	0	0	0	0
TOTAL	76	6	8	14	1

Table 13.9 Decision-maker group responsible for choice of accounting policy

	Internal directors	Auditors	External directors	Contradictory anwers	No answers
Small firms – structured interview	21	3	2	2*	2
Small firms – questionnaire	18	1	4	0	4
Large firms – questionnaire	21	0	1	0	5
Indeterminate size – questionnaire	6	1	0	0	0

Note:
* In these two firms the Finance Director suggested that the auditors had decided on the policy, while the Technical Director believed it was the external executive.

all R & D expenditure (80 per cent or more). Approximately 20 per cent of small companies, at least occasionally, capitalized development expenditure, whereas for large companies this figure was less than 10 per cent. Market (i.e. analysts') pressure for expensing is probably greater for large companies, and the impact on profitability is likely to be less than in small high-tech firms which may be rapidly growing.

The groups which were reported as being responsible for the choice of accounting policy are shown in Table 13.9. On the whole it appears that accounting policies have been chosen by internal managers, and that these policies have been consistently followed since the foundation of the company. Only one company had actually changed its policy to capitalization, as a result of the changing nature of its R & D activities, while others suggested they might change policy once suitable data collection systems had been established. One capitalizer, which was involved in developing satellite-based navigational systems, changed to expensing when the Challenger disaster made the (capitalized) development work valueless.

When asked about the motivation for adopting a particular accounting policy, expensers tended to quote reasons associated with prudence, 'normal' behaviour, reacting to auditor's advice and doubts about the value of R & D; capitalizers tended to stress the maintenance of profit levels and confidence in the real and exploitable value of their R & D. Seven of the companies (two capitalizers and five expensers) involved in the structured interviews felt that their accounting policies influenced their level of R & D expenditure. Both capitalizers argued that they would decrease R & D expenditure if unable to capitalize. The five expensers stated, in various ways, that projects were constrained by R & D expenditure. Although two realized that capitalization might be a possible solution, they seemed inhibited by external pressures from making the change.

Companies were asked if their decisions on R & D would change if capitalization of all R & D costs was allowed. The following responses were obtained from the structured interviews:

Yes	5
No	22
Disagreement between technical and financial officer	3

Three of the six capitalizers gave a positive response to this question, the other three saw little advantage in the change since only a very small proportion of their expenditure was non-qualifying research and development in any case. Only two expensers unequivocally wished to capitalize. Reasons given were confidence that excellent profits would result from their products. Capitalization was already an available option for these companies, which might suggest that reduced external pressures would encourage capitalization; a change in the accounting standard would probably achieve little. Similar results were obtained in the postal survey.

Companies were also asked how they would react to accounting policies which obliged companies to expense in the current year, as in the United States. Most expensers, of course, were relatively unconcerned. Four of the six capitalizers in the structured interviews expressed definite concern with comments such as:

- Unhappy; it would affect profit.
- We would not spend on R & D at all.
- We would not be as successful.
- We might not go ahead with projects having high development costs.

Capitalizers in the postal survey expressed similar misgivings.

The amount of R & D expenditure which qualifies for capitalization is of significance and this question was included in the postal questionnaire. Only a limited number of usable replies were received and these are summarized in Table 13.10. Some reservations must be expressed about the 0 per cent and some of the 100 per cent responses – these respondents may well have misinterpreted the question. Taking the remaining data it is possible to suggest that between 50 and 60 per cent of R & D expenditure may be eligible for capitalization.

Table 13.10 Proportion of R & D costs qualifying for capitalization

| | Number of firms with stated % of qualifying R & D expenditure | | |
	Small firms	Large firms	Indeterminate
0%	5	2	1
1–19%	0	1	0
20–39%	1	0	1
40–59%	5	2	0
60–79%	1	1	0
80–99%	1	1	0
100%	3	6	1
Usable responses	16	13	3

Companies were asked whether they disclosed R & D expenditure in their financial accounts. Results are shown in Table 13.11. The structured interview small companies showed a two to one majority in favour of disclosure, although the questionnaire responses are significantly different. The majority of large companies were disclosers. Most of the companies which did disclose gave very positive reasons for doing so. These included:

- The need to demonstrate their commitment to new developments and maintain the company's reputation as 'leading edge'.
- For market purposes or for evaluation of performance by shareholders.

Some large companies stated that they had already begun to disclose before SSAP 13 (revised) had been introduced. Those companies which did not disclose generally stated that this was sensitive information in an extremely competitive market. One or two added that they were not particularly proud of their level of expenditure.

Table 13.11 Number of companies disclosing R & D expenditure in their financial accounts

	Small firms (structured interview)	Small firms (questionnaire)	Large firms (questionnaire)	Indeterminate size
Disclose	20	11	17	3
Don't disclose	10	16	9	4
No response	0	0	1	0

Small companies on the whole felt that the disclosure requirement of SSAP 13 would have little effect on them individually since most would be exempt under the small company amendment. Some large companies, however, had reservations. There was also some feeling that the effect on industry as a whole could be positive with disclosure putting upward pressure on R & D expenditure in general.

Conclusions

This part of the study was designed to investigate a number of questions about Research and Development, including whether the provisions of SSAP 13 (revised) with regard to expensing of R & D costs disadvantage small high-tech companies. The study showed that while small firms make more use of the existing provisions for capitalization of development expenditure than large ones, only a minority (around 20 per cent) do so. It was found that most of the others do have the necessary detailed information but choose not to capitalize for reasons of prudence or fear of external judgements. Even among the companies which do capitalize, a substantial proportion did not want the current provisions to be further extended to research itself.

On the other hand, previous and current year profits do appear to be a moderately important factor in setting the level of the R & D budget, so if a policy of capitalization of development costs were adopted by more firms, it might indirectly contribute towards an increase in R & D expenditure. However, most small companies were satisfied with the current situation. A minority of expensers showed some frustration and a desire to change but seemed to be inhibited from capitalizing, more by internal or other external pressures, than by the provisions of SSAP 13.

Thus, overall this study did not show that the accounting standard disadvantages small high-tech companies. The provisions for capitalization that already exist (and the study suggested that between 50 and 60 per cent of R & D expenditure might currently qualify) are generally not taken up and the accounting standard is generally not an important deterrent among those wishing to change. There may be an argument for highlighting existing possibilities for capitalization and encouraging decision-makers to make their decisions in the light of the real financial and economic needs of their companies rather than abstract and ill-defined notions about prudence.

The second question related to whether incentive schemes for managers have any influence on R & D decision making. The study indicated that most companies have incentive schemes and in general they are profit related. There was no evidence to suggest that this provides an incentive to capitalization (which in the short term would provide higher profits and therefore higher bonuses). Nor was there any evidence that companies might tend to cut R & D to maintain profits for this reason; indeed, many respondents seemed genuinely puzzled by this question. In order to investigate this question fully, it would probably be necessary to contrast the R & D investment behaviour over time of a group of companies with and without profit-related incentive schemes.

The third issue considered whether expensing of R & D costs might hinder the raising of finance. Generally few companies saw any relationship between accounting policies and their ability to raise finance. Only five (one capitalizer and four expensers) of twenty-seven large firms thought that their accounting treatment of

R & D helped with finance raising. Amongst small firms, nineteen (fourteen expensers and five capitalizers) out of the fifty-seven thought that fund-raising was influenced by conventions chosen. Comments made by expensers all related to the importance of expensing in order to maintain company image with analysts. Three of the capitalizers pointed to the fact that enhanced R & D assets were important to industrial investors. If, as Part I of the study indicates, analysts 'see through' different accounting conventions, then accounting treatment may indeed be irrelevant.

The final question asked whether mandatory disclosure of both expensed and capitalized R & D might discourage R & D expenditure. Many small companies are proud of their technological development and therefore already disclose as a matter of policy. Some small firms, particularly those with a small number of products, were worried about disclosure of commercially sensitive information, but these have generally been satisfied by the SSAP 13 exemptions from disclosure for small companies. The majority of respondents viewed mandatory disclosure as a positive development and there was some feeling that resulting comparisons might be a subtle influence leading to an overall increase in R & D work.

13.5 OVERALL CONCLUSIONS

The main objective of the project was to investigate whether the accounting treatment of R & D expenditure was likely to have any impact on R & D investment. Company management make decisions on how much to invest on R & D and therefore, for the accounting treatment to have any impact, it must affect company management. In the current survey of the opinions of managers in mainly smaller companies, in contrast to some previous research (Horwitz and Koldny 1980, Fisher and Lothian 1987), accounting for R & D did not seem to be a major issue. Many managers show concern for how their company is perceived by the stock-market and by analysts in particular. Some have expressed publicly the view that analysts have 'short-term' horizons and that R & D investment decisions must be taken with this in mind. The evidence from the current research suggests that analysts do appear to place value on R & D investment, up to the level of the 'industry-norm', and, in aggregate at least, are not 'fooled' by accounts which report higher profits and higher assets, solely as a result of the choice of R & D accounting method. It would be interesting to know whether these results might persist across different industrial sectors and over time. On the basis of this study, there is no evidence to suggest that the low level of R & D investment might be attributable to the accounting method chosen for reporting purposes.

NOTES

1 The results of the study have been reported previously in a professional journal (Goodacre 1991) and in papers presented at various conferences (Goodacre *et al*. 1990a, 1990b), and the authors are grateful for comments received at these presentations.
2 Research subjects were identified from various yearbooks and directories of investment intermediaries, with an additional random sample of names and addresses provided by the Society of Investment Analysts from its list of members.
3 A lower PE ratio is also consistent with analysts' expressed preference for R & D write-off (Gray 1986) rather than 'capitalization'. This might manifest itself in a feeling that the Capitalizer company is, in some sense, riskier and that its cash flows should be discounted at a higher rate of return, or a lower PE multiplier applied.
4 This part of the chapter draws heavily upon a previous reporting of the results in: Ball *et al*. (1991).
5 'Small is here used in the sense of SSAP 13 – that is, with less then £80m turnover, or less than £45m balance sheet, or less than 500 employees (two of these three being satisfied).

REFERENCES

Abdel-Khalik, A. R. and Keller, T. F. (1979) 'Earnings or cash flows: an experiment on functional fixation and the valuation of the firm', *Studies in Accounting Research* 16 (American Accounting Association).

Abdel-Khalik, A. R., Thomson, R. B. and Taylor, R. E. (1978) 'The impact of reporting leases off the balance sheet on bond risk premiums: two exploratory studies', in *Economic Consequences of Accounting Standards: Selected Papers*, Stamford, Conn.: Financial Accounting Standards Board.

——, —— and —— (1981) *The Economic Effects on Leases of FASB Statement No. 13, Accounting for Leases*, Stamford, Conn.: Financial Accounting Standards Board.

Ball, R. Thomas, R. E. and McGrath, J. (1991) 'Influence of R & D accounting conventions on internal decision-making of companies', *R & D Management* 21(4): 261–9.

Drebin, A. R. (1966) 'Accounting for proprietary research', *The Accounting Review*, July: 413–25.

Dukes, R. (1976) 'An investigation of the effects of expensing research and development costs on security prices', in M. Schiff and G. Sorter (eds) *Proceedings of the Conference on Topical Research in Accounting*, New York: Ross Institute of Accounting Research, School of Business, New York University, pp. 147–93.

Dukes, R., Dyckman, T. and Elliot, J. (1980) 'Accounting for research and development costs: the impact on research and development expenditures', *Journal of Accounting Research* (Supplement): 1–37.

Elliot, J., Richardson, G. Dyckman, T. and Dukes, R. (1984) 'The impact of SFAS no. 2 on firm expenditures on research and development: replications and extensions', *Journal of Accounting Research*, Spring: 85–102.

Estes, R. and Reimer, M. (1979) 'An experimental study of the differential effect of standard and qualified auditors' opinions on investors' price decisions', *Accounting and Business Research*, Spring: 157–61.

Fisher, J. and Lothian, N. (1987) *The Management of the Research and Development Function in United Kingdom Corporations: Some Empirical Evidence*, Edinburgh: Institute of Chartered Accountants of Scotland.

Goodacre, A. (1991) 'R & D expenditure and the analysts' view', *Accountancy*, November: 78–9.

Goodacre, A., Ball, R. McGrath, J. Pratt, K. C. and Thomas, R. E. (1990a) 'Perceptions of accounting disclosure of R & D expenditure: an experimental study', first presented at The Institute of Quantitative Investment Research (INQUIRE), Autumn Conference, Cambridge.

—, —, —, — and — (1990b) 'How do firms and financial markets regard R & D expenditure?', presented at the ESRC Dissemination Conference 'Financing Marketing and Adoption of New Technologies in the UK', London.

Gray, R. H. (1986) *Accounting for R & D: A Review of Experiences with SSAP 13*, London: Institute of Chartered Accountants in England & Wales.

Hope, T. and Gray, R. H. (1982) 'Power and policy making: the development of an R & D standard', *Journal of Business Finance and Accounting* 9 (Winter): 531–58.

Horwitz, B. N. and Kolodny, R. (1980) 'The economic effects of involuntary uniformity in the financial reporting of R & D expenditures', *Journal of Accounting Research* (Supplement): 38–74.

Horwitz, B. N. and Normolle, D. (1988) 'Federal Agency R & D contract awards and the FASB rule for privately-funded R & D', *The Accounting Review*, July: 414–35.

Lev, B. and Ohlson, J. A. (1982) 'Market-based empirical research in accounting: a review, interpretation and extension', *Journal of Accounting Research* (Supplement): 249–322.

Marsh, P. (1990) *Short-termism on trial*, Institutional Fund Managers Association, reviewed in S. Holberton, 'Cutting through the conceptual fog', *The Financial Times*, 7 November, p. 17.

McGee, R. W. (1984) 'NAA research: software accounting, bank lending decisions and stock prices', *Management Accounting (USA)*, July: 20, 23.

Schwan, E. S. (1976) 'The effects of human resource accounting data on financial decisions: an empirical test', *Accounting, Organizations and Society* 1(2–3): 219–37.

Sunder, S. (1973) 'Relationships between accounting changes and stock prices: problems of measurement and some empirical evidence', *Journal of Accounting Research* (Supplement): 1–45.

—— (1975) 'Stock price and risk related to accounting changes in inventory valuation', *The Accounting Review*, April: 305–15.

Wilkins, T. and Zimmer, I. (1983) 'The effect of leasing and different methods of accounting for leases on credit evaluations', *The Accounting Review*, October: 749–64.

Wilner, N. and Birnberg, J. (1986) 'Methodological problems in functional fixation research: criticism and suggestions', *Accounting, Organizations and Society* 11(1): 71–80.

14 R & D Intensity and Firm Finance: A US–UK Comparison

John Board, P. J. Robert Delargy and Ian Tonks

14.1 INTRODUCTION: SSAP 13 AND PREVIOUS ACCOUNTING POLICIES

In January 1989 the Accounting Standards Committee introduced a new standard of accounting practice for the United Kingdom. Statement of Standard Accounting Practice, SSAP 13 (revised), requires the publication of expensed amounts of R & D. Before the introduction of the new standard the decision whether or not to disclose R & D expenditure was made by individual firms. The standard applies to financial statements for accounting years ending on or after 1989 and extends 'in effect to companies which are public limited companies, or special category companies, or subsidiaries of such companies, or which exceed by a multiple of ten the criteria for defining a medium-sized company under the Companies Act 1985'. Those companies covered by the standard[1] are now required to disclose the full amount of R & D expenditure incurred each year.[2]

SSAP 13 now allows identification, for the first time, of the amount of R & D undertaken by large companies. This disclosure is a valuable addition to the information available to investors, particularly because R & D-intensive companies are often grouped within a few specialist industries (e.g. Aerospace), and therefore it was difficult to construct industry-matched samples to estimate the extent of a non-disclosing company's R & D activity.

In this chapter we examine the link between a firm's debt-equity ratio and its R & D expenditure, comparing the results to those from similar tests for the United States. We also compare the intra-national differences between the financing structures of those firms who are relatively R & D intensive, those that are relatively non-intensive R & D investors and those which perform no R & D at all. We show that there are marked differences between the UK and US financing structures and suggest that UK firms may under-utilize financial instruments such as convertibles.

14.2 THE FINANCING DECISION OF THE FIRM

In the context of R & D, undertaking a positive net present value investment opportunity involves a commitment of funds to R & D in the expectation that the subsequent discounted new cash inflows outweigh the initial costs. This calculation requires that a probabilistic series of cash flows is estimated by the investor, and one definitional feature of R & D investment is that the cash flows are exceptionally risky. Not only is it often impossible to accurately forecast, at the initiation of the project, what inputs will be required, but it is equally difficult to assign inputs to particular outputs. In part this is because one very important feature of R & D is that it will often not be attributable to specific projects. Instead it will be associated with a programme which will have an unknown number of uncertain benefits arising from it, so that there is a one-to-many relationship between input and output, rather than the conventional one-to-one relation considered in standard investment appraisal. These spillover properties add to the uncertainty about the profitability of R & D projects.

Capital structure theory

Suppose that a firm has decided, using an appropriate investment appraisal technique, that the commitment of funds to R & D is justified. The problem the firm now faces is how to finance the R & D expenditure. External finance falls into two main categories: new equity and new debt. The mix between equity and debt in a firm's balance sheet is referred to as the firm's capital structure and, since the seminal paper by Modigliani and Miller (1958), there has been debate over whether an optimal capital structure exists for a firm.

Equity gives legal ownership of the firm's assets and entitles the equity holders to some share of the future profits of the enterprise, which are, of course, uncertain. Debt (or bonds) guarantees that the debt holders receive a series of fixed interest payments until the maturity of the debt when they also receive the repayment of principal. Therefore, equity in a levered firm is riskier than equity in an unlevered firm and the equity holders in a levered firm will require a higher expected return in compensation; there is a risk premium associated with equity in the presence of debt. However, Modigliani and Miller (1958) show that there is a precise risk-return trade-off, so that capital structure does not affect the value of the firm. Subsequently, Modigliani and Miller (1963) showed that, if interest payments on debt are tax deductible, debt becomes the preferred method of finance. Four arguments have been advanced to counter the implication that firms should be financed entirely by cheap debt:

- Bankruptcy and liquidation costs mean that bond holders are not unconcerned about the capital structure of the firm and will require higher marginal returns on debt to compensate them for the increasing risk of their investment (Warner 1977, Altman 1984). Even if debt is risky, so that the debt holders acknowledge the possibility of default, the Modigliani-Miller capital structure irrelevance result still holds provided that there are no costs of financial distress. However, these conclusions are altered if there are costs of bankruptcy.
- The interaction of the corporate and personal taxation systems means that a particular capital structure, of less than 100 per cent debt, may minimize the tax burden faced by investors (Miller 1977, DeAngelo and Masulis 1980).
- Agency costs may be reduced with a certain level of debt in the capital structure of a firm (Jensen and Meckling 1976, Haugen and Senbet 1988).
- Asymmetric information about future cash flows leads to signalling models of capital structure, in which high-quality firms signal their quality to the market by undertaking levels of debt that cannot be replicated by low-quality rivals (Ross 1977, Leland and Pyle 1977, Harris and Raviv 1991).

These arguments imply that there may be an optimal capital structure for an individual firm.

R & D and capital structure

In the context of bankruptcy costs, R & D specific costs may arise from the inability of the owner of the R & D assets to receive a fair price in the event of insolvency, since the assets purchased for an R & D investment are likely to be difficult to resell. For R & D undertaken by new firms, not only are the future cash flows highly uncertain but R & D investment is likely to be the major component of the firm's investment. As there is a high probability that early in the life of the firm the profits generated by the R & D project will be insufficient to cover the interest payments (forcing the firm into liquidation), new firms will be reluctant to use debt to finance R & D. Similarly, potential debt holders may be unwilling to purchase a new firm's debt since they realize the inherent risk and, perhaps more importantly, are unable to secure their loan against any fixed assets (because some R & D investment will have a low resale value). These arguments suggest that new companies are unlikely to finance their new R & D investments by issuing debt. We expect these firms to be more likely to use equity as a source of finance.[3]

The situation for existing companies is somewhat different, as they can cross-finance their activities. An existing firm could also use existing assets as security against loans raised. We might therefore expect that large diversified firms are as likely to use debt as equity to finance R & D, whereas smaller undiversified firms are more likely to finance R & D by issuing equity.

If we consider both new and existing companies, DeAngelo and Masulis (1980) argued that any unused tax allowances will offset the tax advantages of debt finance. Generous investment credits on R & D expenditure (Cordes 1989) will result in R & D-intensive firms being less likely to employ debt in their capital structure, since the tax benefit of debt will be smaller, and we would expect to see R & D-intensive firms with low levels of leverage.

Information asymmetries between firms and the suppliers of capital have led to the 'Pecking Order' theories of financial structure based on the premise that internal finance (e.g. retained earnings) is preferred to debt which, because it does not constitute a sale of a portion of the firm at a price which may undervalue the firm, is preferred to equity (Myers 1984, Myers and Majluf 1984). We again suggest that companies who perform R & D are likely to prefer equity to debt, since the cost of debt will be unusually high for these companies. Also, the likelihood of asymmetric information is greater the greater the riskiness of the company's activities.

Finally, this preference for equity finance of R & D is reinforced once the equity of a firm is seen as a call option on the projects undertaken (Myers 1977). Since a rise in the volatility of the project will result in a rise in the value of the call option (i.e. equity), it will be in the interest of the equity holders to undertake risky R & D. Furthermore, if the firm attempts to finance this risky R & D without issuing debt, it avoids raising the exercise price of the implied option which would, *ceteris paribus*, lower the value of the option.

These arguments suggest that (1) R & D undertaken by small and/or undiversified public companies[4] is more likely to be financed by equity, and hence the percentage of debt in the capital structure of these firms should be lower then for larger and/or diversified firms, and (2) firms which undertake R & D will have lower levels of leverage than those who undertake a lesser quantity of R & D (or none at all), and this will lead us to expect a negative correlation between R & D and gearing.

14.3 DATA

The source of our data is Datastream International's share service. We use their definition of the debt-equity ratio, defined as debt as a proportion of debt plus equity.[5] Our definition of R & D-intensity is the expensed R & D of the firm[6] divided by the total sales of the firm.[7] This adjusts R & D expenditure for the scale of a company's activities.

In the United Kingdom R & D may be capitalized or expensed. Capitalization has, at least in theory, the implication that there is a certainty equivalent future stream of earnings from the investment. This is not appropriate for the 'pure' R & D which we wish to consider. Hence, capitalized R & D was excluded and in the analysis below, any firm having both expensed and capitalized R & D was omitted. (This had little effect on the sample, because only a few firms had any capitalized R & D; these were mainly in the oil industry.)

The distribution of companies by R & D intensity is shown in Figures 14.1 and 14.2.

Figure 14.1 shows companies which declared positive R & D expenditure and reveals that about 50 per cent of United Kingdom companies had R & D intensity of less than 1 per cent. In contrast, the figure shows that the distribution of R & D intensity for US firms is more uniform and has very few firms which declare R & D of less than 1 per cent of sales. Figure 14.2 shows a more detailed breakdown of the group of low-R & D-intensity companies.

In Section 14.4 we use regression analysis of two cross-sectional samples, one for the United States and another for the United Kingdom, each consisting of a mixture of R & D-intensive and low-R & D firms to examine the relation between the gearing ratio and the intensity of R & D expenditure. In Section 14.5 we compare

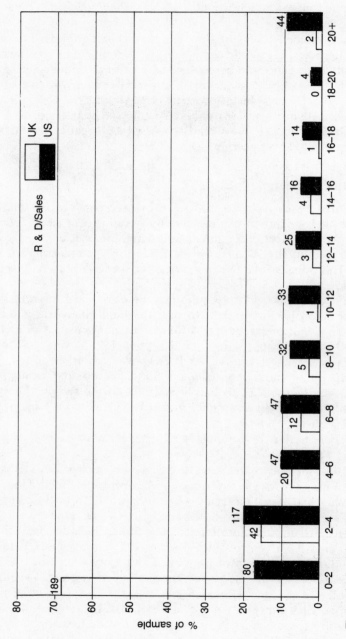

Figure 14.1 Distribution of R & D intensity

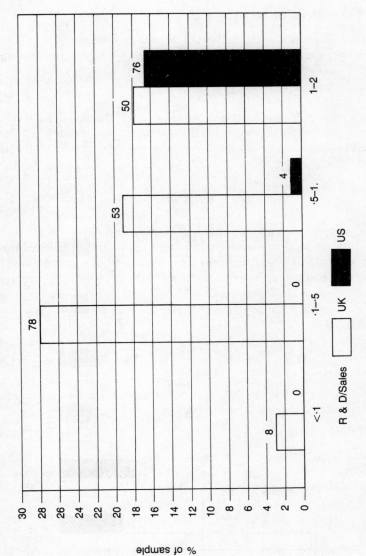

Figure 14.2 Distribution of R & D intensity: very low intensity

the average gearing in companies with positive R & D with those having no R & D expenditure.

14.4 RELATION BETWEEN R & D AND GEARING

The firm chooses the capital structure which maximizes its value. This is equivalent to minimizing the weighted average cost of capital (WACC), which is:

$$\text{WACC} = r_E(1 - \Theta) + r_D\Theta \tag{1}$$

where r_E is the required return on equity, r_D the required return on debt and Θ is the ratio of the market value of debt to the value of the firm. To find the optimal Θ, differentiate (1) with respect to Θ:

$$\frac{\partial \text{WACC}}{\partial \Theta} = -r_E + (1 - \Theta)\frac{\partial r_E}{\partial \Theta} + r_D = 0 \tag{2}$$

No arbitrage implies a linear relationship between r_E and $\Theta/(1 - \Theta)$, so that an optimal capital structure from (2) is indeterminate: this is the Modigliani–Miller theorem. However, suppose that there are substantial bankruptcy costs that the firm incurs in the event of financial distress, and that expected bankruptcy costs Ω increase as Θ increases. Then, since r_E and r_D will now depend on Ω, equation (2) becomes:

$$\frac{\partial \text{WACC}}{\partial \Theta} = -r_E(\Omega) + (1 - \Theta)\frac{\partial r_E}{\partial \Omega}\frac{\partial \Omega}{\partial \Theta} + r_D(\Omega) + \Theta\frac{\partial r_D}{\partial \Omega}\frac{\partial \Omega}{\partial \Theta} = 0 \tag{3}$$

The first-order condition (3) defines the optimal capital structure as a function of expected bankruptcy costs:

$$F(\Theta^*,\Omega) = 0 \tag{4}$$

Linearizing the implicit solution to (4) and proxying the expected bankruptcy costs by the amount of research and development expenditure, we may write the capital structure decision of firm i as a linear function of its R & D. The estimated equation is:

$$\Theta_i = \alpha_1 + \alpha_2 \text{ R \& D}_i + \varepsilon_i \tag{5}$$

To examine the effect of SSAP 13 on the correlation between R & D and gearing, we considered an expanded form of (5) with R & D scaled to allow for the size of company activities, in a cross-section model of the form:

$$\text{GEARING}_i = \gamma_0 + \gamma_1 (\text{R \& D}_i/\text{SALES}_i) + \gamma_2 \text{BETA}_i \qquad (6)$$

where BETA_i is the equity beta of the ith firm.[8] This model was applied to a random sample of 114 US firms, 57 with greater than 5 per cent R & D/SALES and 57 which declared amounts between zero and 5 per cent R & D/SALES, with the results given in the first panel of Table 14.1 in models 1 to 4. The signs of the variables are as hypothesized above with a negative relationship between GEARING and R & D/SALES. The t-tests of R & D/SALES are significant while those of BETA are insignificant. While the F-statistic is significant in all four cases, the R^2 values suggest only a small explanatory value for the regressions.

There are two problems with this model. The first is a possible simultaneous relationship between R & D and SALES, so that γ_1 may actually reflect a pure sales effect, an absolute R & D effect or a R & D-intensity effect. The second is the usual problem of heteroskedasticity in cross-sectional models. This arises because different firms have different error variances in (5), and its effect can be assessed through the Goldfeld-Quant test for heteroscedasticity. The results of this test, when the data are ordered by ascending magnitude of the variable SALES, are given in the final column of Tables 14.1 and 14.2. For the United States, this indicates significant heteroskedasticity (driven by sales) for 1988, 1989 and 1990. There was no evidence of heteroskedasticity in the 1987 United States (or for the UK sample in any year).

To allow for both problems, a log-linear form of the model was considered:

$$\text{GEARING}_i = \delta_1 + \delta_2 \text{Ln}(\text{R \& D}_i) + \delta_3 \text{Ln}(\text{SALES}_i)$$
$$+ \delta_4 \text{Ln}(\text{BETA}_i) \qquad (7)$$

It was found that the separation of SALES from R & D in this way removed the heteroscedasticity. The results for the United States 1987–90 are presented in the second panel of Table 14.1. in models 5 to 8 Both $\text{Ln}(\text{R \& D}_i)$ and $\text{Ln}(\text{SALES}_i)$ are statistically significant at the 5 per cent level and of the expected sign. Once again BETA is not significant. The logarithmic transformation provides a substantial increase in explanatory power (the lowest R^2 is now 0.142) which would appear to result from the separation of sales (which has a positive and significant effect on gearing) from R & D (which has a negative effect on gearing) as well as the removal of the heteroscedasticity from the residuals (indicated by the low Goldfeld–Quandt test statistics).

Table 14.1 Regressions for the United States

Model	Year	INTERCEPT	R & D/Sales	Ln(R & D)	Ln(SALES)	BETA	Ln(BETA)	F-statistic	ADJUSTED R^2	G-Q
1	1987	25.483** (2.83)	−84.269* (−2.20)			2.425 (0.323)		2.8	0.031	0.419
2	1988	29.247** (3.97)	−62.180 (−1.95)			−2.156 (−0.354)		2.9	0.033	6.299
3	1989	32.558** (3.58)	−103.040** (−2.69)			0.246 (0.032)		4.8	0.062	7.864
4	1990	29.12 ** (3.04)	−132.14 ** (−3.276)			4.918 (0.614)		6.1	0.081	8.464
5	1987	−1.824 (−1.56)		−0.193* (−2.35)	0.445** (4.10)		0.935 (1.86)	5.9	0.118	0.269
6	1988	−2.025 (−1.76)		−0.179* (−2.33)	0.417** (4.42)		0.599 (1.19)	7.9	0.161	0.355
7	1989	−0.181 (−0.17)		−0.147* (−2.07)	0.3263* (3.50)		0.074 (0.16)	6.0	0.120	0.181
8	1990	−0.078 (−0.06)		−0.224* (−2.69)	0.373* (3.39)		0.078 (0.14)	6.2	0.127	0.104

Note: ** denotes significance at 1 per cent, and * denotes significance at 5 per cent.

Table 14.2 Regressions for the United Kingdom

Model	Year	INTERCEPT	R & D/Sales	Ln(R & D)	Ln(SALES)	BETA	Ln(BETA)	F-statistic	ADJUSTED R^2	G-Q
9	1989	25.80** (4.94)	-0.005 (-0.05)			22.69 (1.25)		0.78	0.008	0.077
10	1990	39.12* (-2.78)	-6.400** (-7.75)			7.41 (0.60)		31.07	0.202	0.623
11	1990	55.88* (2.59)	-13.021** (-10.30)			-0.55 (-0.03)		53.15	0.482	0.943
12	1989	2.93 (3.75)		-0.120 (-1.75)	0.133 (1.86)		0.288 (1.72)	2.55	0.069	0.943
13	1990	2.44 (5.94)		0.061 (1.94)	0.027 (0.80)		0.332 (1.25)	2.82	0.035	0.966

Note: ** denotes significance at 1 per cent, and * denotes significance at 5 per cent.

Table 14.2 contains the result of application of the linear and log-linear models to UK samples in models 9, 10, 12 and 13, and reveals some striking differences from the US results. The results for 1989 apply to a period before mandatory disclosure under SSAP 13. In this year, the sample consisted of forty-eight firms which voluntarily disclosed more than 2 per cent R & D/SALES and twenty-four firms voluntarily declaring positive amounts between 0 per cent and 0.5 per cent R & D/SALES. For the linear model, the F-statistic suggests that the coefficients should be treated as zero.[9]

In contrast is the result obtained by applying the same model to a sample of 233 UK firms which declared positive amounts of R & D in 1990, in their first set of post-SSAP 13 accounts (note that this sample includes the voluntarily disclosing companies which comprised the sample used for the 1989 regression). Here the independent variables have the expected signs (as in the regressions on US data), R & D intensity is statistically significant at the 1 per cent level, BETA is not statistically significant, and R^2, which is significant at the 1 per cent level, is substantially higher.[10] The SSAP 13 requirement that companies disclose their expensed R & D[11] reveals a consistent relationship both over time and between countries.[12]

It is clear that there is a large improvement in the explanatory power of the 1990 data for the United Kingdom. A possible explanation of this improvement could be the existence of two types of firms which conduct R & D. We suggest that there are:

- firms which undertake 'safe' R & D – these are firms with a good research track record and will therefore be able to borrow at interest rates equal to the market rate;
- firms which practice 'speculative' R & D – these have no track record in R & D and must therefore pay a premium above the market rate on debt.

For the first group, Modigliani–Miller theorems will hold, gearing is irrelevant to value and the source of finance for R & D (or any other investment) will be arbitrary. Thus, for these firms we expect a low association between source and use of funds and hence a low R^2 in estimates of (5). In addition, this group also has an incentive to disclose pre-1990 (if they did not they might be wrongly classified as 'speculative' R & D and therefore face a premium on the borrowing rate due to the lender having asymmetric information about them *vis-à-vis* other firms attempting to borrow).

For the second group, the increased risk means that Modigliani-

Miller theorems fail to hold so that gearing and the investment decision will be related. If the debt premium is related to the project risk, we expect R & D-intensive firms to have relatively little debt outstanding. Thus, fitting the linear model only to these firms should reveal a relatively strong link between R & D and gearing. Note also that these firms (i.e. the real innovators) are those with the strongest incentive not to have voluntarily disclosed their R & D before SSAP 13. Therefore, these companies will be present in the 1990 sample but absent from that of 1989.

If these two groups exist then a sample selection bias is introduced into the 1989 equation, since it will consist of only firms belonging to the 'safe R & D' group. As a test of this, a regression was run using a sample of firms disclosing for the first time in 1990. The results, given in Model 11 of Table 14.2, show a considerable increase in the significance of R & D, together with a more than doubling of the explanatory power of the larger 1990 sample the results of which are given in Model 10. Thus the hypothesis of a division between these two groups is strongly supported by this result.

In summary the evidence supports the hypothesized negative correlation between GEARING and R & D. The results also suggest a rationale for voluntary disclosure of R & D before 1990 by some firms.

14.5 ANALYSIS OF SUBGROUP SAMPLE MEANS

The disclosure required by SSAP 13 also allows the examination of the average gearing of particular groups of firms (e.g. R & D intensive, R & D non-intensive and firms which do no R & D). The levels at which firms are classified as having high or low R & D expenditure are arbitrary. We treated any UK firm with intensity (i.e. ratio of R & D to sales) of more than 2 per cent as being a high-intensity firm. Before 1990, when disclosure became mandatory, we regarded low-intensity firms as those with R & D intensity of less than 1 per cent. After 1990, we redefined low intensity to include only those firms with intensity of less than 0.5 per cent. The US population from which we drew our sample was much larger so that we were able to define high-intensity firms as those spending over 5 per cent of their sales revenue on R & D. We consider as low intensity those US companies which declared an amount that was positive but less than 0.5 per cent.

For the US samples, we were able to require that the companies met the appropriate criterion in each of the four years considered.

Such a requirement was not enforceable for the United Kingdom. This is an important difference in the samples since, while we can claim that the high-intensity group for the United States contains consistently high spenders on R & D, all we can claim for the UK firms is that they spent considerable amounts on R & D in at least one period.

The results for the US samples are given in Table 14.3. It is clear that there is a statistical difference of the mean gearing of the groups at the 1 per cent level. It can be seen that the estimates of the average gearing of the R & D-intensive firms are smaller than the estimates for the low-intensity R & D firms. This is consistent with the earlier arguments. A smaller sample in which R & D intensive companies were matched by industry and size to non-declaring companies contained twenty-three matched pairs of companies and yielded the results shown in Table 14.4.[13] In all years except 1985 there is a statistical difference between the high-R & D sample and its matched non-disclosing sample with the non-disclosing sample means exceeding the average value of the high-R & D sample. This further confirms the result that US R & D-intensive companies have a below-average level of gearing.

Table 14.5 shows that the evidence for the United Kingdom is somewhat different.[14] What emerges from this table is the suggestion that the average gearing ratios of the R & D-intensive sample are not statistically different from the average of the non-declaring firms, but that the low-intensity R & D practitioners' average substantially exceeds (and in two years, 1988 and 1989, is statistically

Table 14.3 Mean gearing of US samples

	1990	1989	1988	1987
HIGH R & D				
Sample size	122	122	122	123
Mean	22.76	21.32	20.03	19.40
Std dev.	21.28	19.78	17.54	19.95
Skewness	1.21	1.34	1.05	2.18
LOW R & D				
Sample size	58	58	58	58
Mean	34.76	32.99	28.09	30.00
Std dev.	26.25	25.23	18.34	24.87
Skewness	1.85	1.65	0.27	3.32
t-statistic	3.27	3.38	2.84	3.07

Note: t-statistics are for differences in sample means.

Table 14.4 US R & D-intensive companies: matched samples, average gearing

	1990	1989	1988	1987
MATCHED SAMPLE (high R & D vs no R & D)				
Sample size	23	23	23	23
Mean	−15.47	−17.18	−18.27	−17.43
Std dev.	29.25	28.25	24.63	19.99
Skewness	−0.12	−0.40	−0.26	−0.17
t-statistic of mean	2.54	2.92	3.56	4.18

Table 14.5 UK firms matched by industry grouping: average gearing

	1990	1989	1988	1987
MATCHED SAMPLE (high R & D vs no R & D)				
Sample size	47	50	33	25
Mean	−9.47	−2.32	−4.78	7.47
Std dev.	67.09	26.99	24.80	23.36
Skewness	−4.58	0.50	−0.03	−1.31
t-statistic of mean	0.97	0.61	1.11	1.60
MATCHED SAMPLE (low R & D vs no R & D)				
Sample size	34	35	28	20
Mean	11.26	16.05	10.47	0.76
Std dev.	36.29	45.20	21.67	26.38
Skewness	−0.08	1.20	1.15	0.51
t-statistic of mean	1.81	2.10	2.56	0.17

different from) their matched sample of non-declaring firms. This pattern carries over to the 1990 sample, where the mean and standard deviation of the difference of an R & D-intensive sample of forty-seven firms and its non-declaring sample match are respectively −9.07 and 67.49, indicating no statistical difference at the 5 per cent level.[15]

These results are not inconsistent with the suggestion outlined above that gearing will be negatively related to R & D. They also apply in both the United Kingdom and the United States. They do suggest consistent differences in the assessed riskiness of R & D projects adopted between the United States and United Kingdom.[16] The fact that R & D intensive companies in the United Kingdom tend to use as much (financially risky) gearing as companies who perform no R & D points to a possible risk disadvantage for UK companies *vis-à-vis* United States firms if the Modigliani-Miller capital structure irrelevance propositions do not hold in the United Kingdom.

In the final section of this chapter we consider a method of finance which may disperse some of the financial effects of the riskiness of R & D. We find that this method, the use of convertible bonds, although used extensively in the United States is rarely used in the United Kingdom. Hence we would argue that, given two firms, one UK firm and the other a US firm, facing the same investment opportunites, the UK firm is more likely to have to pay a risk premium for its capital.

14.6 CONVERTIBLES

Although we have distinguished between the two main sources of external finance as being equity and debt, in fact there are many hybrid versions of this simple classification. One source particularly appropriate to the finance of speculative R & D investment is a convertible bond issue. A convertible bond is a fixed-interest bond which allows the owner the right to convert into equity at a specified conversion price up to the maturity of the bond. It is similar to a package of a straight bond and a warrant. A warrant allows the owner the right to purchase equity at a specified exercise price.

The value of a convertible can never be less than the value of a similar straight bond or the conversion value into equity:

Value of convertible > MAX (value of straight bond, conversion value)   (8)

where the conversion value is the market price of the equity multiplied by the conversion ratio, which is the number of shares exchanged for a specified face value of debt. The value of a straight (but risky) bond will be a concave function of the value of the firm. As firm value increases, the bond becomes safer and eventually approaches the value of a risk-free bond. Since the conversion ratio is specified when the convertible is issued, the conversion value increases linearly with share value. From equation (8) we can see that the value of the convertible must lie above both the bond value and the conversion value. In fact the difference between the value of the convertible and the lower limit is the value of the option to convert:

Value of convertible = Value of conversion option
+ MAX (value of straight bond, conversion option)   (9)

Hence the value of the convertible includes the valuation of the conversion option. The reason why convertibles are a particularly useful way of financing R & D is because of the speculative and risky nature of R & D (Brennan and Schwartz 1982). The value of a convertible is relatively insensitive to the risk of the underlying asset. This is because a risky investment reduces the value of the straight bond (since default is more likely) but increases the value of the conversion option since option values are an increasing function of the risk of an underlying asset (Merton 1973). Therefore, if the R & D is perceived by some investors as being risky but by others as being safe, the convertible will sell for approximately the same value to both groups of investors since both will attach approximately the same value to the financial instrument, even though they value the different components of the instrument differently.

Table 14.6 shows that there is a contrast between the financing of US and UK companies which disclose R & D expenditure. While almost one-third of R & D-intensive companies and about a quarter of non-intensive R & D companies in the United States have issued some convertibles, only eleven companies in the samples of UK companies (over 100 different companies in all) considered in the industry matchings of Table 14.5 for 1987 to 1989 had issued any convertibles. Over the three-year period 1987 to 1989 the highest percentage of convertibles to total finance of a UK firm was 10 per cent. The same apparent reluctance to use convertibles is seen if we examine all companies declaring R & D in 1990.[17] Of 280 firms only fifteen have any convertibles at all. If we consider only these fifteen companies, the average of convertibles to debt plus equity is 8 per cent with the maximum percentage held by one company being 27 per cent. It is obvious that, in contrast to the

Table 14.6 The use of convertibles by US industrial firms, 1987

Year	Maximum	Mean	Std dev.
(A) *Less than 5% R & D/SALES (118 firms, 36 with convertibles)*			
1986	72.17	3.35	10.61
1987	47.62	5.82	12.48
1988	54.63	5.40	11.88
1989	72.76	4.96	11.52
(B) *Between 0% and 0.5% R & D SALES (36 firms, 9 with convertibles)*			
1986	22.64	1.57	5.09
1987	48.07	2.32	8.74
1988	45.69	2.38	8.10
1989	42.59	1.99	7.29

United States, in the United Kingdom convertibles are not being used to minimize the impact of risk in R & D-declaring firms.

In contrast, not only do a greater proportion of US firms avail of this financing instrument but the average values of convertibles as a percentage of finance for the 118 R & D-intensive firms substantially exceed the average values of the thirty-six low-intensity R & D firms in all years considered. Another contrast is that the maximum percentage held was as high as 72.76 per cent of the total finance of the company.

It is unclear why this difference should exist but the inability or unwillingness to use convertibles may be linked to one of the following.[18] First it could be a perceived absence of a particular type of risk that it is generally felt that convertibles counter. That is the moral hazard problem that, either by subsequently issuing debt with priority over existing debt or by engaging in excessively risky ventures, management will subject the bond holder to a risk he cannot anticipate when purchasing the debt. Convertibles insulate a bond holder against such a risk since if the risk is taken by management he also will participate in the rewards of a successful outcome. Alternatively, it may be that the hypothesis of Fama and Jensen (1983) that firms issue only straight debt or equity because this allows specialist risk-bearing (and imposes costs of monitoring contract fulfilment, by management and equity holders, only on bond holders) holds for the UK market but not for the US market. Such a situation could exist if it were easier for shareholders to ensure contract fulfilment by bond holders in the United States. There would then be less cost involved to shareholders in monitoring the activity of bondholders within the firm. However, there is no evidence to suggest that either of these reasons for the lack of use of convertibles exists in practice. So we are confronted with a possibility (with all its ramifications for the international cost of capital) that the UK financial market has not exploited a major financial innovation.

14.7 SUMMARY

The new accounting standard, SSAP 13 (revised), has enriched the data available to financial economists and enabled several comparisons to be made between the United States and the United Kingdom. It has enabled us to identify a clear negative correlation between R & D and capital gearing in both countries. Firms that invest in R & D tend to have less debt in their capital structure.

This result is consistent with the hypothesis that investment in R & D is risky and that the existence of bankruptcy costs means that firms are either unwilling or unable to raise finance for R & D projects by issuing straight debt. We found no evidence of size effects, so that the negative relationship between R & D intensity and leverage applies to large and medium-sized quoted companies. We found that, in the United States, R & D-intensive firms made use of convertible debt to finance their investments, but that firms in the United Kingdom did not take advantage of this source of finance (which may be argued to be particularly appropriate for R & D projects).

NOTES

1 In practice this means that the largest 300 companies are required to disclose their R & D expenditure.

2 Under the new United Kingdom standard, there is no change in the conditions under which R & D may be expensed (i.e. treated as an expense against income for the current year) rather than capitalized (i.e. shown in the balance sheet). To be capitalized, assets are required to meet the criterion of being 'fixed assets required or constructed in order to provide facilities for research and development' (Deloitte, Haskins and Sells, 1990). The only change enforced by SSAP 13 is that expensed R & D must now be separately revealed in the Income Statement. Thus, there are no cash-flow or tax consequences of this change. This is in contrast to the position in the United States. For a number of years the United States has enforced 'FASB Statement 2', which requires all R & D to be declared as an expensed item. The implication of this requirement was that some R & D, which had previously been capitalized, had to be treated as an expense for the year. Thus this change will have real implications for firms (i.e. on their tax payments). This has given rise to a number of studies examining whether an economic inefficiency is imposed when companies cannot capitalize some or all of their R & D. Horwitz and Kolodny (1980) find some evidence that the R & D undertaken by small high-tech companies declined on introduction of FASB 2. An alternative test of the effect on small companies by Dukes *et al.* (1980) found no evidence of a decline caused by FASB 2. Other treatments focus on precise reasons why expensing should be prejudicial to small firms' research capability. An example is Horwitz and Normolle (1988), which presents evidence that the increased volatility in accounting ratios induced by mandatory expensing of R & D is discounted by government agencies awarding contracts. SSAP 13 does not inflict any economic inefficiencies comparable to those it is suggested that FASB 2 might impose and represents pure information disclosure by companies.

3 These arguments apply to new public companies who have access to

the equity markets. Small single proprietorships and partnerships may be forced to use bank loans or venture capital arrangements.

4 Which may have a few assets on which to secure loans and/or other activities capable of generating income which could underwrite interest payments.

5 Datastream item 731 in their accounting definitions. This is Preference Capital plus Subordinated Debt plus Total Loans Capital plus Borrowings Repayable Within One Year divided by Total Capital Employed plus Borrowings Repayable Within One Year minus Total Intangibles.

6 Datastream accounts definition item 119.

7 Datastream accounts definition item 104.

8 The source is Datastream item BETA. This is the slope coefficient of the market model (a time series regression of the return on each company on the return of the market index).

9 An application of this model using only the forty-eight companies with more than 2 per cent of R & D intensity gave a markedly worse fit.

10 Attempts to extend this model by including additional variables (e.g. taxes paid, company earnings and industry dummies) left these results unchanged.

11 One interpretation of this result is that the substantial increase in explanatory power between 1989 and 1990 suggests that the market ignores voluntarily disclosed information. This argument is based on the idea that voluntarily disclosed information may be less accurate than required information. However, it fails to allow for the fact that all published information, whether mandatory or voluntary, is audited. We advance alternative explanations for our results below.

12 Of course, the correlation between current R & D expenditure and the stock variable GEARING is only part of the basic relationship between gearing and investment in research programmes (of which each annual R & D expenditure is only part). In reality, gearing will consist of numerous increments which, over a period of years, will have provided financing for previous R & D expenditures (as well as many other types of expenditure). In other words, gearing will be sticky so that small changes in R & D intensity will not necessarily be reflected in changes in gearing, unless the new level of expenditure on R & D is expected to persist.

13 We attempted to create matched samples of R & D-intensive and non-declaring companies, matching both by size and by industry grouping. For the United Kingdom we chose companies from the aerospace, electrical, chemicals, health and household, and manufacturing industry groups. Unfortunately, for almost every industry group the small numbers of voluntary disclosers made definite conclusions about statistical differences between groups difficult. In 1990 the constraint on the sample size became the identification of similarly sized matching non-disclosing firms. An even greater problem occurs when we come to the US samples since both high-intensity companies (>5 per cent) and low-intensity companies (0 < intensity ≤ 0.5 per cent) are so concentrated within a few industries (e.g. electronics and instruments) that no meaningful match to non-declaring companies could be constructed. Therefore no attempt was made to match samples by industry and the samples

were based on intensity of R & D expenditure alone. However, those matches already discovered between firms of the same size were carried over to the industry matched groups, with the result that between 40 per cent and 50 per cent of these samples also match by size.

14 Post-SSAP 13 (i.e. for 1990), we can interpret 'non-declaring' companies as those which perform no R & D (at least in the absence of evidence, such as auditor's comments, of non-compliance). Unfortunately, pre-SSAP 13 no such interpretation is possible.

15 The results in this table are not inconsistent with those in Table 14.2 (which showed a negative correlation between gearing and R & D). The reason is that the characteristics of the two control portfolios (matching the high- and low-intensity R & D firms) are different (recall that the matching process will result in the two control portfolios having different industry and size characteristics from each other). The mean gearing of the low-intensity control group substantially exceeds that of the high-intensity control group.

16 One possible cause of such a difference would be the greater and more varied infrastructure of R & D enterprise available to firms in the United States. Another might be the higher probability of adoption of an innovation by firms due to the greater number of firms available as outlets.

17 It is desirable to examine these as a separate, single-year sample, since as shown above, there is some bias within the earlier years due to observing only voluntary disclosers.

18 In efficient markets it is no longer admissible to assume that both buyers and sellers of stock treat convertibles as cheap finance and ignore the changes in the average cost of capital that issuance of convertibles creates.

REFERENCES

Altman, E. I. (1984) 'A further empirical investigation of the bankruptcy cost question', *Journal of Finance* 39(4): 1067–89.

Brennan, M. J. and Schwartz, E. S. (1982) 'The case for convertibles', *Chase Financial Quarterly* 1, Spring: 27–46.

Cordes, J. J. (1989) 'Tax incentives and R & D spending: a review of the evidence', *Research Policy* 18: 119–33.

Deloitte, Haskins and Sells (1990) *UK Accounting Standards*.

Dukes, R. E., Dyckman, T. R. and Elliott, J. A. (1980) 'Accounting for research and development costs: the impact on research and development expenditures', *Journal of Accounting Research*, Supplement.

DeAngelo, H. and Masulis, R. (1980) 'Optimal capital structure under corporate and personal taxation', *Journal of Financial Economics* 8(1): 3–29

Fama, E. F. and Jensen, M. C. (1983) 'Agency problems and residual claims', *Journal of Law and Economics* 26: 327–49 (June).

Harris, M. and Raviv, A. (1991) 'Theory of capital structure', *Journal of Finance* 46: 297–355.

Haugen, R. A. and Senbet, L. W. (1988) 'Bankruptcy and agency costs:

their significance to the theory of optimal capital structure', *Journal of Financial and Quantitative Analysis* 23(1): 27–38.

Horwitz, N. B. and Kolodny, R. (1980) 'The economic effects of involuntary uniformity in the financial reporting of R & D expenditures', *Journal of Accounting Research*, Supplement 18, 38–74.

Horwitz, B. and Normolle, D. (1988) 'Federal agency R & D contract awards and the FASB rule for privately-funded R & D', *Accounting Review*, July 414–35.

Jensen, M. C. and Meckling, W. H. (1976) 'Theory of the firm: managerial behaviour and ownership structure', *Journal of Financial Economics* 3(4): 305–60.

Leland, H. and Pyle, D. (1977) 'Information asymmetries, financial structure and financial intermediation', *Journal of Finance* 32: 371–87.

Masulis, R. W. (1980) 'The effect of capital structure on security prices', *Journal of Financial Economics* 8: 139–78.

Merton R. C. (1973) 'Theory of rational option pricing', *Bell Journal of Economics*, 4: 141–83.

Miller, M. H. (1977) 'Debt and taxes', *Journal of Finance*, May: 261–75.

Modigliani, F. and Miller, M. H. (1958) *The cost of capital, corporation finance and the theory of investment'*, *American Economic Review*, June: 261–97.

—— and —— (1963) 'Corporate income taxes and the cost of capital: a correction', *American Economic Review*, June: 433–43.

Myers, S. C. (1977) 'Determinants of corporate borrowing', *Journal of Financial Economics* 5: 147–75.

—— (1984) 'The capital structure puzzle', *Journal of Finance*, July: 575–92.

Myers, S. C. and Majluf, N. (1984) 'Corporate finance and investment decisions when firms have information that investors do not have', *Journal of Financial Economics*, June: 187–221.

Ross, S. (1977) 'The determination of financial structures: the incentive signalling approach', *Bell Journal of Economics* 23–40.

Scholes, M. and Williams J. (1977) 'Estimating betas from nonsynchronous data', *Journal of Financial Economics* 5(3): 309–27.

Warner, J. B. (1977) 'Bankruptcy, absolute priority and the pricing of risky debt claims', *Journal of Finance* 32(2): 337–48.

Part V

Collaboration in new technology

15 Management of international collaboration

Luke Georghiou and Kate Barker

15.1 INTRODUCTION

The rise of technological collaboration has been observed since the early 1980s and appears to be linked with the need for firms to collaborate with others to gain access to new technologies as a source of competitive advantage. This collaboration may cover a variety of activities, ranging from so-called 'pre-competitive' research, promoted by national governments and the European Commission, to joint market-oriented activities involving shared exploitation of technology. In several technology-intensive sectors firms have gained over the last decade a considerable body of experience in the management of collaboration, often having participated in joint technology projects in national and European programmes. Others have become skilled in collaboration outside the subsidy and support of public sponsorship.

Many of the assumptions and practices for successful management and exploitation of R & D developed within the perspective of the single firm are not appropriate when two or more firms work together. (For a more theoretical treatment see Georghiou *et al.* 1990.) Added complexity results when collaboration extends across international borders, accentuating problems of distance and differences in culture, among other factors. This chapter follows the contributions of others in the initiative which describe firms' management of technology and strategies towards it. Our research looked in depth at how firms manage international technological collaboration. We describe our study, which aimed to identify the factors underpinning successful collaboration between firms at the R & D stage and beyond, and draw lessons about best practice in the formulation and management of collaborations. At the outset we identified questions regarding both the circumstances under which firms choose to collaborate, and how they structure and operate the collaboration to promote a beneficial outcome. Within these broader issues, a number of subsidiary questions were followed up, for example the effects of government involvement, and more specific topics such as collaboration with Japanese firms.

International technological collaboration

Prior to this project, empirical studies of collaboration had tended to fall into three categories: one group concentrated on compilation of data-bases on the number of interfirm relationships (see below) a second concentrated on collaboration in major projects such as the aerospace and nuclear industries (e.g. Mowery 1989); while the third examined collaboration through evaluations of government-sponsored collaborative R & D programmes which began in the 1980s.

Data-bases of collaborations compiled from public sources have shown them to be concentrated in relatively few industries (aerospace, telecoms, motor vehicles and computers) (Morris and Hergert 1987). It can be postulated that collaborations here are driven by high entry costs and the large risks of new technological development. Indeed, these sectors have typically won public support justified by such reasons. However, data including all announced alliances between firms are potentially misleading, because they mass agreements outside the scope of technology which may be different in nature from the topic of interest here (Mariti and Smiley 1983). When data are restricted to inter-firm collaborations which specifically include technology (technology transfer, joint research, research exchange), the rise is even more pronounced, particularly that of joint R & D outside the framework of joint ventures (Hagedoorn 1990).

The data suggest that technological collaborations are concentrated in 'high technology' sectors. Although seemingly having little in common when large-scale international industries such as IT and aerospace are put beside smaller scale and still partly laboratory-based sectors such as biotechnology, they do have the common characteristics of knowledge-intensity and pervasiveness (Georghiou and Metcalfe 1990). This suggests that a single firm is under competitive pressure to ensure that its knowledge base contains the necessary components to stay in the market. Collaboration is not the only option open, but the firm may often require access to knowledge which is held by others. The knowledge held by high-technology firms is often tacit and proprietary, and so collaboration for innovation is significantly concerned with knowledge transfer in the tacit dimension. This view of the underlying reason for the increase in technological collaboration is expressed by Teece in terms of firms' needs to gain access to complementary assets and the appropriability regime of the technology being suitable for joint action with a partner (Teece 1989).

The second characteristic of sectors where we see a high degree of inter-firm collaboration is that the technology is pervasive, that is it underlies a range of products and processes. Here we see the rationale for the public support of collaborative research projects and academic-industrial programmes, such as Alvey in the United Kingdom and the EC's Brite and Esprit programmes. At the time these programmes were established it was politically convenient to describe the research they supported as pre-competitive, whereby participants would work together in the R & D phase, sharing costs and risks, and then subsequently compete in the market. Evaluations have since demonstrated that this was often not the case, with collaborations being based on more complex motives and often persisting beyond the R & D phase (Guy *et al.* 1991).

The data-base approaches, while providing some contextual information, suffer from limitations of data, and disguise a wide spectrum of different activities which are termed 'technological collaboration'. Evidence from collaborative programme evaluations points to more intricate rationales for joint research than were assumed by policy makers. A closer examination of the behaviour of collaborating firms, and a better understanding of the technological flows which take place, is required. Our aim was to build on previous work by examining in greater depth the processes by which collaborative projects are managed.

Approach of the study

The research approach was to carry out fifteen case studies covering a range of collaboration types in different industries. Collaboration in technological development consists of a complex set of interactions between the technological and competitive environments, mediated by the structures of the collaboration and the motivations of the participants. The case studies offered the opportunity to bring out these interactions and to formulate guidelines which related broader principles to specific examples. Selection of the cases was driven by the need to cover a wide range of circumstances. Table 15.1 shows their main characteristics. Three gained support from public schemes (Eureka, BRITE and ESPRIT), and one investigated at a broader level the setting up of a European collaborative R & D programme (JESSI).

Two collaborations for the development of standards were investigated, each involving co-ordination of many partners. Another study looked at a joint industrial research facility. Two of the partnerships covered 'pre-competitive' research only, but the others encompassed varying degrees of involvement in product development, production and marketing tackled through joint ventures. Joint technical development with a licence was included where there was a genuine exchange of knowledge. Different motivations were covered in the set: complementarity in technology or markets, cost-sharing and access to markets. The industrial sectors covered were broad-ranging and not all in high technology. About half the cases were on-going collaborations of several years' duration, enabling us to study the development and changes in collaborative relationships over time. All studies involved British partners, but in each case at least one foreign partner was interviewed. Contact with the companies was at senior management (usually board) level.

15.2 A MANAGEMENT FRAMEWORK

To structure the investigation, a simple chronological model of the process of collaboration was developed. This is shown in Figure 15.1. Three main phases are distinguished: the decision on whether to proceed with a collaborative approach, the implementation of the collaboration, and exploitation of the knowledge generated. Within each phase, some more detailed issues were found to recur in most of the studies. As we shall see, these may come into prominence at different times in the life cycle of the collaboration, but they are frequently closely related, particular structures, for example, being associated with certain types of collaboration. As

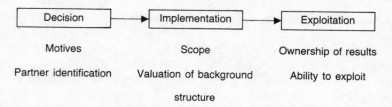

Figure 15.1 A management framework for collaboration

Table 15.1 Range of the case studies

Sector	Collaboration in:			Publicly sponsored scheme	No. of industrial partners	Academic partners	Partners UK and:
	Research	Development	Production/ research				
Aerospace		+(JV)	+(JV)	–	7	–	US, Japan
Scientific instruments	+	+	+(JV)	EUREKA	2	2	European
Chemicals	+	Standards		BRITE	2	1	European
IT		+	+(JV)	ESPRIT	10+	2	European
Nuclear	+				3	–	European
IT	+	+		Joint facility	3	–	European
IT				Scheme level (JESSI)	Many	Many	US Others
Telecoms		+ Standards		International collab. for standards	Many		Japanese
Machine tools		+	+ licence	–	2	–	Japanese
Metals		+	+(licence)	–	2	–	Japanese
Machine tools	+	+	+(JV, licences)	–	2	–	Japanese
IT		+	+	–	2	–	Japanese
Motor industry		+	+	–	2	–	Japanese
IT		+	+(licence)	–	2	–	Japanese
Medical magnets		+	+(JV)	–	2	–	Japanese

we proceed through the management framework certain points will be illustrated by examples drawn from the case studies.

Making the decision

Motivation for collaboration

A prerequisite to entering a collaboration is to know under which circumstances it is a viable option. It helps to clarify the motivations for collaborating in the first place. Table 15.2 sets out the five main categories identified in the study. Firms may be driven by more than one motivation simultaneously, and the principal motivation may alter during the life of the alliance. While examples of all the above types were evident in our research, the case studies supported the finding from our own evaluation studies that risk- and cost-sharing are not the dominant motive in most cases. Complementarity and strategic motivation appear to predominate. One explanation of this is that the latter two categories do not normally entail working with close competitors. Firms naturally prefer to avoid this as competitive advantage lies in differentiation of technology. Collaboration implies the possibility of 'leakage' of knowledge to competitors, both from the project itself and beyond, in areas such as markets and organizational solutions. Nevertheless, when competitive pressure from third parties is strong, or costs and risks rise to levels which single firms cannot bear alone, cost- and risk-sharing collaborations do occur as firms seek to improve the time-cost trade-off. Here firms combine resources to bring a product or technology to a state of development for the market more quickly than can a competitor.

One illustration of a cost sharing collaboration which was investigated in the study is found in the nuclear industry, which has characteristically high entry costs. British, Dutch and German producers of enriched nuclear fuel discovered that they were independently developing a new approach to enrichment, centrifugation, at the end of the 1960s. Under severe competitive pressure from other producers they agreed to share the large costs involved carry out joint development, and jointly market the product, which has a world market and requires long-term negotiations with customers. Together they developed a competing technological paradigm for nuclear enrichment against the less efficient diffusion technology supported by the French nuclear industry. Initially the partners shared their technical knowledge, but each developed their own

Table 15.2 Motivations for collaboration

Motivation	Description	Benefits	Constraints
Risk-sharing	Pursuit of separate R & D routes while agreeing to share results	Covers wider range of options when technological outcome uncertain	Dependent on successful technology transfer at end of project
Cost-sharing	Combining resources with other firms to achieve minimum necessary level	Allows indivisible assets such as facilities or critical mass to be achieved	Requires agreement on detail of shared assets. Usually means working with competitors
Establishment of standards	Working together on technological underpinning of new standards	Helps firms' choice of standards to get adopted	Benefits free-riders. May be wrong standard
Complementarity	Combining different knowledge bases or competences	Creates new possibilities. If collaboration is with user, allows early feedback/experience	Generally needs to be maintained in the exploitation phase
Strategic motivation	Motivated by factors peripheral to project such as gaining access to foreign market or funding, or as precursor to mergers etc.	Relatively cheap way to explore these options	Partner or outside sponsor may object

plant using their own centrifuge designs from a common base. However, after fifteen years all three plants have converged to the same technology. The marketing is run through a joint venture based in the United Kingdom. The next technological generation for fuel enrichment – laser separation – is being investigated jointly by the partners. Again, cost- and risk-sharing drive the collaboration.

Motivations of complementarity drive many firms when collaborating to develop a technology which is new to them, or where novel products and processes are planned by combining different areas of technology. Here, collaboration is chosen above takeover or buying in of the required expertise. Our case study examined collaboration between a British manufacturer of chemical reagents working with a French instrumentation company to develop and market a series of automated instruments and associated biochemical reagents for molecular biology. Neither could proceed without the technical skills of the partner. The firms are in no way rivals, and the complementarity extends beyond the division of technological skills to include combination of expertise in project management and the target world market.

Finding a partner

Identification of a suitable partner is, not surprisingly, usually the first concrete problem to be encountered by managers. The most obvious solution is to collaborate with firms already known to the prospective collaborator. As well as overcoming the barrier of knowing which potential partners exist and where, there may already exist a set of personal relationships between managers and research teams which can underpin the mutual trust which is essential for collaboration. The advantage of previous links is demonstrated empirically by findings from collaborative programmes, where early entrants often upgraded less formal links, while the current second- and third- generation collaborators typically work with at least some of their previous partners. Skills of collaboration have themselves become a desirable attribute (Lyles 1988). Many firms avoid partners who have yet to enter the learning curve.

For those who lack suitable existing connections, international collaboration may entail a difficult and costly search process which forms a significant barrier for small firms. Some attempts at marriage-broking take place in government-sponsored programmes, but these are limited in scope. A niche has emerged for professional brokers, a function which already existed in the context of mergers and acquisitions. Generally speaking, the greater the physical and cultural distance, the harder the process becomes. Nevertheless, our cases show that persistence is rewarded.

Systematic search by a small firm is illustrated by a British machine-tool manufacturer which was seeking a more technologically advanced product than it had, to extend its range and raise its general technology level and profile with customers. This was a central part of its technology and competitive strategy. A company strategist researched the 'market' of potential partners and products which would be suitable for it to make and sell, taking into account the existing markets, and their technological requirements. Over a hundred possibilities were identified world-wide. A shortlist of firms was compiled, all of which turned out to be in Japan. Following a visit to the short-listed firms by the British managing director and assistance by a Japanese employee of the UK firm, a long-standing relationship was established with a small family-owned Japanese machine-tool manufacturer. Thus, investment in researching the desired characteristics of collaborative partners and investigation face to face of potential partners was worthwhile in reaping a long-term technology-based relationship, allowing the British firm to improve quickly its competitive position.

Larger firms may be able to use their existing networks, particularly for international partnerships. We studied a small technology start-up which was a subsidiary of a large British manufacturing company. It had developed a novel micro-electronics technology which it was seeking to license to major manufacturers, neither itself nor the parent being in a position to set up competitive manufacturing. The strategy of the subsidiary was to form partnerships with globally competitive electronic devices manufacturers, and naturally this would include one of the Japanese players. Systematic search, as in the case above, is much more difficult when dealing with very large corporations in a globalized industry, especially when trying to gain the interest of a Japanese concern. A different approach was required. In order to overcome the barriers of cultural and business practice in Japan, the subsidiary used the influence of its parent company's connections there. The parent company's merchant bank in Japan undertook to canvas interest in the technology and approached the large electronics firms. The combination of the parent company's reputation in the country (even though it was in a completely different area) and the standing and local knowledge of the bank caused the approach to be taken seriously, a rare occurrence for unsolicited technological solutions. A partner was found and joint development is proceeding. This search did not remove the necessity on the part of the subsidiary to put forward a convincing case for their new technology, and lengthy negotiations of technology transfer. This case is rather unusual, and the Japanese merchant bankers would not normally become involved in such relatively small-scale deals. However, it does demonstrate that creative solutions and use of existing links –

particularly in Japan, where new relationships are treated with extreme caution – can be worthwhile (Loveridge *et al.* 1992).

Implementing the collaboration

Once a decision has been made to collaborate and partners have been identified, then implementation can begin. As noted in the introduction, the assumptions and lines of authority which are well defined in a single firm do not necessarily hold when two or more are involved. In a formal sense they need to be supplanted by structures and agreements, and on a working level practices and routines need to be established.

Scope and valuation of background

Certain issues are best resolved at the outset, notably the scope to be encompassed by the partnership. This is not solely a technological matter but involves as well a consideration of what parts of the firm are to be involved: is it solely an R & D exercise, or are other functions such as marketing and sales to be drawn in? The level of decision-making and reporting will have to be decided. There are trade-offs in the degree to which a firm allows itself to become involved. 'Deep' collaboration, involving the core business of the firm in organizational or technological terms, facilitates the flows of knowledge across the firm's boundaries, but this is a double-edged sword as easy absorption may be offset by 'leakage' to the partner. If the latter is seen as a threat, it may be contained by collaborating through a subsidiary or interface unit, such as a joint venture or by erection of internal barriers. The structure will depend on the appropriability of the firms' technology and its existing organization (see Ch. 1 of this volume, by Kay and Willman, for a discussion of architecture and appropriability).

An example of a collaboration which was tightly defined in scope in order to protect competitive interests of the partners, was studied. An international joint venture in aeroengine development and construction involves two technologically equal lead partners and five minor partners. The lead partners were motivated by their need to share costs and risks in the development of this medium sized engine. Their problem was that they are fierce competitors in other sizes and types of engine, and, furthermore, they wished to minimize technology transfer to the junior partners. The solution adopted was to assign each partner specific segments by tightly specified interfaces.

The scope of the collaboration was defined from the beginning to include joint production, marketing, sales and service, and was implemented through a joint venture.

The tight definition and allocation of tasks in order to minimize leakage was possible partly because the venture did not represent novel technology. Both lead partners could have designed and built the engine alone. This gave the collaboration a degree of technological certainty which allowed rigid definition of scope. Approaches to partners also may involve the assessment of whether they possess the required knowledge, and how to value the background each brings in. Sufficient information needs to be revealed to maintain interest without giving away commercial secrets. The problem may be that the firm does not have a full apprehension of its own knowledge base. Frequently partners tend to overvalue their own background. If an agreement is not made to share background, imbalances are offset by cash payments, or technology exchange in some other areas of mutual interest.

One collaboration which we studied tried to overcome the problem of attribution of background at the early stage of joint definition of a novel product which was destined for selling to research scientists. Academic partners took part in brainstorming sessions with two firms during the feasibility stage of the project. The academics (employed by a charitable foundation) were concerned that their background expertise should be adequately rewarded. A 'brown envelope' system was adopted whereby ideas could be recorded by an individual prior to the meeting and lodged with the chair. Ideas produced during the meeting would be common property unless claimed in this way. Such formal systems have to be implemented where partners are unhappy about potential rewards from their input, but often are forgotten when the collaboration is well under way. Firms taking part in government-sponsored programmes often report that collaboration agreements, which cover valuation of background, may take a while to draft and agree, but in a good relationship remain in a drawer throughout the partnership.

Structures

A number of dimensions, physical and legal, define the structure of a collaboration. These include location, control by the partners and ownership of the results. In terms of location, three basic options exist: carrying out the work on one partner's premises, distributing it between premises, or establishing a special location for the purpose of collaboration. The appropriate option may be associated with particular motivations. For example, cost-sharing often demands a single site and risk-sharing a distributed structure. For other forms of collaboration the choice is less obvious. A single location is more conducive to the pursuit of common goals and to project management in general. On the other hand, a collaboration removed from the main body of a firm's activities risks losing touch with market priorities and requires additional attention to be paid to technology transfer. Personnel management considerations are important. If staff are to be concentrated in a special location, they must be willing to make the move, often a secondment. This involves risk for both employer and employee. Secondees are often unwilling to return, making employers reluctant to release key personnel. From the employee's perspective, there are career risks in being removed from the main locus of the firm's activities. One solution is to hire personnel for the collaborative project on the open market. A joint industrial research facility illustrates these points. In the early 1980s three European computer manufacturers established a jointly owned research establishment to carry out longer-term research in areas of exploitable technology. An environment was deliberately created (including a desirable location and relative freedom from bureaucracy for researchers) to attract high-calibre researchers from around the world in areas where they were at that time in short supply. Some staff are seconded while the rest are hired directly and subsequently 'sponsored' by a partner firm. Each partner has its own approach to transferring the knowledge and technology developed in the centre back to parent firm, ranging from emphasis on receiving written reports, through temporary placement of non-centre staff, to organizing joint projects with the facility. The centre is run as a joint venture in equal shares by the partners, and technical decisions are made by committees. The partners reported that they found the centre to be value for money in terms of exploitable research. A danger in creating a separate entity for collaboration is that it develops a life of its own and is difficult to shut down. Indeed, after a recent phase of uncertainty due to the takeover of one of the partners, the centre is set to continue, albeit in a modified form (Barker and Ray 1991).

Project management and control may often entail codifying routines which within a single firm are tacit, covering areas such as reporting arrangements, the relationship with parent companies, and the daily procedures including meetings. Linguistic barriers and differences in managerial culture can lead to misunderstanding.

Frequency and style of meetings depend on the project, and involve a balance between an unnecessary overhead and good communication. A crucial part of many technological collaborations is the work that is done during meetings of the partners. For standards projects this is particularly true, since the object is to share technical knowledge to create common solutions which will be defined in the standard itself. We studied a large standards project in the area of manufacturing technologies. It involved vendors and users of equipment and aimed to write and validate requirements for communications standards for integrated manufacturing technologies, and to demonstrate the results in real production facilities. Collaboration was intense during the specification of the standards and source codes. It took place at frequent technical meetings which involved fifty delegates meeting for around ten weeks a year. Management meetings every eight weeks dealt with non-technical issues. Although many partners were present, in practice only a few contributed actively, the others keeping a watching brief. Free-riding is not a problem, because the proactive partners gain the opportunity to shape the standard to their requirements, and at the same time have a built-in constituency for diffusion of the standard.

Exploitation

Industrial collaborations in technology take place to gain market benefits. For the results to be exploited a framework is necessary for treatment of intellectual property. In some cases the exploitation route is far from linear and will often be through knowledge-enhancing tools and techniques. In other, more downstream arrangements, licences and joint ventures are the dominant features.

However, it is important to remember that fair collaborative conditions do not lead to partners benefiting equally from the results. The differences may lie in their respective environments, for example a better home market base or regulatory regime. Alternatively, the firms themselves may be better equipped to exploit a particular set of results, either through better innovation ability or because the knowledge created has a better 'fit' with their existing skills and experience. Japanese firms are particularly assiduous in demanding and using agreed knowledge transfers. If one partner is dependent upon the other as a route to exploitation, then it is vulnerable to strategy changes by the latter. In the longer term, changes in the relative standing of partners may overtake initial agreements. For example, in the 1970s a UK firm established a joint venture with a Japanese machine tool manufacturer. The UK firm licensed its technology to the joint venture in return for a dividend and for on-selling of its products in Japan. Technical change has led to a substitute technology which the Japanese parent company developed independently, having in the meantime levelled with the United Kingdom in technological expertise. The original partnership has continued, but profits are low and relations strained. The original agreement did not allow for transfer of technology from the Japanese parent to the UK firm, although the UK firm had agreed to provide technical reports and assistance to the Japanese partner.

15.3 CONCLUSION

It emerged from this study that the management of international collaboration involves careful planning and execution, with a need to match projects with particular motivations to the appropriate form of structure. The management framework provides a useful structure both for practical guidance and in providing a linkage with underpinning theories of technical change. We conclude this chapter with some of the main themes emerging from the project:

- *Collaboration is a strategic instrument.* The review of motivations emphasized that collaboration provides firms with an instrument for achieving objectives which would not be possible alone. In the simplest cases it provides more resources (and time) but often it enables combinations of technological and market skills which one firm cannot achieve on a reasonable timescale. Broader strategic goals such as entry to new markets may also be pursued through collaboration.
- *Management of collaboration requires specific skills.* There appeared to be substantial learning benefits in the management of collaboration. However, these acquired skills are quite frequently personalized in the form of key individuals who hold the trust of partners. To avoid allowing these skills to atrophy it is necessary for suitable training to be provided, with more experience being codified.
- *Response to changing circumstances is needed.* The circumstances described in Section 15.2 generally apply at a point in time during a collaboration. When analysing the factors behind longer-lasting collaborations (one indicator of success), it emerged that the ability to respond to change in the circumstances of the project or partner is a key feature. Changes may occur as the project matures in technical and market terms, because the relative technological

standing of the partners has changed, or because the market relationship of the partners changes, for example because of a takeover. Robust collaborations need a careful balance between sufficient flexibility to adapt arrangements and rigidity to stabilize the collaboration against short-term fluctuations (Georghiou and Barker 1991).

- *Collaboration with Japan can be highly beneficial.* In general both parties were satisfied to a greater or lesser extent in the nine Anglo-Japanese collaborations which we examined. Elements of good practice emerging included (1) the British firm having a Japanese national in its employ, or representing it, to facilitate negotiations through cultural and linguistic barriers, (2) the need for top management to make clear its commitment and develop a personal relationship and (3) the need for patience on the part of the UK company while the Japanese company made a decision. Once made, the commitment tended to be implemented quickly and would survive for relatively long periods. A particular benefit available from a collaboration with Japan is exposure to the exacting requirements of Japanese customers, whose input raises product quality. Factory practices disseminated in both directions. This finding is in sharp contrast to the earlier alarmist literature about Japanese firms as partners (Reich and Mankin 1986). A lesson is to be learnt from the skills of the Japanese in setting up mechanisms for learning from technological partners (Hamel *et al.* 1989).

- *Government has a catalytic role to play.* For those collaborations involving government support, this appeared to be a crucial element, both in catalysing the activity in the first place and in helping company managers to gain internal acceptance for the project by dint of prestige value or by helping to demonstrate that the work was pre-competitive. Outside these circumstances, there was a further role for government in providing guarantees, and encouraging the development and dissemination of standards. With the growth of international publicly sponsored collaborative schemes like Eureka, government involvement in collaboration seems likely to stay. Therefore it is relevant to retain lessons about the management of collaboration and keep a watch on its contribution to firms' and policy makers' goals.

ACKNOWLEDGEMENTS

We would like to thank all managers and firms who provided time and materials for our case studies. In particular we would like to thank staff at the British Embassy in Japan for invaluable assistance in arranging our visits to Japanese managers and policy makers.

REFERENCES

Barker, K. and Ray, T. (1991) 'Under one roof: management of collaborative IT research centres in Europe, Japan and the US', paper presented to the ESRC New Technologies and the Firm/ Industrial Economics Joint Study Group, 22 November.

Georghiou, L. and Barker, K. (1991) 'Growing together or growing apart: managing collaboration under conditions of change', paper presented to the colloquium on Management of Technology: Implications for Enterprise Management and Public Policy, a session at the international symposium entitled Europe-USA: New Frontiers in Science and Engineering in a European Perspective, Paris, 27–8 May.

Georghiou, L. and Metcalfe, J. S. (1990) 'To have and to hold: research administration and intellectual property rights' in J. De La Mothe and L. Ducharme (eds) *Science and Technology under Free Trade*, London: Pinter.

Georghiou, L., Barker, K. and Williams, R. (1990) 'Strategic management of international collaboration', paper presented at the Anglo-Danish workshop on Process of Knowledge Accumulation and the Formulation of Technology Strategy, May, Rosnaes, Denmark.

Guy, K., Georghiou, L., Quintas, P., Cameron, H,. Hobday, M. and Ray, T. (1991) *Evaluation of the Alvey Programme for Advanced Information Technology*, London: HMSO.

Hagedoorn, J. (1990) 'Organisational modes of inter-firm co-operation and technology transfer', *Technovation* 10(1): 17–30.

Hamel, G., Doz, Y.L., Prahalad, C. K. (1989) 'Collaborate with your competitors and win', *Harvard Business Review* 67: 133–9.

Loveridge, D., Barker, K. and Georghiou, L. (1992) 'Managing technology transfer as corporate strategy: licensing technology to Japan', paper presented at the Technology Transfer and Implementation Conference, Queen Elizabeth Centre, London, 7 July.

Lyles, M. A. (1988) 'Learning among joint venture sophisticated firms', in F. J. Contractor and P. Lorange (eds) *Cooperative Strategies in International Business*, Lexington, Mass: Lexington Books.

Mariti, P. and Smiley, R. H. (1983) 'Co-operative agreements and the organisation of industry', *Journal of Industrial Economics* 31(4): 437–51.

Morris, D. and Hergert, M. (1987) 'Trends in international collaborative agreements', *Columbia Journal of World Business* 22(2): 15–21.

Mowery, D. (1989) 'Collaborative ventures between US and foreign manufacturing firms', *Research Policy* 18: 19–32.

Reich, R. B. and Mankin, E. D. (1986) 'Joint ventures with Japan give away our future', *Harvard Business Review* 64: 78–86.

Teece, D. (1989) 'Profiting from technological innovation: implications for integration, licensing and public policy', *Research Policy* 18: 19–32.

Summary and conclusions

Chapters 1 to 5 address 'core' issues in the management of technology. Chapter 1 develops an approach to the study of technological change which locates it squarely in the context of firm organization, employing ideas from industrial economics and organizational sociology. The three main issues in that framework concern centrality of technology, firm-specific knowledge and the contractual structure of the firm. Where technology is central to the firm, the long-term commitment to a technology-based value system allows informal contracting between the firm and those who contribute technological expertise. When technology is non-central, however, this is necessarily the subject of an explicit contract. The chapter concludes that firms which implement technology successfully do so because they take the development of firm-specific knowledge beyond the point required by the nature of the technology itself. In some cases firms encourage the development of further technological expertise because they are confident that this will in the long run enhance commercial know-how. Finally they conclude that organizations which are successful in implementing technology tend to have some form of relational contracting, which is reflected in the pay and remuneration structure and in the form of organizational controls over employees.

Chapter 2, building on the same research project, outlines the framework for relating the management of technology to the performance of the firm and summarizes some of the case-study results. Six main themes emerge from these case studies, and are developed in a theoretical framework. First, the issue of technical and commercial capability. These case studies give examples of institutions which have used technically modest systems but with development staff experienced in the organization and sensitive to user needs; these institutions have had considerable success at introducing information technology. Conversely the chapter gives examples where a company's technical brilliance is not matched by its commercial capability. The second issue is integration and learning. The cases find how important it is that close contact is maintained between design, manufacturing and marketing. This is especially true in the electronics group of cases. The third issue is that of appropriability, including external appropriability and internal appropriability. One case shows how individual engineers, who have grown up with the firm, find it difficult to take their skills outside and competitors were unable to duplicate such a team. The fourth issue is centrality, which was developed in some detail in Chapter 1. The fifth issue is that of the appropriate architecture for the firm, and the cases included examples where firms successfully used a flat organizational architecture, and conversely where a hierarchical holding company, managed by a non-technical chief executive, has had difficulty developing and exploiting innovation. The final issue is that of ownership and finance: an example is given of how an inappropriate ownership structure and financial preoccupations can constrain the firm from successful innovation.

The evidence in Chapter 3 confirms the view that most of the significant innovations introduced into the United Kingdom by the small-firm sector were concentrated in a few industries, including electronic data-processing equipment; electrical and electronic components; measuring, checking and precision instruments; medical and surgical equipment, and plastic products. It also finds that most innovators were established in the industry some time before innovation, and hence innovation does not necessarily coincide with new firm formation. Most of these small firms were operating in niche or specialized markets. The chapter concludes that the capacity for innovation does seem to be associated with the capacity to survive and to create employment. There are important sectoral and regional differences in their results; for example, post-innovative survival is highest in medical and surgical equipment, but lowest in electronic data-processing equipment, while the innovative firms in the South East seem to outperform those in other regions. In summary, the authors conclude that this type of firm is unlikely to have more than a marginal impact on current economic problems either at a national or a local level.

Chapter 4 argues that the formulation and implementation of technology strategy are critically important influences on the pattern of technological innovation, and indeed on the competitive advantage of firms. The chapter examines the 'agenda-setting' process in two major companies. The chapter concludes that firms would benefit from a clear understanding of the structure and logic of their own strategic paradigms, which in some cases they may perceive only imperfectly. This understanding would promote a greater awareness of and sensitivity to changes in the external competition environment, and a realization that the current set of organizational structures can *both contribute to and limit* strategic vision. The authors show that conceptual tools for mapping technology and the concepts of internal and external knowledge bases play an important role in developing this understanding.

Chapter 5 examines case studies of the shift from a functionally divided organizational structure to a more entrepreneurial structure, and its implications for the management of supplier-user relations. Since expertise is embedded in management control structures, its deployment is bound to be affected by such restructuring, which in turn is rarely uncontroversial because the allocation of resources to different specialisms becomes a political issue. Structural change moreover is not just threatening to traditional technical functions, but also poses a threat to conventional management control systems. The entrepreneurial organization requires managers and 'professionals' in occupational niches to integrate their different types of knowledge. The authors show why managers experience a loss of control under these new conditions, and faced with what they perceive to be a threat, managers can inhibit the very changes they were meant to be facilitating. In short, not only do managers need to be educated in the techniques of supply-chain management, they also need to understand and negotiate relationships within the firm.

Chapters 6 and 7 are concerned with skills and expertise. Chapter 6 studies the skills and training issues arising from the use of new technologies (especially robots, CAD and CAD/CAM) in a sample of large plants in traditional manufacturing industries. Skills shortages seem to have affected a significant number of establishments using new technology, but labour-related issues were less of a constraint on technology adoption than financial constraints. The main skill shortages related to traditional skills, rather than technology-related skills, though the latter were very important in a small number of cases. Training needs were increased by the adoption of new technology, but gaps in the provision of training were still evident. A major policy implication is that local training co-ordinators (such as TECs) need to identify training needs very carefully, and may need larger *discretionary* budgets to achieve more effective targeting.

Chapter 7 examines the differences in the way different companies employ professional scientists and engineers, and investigates the likely consequences of such differences for the performance of companies. The chapter examines two broad questions: first, do key company and industry characteristics explain the differences in use and deployment of scientists and engineers; and second, do companies employing more scientists and engineers in senior positions perform better or worse? As the authors emphasize, these are actually rather difficult questions to answer because the relationships between the deployment of highly qualified personnel, their role in strategic management and dynamic economic performance are very complex. Nevertheless, the authors find several interesting and statistically significant relationships between firm and industry characteristics and the employment of professional scientists and engineers, and also between the deployment of such personnel and dynamic economic success. In particular, there appears to be a clear correlation between the representation of highly qualified people on the board of directors of companies and various measures of 'structure', including firm size, foreign or home ownership, and whether the company is part of a larger group, or completely independent. The use and deployment of highly qualified scientists and engineers is also found to be linked to various measures of technological performance (such as whether or not particular technologies are in use, or the total number of technologies adopted).

Chapters 8 to 11 are concerned with market issues. Chapter 8 summarizes the results of econometric studies of the diffusion of computer numerically controlled (CNC) machine tools across the engineering sector in the United Kingdom, and the diffusion of colour televisions across UK households. In the first of these, the econometric analysis used represents a significant advance on current practice in that it is able to discriminate between three broad groups of diffusion models. The results cast considerable doubt on the validity of diffusion models based on game theory, but find support for models of the 'rank' and 'epidemic' type – these emphasize that diffusion proceeds (for example) from larger firms to smaller firms (or richer consumers to poorer) and that diffusion depends on the spread of information about the new technology or product. The overall findings have an important policy implication. If (as the results suggest) diffusion is constrained by the rate at which information spreads then government policy should be directed at stimulating the spread of information; if it is not, then such a policy would neither be necessary, nor would it work.

Chapter 9 examines whether the performance of small high-tech firms might be improved by adopting a more proactive approach to marketing. In particular, the research analyses the value of marketing assistance and customer evaluation surveys supplied by the research team. The authors conclude that such assistance and surveys produced substantial benefits to a number of the assisted firms, and that there is considerable scope for an agency that provides such services on a substantial and regular basis. The rationale for such an agency being external to the firm is that there is insufficient in-house time and expertise. While government might be involved in initiating such an agency, it is argued that such an agency would probably be more successful in the medium to long run as a self-sustaining private-sector body.

Chapter 10 examines the hypothesis that if rapid technology change is consistent with widely held 'visions of the future' for that technology, then it is likely to lead to a more concentrated market structure, while if it runs contrary to widely held 'visions', then the outcome is deconcentrating. The case-study evidence presented there is broadly supportive of this hypothesis. Radical innovations lead to a disruption of market structure initially, though later in the product life-cycle there could be a reconcentrating trend, either as the older established firms recapture market share, or alternatively if the pioneer of the radical innovation grows rapidly and consolidates its market position. Even in capital-intensive industries, radical innovations can still be contrived which the smaller firm is best able to exploit, and even if these radical innovations are infrequent, their economic significance is out of proportion to their frequency.

Chapter 11 analyses the innovation process in consumer IT products. The authors see innovation as a dynamic and cyclical process encompassing the sale of the products as well as their research, development and design. They develop the idea of a product space to analyse how technological spin-offs and convergences can present opportunities for new products, and examine those factors that affect the boundaries of this product space. They give particular attention to organizational factors within the firm and inter-firm collaboration, noting that in consumer markets the role of such structures is to collect and interpret data on market characteristics. In addition, they find that firms often place considerable weight on anecdotal and indirect evidence of consumer preferences and behaviour, but less on standard market research techniques, in part because of the difficulty of applying the latter with radically new technologies.

Chapters 12 to 14 are concerned with financial issues. Chapter 12 concludes that, of the many factors within the organization that influence the decision to invest in new technology, the dominant influence is corporate strategy and the fundamental beliefs of top management that underpin it. When technology-based new product and process development is at the hub of corporate strategy, financial controls will not constrain investment in innovative technology. External constraints on genuinely innovative firms seem to be more important for enterprises that are new or small, or have undertaken ambitious expansion programmes that further weaken their financial position. The authors examine the implications of these external constraints on such companies, and come to the striking conclusion that some vulnerable and small companies do not modify investment strategies in the face of cash-flow pressures. The corporate culture of these companies is so committed to innovation that the owner-managers are prepared to risk liquidation by continuing with their chosen strategies.

Chapter 13 investigates whether the accounting treatment of R & D was likely to have any impact on R & D investment. The authors surveyed opinion amongst a sample of managers, and found that in contrast to some earlier research, the accounting treatment of R & D did not seem to be a major issue influencing the R & D decisions made by managers. The chapter also studies whether an analyst is likely to value companies differently according to their accounting treatment of R & D. The evidence from their research suggests that analysts *do* value R & D investment up to the industry norm, and in aggregate are not over-impressed by accounts which show higher profits and assets solely because of the choice of accounting method. These findings cast some doubt on the argument that analysts are short-termist about R & D expenditure, even at a level consistent with the industry norm.

Chapter 14 examines the link between a firm's financing structure and its R & D expenditure, comparing the results to those from similar tests on US data. The authors find a clear negative correlation between R & D and capital gearing both in the United Kingdom and the United States: firms that invest in R & D have less debt in their capital structure. This is consistent with the argument that it is the riskiness of R & D activity that makes firms unwilling to finance R & D by issuing debt. They found no evidence that this relationship was altered by the size of the firm. Moreover, the authors find that there are marked differences between the UK and US financing structures, and suggest that UK firms may under-utilize financial instruments, such as convertibles, which might be especially appropriate for financing R & D projects.

Finally, Chapter 15 examines the management of international collaboration. The authors describe the factors underpinning successful collaboration between firms at the R & D stage and beyond, and draw some lessons about *best practice* in the formulation and management of collaboration. Collaboration is seen as a strategic instrument, to achieve objectives that would not be possible alone. Collaboration calls for specific skills, which are often personalized in the form of key individuals who hold the trust of partners. The response to changing circumstances in the project or the partner needs to be carefully managed, as for example when the project matures or the relative technological standing of the partners diverges. The authors conclude that collaboration with Japan can be highly beneficial, but recognize that several special elements of best practice apply here. Finally, the authors consider that government has a catalytic role to play in encouraging collaboration in the first place, and in helping managers to gain internal acceptance for collaborative projects.

As noted in the Introduction to this book, there are a number of important themes that cut across many of these chapter boundaries, and it is apparent that a full understanding of any of the chapter themes requires some understanding of the others. Much research on the social and economic analysis of new technologies takes the form of interesting fragments from different disciplinary perspectives; much work remains to integrate these many fragments. We hope that the components of this ESRC research initiative, and the linkages between them, will contribute to this process of integration.

Bibliography of work arising from the Initiative

This does not represent an exhaustive list of all the output arising from the Initiative, but includes the main works identified by each research team. Many of the unpublished papers here will be published in due course. The affiliations indicated after each author (or group of authors) identifies the institution at which the Initiative project was based; not all authors are necessarily still based at the same institutions. Finally, in what follows, NTI stands for the ESRC/DTI New Technologies Initiative.

Alderman, N. and Thwaites, A. (Newcastle) 'Some problems of stimulating technological change at the local level', *Development International* 6(1): 61–79, 1991

Al-Qudah, K., Walerk, M. and Lonie, A. (Dundee) 'Evidence on the accessibility and perceived usefulness of information relating to the capital expenditure intentions of UK quoted companies', *Accounting and Business Research* 22, Winter 1991

Aston, B. (LBS) 'Unlimited horsepower: innovation at Cosworth Engineering', *Technology Project Paper*, London Business School, April 1991

—— 'Oxford Instruments', *Technology Project Paper*, London Business School, July 1991

—— 'The key to running a high-tech business: relational teams', *Technology Project Paper*, London Business School, December 1991; also in *Business Strategy Review* 2(3), Autumn 1991

—— 'Solid State Logic', *Technology Project Paper*, London Business School, April 1992

—— 'Quantel', *Technology Project Paper*, London Business School, June 1992

—— 'The importance of technocrats to management', *Technology Project Paper*, London Business School, December 1992

—— 'Appropriability and the specialist market', *Technology Project Paper*, London Business School, December 1992

—— 'UEI', *Technology Project Paper*, London Business School, December 1992

Ball, R., Thomas, R. and McGrath, J. (Stirling) 'Influence of R & D accounting conventions on internal decision-making of companies', *R & D Management* 21(4): 261–9, 1991

Barker, K. (Manchester) 'Managing transnational collaboration in science and technology for national benefit', prepared for Commonwealth Consultative Group on Technological Management/Commonwealth Science Council, July 1990

Black, J. and Tonks, I. (Exeter/LSE) 'The decision to disclose R & D expenditure in the presence of a takeover threat', in M. Taylor (ed.) *Money and Financial Markets*, Oxford: Blackwells: 260–76, 1991

Board, J. and Tonks, I. (LSE) 'Disclosure of research and development expenditure by UK companies: a probit analysis', unpublished paper, London School of Economics, October 1989

Board, J., Bromwich, M., Delargy, R. and Tonks, I. (LSE) 'The market impact of enforced disclosure: the case of SSAP 13', LSE Working Paper No. 16, 1992

Boden, M. (Manchester) 'Strategic management of technology: a survey', Discussion Paper, University of Manchester, June 1989

—— 'Technology strategy; a review', Discussion Paper, University of Manchester, February 1989

Boden, M. and Metcalfe, J. (Manchester) 'Strategy, paradigm and evolutionary change', Discussion Paper, University of Manchester, May 1990

Boden, M., Gibbons, M. and Metcalfe, J. (Manchester) 'Technology and knowledge; the strategic dimension', presented at and published in the *Second International Conference on Management of Technology*, Miami, February-March 1990

Bosworth, D. and Warren, P. (Warwick) 'Strategic manpower and patent races under uncertainty: dissembling and learning', presented at Conference on Firm Strategy and Technical Change: Microeconomics or Microsociology?, Manchester School of Management, September 1990

Bosworth, D., Jacobs, C. and Lewis, J. (Warwick) *New Technologies, Shared Facilities and the Innovatory Firm*, Aldershot: Avebury, 1990

Bosworth, D., Wilson, R and Taylor, P. (Warwick) *The Role of Scientists and Engineers in the Process of Technological Change*, Aldershot: Avebury.

Bosworth, D., Lewis, J. and Wilson, R. (Warwick) 'The role of scientists and engineers in the process of technological change: the Swedish case studies', unpublished paper, Institute for Employment Research, Warwick University, 1991

Cawson, A. (Sussex) 'A high-tech industry: consumer electronics', Unit 13 for Open University Course D212, *Running the Country*, Milton Keynes: Open University Press, 1992

Cawson, A., Haddon, L. and Miles, I. (Sussex) 'Delivering IT into the home; interim report', presented to NTI Co-ordination Meeting, University of Warwick, October, 1988

—— 'Producer strategies for the introduction of new information technology products for the home', Conference on Domestic Consumption, CRICT, Brunel University, May 1990

—— 'The shape of things to consume', in R. Silverstone and E. Hirsch (eds) *Consuming Technologies*, London: Routledge, 1992

Cleary, D. (Edinburgh) 'Trouble brewing: managing expertise and IT acquisition in a drinks company', Working Paper, Department of Business Studies, Edinburgh University, 1990

—— 'Theorising organisational change', Working Paper, Department of Business Studies, Edinburgh University, 1990

—— 'How to succeed in business by ignoring your customers: some thoughts on feedback loops and the problem of market responsiveness in the ICT industry', presented to the NTI Co-ordination Meeting, Brunel University, April 1991

Cleary, D. and Webb, J. (Edinburgh) 'The search for true love: the supplier-user relationship', presented to PICT Seminar Series, University of Edinburgh, May 1990

Dyerson, R. (LBS) 'The driver vehicle licensing centre and technological change: one time failure, long term success', *Technology Project Paper*, London Business School, December 1989

—— 'Inmos and the transputer', *Technology Project Paper*, London Business School, April 1992

—— 'VG instruments', *Technology Project Paper*, London Business School, May 1992

—— 'Halifax Building Society', *Technology Project Paper*, London Business School, July 1992

—— 'Inmos: a case of unsuitable corporate governance?', *Business Strategy Review*, 3(1): 13–27, 1992

—— 'Contradictions of entrepreneurial growth: the case of VG instruments', *Business Strategy Review*, 3(3): 1992

Dyerson, R. and Mueller, F. (LBS) 'Managing competencies at Inmos and Rover: lessons for intervention policy', *Technology Project Paper*, London Business School, July 1992

Dyerson, R. and Roper, M. (LBS) 'Computerisation at the Department of Social Security 1977–89: the operational strategy', *Technology Project Paper*, London Business School, December 1989

—— and —— 'Building competencies; the computerisation of PAYE', *Technology Project Paper*, London Business School, August 1990

—— and —— 'Implementing the Operational Strategy at DSS: from technical push to user pull', *Technology Project Paper*, London Business School, December 1990

—— and —— 'When expertise becomes know-how: managing IT in financial services', *Technology Project Paper*, London Business School, May 1991; also in *Business Strategy Review*, 2(2): 55–73, Summer 1991

—— and —— 'Large scale projects in Britain: Department of Social Security and Inland Revenue', *Technology Project Paper*, London Business School, May 1991; also in B. K. Brussaard (ed.) *Informatization in Public Administration*, Amsterdam: Elsevier, 1992

—— and —— 'Implementing the Operational Strategy', in M. Adler and R. Williams (eds) *The Social Implications of the Operational Strategy*, Waverley Paper Series, University of Edinburgh, May 1991

—— and —— 'The computerisation of PAYE', in B. Williams (ed.) *IT and Accounting: The Impact of Information Technology*, London: Chapman and Hall, 1991

—— 'Managing change in Britain: IT implementation in the Department of Social Security and the Inland Revenue', *Informatization and the Public Sector* 1(4): 303–27, 1991

Foley, P. (Sheffield) 'Prospects and problems for Sheffield', *Westside*, June 1990

—— 'Innovation, new technology and economic development: theoretical considerations for high technology centre development', *Proceedings of the Korea-UK International Symposium on High Technology Centres and Urban Development*, Taejon, Korea, September 1990

—— 'Factors contributing to small business success', presented to Sheffield Managing Director's Club, September 1989

Foley, P., Watts, H. and Wilson, B. (Sheffield) 'New technologies, skills shortages and training strategies in local labour markets: a literature review', Working Paper 1, University of Sheffield, 1989

——, —— and —— 'New technologies, skills shortages and training strategies: some evidence from northern industrial cities', Working Paper 2, University of Sheffield, 1989

——, —— and —— 'New technologies, skills shortages and training strategies in Sheffield: preliminary results', Working Paper 3, University of Sheffield, 1989

——, —— and —— 'New technologies, skills shortages and training strategies in Sheffield: major areas for investigation in the survey of new technology adoption in traditional industries', Working Paper 4, University of Sheffield, 1990

——, —— and —— 'New process technology in traditional industries: skills shortages and training', Working Paper 5, University of Sheffield, 1991

——, —— and —— 'New technology, skills and training', presented to the NTI Co-ordination Meeting, Warwick, October 1989

——, —— and —— 'New technology skills shortages and company training strategies', Employment Department: *Training Agency Skills Bulletin* 44: 20–1, 1990

——, —— and —— 'Introducing new process technology: implications for local employment policies', *Geoforum* 23: 61–72, 1992

——, —— and —— 'Local perspectives on new process technology and employment', *New Technology, Work and Employment*, forthcoming

Georghiou, L. (Manchester) 'Evaluating the impact of International Collaboration on National R & D', presented at United National Economic Commission for Europe, Seminar on Evaluation in the Management of R & D, Madrid, April 1989

Georghiou, L. and Barker, K. (Manchester) 'Growing together or growing apart: managing collaboration under conditions of change', unpublished paper, University of Manchester.

Georghiou, L. and Metcalfe, J. S. (Manchester) 'To have and to hold: intellectual property rights and research administration', in J. de la Mothe and L. Ducharme (eds), *Science and Technology under Free Trade*, London: Pinter, 1990

Georghiou, L., Williams, R. and Barker, K. (Manchester) 'The strategic management of international collaboration', presented to the NTI Co-ordination Meeting, Warwick University, October 1989

——, —— and —— 'Strategic management of international collaboration', paper presented to Anglo-Danish Workshop, May 1990

——, —— and —— 'Selected empirical findings from case study work on the strategic management of international collaboration', presented to the NTI Co-ordination Meeting, Brunel University, May 1990

Geroski, P. (LBS) 'Entry, innovation and productivity growth', *Review of Economics and Statistics* 71: 572–8, 1989

—— 'Procurement policy as a tool of industrial policy', *International Review of Applied Economics* 4: 182–98, 1990

—— 'Innovation, technological opportunity and market structure', *Oxford Economic Papers* 42: 586–602, 1990

—— 'Entry and the rate of innovation', *Economics of Innovation and New Technology* 1(4): 203–14, 1991

—— 'Innovation and the sectoral sources of UK productivity growth', *Economic Journal*, 101: 1438–51, 1991

—— 'Vertical relations between firms and industrial policy', *Economic Journal* 102: 138–47, 1992

—— 'Technology and markets', P. Stoneman (ed.) *Handbook of the Economics of Innovation and Technical Change*, Oxford: Blackwell, forthcoming

Geroski, P. and Pomroy, R. (LBS) 'Innovation and the evolution of market structure', *Journal of Industrial Economics*, 38: 299–314, 1990

Gill, J. (Brunel) 'The speed of technology change and development of market structure. 3: memory chips', CRICT Discussion Paper, Brunel University, April 1990

—— 'The speed of technology change and development of market structure. 4: standard logic chips', CRICT Discussion Paper, Brunel University, July 1990

—— 'The speed of technology change and development of market structure. 5: biotechnology (HIV diagnostics), CRICT Discussion Paper, Brunel University, December 1990

Goodacre, A. (Stirling) 'R & D expenditure and the analysts' view', *Accountancy*, April 1991

Goodacre, A., McGrath, J., Pratt, K., Thomas, R. and Ball, R. (Stirling) 'Internal and external perceptions of accounting disclosures of R & D expenditure, Part 1: external perceptions of R & D', presented to NTI Co-ordination Meeting, Warwick, October 1989 and ESRC New Technology Study Group, London Business School, December 1989

——, ——, ——, —— and —— 'Internal and external perceptions of accounting disclosure of R & D Expenditure. Part 2: internal perceptions of R & D', presented at the NTI Co-ordination Meeting, Brunel University, May 1990

——, ——, ——, —— and —— 'Perceptions of accounting disclosure of R & D Expenditure: an experimental study', presented at the INQUIRE Conference, Cambridge, October 1990; at the British Accounting Association Annual Conference, Salford, April 1991 and also at the ICAEW Financial Accounting & Auditing Research Conference, London Business School, July 1991

——, ——, ——, —— and —— 'How do firms and financial markets regard R & D expenditure?', presented at ESRC NTI Dissemination Conference, London, December 1990

Grindley, P. (LBS) 'Turning technology into competitive advantage', *Technology Project Paper*, London Business School, February 1991

—— 'Technological change within the firm: a framework for research and management', *Technology Project Paper*, London Business School, December 1989

—— 'Managing new technology in the firm: the role of strategic and organisational continuity', *Technology Project Paper*, London Business School, October 1990

—— 'Managing technological innovation: culture and organisational relationships within the firm', *Technology Project Paper*, London Business School, October 1991

—— 'The reluctant innovators: price discrimination and diffusion in the presence of externalities', Centre for Business Strategy Working Paper, February 1991

—— 'Price stickiness and diffusion of proprietary innovations', Centre for Business Strategy Working Paper, March 1991

—— 'The open systems revolution in the computer industry', Centre for Business Strategy Working Paper, January 1992

—— 'Winning standards contests: an introduction to strategy', Centre for Business Strategy Working Paper, January 1992

—— 'Standards and business strategy: an overview', Centre for Business Strategy Working Paper, January 1992

—— 'Standards and the open systems revolution in the computer industry', in J. Berg and H. Schumny (eds), *An Analysis of the Information Technology Standardisation Process*, Amsterdam: North Holland 1990

—— 'Standards strategy for personal computers', in J. Berg and H. Schumny (eds), *An Analysis of the Information Technology Standardisation Process*, Amsterdam: North Holland 1990

—— 'Winning standards contests; using product standards in business strategy', *Business Strategy Review* 1(1), 1990

—— 'Turning technology into competitive advantage', *Business Strategy Review*, 1991

—— 'Technological change within the firm; a framework for research and management', in W. Vrakking and A. Cozijnsen (eds), *Handbook of European Innovation*, Oxford: Blackwell, forthcoming

—— 'Managing technology: organising for competitive advantage', *Technology Project Paper*, London Business School, June 1992

—— 'Technological innovation and new ventures: making the transition to stable growth', *Technology Project Paper*, London Business School, June 1992

Grindley, P. and McBryde, R. (LBS) 'Product standards and business strategy: the case of video cassette recorders' Centre for Business Strategy Working Paper, November 1991

—— and —— 'The standards contest for digital audio: compact disc and digital audio tape', Centre for Business Strategy Working Paper, January 1992

—— and —— 'Standards and the development of personal computers', Centre for Business Strategy Working Paper, January 1992

Grindley, P., McBryde, R. and Roper, M. (LBS) 'Technology and the competitive edge: the case of Richardson Sheffield', *Technology Project Paper*, London Business School, December 1989

Grindley, P. and Toker, S. (LBS) 'Regulators, markets and standards coordination: policy lessons for Telepoint', Centre for Business Strategy Working Paper, January 1992

—— and —— 'Standard strategies for Telepoint: the failure of commitment', Centre for Business Strategy Working Paper, January 1992

Haddon, L. (Sussex) 'Home automation', *Screen Digest*, November 1989

Karshenas, M. and Stoneman, P. (Warwick) 'A flexible model of technological diffusion incorporating economic factors with an application to the spread of colour television ownership in the UK', *Journal of Forecasting* 11(7): 577–602

—— and —— 'Rank stock order and epidemic effects in the diffusion of new technology: an empirical model', unpublished paper

Kay, J. (LBS) *The Structure of Strategy*, Oxford University Press, 1992

Kay, J. and Willman, P. (LBS) 'Managing technological innovation: architecture, trust and organisational relationships in the firm', Centre for Business Strategy Working Paper, August 1991

Lonie, A., Power, D. and Sinclair, C. (Dundee) 'The discriminatory impact of interest rate changes on companies, industries and regions', *British Review of Economic Issues* 12(28): 77–106, October 1990

——, —— and —— 'Effects of interest rates on UK companies, recession myopia and the short-termism debate', Finance Discussion Paper, University of Dundee, August 1991

——, —— and —— 'Effects of interest rates on UK companies and the short-termism debate', presented to Fellowship of Engineering Economics Seminar, Royal Society of Arts, June 1991

——, —— and —— 'Interest rates, company vulnerability and the short-termism debate', presented to British Accounting Association (Scotland) Conference, Aberdeen, September 1991

——, —— and —— 'Interest rates and short-termism, *Business and Economics Review* 8: 39–46, 1992

Metcalfe, J. and Boden, M. (Manchester) 'Strategy paradigm and evolutionary change', Discussion Paper, University of Manchester, May 1990

—— and —— 'Innovation strategy and the epistemic connection: an essay on the growth of technological knowledge' *Journal of Scientific and Industrial Research*, 1991

—— and —— 'Evolutionary epistemology and the nature of technology strategy' in R. Coombs *et al.* (eds) *Technological Change and Company Strategies: Economic and Sociological Perspectives*, Academic Press, forthcoming

Metcalfe, J. and Gibbons, M. (Manchester) 'Technology policy in an evolutionary world', *Proceedings of USA-Europe Symposium on Managing Technology*, Paris, May 1991

Miles, I. (Sussex) '<Shift><Control> <Home>', *Futures*, October 1990

—— 'Teleshopping; just around the corner?' *Journal of the Royal Society of Arts*, 180–9, February 1990

Mueller, F. (LBS) 'Strategies for successful innovation in the automobile industry: the importance of technology for differentiation strategies and reputation', *Technology Project Paper*, London Business School, March 1992

—— 'The management of know-how and core assets: organisational change in the automobile industry', *Technology Project Paper*, London Business School, August 1992

Mueller, F. and Roper, M. (LBS) 'Technological innovation and commercial success: the development of the K-series engine at Rover', *Technology Project Paper*, London Business School, November 1991

Nixon, W. (Dundee) 'Accounting for research and development: the need for a new perception', paper presented at Chartered Accountants' Hall, London, May 1990

—— 'The revision of SSAP 13', *Audit Briefing* 1(11), August 1990

—— 'R & D disclosure: SSAP 13 and after', *Accountancy* 107(1170): 72–3, February 1991

—— 'Accounting for R & D: the need for a new perception', presented to Board for Chartered Accountants in Business, January 1991

—— 'A fiscal incentive for R & D disclosure', *Accountancy* 108(1175): 122, July 1991

Nixon, W. and Lonie, A. (Dundee) 'Accounting for R & D; the need for change', *Accountancy* 106(1158): 90–1, February 1990

—— and —— 'A strategic approach to management accounting practice: evidence from 13 case studies', presented to British Accounting Association (Scotland) Conference, Aberdeen September 1991

—— and —— 'Technology, competitive strategies and management accounting: some evidence from 13 case studies', presented to the BAA National Conference, Warwick, April 1992

—— and —— 'Technological innovation and management accounting control: some evidence from 13 case studies', presented to the Second European Management Control Symposium, Jouy-en-Josas, France, July 1992

Oakey, R. (Heriot-Watt) 'Government policy towards high technology small firms beyond the year 2000' in J. Curran and R. A. Blackburn (eds) *Paths of Enterprise*, London: Routledge, 1991

—— 'High technology small firms: their potential for rapid industrial growth', *Journal of Small Business* 9(4): 30–42, 1991

—— 'Innovation and the management of marketing in high technology small firms', *Journal of Marketing Management* 7: 343–56, 1991

Oakey, R. and Cooper, S. (Heriot-Watt) 'The relationship between product technology and innovation in high technology small firms', *Technovation* 11(2): 79–92, 1991

Smith, I. and Thwaites, A. (Newcastle) 'Relationship between technologically advanced SME, large firms and markets', presented to NTI Co-ordination Meeting, Brunel University May 1990

Smith, I. J., Alderman, A., Thwaites, A. T. and Townsend, J. (Newcastle) 'Some influential factors in technology policy for the less favoured regions in the community', presented to Conference on The Local and the International in the XXI Century, Bilbao, Spain, 1991

Smith, I. J., Alderman, A., Tether, B., Thwaites, A. T. and Townsend, J. (Newcastle) 'The environment for innovation in SME's', presented to NTI Co-ordination Meeting, April 1991

Stoneman, P. (Warwick) 'Technological diffusion, horizontal product differentiation and adaptation costs', *Economica* 57: 49–62, February 1990

—— 'Technological diffusion and vertical product differentiation', *Economics Letters* 21: 277–80, November 1989

—— 'Technological diffusion, firm size and market structure', in Z. Acs and D. Audretsch (eds) *Innovation and Technical Change*, Hemel Hempstead: Harvester, 1991

—— 'The intertemporal demand for consumer technologies requiring joint hardware and software inputs', *Warwick Economic Research Papers* 355, June 1990

—— 'Copying capabilities and intertemporal competition between joint input technologies: CD vs DAT', *Economics of Innovation and New Technology* 1(3): 233–42, 1991

—— 'The use of a Levy/Grant scheme as an alternative to tax-based incentives to R & D', *Research Policy* 20: 195–201, 1991

—— 'The adoption of new technology: theory and evidence', presented to ESRC NTI Dissemination Conference, London, December 1990

—— 'Technological change and market structure', in A. Del Monte (ed.) *Recent Developments in Industrial Organisation*, Basingstoke: Macmillan, 1992

—— 'Technological change in neo-classical type macro models', in G. Bell (ed.) *Technology and Productivity*, Paris: OECD, 1991

—— 'Technology policy in Europe', in K. Cowling and H. Tomann (eds) *Industrial Policy after 1992*, London: Anglo-German Foundation 1990

Stoneman, P. and Karshenas, M. (Warwick) 'The role of exogenous and endogenous learning and economic factors in the diffusion of new technology', *Warwick Economic Research Papers* 358, June 1990

Swann, P. (Brunel) 'The speed of technology change and development of market structure. 1: theoretical and measurement issues', CRICT Discussion Paper, Brunel University, April 1990

—— 'The speed of technology change and development of market structure. 2: microprocessors and background to the semiconductor industry', CRICT Discussion Paper, Brunel University, April 1990

—— 'The speed of technology change and development of market structure. 6: PC applications software', unpublished paper, London Business School 1992 (revised)

—— 'Rapid technology change, visions of the future, corporate organisation and market structure', *Economics of Innovation and New Technology* 2(1), 1992

—— 'Rapid technology change, visions of the future, organisational and market structure', paper presented to USA-Europe Symposium on Managing Technology, Paris, May 1991

Swann, P. and Gill, J. (Brunel) *Corporate Vision and Rapid Technological Change: the Evolution of Market Structure*, London: Routledge, forthcoming

Thomas, R., Ball, R. and McGrath, J. (Stirling) 'A survey of relationships between company accounting and R & D decisions in smaller firms', presented to ESRC New Technology Study Group, Stirling University, February 1991

Webb, J. (Edinburgh) 'The "customerising" of sales: preliminary findings from the New Technologies and the Firm Project', Working Paper, Department of Business Studies, Edinburgh University, 1990

—— 'The mismanagement of innovation' *Sociology* 26: 471–92

Webb, J. and Cleary, D. (Edinburgh) 'Experts and expertise', presented to the NTI Co-ordination Meeting, Brunel University, April 1991

Webb, J. and Dawson, P. (Edinburgh) 'Measure for measure: strategic change in an electronic instruments corporation', *Journal of Management Studies* 28: 191–206

Williams, R. (Manchester) 'The case of R & D', in M. Moran (ed.) *States and Markets*, London: Macmillan, 1991

Willman, P. (LBS) 'Bureaucracy, innovation and appropriability', *Technology Project Paper*, London Business School, April 1992

—— 'Playing the long game: reaping the benefits of technological change', *Business Strategy Review* 3(1) 1992

Willman, P. and Holding, M. (LBS) 'Computerization at the Trustee Savings Bank', *Technology Project Paper*, London Business School, March 1990; also in B. Williams (ed.) *IT and Accounting: The Impact of Information Technology*, London: Chapman and Hall, 1991

Wilson, R. and Bosworth, D. (Warwick) 'The role of scientists and engineers in the process of technological change', paper presented to and published by Royal Aeronautical Society, London, 1991

Index